Confluence and Conflict

Harvard East Asian Monographs 450

Confluence and Conflict

Reading Transwar Japanese Literature and Thought

Brian Hurley

Published by the Harvard University Asia Center
Distributed by Harvard University Press
Cambridge (Massachusetts) and London 2022

Printed in the United States of America

The Harvard University Asia Center publishes a monograph series and, in coordination with the Fairbank Center for Chinese Studies, the Korea Institute, the Reischauer Institute of Japanese Studies, and other facilities and institutes, administers research projects designed to further scholarly understanding of China, Japan, Korea, Vietnam, and other Asian countries. The Center also sponsors projects addressing multidisciplinary, transnational, and regional issues in Asia.

A Study of the Weatherhead East Asian Institute, Columbia University

The Studies of the Weatherhead East Asian Institute of Columbia University were inaugurated in 1962 to bring to a wider public the results of significant new research on modern and contemporary East Asia.

Cataloging-in-Publication Data is on file at the Library of Congress.

ISBN 9780674267909 (hardcover)

Index by Harvey L. Gable Jr.

♾ Printed on acid-free paper

Last figure below indicates year of this printing
31 30 29 28 27 26 25 24 23 22

This book is dedicated to the memory of my brother, Thomas Shannon Hurley (1981–2019).

Contents

Acknowledgments

This book was made possible by the generous support of many people and institutions. Before I acknowledge some of them below, I would note that any errors and shortcomings in the analysis that follows remain my responsibility alone.

First and foremost, I thank Alan Tansman, who read and critiqued draft after draft of this project from its earliest stages onward. My conversations with him over the years have shaped my thinking about everything from the big picture of literature and ideas to the finer-grain matters of writing and argumentation. As a graduate student at Berkeley, I benefited from the teaching of Dan O'Neill, Mack Horton, William Schaefer, and Andrew Barshay. I am also grateful to Dennis Washburn, Pheng Cheah, Michael Lucey, and Michael Silverstein for leading seminars that helped me to formulate some of the ideas and arguments in this book. I thank Anthony Chambers for guiding my study of Tanizaki Jun'ichirō. Bruce Caldwell convened a National Endowment for the Humanities Summer Institute at Duke University in 2016 on the history of economic thought, and I greatly benefited from it. I send my thanks to him and to all those who participated in the Duke seminar, and to the NEH for the stipend which allowed me to attend. In Tokyo, Umemori Naoyuki supported my affiliation at Waseda University on three occasions and generously welcomed me to his seminars. Namiko Kunimoto, Keith Vincent, Harry Harootunian, and Max Ward all read and commented on parts of the writing that appear in this book, and I thank each of them for sharing their time and expertise. Ross Yelsey of the Weatherhead East Asian Institute at Columbia University guided me through the publication process. I thank everyone at the Harvard University Asia Center for supporting the book, especially Bob Graham. I also thank the anonymous readers who critiqued my manuscript with great insight.

Some of the research for this book was supported by funding from the Social Science Research Council / Japanese Society for the Promotion of Science, Syracuse University, and the Northeast Asia Council of the Association for Asian Studies. I also thank the Japan Foundation, which supported my position at Syracuse University with an institutional support grant that was secured by Gail Bulman. The Central New York Humanities Corridor enabled my collaboration with colleagues at Cornell University during my time at Syracuse. I also thank the College of Arts and Sciences at Syracuse University for making a sabbatical leave possible, and the University of Texas at Austin College of Liberal Arts for giving me a course release at a crucial time during the final revisions.

For intellectual inspiration and collegial support while working on this book, I wish to thank Angie Chau, Brett de Bary, Pedro Erber, Carol Gluck, George Lazopoulos, Meera Lee, Andrew Leong, Matthew Mewhinney, Patrick Noonan, Romita Ray, Paul Roquet, Matthew Seybold, and Marianne Tarcov. In Austin, my colleagues in the Department of Asian Studies have given me a friendly and supportive environment to continue my work. I thank them all, especially Kirsten Cather and Donald Davis. I also thank the office staff who have supported me at several institutions, and the staff of the many libraries that have made materials available to me.

Portions of this manuscript have appeared in print elsewhere. Parts of chapter 1 were published in "Toward a New Modern Vernacular: Tanizaki Jun'ichirō, Yamada Yoshio and Shōwa Restoration Thought," *Journal of Japanese Studies* 39, no. 2 (Summer 2013). Parts of chapter 4 appeared in the following: "The Priest and the Prophet: Reading the Sign of 'Sōseki'" (*Seishokusha to yogensha: Sōseki no kigo o yomu*), *Bungaku*, November–December 2014 (Japanese-language text); "*Kokoro* Confidential: Edwin McClellan, Friedrich Hayek and the Neoliberal Reading of Natsume Sōseki," *Representations* 134, no. 1 (Spring 2016); "Friedrich Hayek and the Pleasures of Liberal Thought in the 'Great Book' of Modern Japan," in *The Routledge Companion to Literature and*

Economics, ed. Matthew Seybold and Michelle Chihara (2018); and "*Kokoro* and the Economic Imagination," *Review of Japanese Culture and Society* 29 (2017). I thank each of these publishing venues for generously granting me permission to republish material here. I am also grateful to the estate of Friedrich Hayek for granting permission to quote from materials held in the Friedrich A. von Hayek Papers at the Hoover Institution Archives, Stanford, California.

Finally, I wish to thank those closest to me for their encouragement. My parents are both teachers by trade and selfless by nature, and I thank them for their gentle inspiration. My sister Alice has supported me in ways great and small. To Shelby—thank you for being there for me through everything, and for bringing a joy to my life that I never would have known otherwise.

I dedicate this book to the memory of my brother, Thomas Shannon Hurley (1981–2019). Thanks for giving me someone to look up to, Tom. I miss you.

INTRODUCTION

> But as there is no such thing as an innocent reading, we must say what reading we are guilty of.
>
> —Louis Althusser[1]

In 1907, the Japanese novelist Natsume Sōseki (1867–1916) completed *Bungakuron* (A Theory of Literature). He recalled in the preface that before writing anything, "I shut away all of my books of literature in a wicker trunk. I believed that to read literature in order to know what kind of a thing literature is would be a method akin to washing blood with blood."[2] It has been observed that one of the implications of Sōseki's iconic statement seems to have been that the domains of expository argument and literary form are separate, each remaining outside the other, and that however paradoxically, it is actually by leaving the realm of the literary per se that the critic can come to "know what kind of a thing literature is."[3] Broadly stated, this study reflects a similar sort of premise, at least insofar as it reads aspects of modern Japanese literature through the prism of its intellectual other—thought. By the same measure, the chapters that follow also reckon with some of the dynamics of thought in modern Japan by moving outside the realm of intellectual exposition, and into the aesthetic atmospheres of related literary writings.

In the course of reading across the boundaries that separate modern Japanese literature and thought, though, this study ultimately comes to consider how their deeper connections have been forged through the shared medium of language. The Japanese philosopher Tosaka Jun (1900–45) suggested as much in observing that since ideas must be translated into "the image of language" (*kotoba no eizō*), it might be argued that what we refer to as "literature" (*bungaku*) encompasses not only an aesthetic form of expression (*bungei*), but an intellectual undertaking, too, and one that connects the realm of representation to that of thought.[4] He titled a group of essays *Shisō toshite no bungaku* (Literature as Thought, 1933–37) in order to express his perspective that "literature" does not simply signify an isolated artistic practice extrinsic to intellectual life. Taking a cue from recent scholarship on philosophy and the arts in other contexts, we might say that Tosaka's point was in fact that the literary comprised a "ground" for thought itself.[5] This reveals another key dynamic to be explored in this study. For if Sōseki guides our attention to degrees of difference, then Tosaka points to deeper bloodlines linking literature and thought together on an almost genetic level of affinity. And in the pages that follow, this book will take inspiration from both perspectives. It argues that although the cerebral aspect of intellectual exposition and the sensuous aesthetics of literary writing would seem to belong to different narrative universes, they have often "conspired" in modern Japan, or "breathed together" in momentary convergences animated by writers and thinkers who washed the blood of literature with the blood of thought.[6]

One of the most obvious perils of this approach is that it could allow the content of ideas to wash out the appeal of literary form, rendering the aesthetic component of literary language bloodless, as it were. But the literary critic Lionel Trilling would remind us that while the systematicity of organized thought can make us "rightly fear that the intellect will dry up the blood in our veins and wholly check the emotional and creative part of the mind," we should not forget that literature and thought need each other, for "ideas, if they are large enough and of a certain kind, are not only not hostile to the creative process, as some think, but are virtually inevitable to it. Intellectual power and emotional power go together."[7] In a similar spirit, it might be said that the ideas examined in the pages that follow are not ideas that obliterate aesthetic sensibilities, but rather engage them, revealing that intellectual life in modern Japan has long had a literary dimension, just as modern Japanese literature has long conspired with adjacent trends in the realm of thought. This is a study of how their dialogues overflowed the stricter boundaries that are often ascribed to literary and intellectual history as they washed over the borders separating aesthetics and ideas, too.

Following these flows carries my analysis through confluences that produced persuasive intellectual positions and affecting literary texts. But this is also a study of encounters between writers and thinkers, literature and ideas, which were contingent, merely momentary, and later, partly forgotten. The noted thinker Walter Benjamin would suggest that to read these contingencies in the texts that remain to us, we have to question the seeming certitude of our own retrospective gaze today.[8] After all, the scholar looking back can take foregone conclusions for granted, and judge the trajectories of figures from earlier times in relation to endings that seem to have always been pending. But in reckoning with Japanese literary and intellectual history in particular, the telos of linear time contrived by the retrospective gaze can obscure the contemporaneity of what were once overlapping trends in literature and thought. One result can be that looking back, the prominent writer's engagement with intellectual life might seem to have been an anomalous detour from the mainline of his literary trajectory, just as the influential intellectual's interest in contemporaneous trends in literature might later seem to have been no more than a sidelong glance toward an expressive style that he himself never practiced. In this study, however, I uncover more in these unexpected connections by viewing them as telltale signs. And in my view, the tales they tell are of imaginations—whether aesthetic or political, literary or philosophical—that have been pushed to their limits within the contingencies of their moment, and into conversation with their fellow travelers on the other side of the literature-thought divide.

In the pages that follow, this approach reveals how some of the most provocative connections between modern Japanese literature and thought materialized within a volatile transwar chronology ranging from the 1920s to the 1950s. In each of four chapters, I examine a dialogue that emerged between a prominent writer and a thinker during these decades as I explore how distinctive trends in literature and thought conspired in a moment of world historical crisis. The first three chapters focus on the interwar years in Japan as they read the writings of the novelist Tanizaki Jun'ichirō (1886–1965) and the linguist Yamada Yoshio (1875–1958), the novelist Yokomitsu Riichi (1898–1947) and the Kyoto School philosophers, and the Marxist poet Nakano Shigeharu (1902–79) and the Marxist thinker Tosaka Jun. The final chapter then extends the study into the midcentury years as it examines the 1957 English translation of Natsume Sōseki's 1914 novel *Kokoro* that the scholar Edwin McClellan (1925–2009) completed as a graduate student at the University of Chicago while working with the noted economist Friedrich Hayek (1899–1992). As I read these writers and thinkers together, my point is not to show that literature has embodied a related trend in thought, nor that a specific thread of intellectual history is the secret inspiration that explains important literary writing. To make those claims would be to come close to arguing that literature and thought have simply said the same thing in different words—a mistaken conclusion that would dissolve the affecting specificity of literary form into the explanatory content of intellectual argument. Moving in a different direction, this study aims to balance the appeals of aesthetics and ideas by exploring how writers and thinkers in modern Japan have frequently shared an interest that is between (*inter-est*) literature and thought, belonging fully to neither, but overlapping the borders of both in ways that link each to the other.[9] As the study engages these connections in contexts ranging from middlebrow writing to avant-garde modernism, and from the wartime left to the postwar right, it traces a transwar chronology of literature and thought in confluence and conflict through the struggles that writers and thinkers waged through language.

Literature and Thought in Transwar Context

Looking at the history of conceptual art alongside the novel of ideas, the theorist Sianne Ngai observed that seemingly any work of art or literature "transparently promising 'ideas'" will court the suspicion that it is no more than a gimmick that has sacrificed its aesthetic integrity in favor of a ready-made intellectual position.[10] And even when the relationship between the realms of aesthetics and ideas is construed more subtly, literature may resent the suggestion that comparison will raise it to the level of philosophical insight, instead preferring to see itself as the superior form all along. The novelist and critic Mary McCarthy pointed to these tensions at the beginning of *Ideas and the Novel* (1980), where she recalled that the poet T. S. Eliot once praised Henry James as a novelist who "had a mind so fine that no idea could violate it."[11] McCarthy explained that Eliot's statement implied "the snubbing notion, radical at the time but by now canon doctrine, of the novel as a fine art and of the novelist as an intelligence superior to mere intellect."[12] These perspectives on the cantankerous connections between the spheres of aesthetics and ideas reveal that navigating their competing demands connects my study of modern Japanese texts to long-standing controversies about how to balance the respective appeals of literature and thought writ large. As I engage some of these controversies through productive tensions in modern Japanese literary and intellectual history, I read the vexed relationship between literature and thought in ways that bring to light measures of affinity even as I reckon with more fundamental dimensions of difference.

One of the challenges of this study is to demonstrate how this approach can shed new light even on canonical Japanese writers and thinkers who have been studied before, many of them extensively. Without implying that the prominent figures examined here are the only ones that matter, their very familiarity counteracts the possible misapprehension that the intersections of literature and thought described in the chapters that follow are no more than surprising anomalies on the periphery of modern Japanese cultural history. In fact, the point all along is that some of the most widely read and oft-discussed texts of modern Japanese literature and thought breathed with structures of meaning that would be impossible to describe in literary or intellectual terms alone. I study these texts together because as objects of inquiry, they demand a method of analysis that is attuned to specific dialogues between writers and thinkers, but that also allows their perspectives to signify beyond the case-by-case consideration of their individual engagements with one another, and to cumulatively conjure a broader middle ground within the cultural field of modern Japan writ large. The specific writings that I have chosen to examine are far from the only possibilities for pursuing these purposes, to be sure. But the wager here is that the chapters of this study focus on texts that at least number among the many that allow us to center relations between the aesthetic forms of literary writing and the cerebral rigor of the intellectual mind, and in so doing, prompt us to rethink the boundaries of literary and intellectual history in modern Japan more generally.

This study explores how these dynamics appeared in writings from the transwar years of the 1920s to the 1950s in order to show how the sense of world historical crisis that gripped writers and thinkers in these decades brought literature and thought into particularly vigorous conversation. While reckoning with the undeniable division in modern Japanese history between a "prewar" period of imperial expansion abroad and a "postwar" period of superlative economic development at home, my deepest investment is in reading Japanese literature that indexes key contours within a more continuous and global twentieth-century history of ideas that emerged during a time of crisis extending across the midcentury divide. It follows that the organization of the study as a whole works against the sense of an ending in 1945 that might otherwise isolate "prewar" and "postwar" periods of cultural history from each other, and instead frames the global crisis of modernity that materialized in the interwar decades as a not-so-distant past that produced ideological afterlives that developed more fully in the midcentury years that followed, and beyond. The result is a perspective on literature and thought in modern Japan that neither begins nor ends in 1945, but instead coalesces within the contextual coordinates of "transwar" time, remembering, as the scholar of literature Jonathan Abel put it, that "the term *transwar* itself gestures to an nonbounded periodization that bleeds out from an event, and therefore to a mode of thinking that works against the rhetorical constraints underlying most uses of periodization. It makes no claims for either origin or terminus."[13]

The transwar scope of this study puts it into dialogue with a much larger conversation to which several other studies of culture and politics in modern Japan have also contributed. Surveying this vast and various body of scholarship, a key interpretive line comes to the fore—namely, that the ideals of the late nineteenth-century Meiji Enlightenment, which promised greater affluence, freedom, and progress in the modern world, produced irresolvable tensions in the early twentieth century that ultimately became unbearable. Japanese writers and thinkers came to believe that the self-interest sanctioned by the modern ethos of liberal individualism had bred a destructive egotism, for example, and that the increasing integration of the global marketplace had dissolved the cultural particularity of Japan into a soulless and homogenous modern idiom. For many, it followed that "the modern" itself had to be transcended, and a wide range of scholarship has shown how Japanese writers and thinkers tried to "overcome modernity" (*kindai chōkoku*) through appeals to various forms of collectivism, all of which (in different ways) promised to heal what was thought to have been the fractured form of modern society and the modern mind. Writ large, then, Japan's interwar "revolt against modernity" was enacted by cultural actors who felt that they had been "betrayed by modernity's promise," as the scholar of Japanese literature Alan Tansman has put it.[14]

Literature and thought occupy a central place in studies of interwar Japan because part of the "revolt against modernity" associated with these years was a revolt that aimed to resolve a crisis of representation. In early twentieth-century Japan, as elsewhere, writers and intellectuals lost faith in the capacity of received narrative forms to meaningfully render lived experience in a modern world in which "all that is solid melts into air." This is to say that they intuited the lesson that the scholar of modern life Marshall Berman has succinctly articulated: that "to be modern is to find ourselves in an environment that promises us adventure, power, joy, growth, transformation of ourselves and the world—and, at the same time, that threatens to destroy everything we have, everything we know, everything we are."[15] It followed for writers and thinkers in Japan that language and narrative, memory and perception, all seemed to have fractured under the strain of the discontinuities borne by the destabilizing experience of "modern life."[16] This led the historian Harry Harootunian to observe that the "crisis of modernity" that gripped interwar Japan was a crisis "over the stability and reliability of forms of representation" and over "the forms most capable of relaying and communicating the lived experience—the experience of genuine difference—and securing accessibility to a memory that was being shattered into splinters by speed, shock, and sensation."[17] These tensions in the literary and intellectual life of early twentieth-century Japan fueled a modernist efflorescence that brought aesthetics and ideas into intense dialogue, and that is why these years are the focus of the first chapters of this study.

As the literary and intellectual energy of interwar Japan contributed to the revolt against modernity, though, it also came into confluence with the most notorious ideological formation of the age: fascism. To be sure, some have debated the applicability of the term "fascism" in the particular context of interwar Japan, and others have argued that "fascism" in general is a vague concept without concrete definition.[18] But as the historian Andrew Gordon has pointed out, it would seem that the "radical nominalism" that has sometimes derailed the conversation about fascism "leads down a conceptual cul-de-sac," whereas an accounting of contemporaneous historical experience through the lens of "fascism" can understand important differences as "*qualifications* that reveal key variants of a shared historical process or formation, not *disqualifications* that prevent our use of common concepts of analysis."[19] Building on this perspective, I will position parts of my own analyses in dialogue with other studies that have defined fascism as a reactionary modernist ideology that took as its object the overcoming of modernity itself.[20]

One of the implications that follows is that "fascism" in this study names a network of cultural and political responses to the interwar crises of modernity described above and helps us to see that taken together, these responses signified the desire to replace the Enlightenment ideals that were believed to have broken down with new communal bonds forged through blood and soil, myth and magic, authoritarian rule and the beauty of violence.[21] This approach acknowledges that part of what makes fascism difficult to identify and define is that its ideological appeals often appeared through the veils of paradox and irony. The historian Reto Hofmann has observed that fascism in Europe and Japan promised revolution and restoration at the same time, for example, and that it celebrated the particularity of the native and the national even as it became a global phenomenon.[22] And while fascism promised to overcome the unprecedented contradictions of capitalist modernity during the interwar years, it did not endeavor to overcome capitalism itself, but only to ameliorate its undesirable effects, as others have noted.[23] The ideology animating these paradoxes of politics and economics became a matter of culture as it took on aesthetic form, and Tansman's extensive analysis of Japanese fascism showed how the literary in particular proved to be one of its most complex modes of representation.[24]

The first parts of this study engage the robust dialogue about fascism in interwar Japan as they examine key connections in the literature and thought of the age. The purpose of my own analysis, however, is not to redefine the term "fascism" itself, but to extend the received conversation about culture and politics in wartime Japan in new directions that are opened up by the writers and thinkers whom I read through the lenses of middlebrow, worldliness, and prosaics in particular. The first chapters show how each of these keywords identifies a nexus of aesthetics and ideas that produced distinctive Japanese literary writing that breathed with the intellectual life of the period in unexpected ways. Chapter 1 explores how the intense rumination on mythic native essences (*kokutai*) that has usually been understood in terms of a highbrow intellectual discourse also engaged a more modest middlebrow literary culture that aspired to cultural sophistication even though it had little patience for scholarly esoterica. Chapter 2 then examines how the philosophy of "worldliness" that appeared in noted Kyoto School writings drifted beyond the realm of theory and into literary practice, where it informed a "novel of ideas" that linked the forms of text and world in a literary idiom unbounded by purposeful expository rhetoric. In chapter 3, I read the "prosaic imagination" in the texts of leftist writers and intellectuals who responded to the literary abstractions of wartime ideology by rebelling against the regime of literary aesthetics as they understood it, and by drawing fresh inspiration from the socially contextualized language of everyday life. Taken together, these chapters offer a multidimensional profile of how literature and ideas in interwar Japan conspired in nativist, cosmopolitan, and Marxist imaginations of the time.

As I explore these connections, I heed Trilling's warning, expressed in his essay "The Meaning of a Literary Idea," that one must be careful not to confuse the complex dialogue between literature and thought with a simpler relationship of inevitability or embodiment. As he put it in his discussion of European literature and ideas:

> Kafka does not exemplify Kierkegaard, Proust does not dramatize Bergson. One way of putting the relationship of this literature to ideas is to say that the literature of contemporary Europe is in competition with philosophy, theology, and science, that it seeks to match them in comprehensiveness and power and seriousness.
>
> This is not to say that the best of contemporary European literature makes upon us the effect of a rational system of thought. Quite the contrary, indeed; it is precisely its artistic power that we respond to, which I take in part to be its power of absorbing and disturbing us in secret ways. But this power it surely derives from its commerce, according to its own rules, with systematic ideas.[25]

At first glance, literature's "competition" with thought might be more apparent in some of the contexts that I examine in the first chapters of this study (such as Yokomitsu's avant-garde modernism) than in others (such as Tanizaki's middlebrow writings). In reading through a range of registers, though, I remember Trilling's observation that the "commerce" involving "artistic power" and "systematic ideas" can materialize even in the language of writers who disavow all connections to intellectual life. He wrote that Ernest Hemingway and William Faulkner "have insisted on their indifference to the conscious intellectual tradition of our time and have acquired the reputation of achieving their effects by means that have the least possible connection with any sort of intellectuality or even with intelligence."[26] But nevertheless, Trilling added, if we were to explain "a certain commendable quality" in their writings, "we are not called upon by our subject to show that particular recognizable ideas of a certain force or weight are 'used' in the work. Nor are we called upon to show that new ideas of a certain force and weight are 'produced' by the work."[27] All that would matter, Trilling wrote, is a "certain aesthetic effect" created by the literary, which "is to be judged by some of the criteria by which an idea is judged."[28] In making this claim, Trilling suggested that the "meaning of a literary idea" articulates itself by "absorbing and disturbing us in secret ways" through aesthetic language formed in "commerce, according to its own rules, with systematic ideas." This is the case even in literary writings that seem to bear no trace of relation to the realm of ideas at all, for in them, too, Trilling observed, an "aesthetic effect" could depend "in large degree upon intellectual power, upon the amount and recalcitrance of the material the mind works on, and upon the mind's success in mastering the large material."[29]

Exploring these dynamics in the first chapters of this study opens a new perspective on the literature and thought of interwar Japan as it reveals unexpected connections between aesthetics and ideas that might otherwise seem to have had little to do with each other. As the study unfolds, moreover, it positions the interwar crisis of modernity within a global transwar frame. This allows the latter portions of the study to explore how Japanese literary writing can broaden our understanding of an idea that is not always associated with the transwar period at all, but which in fact cast its roots as an intellectual formation in the same time of capitalist crisis that gave rise to the fascist form, too, later developing more fully. This idea is known as "neoliberalism."

The word itself is believed to have been coined during the war years by a transatlantic circle of thinkers who hoped to reinvent the liberal imagination in response to the interwar rise of various collectivisms (including fascism, socialism, and communism). In the midcentury years that followed, the architects of early neoliberal thought set out to rebuild the public faith in free-market capitalism that they believed had been shattered by the disasters of the Great Depression, the failures of classic liberalism, and the vogue of state planning.[30] They countered the fascist appeals to collectivist solidarity and the Cold War specter of communist control by positing the origins of freedom in the marketplace initiatives of individuals acting within universal orders bounded by rules. In so doing, early neoliberal thinkers advocated for a model of subjectivity that was premised on an entrepreneurial self-interest, and for a model of society that was based on law and order, each of which made the neoliberal mind skeptical of the forms of mass empowerment promised by the postwar discourses of democracy and "social justice."[31] It follows that tracing the development of early neoliberal thought in the latter portions of this study complicates the more familiar image of democracy on the rise after 1945 that has appeared in numerous studies of postwar Japan, and directs attention to right-leaning liberal perspectives of the time that were more market oriented. In turn, this illuminates a global transwar frame in which a host of unanswered questions emanating from the crises of the "prewar" years suffused the "postwar" period, too, and opens an interpretive trajectory that accounts for how some of these questions took on ideological lives of their own that have continued to develop over the long duration—up to and including today.

As I approach neoliberalism as an article of transwar intellectual history, though, I must emphasize that it was still a fledgling idea incubating in discourse at this time, and make clear at the outset that there was no such thing as a hegemonic "neoliberal" society or state anywhere in the world in the midcentury years, neither in Japan nor anywhere else. Readers of David Harvey will know a robust "neoliberalism" that is defined primarily in terms of political economic trends and class conflicts that took shape in the 1970s and beyond, and readers of Wendy Brown have engaged "neoliberalism" as a fully formed mode of governing today that comes into conflict with what Brown described as the fundamental principles of democracy.[32] But my approach remembers that these and other analysts—including neoliberalism's most famous interpreter, Michel Foucault—have noted that the deeper intellectual historical roots of neoliberalism formed much earlier, in the interwar age of capitalist catastrophe and collectivist ideology.[33] And in its early stages, neoliberal thought took shape as an idea in the discourse that developed from what the Belgian philosopher Michel Feher has suggested we might call the "right melancholy" of liberal thinkers, who feared that the failures of classic liberal ideals and the rise of collectivist alternatives in the early twentieth century could spell the end of liberal civilization itself.[34] Harvey has pointed out that although neoliberalism is today most often associated with the inhumane expansions of a market logic into previously noneconomic aspects of human life, the neoliberal thinkers of the midcentury years thought of themselves as the defenders of human dignity and individual freedom per se, for "these values, they held, were threatened not only by fascism, dictatorships, and communism, but by all forms of state intervention that substituted collective judgements for those of individuals free to choose."[35] Over the course of the postwar decades, the neoliberal persuasion that first emerged in the transwar years would become a global sensation, giving structure to what Harvey described as a form of cultural common sense.[36]

In tracing the emergence of the neoliberal imagination through a literary lens in the latter portions of this study, I read in contexts both within and beyond the geographical territory of Japan itself as I show how Japanese literary writing can present a new perspective on what is more conventionally considered to be a transatlantic intellectual history of neoliberal thought. To this end, the last chapter of this study examines a dynamic moment in the nascent discursive formation of neoliberal thought at the University of Chicago in the 1950s and shows how this was also an influential context in the early reception of modern Japanese literature in the Anglophone world. Then, in the epilogue, I move on to a time when neoliberal ideology more thoroughly penetrated the cultural common sense of the global 1980s that was refracted through Japanese popular fiction. Reading the literary dimension of neoliberal thought in the 1950s and the 1980s draws an unlikely connection between these two chronologically disparate contexts that might otherwise remain alienated from each other; after all, I will posit the former as an intellectual historical context in the midcentury years that earnestly linked the political imagination to practices of serious literary reading and criticism, and then argue that the latter constituted its 1980s pop cultural other because it seemed to set aside political and historical pretenses altogether. But my goal all along in reading the literary dynamic of these two seemingly unrelated moments is to reveal that although "neoliberalism" today is sometimes caricatured as a simple matter of free-market fundamentalism, it has long comprised a more complicated form of cultural imagination capable of making its appeals at all rhetorical points between the poles of rigorous political argumentation and the more intuitive realm of cultural common sense.

Ultimately, this draws the study to a close with a reflection on the resonances of transwar literary and intellectual history in more recent times, remembering the historian Leslie Pincus's observation in her study of the philosopher Kuki Shūzō that studying aesthetics, thought, and politics can "illuminate the interpretive battles from which history is generated."[37] On the face of it, perhaps, there might not seem to be many afterlives of such "battles" to trace these days. After all, the political philosopher Francis Fukuyama (in)famously announced the "end of history" itself in 1989 and substantiated aspects of this enormous claim with reference to modern Japan as a key context in the global contest of twentieth-century ideas.[38] For Fukuyama, the sort of Hegelian historical consciousness that thrives in moments of ideological struggle had burned bright in the interwar years and later during the Cold War decades, but had weakened at "the end of history" as liberalism vanquished its foes and won the contest of ideas by the end of the twentieth century. In a resonant perspective focused on the literature of modern Japan, the philosopher Karatani Kōjin raised the question of what he called "the end of modern literature" (*kindai bungaku no owari*) with reference to Hegel and Fukuyama, too.[39]

But however paradoxically, Karatani also described how it was precisely in the late 1980s—a time of endings among which numbered the death of the Shōwa emperor, the conclusion of the Cold War, and what Fukuyama called the "end of history" itself—that he in fact became drawn to the literary rendering of historical repetitions. He wrote that "it is actually difficult to directly engage this type of repetitive structure. Historians and sociologists tend to avoid it. On the other hand, the major novelists of contemporary Japan all thematized the repetitive quality of modern Japan. For this reason, I first wrote these essays [later published in the volume *Rekishi to hanpuku* (History and Repetition, 2004)] in the form of literary criticism."[40] This comes closer to the tendency of my own study, which ends by turning to trends in contemporary Japanese literature that complicate the picture of a clean resolution to the ideological contests of the twentieth century at the so-called end of history. Without positing a repetition of history per se, the last part of this study puts recent literary writing from Japan into conversation with perspectives on how the neoliberal condition today stands in relation to its own past, which ranges back to the time of the fascist politics of the war years that the midcentury neoliberal intellectuals promised to overcome. This draws the study to a close by considering how the language of popular fiction in Japan that might seem to have little to do with politics or ideas at all can nevertheless supply a vantage point from which to reflect on the resonances of transwar literature and thought in a time closer to our own.

Outline of the Study

As I approach a range of Japanese writings within the transwar chronology described above, I am mindful of the intellectual Maruyama Masao's implied admonition not to ascribe an overdetermined interpretive structure to texts that belong to what he called a "structureless 'tradition'" (*mukōzō no 'dentō'*). In *Nihon no shisō* (Japanese Thought, 1961), Maruyama argued that the intellectual history of Japan had never coalesced within a single narrative organized by clearly demarcated "axial coordinates" (*zahyōjiku*).[41] To the extent that this is so, perhaps it is a virtue, at least inasmuch as the paradox of a "tradition" without "structure" frees readers to explore how Japanese thought has "conspired" with a wide range of literary aesthetics in ways that more rigid boundaries might have prevented. With that said, however, a tradition without structure is also a perplexing object of study. It presents crossed wires where we might assume closed circuits and asks us to interpret unexpected intersections of literature and thought which, however provocative and productive, were also contingent and ambiguous. Interlocutors once engaged in vigorous dialogue may have subsequently moved in different directions, and connections between aesthetics and ideas that were intuitive in earlier times can come to be divided by the more systematic formulations of literary and intellectual histories that later take shape. At times, too, studying literature in its moments of self-alienation and engagements with nonliterary others can uncover politics and persuasions with which writers themselves might have later liked to forget that they ever sympathized. It can also reveal that received narratives about prominent texts have not fully accounted for some of the fundamental stakes of canonical writings we thought we knew.

All of these issues figure in the pages that follow. Taken together, they reveal that the connections between literature and thought that I examine in the chapters to come are mercurial objects of study because they materialized within the unresolved time of a past present that writers and thinkers themselves "lived feverishly minute by minute," to borrow Jean-Paul Sartre's expression.[42] In retrospect, of course, things look different. After all, the first parts of this study examine aspects of a past that appears to us today to be bounded by an inarguable endpoint: the collapse of the Japanese empire, the atomic bombings of Hiroshima and Nagasaki, and the Japanese surrender that ended the Pacific War all seem to indicate that the Japanese defeat in 1945 signaled a nearly totalized end of an era to which everything preceding inexorably led. And on the other side of 1945, we know looking back that the neoliberal ideas that first gathered in the transwar years would go on to exert a tremendous influence globally. But the neoliberal thinkers of the midcentury years could not have known that, and far from confidently prophesying the triumphant rise of their most cherished principles, they thought of themselves for years as marginalized outsiders clinging to imperiled ideals on the brink of obliteration.

Emphasizing the contingencies of literary and intellectual history reveals that the relations between literature and thought that materialize within the fluctuating boundaries of a perishable present that was "lived feverishly minute by minute" are not relations of complete embodiment, perfect identity, or historical inevitability. Instead, I aim to show in the chapters that follow how literature came into what might be called a "pensive" relationship to thought, remembering that Jacques Rancière once observed in another context that "the adjective ['pensive'] describes a curious condition: someone who is pensive is 'full of thoughts,' but this does not mean that she is thinking them. In pensiveness, the act of thinking seems to be encroached upon by a certain passivity."[43] Extending this formulation, it might be said that the pensive literary writing examined here does not reveal any inevitable effect that was coerced by its intellectual interlocutors. Instead, the "pensive" literary text is "encroached upon by a certain passivity" that leaves room for what Trilling called a "certain aesthetic effect" to work its magic in literary terms, even while the literary writing in question conspires with adjacent structures of thought and engages in a literary "commerce, according to its own rules, with systematic ideas." In this view, the "pensive text" creates a middle ground within the confluences and conflicts of aesthetics and ideas more generally—a "zone of indeterminacy between thought and non-thought, activity and passivity, but also between art and non-art," as Rancière had it in the case of the "pensive image."[44]

One of the main arguments that emerges from this approach is that reading time and text together affords the opportunity to explore some of the perceptions of the historical present within and against which culture and ideology have mutually imbricated. To show how, my readings in the pensive middle ground of literature and thought draw on elements of the interpretive strategy developed by the literary scholars Gary Saul Morson and Michael André Bernstein called "sideshadowing," a neologism that they coined in opposition to the determinism of "foreshadowing" and "backshadowing."[45] Wary of the power of teleological thinking and foregone conclusions, Morson and Bernstein posited "sideshadowing" as a method for melding elements of historical inquiry and literary criticism in an effort to recuperate the field of perceived possibilities that saturate the temporal topos of past presents. But as I consider the implications of Morson's and Bernstein's critiques of linear thinking in the specific context of wartime Japan and beyond, I layer them with the darker implications of perceived possibility that appeared in Tosaka's perspective on the fascist cultural politics of 1930s Japan. One of Tosaka's most important insights was that culture explained away the troubling effects of politics by trafficking in illusory visions of pure possibility.[46] Taken a step further, this would suggest that perceived possibilities became one of the animating forces driving the wartime ideologies of the global 1930s. Culture and ideology also mixed in the unresolved time of the postwar world that Tosaka himself never lived to see, and the latter portions of this study draw inspiration from aspects of his wartime critique as they examine the formation of a nascent neoliberal imagination in the midcentury years through a literary lens.

The chapters that follow trace these dynamics across a spectrum of connections ranging from close collaboration between a writer and an intellectual who coproduced a text to dialogues that materialized within mutually aware literary and intellectual articulations, and to conceptual reckonings that reverberated across contemporaneous texts in a network of political affiliation obscured by the fact that the figures involved never personally collaborated with one another per se. Chapter 1 points to an example of a close collaboration in interwar Japan by taking up the middlebrow rendering of imperial ideology in order to show how the abstract idea of *kokutai* (national polity) community conspired with more modest regimes of bourgeois cultural taste. I focus on the unlikely partnership forged between Yamada Yoshio, a noted linguist and scholar of classical Japanese literature, and the popular novelist Tanizaki Jun'ichirō, both of whom (in different ways) came to believe that the crisis of representation in 1930s Japan was a crisis of modern language first and foremost. I argue that their collaboration on a modern translation of Murasaki Shikibu's *Genji monogatari* (The Tale of Genji, 11th c.) brought forth a "middlebrow" notion of cultural authenticity that reflected Tanizaki's critique of Japan's modern vernacular (*genbun-itchi*), and that evoked the abstract idea of *kokutai* that Yamada also described as coauthor of the 1937 propaganda piece *Kokutai no hongi* (The Essence of Our National Polity). This reveals how their translation allowed a nativist intellectual discourse to conspire with the more intuitive pleasures that characterize middlebrow literary culture. The chapter ends by considering how the middlebrow intersected with a higher-minded discourse that posited *Genji* as a classic of "world literature," and this clears the way to examine more philosophically informed writing and thinking related to the concept of "worldly" relations in the next analysis.

In chapter 2, I turn to the highbrow realm of philosophy and avant-garde modernism in order to examine figures who became convinced that the global 1930s were witnessing a cataclysm of world historical proportions. The chapter revolves around the dialogue that emerged between the novelist Yokomitsu Riichi and his interlocutors associated with Kyoto School philosophy as I read their conversation as a locus in which ideas of world history and practices of world literature breathed together. I begin by examining the philosophical rumination on "worldly" relations that is most often associated with Kyoto School philosophers' expositions, and then inquire after the literary dimension of this discussion by examining the connections between text and world that it implied. This sets the stage for a reading of Yokomitsu's magnum opus, *Ryoshū* (The Melancholy of Travel, 1937–46), a long but unfinished "novel of ideas" (*shisō shōsetsu*) that was inspired in part by Yokomitsu's dialogue with Yura Tetsuji (1897–1979), a minor philosopher in the wider Kyoto School circle. Drawing on the scholar of cosmopolitanism Pheng Cheah's critique of world literature, I illuminate some of the literary implications of the Kyoto School discourse on "worldliness" by asking how the ontology of the literary comes into worldly being as the subjective experience of each individual reader engages the objective forms of language that collectively make up the legible whole of literary narrative. Weaving these threads together leads me to conclude that *The Melancholy of Travel* refracted some of the same ideals of worldly cohesion that also led to ruin in adjacent philosophical writings that justified Japanese imperialism under the sign of a world-making "collectivism" (*kyōdōshugi*).

Chapter 3 then moves away from the middlebrow neoclassicism and highbrow ruminations on "worldly" form that are examined in the early portions of this study, and engages the limits of literature itself through the writings of leftists who believed that modern Japan had been overcome not by modernity, but by the literary. For them, the vogue of romanticism, neoclassicism, and abstract philosophy had severed the bonds by which the most pragmatic, nonaesthetic elements of everyday discourse represent the lived experience of contemporary history. This leads me to reexamine the leftist literary culture of the period by reading the writings of Tosaka alongside those of the Marxist writer Nakano Shigeharu as I limn the possibilities for resistance to wartime ideology that were expressed by the networked articulations of what I call the "prosaic imagination." I start by examining the sociolinguistic and semiotic imperatives of prosaic theory that posited literary meaning in dialogue with everyday life, and then ask how those imperatives informed concrete techniques of literary practice. This leads to a new interpretation of Nakano's writing that focuses on how moments of reading, writing, and speaking that appear in his texts performed what the scholar of French and comparative literature Michael Lucey has called "literary fieldwork," a prosaic practice by which literary writers take up some of the preoccupations of the linguistic anthropologist in order to dig beneath semantic surfaces and excavate the deeper social architecture that is conveyed by each and every contextualized utterance. The chapter then closes by considering how Nakano, as a literary critic himself, showed that the act of prosaic reading could identify the political machinations not only of the authoritarian imagination during the war years, but also of the postwar poetics that came in with the Occupation era that followed.

The study then segues into the midcentury years in chapter 4, which traces the confluence between literary form and early neoliberal thought in the course of considering how a classic Japanese novel was read outside Japan. The analysis revolves around Edwin McClellan's 1957 English translation of Natsume Sōseki's novel *Kokoro*, which McClellan completed while he was still a graduate student at the University of Chicago working with his doctoral adviser, the famed Austrian economist Friedrich Hayek. In the 1950s, Hayek was leading an international group of liberal thinkers who differed from each other in many ways, but who shared the common goal of responding to the rise of fascism in wartime Europe and the continuing threat of communism worldwide with a reconstructed and rejuvenated culture of market enterprise. This group—the Mont Pèlerin Society—has often been cited at the origins of the ideology known as "neoliberalism." As I reconnect the *Kokoro* translation to its original context of production and reception on the liberal right in early postwar America, I also ask how it can be read as a literary aesthetic form through which to rethink the shape of the neoliberal imagination in the global context of the midcentury years writ large. In this light, we begin to see how a modern classic from Japan that is often read in relation to Meiji modernization and framed under the sign of national culture was reborn as an English-language novel that breathed in translation with globally oriented conservative and neoliberal politics.

The epilogue then offers a coda to chapter 4 that sketches the "neoliberal aesthetic" of Japan's flush 1980s in the internationally popular writings of Murakami Haruki (1949–). Focusing on his early novel *Hitsuji o meguru bōken* (A Wild Sheep Chase, 1982), I move my narrative away from elite thinkers and organized movements, and into the realm of pop fiction that rendered the dynamics of the neoliberal condition as a matter of cultural common sense, rather than of intellectual arguments. But as I do so, I also trace the suspensions of a deeper history within the contemporary complexion of writings by a popular novelist and note aspects of the neoliberal condition that have become ironic legacies of the global 1930s—that not-so-distant past in which it originated. My study then ends with a brief consideration of the implications of the neoliberal condition today for the narrative style that I myself have adopted: the academic style of literary scholarship.

CHAPTER 1

Middlebrow as Method

Tanizaki Jun'ichirō, Yamada Yoshio, and *The Tale of Genji* in the Age of Empire

If any human being, man, woman, dog, cat or half-crushed worm dares call me "middlebrow" I will take my pen and stab him, dead.
—Virginia Woolf[1]

The American cultural critic Dwight Macdonald wrote in 1953 that the King James Version of the Bible (1611) "is probably the greatest translation ever made."[2] Macdonald believed that although the translation was not the original telling of anything, it had had an incalculable influence on seemingly everything that came after it in the literature and culture of English-speaking peoples. This was so because in addition to being a foundational religious text, it was also a masterpiece of style, one that appeared "at the end of the Elizabethan age, between Shakespeare and Milton, when Englishmen were using words more passionately, richly, vigorously, wittily, and sublimely than ever before or since."[3] He lamented that its pride of place had been threatened by a mid-twentieth-century upstart. In "Updating the Bible" (1953), Macdonald compared the King James Version to the Revised Standard Version released in 1952, noting that the more recent translation had aimed to combine modern biblical scholarship with a more legible style for contemporary readers. He felt that the quest for accessibility and factual accuracy had succeeded mostly in destroying something sacred and stylish.

To make the point, Macdonald's critique marked its place in time by metaphorically comparing the damage done by the revisers' new translation of the Bible to the wreckage recently wrought by Allied bombings of European cities during World War II:

> Our bombers tried to spare the more celebrated monuments of Europe, though "military necessity" often compelled their destruction. The Revisers' military necessity is the language of the Common Man. Reading their work is like walking through an old city that has just been given, if not a saturation bombing, a thorough going-over. One looks about anxiously. Is this gone? Does that still survive? Surely they might have spared *that!*
>
> And even though many of the big landmarks are left—their fabric weakened by the Revisers' policy of modernizing the grammatical usage—so many of the lesser structures have been razed that the whole feel of the place is different. In Cologne, in 1950, the cathedral still stood, alone and strange, in the midst of miles of rubble.[4]

Macdonald's incendiary metaphor for translation pointed to the alterations in textual topography that inevitably materialize when older classics are replaced by updates geared to the sensibilities of later readers who never set out in search of the "original" of anything. And in the context of reading *Genji monogatari* (The Tale of Genji, 11th c.) in early twentieth-century Japan, this is a good place to start.

After all, the original manuscript in Murasaki Shikibu's Heian hand was long ago lost, and as the scholar and translator Michael Emmerich has observed, *Genji* has long been a classic that has been not so much received as a single textual object endowed with auratic originality as it has been replaced by newer versions that have lives of their own. For this reason, Emmerich wrote that more important than "the text of *Genji monogatari* itself"—which we cannot know—"are its replacements," which "literally take the place of *Genji monogatari*" and become "texts that are read instead of the (unknown and unknowable) original."[5] As I proceed with this in mind, though, I also remember that Macdonald's discussion of different versions of the Bible alerts us to the fact that not all "replacements" convey the same aesthetic power. In the case of bad translations, a lot can go wrong, as Macdonald pointed out in "Updating the Bible." And so the question lingers: What is it that makes for a compelling textual dialogue by which older and newer versions of a classic breathe together without one suffocating the other? In this chapter, I think through this question by examining how the act of translation in interwar Japan allowed high-minded ideas to conspire with more intuitive literary pleasures in the peculiar register of the middlebrow.

My case study is the 1939 modern translation (*gendaigoyaku*) of *The Tale of Genji* that was completed through the collaboration of the novelist Tanizaki Jun'ichirō, the nativist scholar Yamada Yoshio, and the publisher Chūōkōronsha. A "modern translation" of *Genji* is a necessity for any reader who lacks specialist training in the ancient language of the Heian vernacular because these translations rework the antiquated and (for untrained readers) illegible grammar and diction of older versions of the classic into the contemporary idiom. But instead of being a translation premised on traversing a distance measured by space (i.e., the translation of a text originally composed in the language spoken in one place into the language spoken somewhere else), the "modern translation" of *Genji* in question here is a translation premised on traversing a distance measured by time, from the eleventh-century Japanese vernacular of Murasaki's Heian court to a twentieth-century Japanese vernacular more familiar to Tanizaki's readers. And in addition to bridging the divide separating past and present, the 1939 *Genji* translation examined here also had the peculiarity of emerging from imaginations that understood their cultural work within a futural trajectory leading in the direction of imperial grandeur.

We know this because the discourse surrounding the translation around the time of its appearance narrated its significance within a larger cultural historical flow that was believed to have been destined to traverse the horizon of a conflict-riddled present and to deliver readers to an appealing vision of cultural restoration. In this sense, the 1939 *Genji* translation emerged from a collaboration occasioned in part by the perceived open-endedness of its own moment in time, for although Tanizaki and Yamada were always different sorts of thinkers, to be sure, they did breathe together in conversation about their shared perception that the war years were the time to envision a renewed modern vernacular language organic to past centuries of Japanese usage. This envisioned renewal would never be realized, however: soon after the translation was released between 1939 and 1941, the tides of the Pacific War turned against Japanese forces, collapsing the possibility for cultural restoration that its producers had earlier engaged. As those threads unraveled, so, too, did the context in which

Tanizaki and Yamada originally conversed dissolve. The result has been an uneven distribution of judgment casting them in different lights—so different, in fact, that looking back, it might be hard to believe that their earlier conversation was ever possible.

On the one hand, Yamada's contributions to the war effort were so inarguable that he was listed among those literary figures bearing "war responsibility" as early as 1946.[6] His collaboration had been official: he wrote propaganda for the wartime regime and served as the head of an Ise institute that promoted state Shinto, which pushed the question of his complicity with the construction of wartime ideology beyond doubt. But in contrast, Tanizaki's connections to imperial ideology have proven to be more perplexing. Some have harshly indicted his complicity, while others have offered more moderate assessments, or even suggested that he resisted the wartime zeitgeist.[7] One complicating factor is that Tanizaki wrote so broadly and for so long that his corpus presents a mixed record. The multidirectional dynamics of Tanizaki's writings led the film and media studies scholar Thomas LaMarre to emphasize the irreducible ambivalence of their politics. He noted that while many critics had focused either on cultural nationalism or its subversion in Tanizaki's fiction, it would be better to say that the polarity contrasting complicity with resistance obscures their more complicated mixtures in his imagination, making us forget that even Tanizaki's nationalism could be critical and, at times, subversive itself.[8] From this perspective, it would be inadequate to describe Tanizaki's writings either in terms of complicity or resistance, nationalism or cosmopolitanism, tradition or modernity, commitments to the East or the West. LaMarre proposed instead that we delve into how Tanizaki "inhabit[ed] the rupture between" these sorts of polarities, "a site of great discomfort, of anxiety, impossibility, and crisis," and focused on Tanizaki's multidimensional "oscillation."[9]

This chapter understands these "oscillating" movements to have been characteristic not only of Tanizaki's writing in particular, but of an ambivalent "middlebrow" culture that breathed with high and low, politics and pleasure, the aspirational autonomy of art and the pecuniary motives of the market, more generally. As I interpret Tanizaki's relation to Yamada through a prism of middlebrow convergence, I will explore how the pleasures for which Tanizaki's fiction has long been well known (and, for some, much-loved) conspired with the imperial ideology of his age that Yamada had a hand in crafting, too. My approach remembers that their *Genji* translation appeared at around the time that Japanese imperial power in East Asia was at its zenith, and that in this context, Tanizaki's editor, Yamada, had recently coauthored the most widely circulated piece of government-issued propaganda in wartime Japan, *Kokutai no hongi* (The Essence of Our National Polity, 1937). But with that said, I also remember that the scholar of Japanese literature Nishino Atsushi has observed that while the Tanizaki-Yamada *Genji* could be read as a kind of supplement to ***kokutai*** ideology, it contradicted that ideology, too.[10] The historian Max Ward has shown that in legal contexts, ***kokutai*** appeared in debates surrounding the interwar Peace Preservation Law as a term intended to identify a difficult-to-define native essence that was believed to have been threatened by foreign ideologies and nurtured by a "line of Emperors unbroken for ages eternal" (*bansei ikkei no tennō*).[11] Readers of *Genji* know that in contrast, the Heian tale infamously dramatizes the pollution of those very imperial bloodlines and therefore undermines what in other contexts was understood to have been the foundation of ***kokutai*** community itself. And whereas *The Essence of Our National Polity* was notoriously difficult to understand, tending as it did in the direction of recondite language requiring extensive explanatory supplements, the *Genji* translation was a vigorous cultural commodity marketed to middle-class readers as a pleasurable pastime.

These tensions prevented the cultural currents that carried the *Genji* translation forward from ever becoming a simple matter of instrumentalist propaganda or purely autonomous aesthetics. More precisely, these currents flowed into and out from a space of oscillation, to borrow LaMarre's term, a space in which the market matters of cultural capitalism and the earnest claims of Japanese nativism interacted and counteracted one another in the middle ground of the middlebrow. Balancing these dynamics leads me to read the rhetoric of cultural traditions in imperial Japan critically, and to understand it in terms of distinctly modern (rather than uniquely Japanese) forms of ideological articulation, as Ward suggested in his study of ***kokutai*** discourse.[12] It follows that this chapter attunes to layers of irony and paradox (rather than any one-dimensional conviction) as it explores how the all-but-undefinable idea of a mythic native essence (*kokutai*) that so often appeared in the highbrow intellectual discourse of imperial Japan also conspired with a literary imagination that took middlebrow to be its method.

Middlebrow

In "Middlebrow" (1932), a letter addressed to *The New Statesman*, the novelist Virginia Woolf defined a "highbrow" as "the man or woman of thoroughbred intelligence who rides his mind at a gallop across country in pursuit of an idea," contrasting this with a "lowbrow," who is "a man or a woman of thoroughbred vitality who rides his body in pursuit of a living at a gallop across life."[13] Shakespeare is a highbrow in Woolf's estimation, whereas the conductor of an omnibus is a lowbrow. But both the cultural pursuits of the highbrow and the practical labor of the lowbrow were laudable in Woolf's view, and there was, in fact, no tension but only sympathy between the two groups. She wrote that "lowbrows need highbrows and honour them just as much as highbrows need lowbrows and honour them."[14] The problem was with "middlebrows": "They are the go-betweens," Woolf wrote, "they are the busybodies who run from one to the other with their tittle tattle and make all the mischief—the middlebrows, I repeat."[15] While acknowledging the difficulty of definition, Woolf wrote that the middlebrow is "the man, or woman, of middlebred intelligence who ambles and saunters now on this side of the hedge, now on that, in pursuit of no single object, neither art itself nor life itself, but both mixed indistinguishably, and rather nastily, with money, fame, power, or prestige."[16] The links among literary classics, money-making, and middlebrow pedagogy came through as Woolf reported that when she had asked her "lowbrow" acquaintances why they learn Shakespeare from the middlebrows, they told her that it was because "they consider themselves to be common people without education. It is very kind of the middlebrows to try to teach them culture. And after all, the lowbrows continue, middlebrows, like other people, have to make money. There must be money in teaching and in writing books about Shakespeare."[17] Woolf loathed the middlebrow for dissolving authentic cultural authority and bona fide learning into the lower order of self-interested profiteering, and this was why she wrote that "the true battle in my opinion lies not between highbrow and lowbrow, but between highbrows and lowbrows joined together in blood brotherhood against the bloodless and pernicious pest who comes between."[18] The last lines of her letter made her position plain: "If any human being, man, woman, dog, cat or half-crushed worm dares call me 'middlebrow' I will take my pen and stab him, dead."[19]

Woolf's statement implied several of the most familiar tensions evoked by the appellation "middlebrow." They include the need for accessible pedagogy clashing with the prestige of hard-earned erudition, the allure of profits in the culture industry colliding with the priceless authenticity of the aesthetic, and the fate of the classics in the bourgeois hands of the modern middle class.[20] These tensions led Macdonald, in "Masscult and Midcult" (1960), to describe the traffic between higher and lower registers in terms of a cultural smuggling by which the middlebrow keeps its incognito as it assumes some of the trappings of the avant-garde:

> In these more advanced times, the danger to High Culture is not so much from Masscult as from a peculiar hybrid bred from the latter's unnatural intercourse with the former. A whole middle culture has come into existence and it threatens to absorb both its parents. This intermediate form—let us call it Midcult—has the essential qualities of Masscult—the formula, the built-in reaction, the lack of any standard except popularity—but it decently covers them with a cultural figleaf. In Masscult the trick is plain—to please the crowd by any means. But Midcult has it both ways: it pretends to respect the standards of High Culture while in fact it waters them down and vulgarizes them. The enemy outside the walls is easy to distinguish. It is its ambiguity that makes Midcult alarming. For it presents itself as part of High Culture.[21]

To unpack these sentiments, it serves to recall that the scholar of music Christopher Chowrimootoo has observed that "the 'problem' of middlebrow culture lay not just in its ability to mediate between high and low, modernism and mass culture, but also in the distinctive challenges it posed to modernist fantasies of aesthetic autonomy."[22] This is to say that in contrast to the highbrow idealization of art and artist as independent from the vicissitudes of market-mediated valuation and the demands of mass audience popularity, the middlebrow has seemed to some to present a more opportunistic mode of cultural production catering to the market and masses in particular, "as though creator, critic, and audience were involved in a conspiracy," in Chowrimootoo's words.[23]

One of the most basic conditions of possibility for the "conspiracy" of middlebrow literary culture in the early twentieth century was the cohesion of a publishing infrastructure that enabled the proliferation of mass print media on an industrial scale. This media history has already been widely analyzed, and in one study, the scholar Edward Mack noted that the commodification of literature in early twentieth-century Japan prompted a series of debates (*ronsō*) in which writers and critics sought to define literary meaning against the pecuniary interests of the market by asserting "the existence of an alternative economy of value, one that could not be conflated with a text's commercial viability."[24] But as surely as the rise of the print media marketplace instigated these anxious discussions of the value of literature as both art and commodity, so, too, did it distribute the articulation of dangerous political possibilities far and wide. One prominent example from this time was the magazine *Kingu* (King, 1925–57), which the scholar of Japanese literature Nathan Shockey described as a popular entertainment alternative to "highbrow or upper-class magazines (*kōkyū zashi*)" like *Chūō Kōron* and *Bungei Shunjū*, and which in January 1927 became the first magazine to achieve a circulation of over one million copies.[25] Shockey and the scholar of Japanese print media Satō Takumi have noted that the material infrastructure of the print media industry that drove the rise of magazines like *Kingu* proved profitable for its producers and entertaining for its consumers at the same time that it supplied a mass mechanism for disseminating fascistic political appeals, too.[26] And on this score, the Japanese context was but one among many. The art critic Clement Greenberg would write with reference to the transatlantic idiom that the rise of popular culture that he called "kitsch" could prove to be a resource for mass political representation in a way that the more serious, highbrow art of the avant-garde had not:

> As a matter of fact, the main trouble with avant-garde art and literature, from the point of view of fascists and Stalinists, is not that they are too critical, but that they are too "innocent," that it is too difficult to inject effective propaganda into them, that kitsch is more pliable to this end.

> Kitsch keeps a dictator in closer contact with the "soul" of the people. Should the official culture be one superior to the general mass-level, there would be a danger of isolation.[27]

Taken together, these perspectives help us to see that both within and beyond Japan, the rise of mass media in the early twentieth century enabled the lightness of popular entertainment to conspire with the dead seriousness of fascist politics. This is something of a conclusion in itself, given that middlebrow culture often denigrated as opportunistic and inauthentic might not seem to be substantial enough to sustain a political appeal in the first place. After all, few writers have ever self-identified with the appellation "middlebrow," much less aspired to it, and this is no doubt in part because the pejorative connotations of "middlebrow" contrast it with the more prestigious modernist ideal of a cutting-edge "avant-garde." This subordinate status comes through more clearly still in recalling that the "lowbrow"–"middlebrow"–"highbrow" schematic carries within itself an implicit reference to the purported findings of phrenology, an ultimately discredited "science" that once posited (among other things) that the larger one's forehead and the higher one's brow, the greater one's intelligence. In addition to "highbrow," the term "supercilious" also signifies an air of superiority with reference to brow structure (*supercilium*, "eyebrow," plus Latin suffix *-osus*, "full of"), and in more colloquial language, the playfully pejorative "egghead" likewise alludes to the skull structure of those who are supposedly the most brainy.[28] The shadow of the phrenological premise implicit in the "lowbrow"–"middlebrow"–"highbrow" gradation resonates with an imperial pedagogy according to which some groups are naturally entitled to lead others, whether because of their biological traits (as the phrenologists would have had it) or because of their aesthetic and intellectual superiority (as twentieth-century highbrows might have claimed).

But the subjects of this chapter reveal how the claim to privilege could come with a twist: instead of positing the highbrow "eggheads" as the intellectual and cultural vanguard, their work on the *Genji* translation implied a compelling commentary on the fitness of a bourgeois middlebrow culture to hold authority in imperial Japan. These dynamics come into view in considering the range of interested parties who had a stake in producing the translation. First and foremost, it reflected the talents of Tanizaki as a middlebrow maestro. By the late 1930s, he had long been active in the fields of fiction, film, and theater as a kind of pop provocateur whose tastes ranged in the direction of indulgent privilege.[29] His homage to the rollicking Tokyo jazz age in the novel *Chijin no ai* (Naomi, 1924–25) ranks among the best-known renderings of the alluring nightlife, cinematic fantasies, and social politics that filled the world of a recently monied urban middle class. But Tanizaki's collaborator on the 1939 *Genji* translation was another story altogether. Yamada was a nativist scholar who believed in the spirituality of the Japanese language, finding in it a link to the age of the gods. With little formal education, he rose from provincial obscurity to work with the Ministry of Education and publish widely on the history of the Japanese language. He was known for his scholarly erudition, writing numerous book-length studies of classic texts and weighing in on tense debates related to the modernization of various features of modern Japanese language. The force that brought Tanizaki and Yamada together was the corporate facilitator of the translation, Chūōkōronsha, a publishing giant working strategically within the censorship constraints of an increasingly repressive age for print media. The result of this tripartite confluence was middlebrow through and through: it started with a Heian tale (*monogatari*) written in an eleventh-century vernacular that was illegible to most twentieth-century readers, and ended with a modern masterpiece mixing the bawdy tastes of the playboy novelist with the dead seriousness of the nativist scholar, all while serving the commercial interests of a mainstream print media juggernaut and satisfying a mass audience. Composed in the age of imperial arrogance, its influence has ranged more widely; assessing its place within a wider stream of "*Genji* discourse," Emmerich has noted that as the 1939 Tanizaki *Genji* brought together notions of world literature and translation, it placed the tale under the halo of the now-inarguable idea that it is a Japanese classic of global stature, "creating the field within which *Genji* is now almost inevitably apprehended."[30]

Some of the deeper forces in cultural history that propelled the appeal of the *Genji* translation were memorably rendered in Tanizaki's earlier novel *Naomi*, which might be said to have studied the crisis of culture that his later *Genji* translation would try to resolve. It told the tale of Jōji, an engineer from the provinces who comes to Tokyo and marries a young café waitress, Naomi, whose complexion and features remind him of the white American actress Mary Pickford. Their romance was always premised on middle-class fantasies of social status and vapid pretenses to cultural connoisseurship, and as this becomes clear, the novel reveals a self-consciousness of its own superficiality. The knowing parody of an urban middle class in *Naomi* indicated that far more significant than Jōji's personal problems—which include marital betrayal, self-delusion, and shame—are the crises of culture evident in the novel. Narrated in the middle-class spaces of "culture houses," dance halls, and vacation villas, *Naomi* rendered a world of bourgeois pleasure in terms of a mass-mediated simulacrum in which everything is a degraded representation of something else.[31] In so doing, it dramatized the crisis of the bourgeois subject who comes to realize that he lives in a world of bad translations, so to speak—a world in which Naomi stands in as a version of Mary Pickford, for example, and in which awkward dance lessons taught by an aristocratic émigré from Russia replace regal splendor with nouveau riche aspiration. As these substitutions layer over one another, *Naomi* reminded readers of what they lost when they settled for middle-class fantasies and the middlebrow compromises that followed.

But this was ironic, of course, given that the novel itself formulated its perspective from within the very pop cultural idiom that it also critiqued.[32] And this carries implications for how I read the 1939 *Genji* translation below because it reveals a more self-conscious and even strategic middlebrow imagination than the pejorative connotations of the term might lead us to believe possible. In *Naomi*, that is, Tanizaki evoked an imagination in which middlebrow becomes a method: it was for him a technique, and a knowing choice, rather than an inevitable and unthinking capitulation to market forces by a less talented actor in the cultural field. We see this in how he made fun of middle-class fantasies even as he catered to them, and in how he idealized the leisure pursuits of a newly arrived urban class at the same time that he lambasted its philistinism. In this context, the middlebrow functioned through a complex of cultural translations that mediated between high and low, and insofar as these mediations were central to Tanizaki's fiction, it might even be said that he was a writer who made the medium of the middlebrow into the message, as it were. This sheds light on the irony and the aura of the 1939 *Genji* in particular, a text that pointed to a world beyond the vacant simulacra of *Naomi* without ever pretending to overcome the circular paradox that it, too, was always a representation of something else—namely, the imagined "original" of *Genji* itself. In this sense, the 1939 *Genji* promised a good translation that would save middlebrow readers from all the bad translations mired in middle-class striving that they learned about in *Naomi*. Without ever resolving its own paradoxes, the 1939 *Genji* lured readers on with something stylish that was never original, and that was packaged in the sort of accessible and commercially viable middlebrow format whose proliferation had occasioned its own search for authenticity in the first place.

And it worked. Emmerich has noted that the first volumes of the translation numbered among the "biggest literary best sellers of 1939," with sales so vigorous "that the wartime shortage of paper made it difficult to respond to the demand for new copies" after an initial stock of 150,000 sold out as 50,000 new orders poured into Chūōkōronsha.[33] Readers loved it. To mention only one example of the response, it will suffice here to observe that Emmerich has quoted the law professor Nakazawa Zennosuke, who wrote in one advertisement for the translation that the Tanizaki translation is "easy to understand, and it feels like *Genji*."[34] The middlebrow element of Nakazawa's appreciation came through in the implication that one of the virtues of the translation was that it conveyed the full weight of a true classic to nonspecialists with little time for eggheaded esoterica:

> The prose has been rendered into the modern language, but it has that elevated style that is the special characteristic of the classics. I wasn't able to read these two volumes in one sitting, but I'd say it must have taken me a total of only about three or four hours over the course of two or three days to read them all the way through. To be able to read five chapters of *Genji* in three or four hours and, what's more, to be able to take real pleasure in reading *Genji*—for a plain old amateur with no particular connection to the classics of our national literature, this is an astonishing blessing. At the risk of slight exaggeration, I think you might well call this a singular miracle of the Shōwa period.[35]

This helps us begin to see the appeal of middlebrow literature for an audience who enjoyed it, and who never would have denigrated it with that name.

But as Greenberg would remind us, the in-between medium of middlebrow culture can distribute politics as effectively as it does pleasure.

And with this in mind, the joy of easy reading described above must not make us forget that the translation aspired to more than simple legibility. In fact, one measure of the success of the translation was the extent to which it metabolized its connections to a more sophisticated intellectual history that, at its most ambitious, connected aspects of classical Japanese literature to an almost ethereal realm of native sensibility and pathos. This becomes clearer in understanding how the *Genji* translation most often associated with Tanizaki also breathed with Yamada's nativist perspective on Japanese language and literature. He was an authority, not a provocateur, and he was dead serious, rather than ironic. Whereas Tanizaki resembled the bourgeois metropolitan whose tastes blended enlightened skepticism with urbane style, Yamada was more the true believer. Introducing Yamada's life and thought will help us to see how the intellectual history of nativist hermeneutics allowed the middlebrow translation to conspire with higher-minded intentions. And by sensing the aspirational aspect of middlebrow literary culture, we begin to see its deeper relevance for readers in the age of empire in particular.

Highbrow Narrative Neighbors

Yamada's high-minded convictions about the Japanese language originated in his modest provincial upbringing. He was born in Toyama in 1875. Family bloodlines are said to have placed him within a lineage of linked-verse poetry (*renga*) composers.[36] But circumstances of early life forced him to end his formal schooling after only one year of middle school, and he is the only central figure in this study to have lacked an elite education. After leaving school, he took up *kokugaku* (nativist studies) with a tutor in Toyama and later received his teaching license in 1891. Yamada then embarked on a career that would carry him from the ranks of grade school teacher to university professor and beyond. Despite his lack of a prestigious educational pedigree, he rose to prominence as a historian of the Japanese language, an authority on classical Japanese literature, and a frequent public commentator on proposed reforms to language usage.[37] The publication of his 1902 study *Nihon bunpō ron jōkan* (On Japanese Grammar, Vol. 1) set him on this ascendant course, and from 1925 to 1933, Yamada taught at Tōhoku Imperial University in Sendai. He published "Genji monogatari" *no ongaku* (Music in *The Tale of Genji*) in 1934, and soon after, he began his collaboration with Tanizaki on the modern Japanese translation (*gendaigoyaku*) of the classic. Around this time, too, Yamada's concrete involvement in creating and disseminating Japan's wartime ideology deepened. He held positions affiliated with the Ministry of Education at various times in his career, and one of the most notable of these counted him among the intellectuals who served on the committee that collaboratively authored *The Essence of Our National Polity*, the noted propaganda piece published in 1937.

In addition to Yamada's achievements as a scholar of language and literature, he was also influential in the public discussion of Shinto that reached fever pitch during the war years. And in this context, he was more than a commentator: he was a believer. The historian Walter Skya has written that "Yamada is an excellent example of a radical Shintō ultranationalist who came to dominate the prewar Shintō religious establishment," adding that "for Yamada, Japan was the nation of the gods," and elaborating that this perspective followed from the fact that Yamada was "a committed creationist, a true believer in the Japanese Shintō story of creation" who reasoned "that since the imperial ancestors were gods and the Japanese people were descendants of those gods, all of the Japanese people, too, as children of the gods, must also be gods."[38] In 1940, Yamada was appointed president of Jingū Kōgakkan Daigaku, an institute in Ise dedicated to the promotion of state Shinto. He served there until the Japanese surrender in 1945, after which Yamada was blacklisted from jobs in government and education for having supported the war effort. He was awarded the Order of Culture (*bunka kunshō*) in 1957 and died in 1958.[39]

Over the course of a career spanning decades, Yamada's most notorious association was not with Tanizaki, but with the committee of intellectuals and scholars organized by the Ministry of Education to produce the infamous propaganda piece *The Essence of Our National Polity*. Originally released in 1937, this text would have millions of copies in circulation by 1945.[40] And at the time the work first appeared, Yamada's partnership with Tanizaki on the modern *Genji* had already formed around a translation that would be released in 1939, just two years after *The Essence of Our National Polity*. But although both texts had their roles in defining the identity of a nation embarked on an imperial war, it is also true that they afforded reading experiences that could hardly have been more different. In contrast to the *Genji* translation with its marketplace vigor, *The Essence of Our National Polity* was a propaganda tract composed by a committee of scholars working with bureaucratic sanction and instrumentalist intention to disseminate an official line of thinking. And whereas *Genji* was a prose fiction tale about desire and intrigue in the courtly world of Heian Japan, *The Essence of Our National Polity* took as its most potent literary inspiration the recondite poetry found in *Man'yōshū* (Collection of Ten-Thousand Leaves), a Nara-period collection that was completed in the eighth century. Some of the implications of these differences are apparent in considering that the *Genji* translation was supposed to be a joy to read even for casual consumers, whereas the difficult language of *The Essence of Our National Polity* was so esoteric that it occasioned the production of substantial explanatory supplements.[41] And whereas Chūōkōronsha touted Tanizaki's name as a legible sign endowing the 1939 *Genji* translation with the familiar appeal of a popular writer known to contemporary readers, the committee of scholars and intellectuals responsible for *The Essence of Our National Polity* remained anonymous.[42] The scholar Alan Tansman has called it a "bureaucratic document," and "a decidedly prosaic and literarily flat book written for polemical purposes by unnamed members of a government-appointed committee."[43] These descriptions suggest that one of the implicit referents of *The Essence of Our National Polity* was the highbrow intellectual mind itself, as conjured by the cumulative efforts of scholars and intellectuals whose names were nowhere disclosed by their own text.

Far from being a "flat," "bureaucratic document," *Genji* was a romance so scandalous that it was a problem for the wartime authorities who lent their official sanction to *The Essence of Our National Polity*. As is well known, its most unforgiveable sin in the 1930s was its irreverence toward the emperor: whereas *The Essence of Our National Polity* contributed to a state ideology touting a mythical lineage of emperors unbroken throughout the ages (*bansei ikkei*), Murasaki's tale dramatized the pollution of the imperial bloodlines by a libidinous commoner—Genji himself—whose own son rises to the throne, thus implying that the royal blood is not pure and holy (as the wartime regime would have had it), but sullied and degraded by a secret liaison motivated by the basest intentions. This was part of why the scholar Tomiko Yoda, in her examination of *Genji* vis-à-vis the conventional didacticism of "national literature" (*kokubungaku*) in modern Japan, observed that Genji's many sexual liaisons—including most importantly with Fujitsubo—"transgressed the state-endorsed mores at a number of levels."[44] The tension between *Genji* and *kokutai* ideology in the 1930s in particular is perhaps nowhere clearer than in remembering that *The Essence of Our National Polity* was taught to schoolchildren at a time when some versions of *Genji* were being banned. The scholar Kobayashi Masaaki has pointed out that while the amorous elements of *Genji* had long earned the ire of some readers throughout the centuries, the wartime environment of the 1930s marked the first time that "*The Tale of Genji* was not just criticized by scholars, but actively suppressed by the Japanese government."[45] Kobayashi observed that the Office of Security of the Tokyo Police Department banned a theatrical version of *Genji* in 1933 that was to be staged at Shinkabukiza—sold-out performances for which customers had already bought ten thousand tickets—on the basis that the script was "injurious to public morals" because it depicted adultery, among other things.[46] In this climate, the 1939 *Genji* translation was affected, too, most notably in the expurgation of allusions to Genji's liaisons with Fujitsubo (which produced the child who would become Emperor Reizei), as other scholars have pointed out.[47]

Even the two main figures responsible for the 1939 *Genji* had misgivings about the tale. In the first sentence of an essay published in *Chūō Kōron* in 1939, for example, Yamada recorded his ambivalence by declaring that his simultaneous "dissatisfaction and admiration" (*fuman to kyōtan*) regarding *Genji* had long made him of two minds about the classic.[48] He acknowledged that parts of *Genji* "offend the national essence" (*kokutai ni fureru*), while also noting that these troublesome areas were not the central concerns of the tale as a whole, and praising *Genji* as a literary achievement more generally.[49] In the preface to *Music in* "The Tale of Genji," Yamada began by noting that his "sense of morality" (*dōgishin*) made it difficult to approve of *Genji*.[50] For different reasons, Tanizaki was also displeased with some aspects of *Genji*. He noted in *Nikumareguchi* (Some Malicious Remarks, 1965) that he found Murasaki Shikibu's unbounded sympathy for Genji tiresome and that he considered many of Genji's amorous escapades to be superficial and implausible. At one point, for example, Genji simultaneously pursues a secret affair with Fujitsubo, the consort of his father (who is emperor), and another clandestine liaison with Oborozukiyo, a woman aligned with a rival political faction. When his affair with Oborozukiyo is discovered, Genji is forced into exile, though he proclaims his innocence throughout and benefits from the good graces of the gods. Tanizaki disapproved of the sympathetic narration of Genji's exile:

> I suppose that if viewed as an evocation of the pathos of the human condition [*mono no aware*], one might be able to sympathize with Genji's secret liaison with his father's lover [Fujitsubo]—that is, the consort of the ruler of the realm. And yet, even allowing for that, I just cannot forgive him for then simply taking another lover [Oborozukiyo] and showering sweet nothings upon her. I am a feminist, and so I am overly sensitive to these things. If the gender roles were reversed, perhaps I would not feel as I do, but when I read *Genji*, I have always found this point unpalatable.[51]

These objections remind us that the serious tone of *The Essence of Our National Polity* and the more scandalous adventure of Murasaki's *monogatari* cast the state-issued propaganda piece as a highbrow intellectual foil that contrasted with the middlebrow literary appeal of the roughly contemporaneous *Genji* translation.

But as we count their differences, we should also recall that Yamada's participation in the completion of both texts at around the same time suggests that they carried within themselves a kind of genetic reference to one another, as if they were siblings estranged on the level of register, but akin on the level of implication. And that implication was that the intrusions of the Anglo "West" had corrupted the authentic and ancient identity of the Japanese "essence" (*kokutai*). Tansman has observed that if the "meaning" of *The Essence of Our National Polity* were to be rendered as an expository message, it would be simple: in his words, the gist is that "we Japanese are in grave danger, and we need to restore ourselves to our original condition and revive the true meaning of the national essence by wiping away the philosophies that have made us into atomized, Europeanized, individuals."[52] The *kokutai* was offered as an alternative to imported ideologies, and it promised that the Japanese people were more than liberal individuals because they constituted a collective held together by blood and myth. As Tansman had it, *The Essence of Our National Polity* "avers that the notion of the individual as an abstract entity belongs to a tradition that, although it has played an influential role in history, is not 'our' own, no longer has any use, and must be eradicated," and he added that the propaganda tract situates "every individual in the imperial blood lineage of the Japanese people, extending down into eternity."[53]

If this was the higher-minded purpose behind *The Essence of Our National Polity*, then it was also a purpose with literary distributions ranging far beyond the discursive boundaries of that text in particular. Among other things, the idea that nativist literary exegesis expelling foreign influence over Japan could uncover forgotten structures of authentic community was an idea with deeper roots in the imagination of a *kokugaku* (nativist) tradition often associated with the writings of Motoori Norinaga (1730–1801), and with which Yamada himself identified. This is crucial to recall because however problematic *Genji* might have been for twentieth-century censors, it was also true that it had been Norinaga's *kokugaku* hermeneutic that had pioneered the persuasive perspective that *Genji* marked one of the high points of Japanese cultural history. In the 1930s, this nativist perspective recuperated a saving grace to what was otherwise a tale bound to offend the *kokutai* ideologues. Most importantly, it taught the highbrow intellectual mind implicit in *The Essence of Our National Polity* to find its own ideals in the structure of meaning held together by the native vernacular storytelling style of *Genji* itself. This helps to explain why Kobayashi noted in his review of controversies surrounding *Genji* during wartime that the questionable morality of the tale in imperial Japan had to be balanced against the seemingly edifying implications of Norinaga's nativist reading of it, which offered a way of grafting the national prestige of vernacular classics like *Genji* onto the abstract idea of the "national polity" (*kokutai*) that was then being reanimated in the government propaganda of the time.[54] "From the standpoint of the wartime authorities," Kobayashi wrote, "the value of *The Tale of Genji* was a double-edged sword," one which cut against the myth of an unbroken imperial lineage even as it cut to the heart of the matter of how to mythologize national culture in the name of political propaganda.[55] This resonates with Nishino's observation that *Genji* supplemented and sabotaged *kokutai* ideology at the same time.[56] And this doubled nature of the tale was a crucial part of what I would call the middlebrow dynamic of the 1939 *Genji* translation: as a cultural text inextricably lodged on the borders of high and low, *Genji* promised something scandalous and something sacred all at once. For this reason, the 1939 translation could neither fully cooperate with nor completely rebel against the perspective articulated by official propaganda texts like *The Essence of Our National Polity*. More precisely, it smuggled their high-minded intentions given weight by "eggheaded" esoterica into the more middling forms of the vernacular imagination, where high and low could breathe together in a literary confluence mixing aesthetics and ideas, pleasure and politics.

And the vernacular imagination required vernacular language.

The Vernacular

In *De vulgari eloquentia* (On Eloquence in the Vernacular, early 14th c.), the great poet of the Italian vernacular Dante Alighieri wrote that the vernacular language "which we learn without any formal instruction" is more "noble" than the acquired second languages "which the Romans called *gramatica*," and which "can only be developed through dedication to a lengthy course of study": "Of these two kinds of language, the more noble is the vernacular: first because it was the language originally used by the human race; second because the whole world employs it, though with different pronunciations and using different words; and third, because it is natural to us, while the other is, in contrast, artificial. . . . This, in truth, is our primary language."[57]

As in Dante's Italy, the primacy of the native vernacular as a "noble" literary language would not have been a foregone conclusion in Muraskai's Japan. The vernacular could always be denigrated as a middling register that aspired to artistic appeal even though it lacked the sort of prestige that Latin held in Europe, or that Chinese wielded in East Asia. In a sense, vernacular fiction in Heian Japan may have even suffered from some of the pejorative associations that "middlebrow" implies today: a literature too lusty, too superficial, or too altogether fictional to be taken seriously. Perhaps in centuries past, the vernacular could never escape the ironies of the middle register; after all, when Dante wrote *De vulgari eloquentia*, he wrote it in Latin.

As is well known, the problem in Murasaki's Heian Japan was that the vernacular tales known as *monogatari* were thought to have lacked edifying value, and to have been full of falsehoods and immoral temptations, to boot.[58] In the years before Murasaki would begin writing *Genji*, for example, Minamoto no Tamenori critiqued *monogatari* in "Sanbōe-kotoba" (Illustration of the Three Jewels, 984), arguing that they "ramble on and on with meaningless phrases like so much flotsam in the sea" and admonishing readers: "Do not let your heart get caught up even briefly in these tangled roots of evil, these forests of words."[59] In "Genji monogatari" *Tama no ogushi* (*The Tale of Genji:* A Little Jeweled Comb, 1799), though, Norinaga famously recuperated the virtue of native vernacular tales (*monogatari*) by arguing that texts like *Genji* were redeemed by their portrayals of "pathos" (*mono no aware*).[60] This elevated *monogatari* to a realm of humane truth unparalleled by more "serious" writings:

> What, then, is the nature of [these tales], and why do we read them? Tales depict the myriad aspects of life [*yo*]: the good and the bad, the fantastic and the amusing, the intriguing and the moving [*aware*]. Some may even include illustrations of such scenes. In our idle hours they amuse us. When our hearts are troubled and we are beset by worries, they console us. They help us understand our lives in this world [*yo no naka*] and the workings of the emotions [*mono no aware o shiru*].[61]

Although the "worldliness" of *Genji* is today most often associated with its international circulation and discussion of its features in global discourse, Norinaga's nativist perspective excerpted above suggests that Murasaki's *monogatari* comprised a worldly narrative in a different sense—in the sense that it allowed readers to know the truth of "the world" (*yo*) and what it means to live "in the world" (*yo no naka*). Taking inspiration from Pheng Cheah's theorization of world literature in another context, it might be said that quite apart from the travels of the tale in the international space of global discourse, Norinaga's reference to the "world" of meaning held together and opened up by *Genji* indicated a world of greatest possible implication.[62] This was so, Norinaga suggested, because the binding force of pathos (*aware*) structured the most extensive scale of human relations and lived experience just as surely as it gave form to the deepest profundities of Murasaki's fictional *monogatari*. The result was a literary text of maximal proportions, one that seemed to contain everything.[63] That is why Norinaga wrote that Murasaki had observed "carefully with her own profoundly sensitive faculties [*fukaku mono no aware o shireru kokoro ni*] the nature of all there is in this world [*yo no naka ni*]—the good people and the bad, their thoughts and their deeds."[64] He wrote that "of the entire range of emotions in this world [*yo no naka no mono no aware no kagiri*], there are none not to be found in this tale."[65] He concluded that what had been explained in more prestigious registers of a foreign idiom could only be felt as real in the form of a *monogatari* composed in the native vernacular. "As a means of acquiring a thorough knowledge of what Chinese books describe as 'human feeling and the ways of the world [*ninjō setai*],'" Norinaga wrote, "I doubt there is anything to equal reading this tale."[66]

It followed that if the eloquence of the Heian vernacular had been forgotten by modern readers who had sacrificed their own cultural sovereignty in the name of global assimilation, a modern translation (*gendaigoyaku*) of *Genji*—composed in dialogue with the latter-day nativist Yamada himself—would offer a conduit to a *kokutai* that had been abandoned by modern Japan, but never destroyed, eclipsed, or conquered. These higher-brow aspirations of the translation come through in considering how Yamada drew inspiration from the nativist tradition himself. He was a pedagogue in the conventional sense of an educator, having worked with the Ministry of Education, taught language and grammar in schools, and written extensively on the history of the Japanese language. In *Kokugaku no hongi* (The Essence of Nativist Studies, 1942), he explained that the study of Japanese language, literature, and history from a nativist perspective could take many forms and go in many directions, but always returned to the ultimate purpose of clarifying the national essence (*kokutai no senmei*). As he put it:

> What is called the national essence [*kokutai*] is the true substance [*jittai*] that binds the emperor [*tennō*], the people [*kokumin*], and the land of the nation [*kokudo*]. That which upholds the national essence [*kokutai*] and eternally brings forth new life is what is called the single exalted Way that extends from ancient times through to the present. This Way takes several forms, appearing as Shinto, the spirit of the people [*kokumin seishin*], the morals of the people [*kokumin dōtoku*], and the national essence [*kokutai*].

> Nativists [*kokugakusha*] from ancient times to the present have completely devoted themselves to their research for the purpose of illuminating this one great Way.[67]

For Yamada, these features distinguished *kokugaku* from philology (*bunkengaku*). The difference was in their purpose (*mokuteki*), he explained. He argued that while it was true that both philology and *kokugaku* took as their object the close analysis of ancient texts and the clarification of ancient language, the purpose of *kokugaku*—unlike philology—was not merely textual, nor analytical: beyond any strictly interpretive matters, *kokugaku* took as its highest purpose the understanding of the "way of the nation" (*kuni no michi*).[68] This reflected the underlying assumption that "the greatest significance of *kokugaku* is to clarify the *kokutai*."[69] For Yamada, this was a purpose that made *kokugaku* a scholarly practice (*gakumon*) peculiar to Japan, and unique in the world.[70]

This helps to contextualize moments in Yamada's readings of Japanese literature that brought out more than information. At their most ambitious, his readings pushed toward a spiritual history of the Japanese people (*minzoku*) rendered legible by the auratic forms of native language. His writings on *renga* (linked-verse poetry) presented one particularly compelling example from around the time of the 1939 *Genji* translation and the 1937 release of *The Essence of Our National Polity*. In *Renga gaisetsu* (An Introduction to *Renga*, 1937), Yamada wrote that a *renga* sequence was not made as much as it was born because the poet who gave the first link, or *hokku*, could not anticipate how the sequence would evolve, nor could the subjectivity of any single author (*sakusha no shukan*) control the complete composition; instead, *renga* was an art form that surrendered to a more natural outpouring of expression (*shizen no ryūro ni makase*).[71] He understood the unique sociality of *renga* composition to produce an economy of language that amalgamated the aesthetic common sense of the ancients with modes of representation organic to their particular community, allowing a collective soul to fossilize in the clay of *kotoba* (words):

> A *renga* sequence can be none other than the literary product birthed from the spiritual resonance [*seishin no kyōmei*] of the people who participate in its composition. In this regard, *renga* really is a literary art without peer in the world, and could it not be said that it truly is something produced by

> the spirit of the Japanese race [*Nihon minzoku no seishin*], and in which the spirits of individuals [*kojin no seishin*] amalgamate to form a single spirit of the race [*minzoku seishin*]?[72]

In this sense, Yamada's reading of *renga* implicitly identified a discursive economy premised on structured improvisation that avoided the discord that follows from the modern notion of liberty. That *renga* had no cognate in the transatlantic world was not lost on him, and this led him to claim that its deepest profundities could never be understood through the hermeneutics developed abroad for the study of distinctly European literatures and languages.[73]

Although Tanizaki and Yamada were always different sorts of figures, their understandings of the relationships among vernacular language, native identity, and the age of empire sometimes intersected, as Tanizaki made clear in 1942:

> Professor Yamada Yoshio mentioned in the September issue of *Bungei shunjū* regarding the essence of our language [*kokugo no honshitsu*], "It is a travesty of the very traditional spirit of Japan to indiscriminately declare this usage or that more convenient, and thereby rashly alter our language." He is exactly right, considering that as we try to spread our national language [*kokugo*] and script [*kokuji*] abroad, there are such ludicrous notions as simplifying our language to be easier for foreigners to grasp, and such absurd ideas as making the content of our films easier to understand by eliminating some of the multivalent complexity of our lives. The proverb tells us "When in Rome, do as the Romans," but the English, quite to the contrary, refuse to change their ways wherever they go and instead force their customs on native peoples the world over. We would do well to imitate their audacity.[74]

What Tanizaki feared was that the modern Japanese vernacular (*genbun-itchi*) had become increasingly Anglicized since the Meiji years, taking on more and more foreign loan words and Europeanized inflections. He sensed that as a result, the modern Japanese vernacular had become less like a vernacular altogether as it came to imitate the more prestigious languages of Europe that were presumed to be the authoritative modern tongues. What his essays on language sought to reclaim was the eloquence of an older style, and this reclamation project would assume its most ambitious articulation in the form of the 1939 *Genji* translation itself. In navigating Tanizaki's interest in older styles of language, though, we should remember the pervasive ambivalence running through his writing in general, and that LaMarre reminds us that "despite his readiness to speak as a Japanese man in praise of Japan's Oriental traditions, Tanizaki's writings are difficult to characterize as straightforward endorsements of cultural nationalism."[75] One layer of ambiguity is that Tanizaki's cultural nationalism served both as an anti-imperialist critique of Anglo-European interventions in Japan and as an imperialist politics of its own that implicitly justified Japanese colonization of East Asia.[76] But another ambivalence was that at the same time that Tanizaki viewed his age in terms of ambiguities and mixtures, he also wrote about it in terms of hierarchies of power that left some cultures, traditions, and languages threatened with domination and even extinction at the hands of others.

This becomes clearer in revisiting Tanizaki's critique of the modern Japanese vernacular that began in the essay "Gendai kōgobun no ketten ni tsuite" (On the Shortcomings of Modern Vernacular Japanese, 1929) and expanded in *Bunshō tokuhon* (A Manual on Style, 1934). The crux of Tanizaki's argument was that the modern vernacular Japanese language (*genbun-itchi*, *kōgotai*, *kōgobun*) that developed in the late nineteenth century mixed native elements with modes more common to European languages, with the result that writing and thinking in a modern Japanese language autonomous from Western influence had become impossible. The scholar Tomi Suzuki observed that Tanizaki found the Anglicized and hybridized modern Japanese vernacular to be optimized for the precision and clarity of scientific and philosophical forms of argumentation, but not for more literary turns of aesthetic or poetic expression, and I would add that this suggests how his critique of modern language broadly contributed to the interwar revolt against Enlightenment rationality more generally.[77] What Tanizaki called for was a renewed dialogue with the classics: "The urgent matter of the day is to tighten up the loose usages of modern vernacular Japanese by simplifying it as much as possible," he wrote. "Ultimately, however, this amounts to revivifying the spirit of classical language."[78] The conservative politics behind Tanizaki's perspective come through in considering that he believed the hybridized modern Japanese vernacular to mark an aberrational break from the stylistics and usages that he argued had organically evolved over the course of centuries in league with the Japanese "national character" (*kokumin-sei*). From this point of view, the modern innovation of *genbun-itchi* was a rootless philistine's tongue because it cut off the speaker from ages of cultivated usage: "Ideally, we could make the most of those parts of classical grammar that are still useful in modern times, but it is my belief that the present vernacular style [*kōgotai*] completely annihilates the unique virtues and advantages of the Japanese language [*kokugo*]."[79]

Tanizaki claimed that the increase in foreign loan words in the Japanese lexicon during and after the Meiji period had been a corrosive development because native and foreign words functioned in fundamentally inassimilable ways. He argued in *A Manual on Style* that Japanese words were "elastic" (*yutori no aru kotoba*), meaning that a single term could encompass various nuances, meanings, and implications. He wrote that by contrast, the robustness of European lexicons limited the signifying range of each term to a smaller group of direct referents, producing a degree of clarity unknown in Japanese. In *A Manual on Style*, Tanizaki argued that good style in European languages dictated delimiting the signifying range of each term in order to speak or write with precision—the very opposite of what he thought of as good style in Japanese:

> Instead of expending useless energy [piling up descriptors, like Theodore Dreiser and other Western writers], we Japanese writers purposely use words with elasticity [*yutori no aru kotoba*], broad terms that accommodate several meanings. We let the sensuous elements of language, including tone, the written appearance of the characters, and rhythm, compensate for what has been left out. This is what I meant when I said earlier that in classical prose style, each word has a shadowy depth like the halo surrounding the moon. To put it differently, a few words become the hint that activates the reader's imagination, stirring the reader to compensate for any insufficiencies. The writer's brush is used only to invite the reader's imagination. Such is the spirit of classical writing. In the Western style of writing, one must delimit meaning to the most precise range possible, for the slightest shadows are forbidden and a writer reserves no domain for readers' imagination.[80]

Tanizaki's praise of the allusive aesthetics of Japanese language coalesced in a term that he claimed articulated the paramount virtue of native language: *ganchiku* (nuance and implication). In *A Manual on Style*, he defined *ganchiku* as "avoiding verbosity" (*jōzetsu o tsutsushimu koto*), "avoiding excessive description" (*amari hakkiri saseyō to senu koto*), and "leaving gaps in chains of signification" (*imi no tsunagari ni sukima o oku koto*).

But Tanizaki argued that Japanese expression became only more verbose and trite—the opposites of *ganchiku*—as it imitated European languages. In "On the Shortcomings of Modern Vernacular Japanese," for example, he argued that the subjectless sentence, commonplace in classical Japanese style, had become less and less familiar to readers since the Meiji years as writers attempted to strictly delimit the signifying range of each utterance, forsaking more allusive modes of meaning in the process. He wrote that although the Japanese language does not have gendered masculine and feminine inflections of nouns and adjectives in the same way that European languages do, it was nevertheless true that Japanese featured so many gender-specific speech patterns that "even on reading the quoted speech [*kaiwa*] in a novel, it is immediately apparent whether a man or a woman is speaking."[81] He wrote that this was so because women ended sentences with telltale inflections, such as "ne," "wa," "wa yo," and "da wa yo," for example. In Tanizaki's mind, in fact, geography and gender mixed in the social indexes of native language: he wrote that women in western Japan (Kansai) would never describe a meal with the word *umai* (tasty); according to Tanizaki, they would say *oishii* (delicious).[82] For Tanizaki, these were the minor matters that gave texture to the social life of the Japanese language. But the appearance of stylistic elements unknown or uncommon in classical Japanese (such as quotation marks, for example, and attributions of quoted speech with markers like "he said") were ominous signs of modern demise. For Tanizaki, these alterations evidenced the corruption not only of language, but of cultural consciousness. As he put it in *A Manual on Style*:

> Our vocabulary has suddenly grown as we have added Chinese and Western terms, and now finally we have gone so far as to add translated terms [*hon'yakugo*]. As I have mentioned repeatedly, because of these additions, we have come to rely on the power of words too greatly, we have become given to verbosity, and we have forgotten the effects of silence.
>
> The language of a nation is inseparably linked to that nation's character [*kokuminsei*]. That the Japanese language has a small vocabulary does not

> mean that our culture is inferior to that of the West or of China. Rather, it is evidence that by nature, our national character [*kokuminsei*] is not given to verbosity.[83]

In these ways, the conservative rhetoric of Tanizaki's essays on vernacular language conjured the higher-minded virtues of national identity and cultural sovereignty that were also apparent in the wider discourse of *kokutai*. But what was more distinctive about these essays was that they made their appeals to authenticity without abandoning more modest concerns about bourgeois taste. Alongside the parodic *Naomi*, his most lucid rendering of the cultural crisis to which his search for authentic language responded came in *In'ei raisan* (In Praise of Shadows, 1933–34), an iconic and ironic literary essay that ambivalently juxtaposed pretensions to connoisseurship with a more practical acquiescence to the easy convenience of commodity culture. Broadly stated, the essay expressed the pedagogical imperative of the middlebrow imagination that was also implicit in Tanizaki's writings on language: in the same way that *A Manual on Style* set out to teach readers how to feel the aesthetic valence of what he argued was authentic vernacular language in the practical realm of everyday life, *In Praise of Shadows* offered itself as an appreciation of architecture and cultured lifestyle, which Tanizaki believed had become expressions of the Japanese identity articulated through the register of daily living. In both texts, Tanizaki struck the pose of the middlebrow connoisseur curating a learned style of everyday sensibility that was available for like-minded readers to adopt, at least aspirationally. And when read in dialogue with the higher-minded *kokutai* discourse of its time, this pose might be said to have plied readers with a "soft sell," so to speak, persuading them to sympathize with the nativist side as a matter of cultivated taste—and to do so whether or not they would have felt themselves convinced by the more potent highbrow rhetoric of gods and myths with which Yamada infamously inscribed roughly contemporaneous *kokutai* discourse.

Far from the realm of myth, in fact, *In Praise of Shadows* peddled the soft sell through the practical problems of dwelling. The basic premise of the piece was Tanizaki's hypothetical struggle to build a Japanese house that preserved what he understood to have been the aesthetics and materiality of traditional Japanese daily life. In the essay, he fantasized about a dimly lit room in which he could ponder the murky depths of miso soup served in a black lacquer bowl, for example, and lauded the sublimity of Japanese outhouses as a space of spiritual repose. But Tanizaki also conceded throughout *In Praise of Shadows* that the aesthetic produced by Japanese material culture had been irreversibly displaced by more convenient and efficient modern commodities imported from abroad: he admitted that candlelight would never overcome the practical virtues of light bulbs, for example, and that a modern white-tiled bathroom with a Western porcelain toilet was irrefutably more sanitary than the wood-planked outhouse of his dreams, whatever the compromise. Although Tanizaki indulged in an aesthetic fantasy at some length in *In Praise of Shadows*, he ultimately upheld the pragmatic appeal of modern amenities, suggesting that much of the essay was more of a eulogy for an imagined past that could never be recalled than a nativist manifesto. In this sense, the tone of *In Praise of Shadows* was the opposite of propagandistic: the bourgeois antiquarian at the center of the piece admitted to his own defeat, and instead of issuing a call to arms, he was the first to acknowledge that his own ideals were impractical and outdated.

But by the same measure, this is the art of the soft sell that takes its critics' objections into account in advance. And at this point, my reading of Tanizaki's politics enters into deeper water. On the one hand, Tanizaki's writings are so full of ambivalence and contradiction, humor and irony, that they will appear to some readers to safeguard themselves against the heavy-handed ideology of his age. But if we allow ourselves to proceed in reading Tanizaki's ambivalences not only as a matter of his personal taste, but also as a product of the middlebrow idiom that he manipulated, then we begin to see that he at times encourages readers to peel back the veneer of irony and hyperbole with which he lacquered the language of *In Praise of Shadows*. In these instants, readers momentarily encounter something more volatile, and come to sense that this is not only an essay about tableware and décor, but a rhetorical structure that mobilizes metaphors in order to portray Anglo-Europeans as conquerors. The essay never explicitly says any such thing, of course: the soft sell pads its rhetorical gymnastics and supplies emergency exits left and right to readers wishing to escape into the reassuring promise that Tanizaki does not really mean it. But by the same measure, this could be read as a middlebrow strategy that hides something in plain sight. And read this way, we begin to wonder if beneath the pose of the defeated antiquarian, *In Praise of Shadows* might have conspired with the imperial politics of its age by subtly insisting that the inassimilable aesthetic sensibilities of Japanese and Anglo-Europeans had become ground zero of a racial conflict of world historical proportions—a conflict that threatened to destroy the Japanese identity for all time.[84]

If so, then the physical household described in architectural terms by the essay could be taken for a metaphorical structure of meaning in which the ***kokutai*** and the ***kokuminsei*** (national character) dwell. This would indicate that the deterioration of the household corresponds to the deteriorated conditions of possibility for the Japanese ***kokutai*** itself to survive in an inhospitable modern world. These threads come together in noticing that Tanizaki conceived of the cultivation of cultural taste as a metonym for racial identity: the shadowy aesthetic favored in Japan, he wrote, was linked to Japanese skin, which "no matter how white, is blotted by faint shadows within its whiteness," whereas Anglo-Europeans' preference for brightness followed from their complexion, which, Tanizaki argued, "even if turbid on the surface, has a bright clarity underneath. Nowhere are Western bodies tinged by dingy shadows [of the sort that characterize the Japanese complexion]."[85] Correspondingly, Tanizaki linked Anglo-Europeans' preference for brightness to an aggressive "psychology that in the past made the white races despise the colored races," as during the American Civil War, when, according to Tanizaki, "whites' hatred and contempt was not directed only at blacks, but extended even to the mixed-race children of interracial couples, the mixed-race children of mixed-race parents, and the mixed-race children born to one white parent and one mixed-race parent. Whites relentlessly sought to track down and persecute anyone with the slightest trace of black blood, including those who were half black, a quarter, an eighth, a sixteenth, a thirty-second."[86] Tanizaki implied that this racial violence was coterminous with a telos of technological development leading to a literally whiter world: "The progressive Westerner always presses for improvement. From candlelight to kerosene lamplight, kerosene lamplight to gaslight, gaslight to electric light, the Westerner quests unceasingly for greater and greater luminescence, straining himself to eliminate even the faintest shadows."[87] This suggests that what the soft sell of *In Praise of Shadows* sold was the idea that even unremarkable practices in the realm of daily living were in fact tiny battlefields imbued with larger implications. In the same way that Tanizaki viewed the small details of grammar as arenas of contestation, so, too, did he encourage readers to imagine that using an inkstone and brush instead of a fountain pen meant something, and that the visual composition of miso soup served in black lacquerware within the dark recesses of a Japanese teahouse could go away forever. Without ever being doctrinaire, nor even all that consistent, Tanizaki softly implied in his own ambivalent way that everything is political.

His next step was to move the learned poetics of bourgeois dwelling toward a middlebrow politics of empire. And this was where literature and language came in. At the end of *In Praise of Shadows*, Tanizaki concluded that the only way out of the Anglocentric telos of modernity was through the cultural property least susceptible to technological change which still conveyed the shadowy world that he believed to have been favored by the Japanese *kokuminsei*. And that property was native literary language full of *ganchiku*. It became for Tanizaki the last bastion of Japanese autonomy because language could yet be rehabilitated to conform to the intuitive tastes of the Japanese *kokuminsei* in ways that material culture could not. This is why the last lines of *In Praise of Shadows* called language and literature the last "sanctuary" (*dendō*) for the threatened Japanese identity:

> In the end, these are petty gripes, for even I am well aware of the many virtues of the age, and give thanks for them. Whatever may be said now, Japan has already stepped into line with Western culture, and there is nothing to be done but to leave the elder generation behind and proceed steadfastly. Yet, we must be aware that, as long as the color of our skin remains unchanged, we shall forever bear the burden of a loss known to us alone. My hope in writing this is that somehow there might yet remain a way of compensating for that loss—perhaps through literature and the arts. I would like to call back the world of shadows that we are losing at least in the domain of literature. For the sanctuary of literature, I would like to make the eaves deep and the walls dark; I would like to push back into the darkness that which is too plainly visible; I would like to remove the useless décor from the interior. I would not insist on this everywhere, for it would suffice if but one such structure remained to us. What would it be like if for once we tried turning off the lights?[88]

By linking literature to architectural form, Tanizaki merged his pedagogies of language and lifestyle as he suggested how readers could learn to dwell poetically in words that substitute for objects, sentences that take the place of corridors, and pages of literary atmosphere that conjure the warm recesses of darkened interior spaces. In so doing, Tanizaki's perspective implicitly echoed the lesson that Harootunian has argued the nativist reading of *Genji* had earlier taught Edo period townspeople—namely, "the necessity to accept and even valorize the common world of things encountered in daily life and to grasp it from the heart, to see it anew, as something different from what it seemed to be."[89] Most notably, this was the perspective on daily life imbued with *aware*, and Harootunian has added that "it was also a view of daily life removed from the mediations of metaphysics, which corralled people into unnatural, normative grooves of existence and told them what they should see and how they should behave."[90]

By extension, perhaps it could be said that at the end of *In Praise of Shadows*, Tanizaki implicitly breathed with this earlier nativist inclination to teach bourgeois contemporaries to live within the nativist sentiments of a rediscovered everyday life, and emboldened them to do so through words if it had become difficult to do so through things. It followed that the task of his first *Genji* translation was to answer the question he posed at the end of *In Praise of Shadows*: What might readers discover in their own language once the intrusive lights of the Anglo West were turned off? Put differently, what would the modern Japanese vernacular have looked like if it had descended from the Heian period archetype of vernacular eloquence without any Anglo-European influence whatsoever, and been spared the indignities of *genbun-itchi*? Read this way, another layer of middlebrow emerges as we begin to sense that the language of his *Genji* translation emerged in between a conservative antiquarian pursuit and an avant-garde experiment in literary speculation.

Genji *in the Global 1930s*

One of the ironies that complicates any interpretation of the nativist ideals described above is that Tanizaki and Yamada's 1939 translation was preceded by a prominent English-language counterpart: Arthur Waley's legendary rendering of *Genji*, which was published in six parts from 1925 to 1933. Examining the lengthy process by which *Genji* was canonized as a classic of world literature, Emmerich has emphasized the role of essays written by the novelist and critic Masamune Hakuchō regarding Waley's translation, observing that Hakuchō's encounter with *Genji* in Waley's English-language version "pave[d] the way for Tanizaki's first [1939] translation."[91] Emmerich noted that Hakuchō wrote in 1926 after reading *Genji* in Japanese that he felt "hatred" for the tale, adding that "the fact is that I have never before encountered a work so hard to read" and that "I am sure even *Genji monogatari* would be more interesting when read in an English translation."[92] In the years to come, Waley's translation of the tale persuaded Hakuchō to fall in love with *Genji*. Emmerich has observed that the novelist wrote in 1933 that "I have always found it [*Genji*] a very boring book—limp and slippery and devoid of anything that might strike a chord in readers' hearts," but that Waley's translation had finally made the classic legible and enjoyable, noting that "if this English translation were translated anew into Japanese, it might attract a large and avid readership that would enjoy it as one of the great novels of the world."[93] Emmerich concluded that "Hakuchō ends up being right, of course," adding that "the particular translation that paved the way for the tale's rapid rise to prominence during the postwar period is the first of Tanizaki Junichirō's three modern-Japanese renderings, published in the midst of the Second Sino-Japanese War, between January 1939 and July 1941."[94]

This alerts us to a crucial dialogue about translation and *Genji* that reverberated across English- and Japanese-language renderings of the tale in the 1930s. In the wake of Waley's inspiring translation, Shimanaka Yūsaku, president of Chūōkōronsha, lamented that a similarly pleasurable literary translation did not exist in Japanese. He explained in a January 1939 essay published in *Chūō Kōron* that the point of departure from which the Tanizaki translation of *Genji* had emerged was in fact a request he had made as a reader of the famously difficult text himself. The problem, he confessed, was that he had only understood what the tale was about through explanatory supplements, and had never been able to savor *Genji* as a literary text per se.[95] So he petitioned Tanizaki, by then well known for his skillful imitation of classical literary stylistics, meditations on classical Japanese aesthetics, and a recent string of neoclassical novellas, to undertake a literary translation of the ancient tale. Tanizaki agreed, but requested the help of an editor (*kōetsusha*) to assure that the translation would accurately replicate the nuance of the source text. Chūōkōronsha paired him with Yamada, a scholar known for his expertise in the history of the Japanese language. Yamada reviewed Tanizaki's drafts and consulted with the novelist about ambiguous passages in order for the translation to present a modern language as closely aligned with classical precedent as possible. On the release of the translation in 1939, Shimanaka praised Tanizaki's ability as a novelist to artistically render the "fragrance, elegance and nuance" of the source text in modern Japanese, adding that his collaboration with Yamada endowed their "transplantation" (*ishoku*) of eleventh-century language and style into twentieth-century prose with a philological rigor and scholarly accuracy "beyond critique even from the perspective of linguistics."[96]

Emmerich has suggested that this chain of events was set into motion partly by Hakuchō's appreciation of Waley's translation, and to that extent, the nativist *Genji* was ironically occasioned by its English-language other. But in addition to considering Hakuchō's appreciation of the tale, we should also remember that Tanizaki himself wrote about Waley's *Genji*, too, and in ways that reveal how he understood the differences separating the language of Waley's English-language style and the forms of the Japanese language in the source text. Tanizaki was fluent in literary English, but as much as he admired Waley's style, his reading of the Waley *Genji* focused on the differences in form created by the act of translation, rather than positing a greater whole revealed by the proliferations of the tale in different vernaculars. In this sense, Tanizaki suggested that the deepest profundities of *Genji* had less to do with its international reception and global circulation, and more to do with the world of forms—the household of meaning—held together by the Japanese language. Tanizaki's critique of Waley's English-language *Genji* is all the more striking in considering that he held Waley in great esteem. When Chūōkōronsha sent a copy of Tanizaki's *Genji* translation to Waley in London, for example, Waley wrote to Tanizaki, stating, "Now that the whole series is finished, I feel I must write and congratulate you on having so superbly carried through this great task and given your countrymen a *Genji* that they can really feel at home in."[97] And when Tanizaki completed his lengthy novel *Sasameyuki* (The Makioka Sisters, 1943–48), he sent the manuscript to Waley in the hopes that he would translate it into English; although

Waley declined, he wrote to Tanizaki, "I cannot tell you how thrilled I was when I saw your dedication in *Sasame-yuki*. I have admired your writings for many, many years."[98]

In *A Manual on Style*, Tanizaki offered a reading of Waley's recently completed translation of *Genji*. He focused on the opening lines of the "Suma" chapter, in which Genji is exiled from the capital for having offended his political rivals. Since the chapter brings forth a sentimental language occasioned by parting, longing, regret, and transition, it presents a dense weave of the pathos for which *Genji* has long been lauded. Tanizaki first addressed the clarity of Waley's language: "[Waley's] English prose is more precise than the original, and leaves nothing unclear. Whereas the original endeavors to leave unsaid that which could be understood without being stated explicitly, the English translation clarifies even that which is already clear enough."[99] Tanizaki implied that in Waley's English translation of *Genji*, the Japanese preference for allusive shadows was overcome by the Anglo-European taste for rational precision—a repetition of what *In Praise of Shadows* had described as the basic problematic of Japanese modernity. Tanizaki's point, however, was not that Waley's translation was poor (he in fact praised it elsewhere); rather, the point was that translating *Genji* into English or Anglicized Japanese inevitably vitiated the shadowy aesthetics of language (*ganchiku*) that defined the nuance and appeal of the source text.

For Tanizaki, then, Waley's translation demonstrated how the aesthetics of authentic Japanese language could never be assimilated (or translated) into an Anglo-European idiom because, as Tanizaki pointed out next, the English language itself could not accurately reproduce the referential patterns of Murasaki Shikibu's eleventh-century vernacular:

> Yet, even the original language is not necessarily unclear. Certainly, it would be easier to understand [Waley's translation] "being separated from all those whose society he liked best" than [the original] "his home faded" [*furusato obotsukanakaru beshi*], but there is more to it than simply Genji's sadness at being far removed from the capital and his loved ones there. Surely we also feel all manner of helplessness [*kokoro bososa*], melancholy [*sabishisa*], and disconsolation [*yarusenasa*]. [In the Japanese,] all of these emotions are consolidated into the single phrase "His home faded" [*furusato obotsukanakaru beshi*]. [Waley's] English is more clear, but at the expense of limiting meaning and becoming shallow.[100]

According to Tanizaki, then, Waley's translation revealed how Anglo-Europeans' preference for clarity limited the referential capacities of English locutions: Waley's desire for precise semantics delimited the signifying range of the language of his translation, yielding an explicit but superficial summary of the content of the original Japanese.

To be sure, this is not a perspective limited to the intense ideological battles of imperial Japan. In fact, it was echoed implicitly in Masao Miyoshi's much later review of Edward Seidensticker's 1976 English-language *Genji* translation. Miyoshi's review never cited Tanizaki, and it did indicate that the language of Virginia Woolf (an acquaintance of Waley's) "has features uncannily like those of Lady Murasaki's as I read the two women writers from two vastly different traditions and times."[101] But like Tanizaki in *A Manual on Style*, Miyoshi remarked on what he viewed as the basic incommensurability of the *Genji* world and the English language. He wrote that "in the Heian tale, plot and character, together with syntax, fuse into an all-embracing time-flow which affords the reader an occasion to feel and reflect on his being and non-being in life (which may be at the same time non-life). Mr. Seidensticker's rendition tends to convert these shadowy palaces, temples, and hamlets inhabited by princes, princesses, and hermits into well-lit salons crowded by modern Western ladies and gentleman."[102] Miyoshi later elaborated:

> The original *Genji*, I repeat, flows and drifts. At every turn, the stream of narrative opens up an unexpected perspective which also revises what has come before. The subject of a verb is often unknown, then is revealed, then is lost again; the narrator blends with characters, who also subtly intermingle with each other and with their environments. Such, it seems to me, is the world where the Radiant Prince of Genji and Princess Aoi, Prince Kaoru and Princess Ōigimi, flow with time. Can this world be re-created in the modern English language with it fixed syntactic expectations? Maybe not.[103]

This helps us to see that Tanizaki's reading of Waley's translation was less a critique of one translator's efforts in particular, and more a broader meditation on how the forms of language separated by time and space cannot always fit together. For Tanizaki, moreover, Waley's translation attested to a distinctly Anglo-European drive for clarity that corrupted the household of meaning held together by the language of *Genji* by reducing its maximal poetic capacities to the more circumscribed domain of explanatory prose. He made this point in unpacking the specific expression *furusato obotsukanakaru beshi*:

> If one were to scrutinize the myriad emotions collected under this one term ["His home faded," *furusato obotsukanakaru beshi*] and sought to name them all one by one, one would wind up with something like my translation of [Theodore] Dreiser's prose: the piling up of descriptors would not only make things more difficult to understand, but one would very likely find that no matter how many words one had piled up, there would never be a moment of satisfaction at which all had been said. On close inspection, one finds that the sadness of this passage is limitless, and it is therefore only natural that one cannot explicitly and completely articulate its contours.[104]

In lauding the infinitude of the sentimental economy in *Genji*, Tanizaki implicitly communed with the worldly vision of the tale that Norinaga put forward more than a century earlier, according to which *Genji* contains a world of human emotion because its language articulates each and every sentiment that could ever be experienced. From this perspective, *Genji* is an inexhaustible structure of meaning in which a humane pathos (*aware*) dwells in the literary language of the native vernacular. This perspective is illuminated in recalling that the poet, translator, and classicist Anne Carson has written of a Greek word often translated as "sympathy" or "pathos" that it "implies some shared movement of soul between writer and reader, as if words could have a power to enter the reader and design an emotion there from inside his own voice."[105] In *Genji*, too, Tanizaki found in the *aware* (pathos) of the tale a conduit commuting a spirit or soul of Japanese being from ancient times to modern through the surfaces of vernacular language. In a two-way dialogue occasioned by the act of sympathetic reading, the receptive interlocutor could receive this language, taking it within himself while also entering the complete world of human sentiment held together by the text itself. In this context, reading becomes an act by which readers learn to breathe with a text, taking in its inspiration and allowing it to teach them to exhale expressions of their own place in the household of human pathos.

This perspective on *Genji* informed the extraliterary rhetoric surrounding the 1939 translation. Yamada wrote in 1939 that not only does *Genji* "attest to the transcendent skill of the Japanese literary arts [*kokumin no bungei*], but it also testifies to the warmth of our Japanese sense for humanity [*waga kokumin no ninjō*], and to the graceful elegance of our sense for taste. It is therefore something we should be proud of before the world. In working with this great classic, my desire for modern people to feel it with intimacy, and to experience its refined beauty, has never strayed from my mind."[106] Yamada also claimed that modern readers could only "feel" *Genji* when immersed in the affective valence of its language, including its "way of speaking" (*iikata*), "rhythm" (*bunsei*), and "narrative pacing" (*jojutsu no kankyū*):

> I need not even mention that this work of Tanizaki's is not a translation into the contemporary vernacular, nor is it a literal, word-for-word translation. But neither is his a work that wantonly departs from the language of the original. At times, the language has been altered or adjusted, and the number of words in some passages has at times been increased; yet, we have tried to feature the way of speaking of the original and its rhythm so that even its narrative pacing becomes palpable [*ajiwaiuru yō ni natteiru*].[107]

But what were the forms of modern language that conveyed the feeling of pleasure (*ajiwai*) that Yamada praised in the classical source text?

The following is an excerpt of Tanizaki and Yamada's 1939 translation of the same "Suma" passage on which Tanizaki based his critique of Waley's translation in *A Manual on Style.* The nonitalicized text denotes portions of the classical source text that Tanizaki and Yamada preserved, and the *italicized* portions represent what I understand to have been significant departures from the source text:

> Ano Suma *to iu tokoro* wa, mukashi koso hito no sumika nado mo atta monono, ima wa *taisō* hitozato o hanareta, *mono* sugoi *tochi ni natteite,* ama no ie sae mare de aru to kiiteoide ni naru keredomo, *amari ningen no deiri no hageshii, ōbirana atari ni* sumai *o suru no* wa *fu*hon'i *de arushi,* sōka to itte miyako o tōku satte iku no mo, furusato *no koto ga kigakari de arōshi nado to, hata no miru me mo kimari ga* warui *hodo omayoi asobashite,*

> kishikata *no koto ya*, yukusue *no koto ya*, yorozu no koto o oomoitsuzuke ni nari, samazama no kanashimi ga *mune ippai ni onari ni naru.*[108]

In Waley's translation, the same passage reads:

> There was Suma. It might not be such a bad place to choose. There had indeed once been some houses there; but it was now a long way to the nearest village and the coast wore a very deserted aspect. Apart from a few fishermen's huts there was not anywhere a sign of life. This did not matter, for a thickly populated, noisy place was not at all what he wanted; but even Suma was a terribly long way from the Capital, and the prospect of being separated from all those whose society he liked best was not at all inviting. His life hitherto had been one long series of disasters. As for the future, it did not bear thinking of![109]

In many cases, Tanizaki and Yamada's 1939 translation preserved the same or nearly equivalent diction as that found in the source text. Even when they altered the diction, moreover, they often succeeded in maintaining much of the allusiveness of the source language. For example, the phrase that Tanizaki lauded as exemplary of the *ganchiku* aesthetic in *A Manual on Style*, *furusato obotsukanakaru beshi* ([His] home faded), became *furusato no koto ga kigakari de arōshi nadoshi* (Thoughts of home surely made him uneasy). Tanizaki and Yamada's translation maintained the term *furusato* (which connotes one's native place, home, and, in this case, the capital and imperial court) and the expression *kigakari* (fear, anxiety) maintained the senses of vague foreboding and unnamed anxiety that Tanizaki praised in the original locution, *obotsukanakaru beshi* (faded, became vague or unclear). The speculative verb *arō*, like *beshi* in the source text, suggested that Genji "must have been" anxious, replicating the conjectural nature of the original narration. Adding *shi* and *nado* (each meaning something like "etcetera") implied a constellation of anxieties that are unnamed but exist, further strengthening the allusive implication of Tanizaki and Yamada's prose in much the same way that Tanizaki argued the original language expressed a limitless expanse of anxiety, disquiet, and unease. The success of this translation in modernizing several formal elements of the original source language, preserving much of the older diction and creatively reworking seemingly untranslatable archaisms, reflected Tanizaki and Yamada's desire for a renewed modern Japanese language that would draw on premodern inspirations in the late 1930s.

Other aspects of Tanizaki and Yamada's translation, however, revealed that the language they constructed remained an imperfect, experimental vision of a rejuvenated modern Japanese vernacular rather than a perfect embodiment of their ideals. Yamada and Tanizaki's translation often succeeded by their lexical restorationist standards, but it also sometimes vitiated the rhythm of the original that Yamada had described as indispensable for readers to "feel" (*ajiwau*) its language, and that Tanizaki had described as fundamental to the *ganchiku* aesthetic that he thought defined the classic. Their translation of the "Suma" excerpt, for example, was (ironically) far longer than the original and Waley's supposedly "verbose" English translation. By my count, the original (*genbun*) contained 169 syllables, Waley's translation 165, and Tanizaki and Yamada's—by far the longest—244.[110] Tanizaki and Yamada's prose in the "Suma" excerpt, furthermore, was padded with circumlocutions and additions such as *to iu tokoro* (a place such as [Suma]) and *no koto ya* (and so on) that altered its rhythm and density of expression. They also elaborated some dense expressions into wordier formulations: *Hito shigeku*, for example, is a pithy description of a place with "lots of people," but it became *amari ningen no deiri no hageshii* (a place where the comings and goings of individuals are much too furious) in Tanizaki and Yamada's more prolix modern prose. As this suggests, the language of Tanizaki and Yamada's translation successfully transplanted several allusive referential patterns from Murasaki Shikibu's eleventh-century prose to a modern idiom, but it also retained some vestiges of modern language that they had criticized.

In 1939, though, Tanizaki and Yamada considered their translation to be a significant contribution to a broader cultural restoration that they thought was on the cusp of remaking modern Japan and East Asia. Emmerich has even pointed out that when the president of Chūōkōronsha, Shimanaka Yūsaku, advertised the translation in the *Tōkyō nichinichi shinbun* on January 2, 1939, he linked the modernization of *Genji* to the revitalization of Asia, writing:

> As we enter the spring of this third year of glorious success on the battlefield of the Japan-China Incident, we wish, first of all, to offer our most

> humble thanks to the loyal and brave officers and men of our army and navy. At present, however, the Incident is advancing from the stage of military conquest to the stage in which we establish order, and the future before us is still fraught with innumerable difficulties and complications. These are the pitifully weak first kicks of a New East Asian culture, the agonies of new shoots budding forth over the dead ashes. How can we, blessed with the good fortune to participate in this sacred war of culture, if only in a minor way, fortify these fragrant buds? It is foolish even to hope that we might push back the onslaught of European and American culture. But surely we have long since awakened from that adoring dream of red-haired foreigners in which we forgot the unique culture of our own nation? Cultural development in this sense must give life to the traditions that flow in our bloodstream, and strive to lift up that which is Japanese, making it that which is of the world.[111]

In the latter portion of the New Year's felicitation, Shimanaka explicitly connected the making of a modern *Genji* to the larger project of building a "New East Asian culture":

> The fourteenth year of the Shōwa period [1939] is indeed a period of great transition in our nation's culture and a period of great discovery for the new East Asian culture. We do not "look into the past in order to know what is new." That which is old and eternally great is itself already new. The fourteenth year of Shōwa is, then, the moment for us to look anew with fresh eyes at our nation's great and unique literature as it becomes the blood and flesh of the new order we are establishing. This is precisely why, at long last, voices have begun crying out for the revival of classical literature. And this is precisely our intention in resurrecting *Genji monogatari*, giving it a modern life. At the dawn of this new spring, our bodies secretly abrim with confidence, we are pleased to share with you this small measure of our ambitions. Nothing could satisfy us more than for you to show us the great kindness of understanding the cause to which we are so sincerely and passionately devoted.[112]

In a resonant vein, Tanizaki's preface to the translation revealed his optimism that what he viewed as a Japanese renaissance underway in the 1930s was succeeding, and that the 1939 *Genji* translation was part of a broader reformation in East Asia: "Looking back, society has changed dramatically in the four years since I began work on this translation. Today, our nation from top to bottom is cooperating in rebuilding East Asia [*tōa saiken*]. In such an age, to introduce to the modern world anew the crystallization of our illustrious classical literature, a work which we believe stands against any in the world, might also signal some sort of opportunity."[113]

These statements remind us that all pedagogy orients itself toward the future because it implies a form of leadership guiding the imagination to something it does not already know. The time of imperial expectation and the pedagogical leadership of the middlebrow came together in Tanizaki and Yamada's efforts to reclaim for their own precarious present something of the aristocratic authority of vernacular storytelling in Murasaki's Heian tale. In a translation that never promised to tell any original story for the first time, a feel for language was nevertheless imagined to have wielded a rejuvenating force.

Middlebrow World Literature

This chapter has explored how a modern translation of *Genji* allowed aspects of a high-minded intellectual discourse on native language in imperial Japan to conspire with the pleasures of middlebrow literary culture. In so doing, it has framed the interplay of belief in the sacred and the allure of the stylish in terms of modernist matters that are well known to the bourgeois imagination in particular. Roughly a decade before Tanizaki's collaboration with Yamada, the philosopher Bernard Groethuysen described the emergence of bourgeois skepticism in a world of religious faith as a mix more complicated than any simple rejection or acceptance of belief. In *The Bourgeois: Catholicism vs. Capitalism in Eighteenth-Century France* (*Origines de l'esprit bourgeois en France*, 1927), he noted that "although the bourgeois had eliminated certain truths or, rather, allowed them to wither in his soul, he had retained others, transforming them by taking away their specifically religious character and secularizing them by integrating them in his nonreligious world. Thus a bourgeois did not say, simply, 'I don't believe in God.' Indeed, he might readily admit the existence of God. But his concept of God was different."[114]

Recalling aspects of the cultural mixing of high and low that also play out in middlebrow culture, Groethuysen limned the position of the bourgeois subject in between faith and doubt, writing that the bourgeois acted as a middle agent who complicated the definitions of each:

> It would be altogether misleading, therefore, to reduce the religious problem of bourgeois emancipation to the terms "I believe" or "I don't believe." It would be more accurate to speak of a continuous movement, punctuated by sudden jolts both on the individual and on the collective level, but one which on the whole developed less in the form of great battles in which the adversaries pitted principle against principle, than through successive and constantly renewed struggles in the course of which the bourgeoisie often took over certain positions of the other side and incorporated them in its own.[115]

The language of literature leaves one record of these "constantly renewed struggles," and that is why the scholar Franco Moretti wrote in *The Bourgeois: Between History and Literature*, "Stories, and styles: that's where I found the bourgeois," adding that in his study, "the peculiarities of bourgeois culture will emerge from the implicit, and even buried dimension of language: a 'mentality' made of unconscious grammatical patterns and semantic associations, more than clear and distinct ideas."[116] In a resonant vein, this chapter has linked this bourgeois "mentality" to a middlebrow literary mode in interwar Japan, and explored how it found something sacred to believe in the "unconscious grammatical patterns and semantic associations" of *Genji*, yet something that was also cloaked in a style so alluring that it never asked readers to explicitly declare "I believe" at all.

The last installment of the translation was released in 1941, the same year as the Japanese attack on Pearl Harbor. In the years to come, the Pacific War would turn the tides against the Japanese forces that Tanizaki himself had earlier praised, and that Yamada's propaganda had exhorted to battlefields across Asia and the Pacific. After the surrender in 1945, a vigorous debate about the literati's culpability in advancing the wartime ideology gained steam, and as a result, many prominent writers and thinkers (including Yamada) were condemned to infamy by the damning charge of complicity. But one of the peculiar effects of middlebrow in the age of empire is that it seems both to have enabled Tanizaki's casual association with the toxic wartime ideology of ***kokutai*** and, after the defeat, to have protected him from its stain. After all, Tanizaki's career following the 1945 surrender was prosperous and successful. It helped that for Tanizaki, the politics of the war years could be left behind, and perhaps in this sense, he showed himself to have been something of the middlebrow opportunist who engaged the wartime ideology in its moment of ascendance only to abandon it later as the temper of the times changed.

After the war, Tanizaki expressed his disdain for the very militarists whose imperial advances he had himself condoned just years earlier. He expressed his support of the war several times, in fact, as in 1942, when he took to the national radio airwaves to deliver a speech commending the Japanese military victory in Singapore and calling Japan's mission a holy war (*seisen*) for the "liberation of all East Asia."[117] The scholar Hosoe Hikaru has pointed to other writings in which Tanizaki voiced his support for the war, too, such as in 1935, when he declared that he was "happy about the broadening of the empire and eager for there to be an augmented Japanese cultural sphere. The earning potential for a writer will no doubt become only greater."[118] But after the war, Tanizaki revealed that military pressures and censorship greatly influenced how he translated *Genji*. In the preface to his second modern translation of *Genji*, published in 1951 to 1954 with censored passages restored, he blamed the zeitgeist of the wartime for deficiencies in the first translation, which he lamented had to be strategically altered to overcome wartime publishing restrictions:

> The clumsy style of the first translation was not the only thing that left me dissatisfied. It was published in an era when the bigoted ideologies of militarist nationalism were rampant. In order to avoid the censure of ignorant militarists, I was forced to minimally twist, cut, adjust, and color the original story. Additionally, in the five or six years I worked on the project, the state of affairs gradually worsened and military coercion intensified, and so I was left with no alternative but to expurgate and distort even more of the original than I had at first anticipated. . . . Knowing that the dark age of war could not continue forever, I privately waited expectantly for the inevitable return to an era of freedom [*jiyū na jidai*]. Thereafter, our nation recklessly plunged into the Greater East Asian War, but as a result of meeting with calamitous defeat, the era of freedom for which I had hoped came sooner than I had anticipated.[119]

While Tanizaki's modern *Genji* had to wait until the end of the war to be completed—for only then could previously expurgated portions be restored—it is also true that the middlebrow *monogatari* produced during the time of world war had already completed some of the most important work of canonizing *Genji* as a classic of world literature.

Emmerich traced this process of canonization through a longer discourse stretching back decades, to the late nineteenth century, while also showing how some of the most important links in the discursive chain he examined formed around the time of the 1939 translation examined in my analysis, too. He wrote that "*Genji*'s contemporary existence might be envisioned as a triangular field delimited by three conceptual lines: *Genji* as a work of world literature, *Genji* as a work that exists first and foremost in translation, and *Genji* as a work that is discursively figured as participating in world literature through translation." One conclusion that followed from this perspective was that "the moment when the three lines finally clicked into place, creating the field within which *Genji* is now almost inevitably apprehended" was "the publication between 1939 and 1941, during the final years of World War II, of the first of Tanizaki Jun'ichirō's three modern-Japanese translations of *Genji monogatari*."[120] Although the sometimes pejorative appellation "middlebrow" might seem to present itself in opposition to the more exalted sign of "world literature," Emmerich's analysis, combined with my own, would suggest that they crossed paths within the same cultural historical field, more or less, and that various middlebrow cultural translations—especially Tanizaki's—might well have occasioned some of the "replacements" and discursive reckonings that, over time, both in Japan and abroad, had the effect of canonizing *Genji* as a masterpiece of global stature.

More recently, though, aspects of the theories of world literature that had earlier been put forth by the scholars David Damrosch, Pascale Casanova, and Moretti have been challenged in ways that raise new questions for our understanding of the worldly imagination that surrounded the 1939 *Genji*. The most powerful critique has come from the literary scholar and intellectual historian Pheng Cheah, who has argued that earlier theories of world literature did not adequately conceptualize what a "world" actually is, instead taking "world" and "globe" for granted as synonyms, with the result that "world literature" is that literature which circulates through circuits created by the market forces of globalization. For Cheah, the global movements of a text and its discursive reception in global space do not allow us to fully consider the world-making potential of literary form itself. This is why he wrote that earlier theories of world literature "equate the world with circulatory movements that cut across national-territorial borders. They are primarily concerned with the impact of these spatial movements on the production, reception, and interpretation of literary texts instead of world literature's impact qua literature on the world. As I will show, they reduce the world literature's normative force to the barest minimum."[121] As a corrective, Cheah averred that a "world" is not something that can be perceived intuitively, or physically, but is, rather, something that "is given to us by the imagination."[122] Drawing on a complex philosophical lineage of worldly rumination, Cheah posited a notion of "world literature" that draws a more intimate relation between literary form and worldly being, and that sets aside the familiar preoccupation with the international circulation of texts about the globe.

I delve more deeply into the implications of Cheah's critique in the next chapter. But in transitioning to that analysis, it will suffice to say in closing this one that Cheah reminds us that literary form itself can be endowed with a normative worldly force that is irreducible to the circulations of a text-as-object in global space. Of particular relevance to my reading of the politics of middlebrow *monogatari* here is the related implication that the worldly form of the literary can be disruptive to the global system as given if it opens up futural trajectories of imagination that are not congruent to the hierarchies of cultural power East and West that weigh on the reception of literary writings by foreign audiences in translation. From the nativist-nationalist perspective in Japan's age of empire, these disruptions would have held particular promise as openings leading away from the problematic present and toward a futural catharsis. After all, the nativist imagination examined here pursued the fantasy of finding the form of the future in the prose of the past. It clung to the perspective that however far modern readers might be removed from the imagined "original" composed by Murasaki's own Heian hand, and however many distortions have accumulated through all the translations, supplements, and replacements that have appeared over the centuries, they still knew enough a millennium after Murasaki first wrote the tale to know that *Genji* was a "worldly" text long before it ever circulated internationally, and before anyone in the global discursive sphere could have ever called it "world literature" at all. From their perspective, the modern discourse that "discovered" in *Genji* the elements of what it recognized to be "world literature" was a descriptive epiphenomenon. The crux of the matter in their eyes was that as an irreducibly literary structure of meaning, the grammar of *Genji* had always ordered a complete poetics of human pathos.

This helps us begin to see that within the layers of literary atmosphere created by the collisions and collusions of aesthetic form and intellectual history, the act of reading the modern *Genji* allowed a translated language to nevertheless feel authentic. Past breathed with present as this language made its most forceful appeals through a collapsing of time that opened up a conduit to the sort of power that other expressions of *kokutai* ideology promised in more mythic terms. However paradoxically, in fact, the pedagogy of the middlebrow *monogatari* posited that the precarious present of the war years could be saved through a future-oriented meditation on an earlier age that could hardly have been more different from the modern world of Tanizaki, Yamada, and their readers. As Virginia Woolf put it in her 1925 description of Murasaki's eleventh-century Japan: "The accent of life did not fall upon war; the interests of men did not centre upon politics. Relieved from the violent pressure of these two forces, life expressed itself chiefly in the intricacies of behaviour, in what men said and what women did not quite say, in poems that break the surface of silence with silver fins, in dance and painting, and in that love of the wildness of nature which only comes when people feel themselves perfectly secure."[123]

These were the rhythms of an inspired life bathed in a redemptive light promising pleasure to middlebrow readers whom Woolf herself elsewhere derogated. And as these rhythms amplified within a bourgeois cultural style, they carried within themselves the authorization to recuperate an aristocratic privilege that was coded by the lost language of Heian vernacular eloquence. In the architecture of *Genji*, then, readers embarked on an imperial war and living in an age of uncertainty could finally dwell within the shared time of *kokutai* community held together by the "sanctuary of literature." And as the middlebrow *monogatari* taught them how to breathe with the courtly vernacular style of Heian eloquence, it also taught them to conspire with each other by believing in their own legitimacy to lead in a moment of world historical struggle.

The next chapter continues the discussion of literature and thought in interwar Japan as it turns to the highbrow realm of avant-garde modernism and cosmopolitan philosophy by engaging perspectives on "worldliness" in the writings of novelist Yokomitsu Riichi and his Kyoto School contemporaries.

CHAPTER 2

A Worldly World in Fiction and Philosophy

Reading Yokomitsu Riichi's *The Melancholy of Travel* as a "Novel of Ideas"

> Novel of ideas. The character of each personage must be implied, as far as possible, in the ideas of which he is the mouthpiece. In so far as theories are rationalizations of sentiments, instincts, dispositions of soul, this is feasible. The chief defect of the novel of ideas is that you must write about people who have ideas to express—which excludes all but about .01 percent of the human race. Hence the real, the congenital novelists don't write such books. But then, I never pretended to be a congenital novelist.
>
> —Aldous Huxley, *Point Counter Point* (1928)[1]

It might be said that the writer Yokomitsu Riichi "never pretended to be a congenital novelist." Instead, he engaged ideas even in his literary fiction, betraying a hybrid self-identity as part novelist, part intellectual. His two sides breathed as one at a roundtable discussion devoted to his essay "Junsui shōsetsu ron" (A Theory of the Pure Novel, 1935), where he declared that his future fiction would feature what he called "fourth-person perspective."[2] Yokomitsu had introduced the idea of "fourth-person perspective" in the essay, and it has long been regarded as one of the most provocative ideas to have appeared in writings on literature in modern Japan. But it has also proven to be one of the most perplexing. In "A Theory of the Pure Novel," Yokomitsu offered only a broad explanation of what "fourth-person perspective" actually signified, vaguely suggesting that it involved blending first-person subjectivity and third-person objectivity.[3] Taken in isolation, then, "fourth-person perspective" feels like a modernist description of modernist possibility without any clear referent in the realm of modernist practice itself.

Recently, though, the scholar Inden Masashi has shown that some of Yokomitsu's seemingly inexplicable articulations make more sense when read not only within conventional literary historical contexts, but also in dialogue with contemporaneous trends in neo-Kantian thought that emerged in early twentieth-century Europe and Japan.[4] In particular, Inden observed that some of Yokomitsu's theoretical concerns as a novelist deeply reverberated with those of the German philosopher Ernst Cassirer (1874–1945) and the Japanese thinker Yura Tetsuji—the latter of whom had studied with Nishida Kitarō (1870–1945) at Kyoto Imperial University, later completed his doctoral research under Cassirer's tutelage in Germany, and remained one of Yokomitsu's closest friends from childhood onward. Inden also noted that Yokomitsu's writings resonated with those of Miki Kiyoshi (1897–1945) and the wider circle of "Kyoto School philosophy" more generally. In fact, Miki himself participated in the roundtable discussion on the topic of Yokomitsu's "Theory of the Pure Novel" mentioned above, and that conversation took place shortly before the appearance of the first parts of what would become Miki's magnum opus, *Kōsōryoku no ronri* (A Theory of Imagination, 1937–43), which described the syntheses of subject and object, logos and pathos, that Miki argued emerge from the force fields of cultural "imagination." Inden examined how Yokomitsu engaged Miki's theory of imagination in ways that signaled he may have found in it a conceptual language that aligned with his own attempts, as a novelist, to synthesize first-person subjectivity and third-person objectivity in the form of a "fourth-person perspective" at around the same time.[5]

In the course of exploring these and other connections, Inden identified a crucial nexus of fiction and philosophy in the age of empire. His analysis helps us begin to see that Yokomitsu's literary experiments with narrative perspective conversed with the writings of Kyoto School intellectuals who were then speculating about how to conceive of a world historical standpoint (*sekaishiteki tachiba*) capable of synthesizing a cosmopolitan narrative of greatest possible meaning—a narrative in which provincial parts and cosmic wholes, national particularity and universal humanity, history and being, would all converge. By the 1930s, Miki, Yokomitsu, and their interlocutors had come to believe that the crises of world war and global economic turmoil had indicated the structural failure of worldly relations that had earlier been sustained by distinctly European premises. They sensed that the failures of a Eurocentric epoch had ushered in an age of world historical confusion in which the story of the world itself had encountered a rupture in its own unfolding. In response, they became convinced that repairing the unity of worldly relations could be achieved only through the construction of a new cosmopolitan holism that would ameliorate the antagonisms among all rival "isms" and bring a vast concatenation of cultural and historical phenomena into accord. In some articulations, that holism was to be the Japanese empire itself.[6]

As I read Yokomitsu's literary modernism through this discursive prism, I examine another conjuncture in which literary and intellectual history breathed together. Exploring this connection shifts the overall trajectory of my narrative away from the bourgeois privilege and middlebrow pleasure that figured in the previous chapter, and toward a more philosophically cosmopolitan turn of mind that pursued a globally informed synthesis. In making this transition to the much-studied realm of the Kyoto School thinkers and their interlocutors, I advance the received conversation by focusing on the question of literary form and asking what the orchestrations of a novelist like Yokomitsu reveal that the content of intellectual historical discourse alone does not. It follows that my reading of Yokomitsu's *Ryoshū* (The Melancholy of Travel, 1937-1946) rises from the broad premise that the worldly cohesion of the Japanese empire, which was described in imperial propaganda and conceptualized in philosophical writings by several Kyoto School thinkers, shared some properties with the modernist text that Yokomitsu theorized and composed at around the same time. Drawing on the literary theorist Pheng Cheah's engagement with philosophical writing on the question of "worldliness," introduced in the previous chapter, my approach starts with the observation that like a literary text, the cohesion of the colonial world that was imagined in the philosophy and propaganda of wartime Japan floated in an ontological middle ground between subjective interpretation and objective meaning, remaining irreducible to either and yet contiguous with the borderlines of both. And like the narrative held together by the structure of an endlessly interpretable text, the world created by the culture of empire was imagined to hold together an almost infinite spectrum of meaning—a spectrum far in excess of the scales of meaning measured by the categories of nation and race, class and gender, "ism" and ideology. In an imagination that continually squared the circle of the subjective part and the objective whole in an effort to overcome what was felt to have been the deteriorated episteme of a Eurocentric modernity, the phenomenology of being in the world of capacious meaning sustained by the cosmopolitan culture of empire reverberated with the experience of reading an inexhaustible literary text: the logos of its particular details were legible to anyone even at the same time that the pathos of its ultimate implication exceeded everyone.[7]

This chapter brings these conceptual threads together by reading *The Melancholy of Travel* as a "novel of ideas" (*shisō shōsetsu*) that took shape on the fault lines of fiction and philosophy, and that registered their quaking contiguity. I begin by tracing some of the ideas suspended in the novel to more explicit articulations within the Kyoto School discourse on world history (*sekaishi*). This reveals that some of the connections between the novel and contemporaneous trends in thought developed as Yokomitsu himself composed aspects of *The Melancholy of Travel* after the philosophical itinerary of one thinker in particular who might be loosely associated with the Kyoto School: Yura Tetsuji. After linking the novel to this intellectual historical context, I then develop close readings of selected passages that reveal the idea of "worldliness" moving beyond the plane of theoretical rumination (where it has usually been interpreted in studies of Kyoto School thought) and becoming infrastructural to an actual aesthetic creation—*The Melancholy of Travel* itself. As we sense how the novel allowed the deeper affinities between text and world to conspire with one another, we also begin to see how Yokomitsu's magnum opus rendered the aesthetic dynamic of worldly form in ways that the purposeful language of Kyoto School expositions never could.

Yura Tetsuji and the Worldly Imagination in Philosophy and Propaganda

The scholar of Japanese literature Seiji Lippit has described *The Melancholy of Travel* in terms of a "melancholic nationalism," noting in particular that throughout the text, "the yearning for cultural wholeness and authenticity is tempered by an awareness of the impossibility of returning to any purified 'native' culture unsullied by foreign intervention."[8] These themes are set into motion in the first half of *The Melancholy of Travel*, which is set in Europe (mostly Paris) and centers on the relationship between two Japanese expatriates: Yashiro, a young man of nativist-nationalist inclination, and Kuji, a pedantic Europhile who plays the role of Yashiro's foil. Yashiro is alienated from his surroundings abroad and yearns to return home to Japan; Kuji, in contrast, adores nearly everything that catches his eye in Europe. A third character, Chizuko, joins them in Paris, and it gradually becomes clear that Yashiro is in love with her. But the possibility of romance between them will always be complicated by the fact that she and her family are Catholic, which in Yashiro's eyes endows them with a mixed identity that is part Japanese, part European. In the second half of *The Melancholy of Travel*, the characters return to Japan, where Yashiro searches in vain for the native spiritual and cultural home that he had imagined while in Europe. Kuji is absent from the second half of the novel, save for a brief appearance in the last installments. The novel ends with a rally in Hibiya Park in which Tōno—a pensive haiku poet—imagines the prospects for the Japanese empire in East Asia.

This brief sketch of *The Melancholy of Travel* suggests much of why it might be called a "novel of ideas." In literary criticism, the appellation names a loosely defined style that is known for importing fully formed philosophical perspectives into its narrative plane, staging contrived debates among cerebral characters who become the spokespersons for different intellectual or political positions, and generally straining to square the circle of philosophy and literature, art and thought, in ways that sometimes strike readers as unrealistic.[9] In the case of *The Melancholy of Travel* in particular, we notice that its three main figures—the nativist Yashiro, the Europhile Kuji, and the in-between Chizuko—are all characterized in ways that recall one of the conventions of the "novel of ideas" that was elaborated by Aldous Huxley in the epigraph to this chapter—namely, that the "character of each personage must be implied, as far as possible, in the ideas of which he is the mouthpiece." This aspect of the "novel of ideas" accounts for part of its vexed reputation, and even raises the question of whether it is really a novelistic form at all. In one critique, the literary theorist Sianne Ngai observed that the ironically unnovelistic mixing of literary form and readymade thought can mean that the novel of ideas runs the risk of becoming a gimmick, one that works too hard to import canned philosophical perspectives from beyond its discursive boundaries, only to convince readers too little that they are organically part of the world of the text.[10] Huxley's character in *Point Counter Point* reminds us of this, too, when he observes, "The great defect of the novel of ideas is that it's a made-up affair. Necessarily; for people who can reel off neatly formulated notions aren't quite real; they're slightly monstrous. Living with monsters becomes rather tiresome in the long run."[11]

To the extent that Yokomitsu's novel of ideas belongs to the category, it can hardly be spared the critique that moments in its narration feel contrived, canned, and "slightly monstrous." But with that said, Inden's study helps us to see that other, more compelling aspects of what made *The Melancholy of Travel* a "novel of ideas" come to the fore in realizing that it was drawn in part after the intellectual journey of Yura Testsuji, a minor philosopher who associated with some of the better-known Kyoto School figures.[12] Yura grew up with Yokomitsu and later studied at Kyoto Imperial University with the central thinkers of the Kyoto School, Nishida Kitarō and Tanabe Hajime (1885–1962). He then continued his studies as a doctoral student in Germany from 1928 to 1931 under the tutelage of the philosopher Ernst Cassirer, a towering figure who famously debated Martin Heidegger in 1929.[13] Yura received his Doctor der Philosophie degree in 1931 and then returned to Japan, where in 1943 he took a position at Jingū Kōgakkan Daigaku, the Ise institute for the promotion of Shinto that was headed by Yamada Yoshio, the linguist examined in chapter 1.[14] Although Yura was only a minor figure in the intellectual history of early twentieth-century Japan, he matters in the current analysis because Yokomitsu seems to have composed aspects of *The Melancholy of Travel* in mind of his philosophical sojourn abroad.

The scholar Inaga Shigemi has written that Yura was the real-life model for the protagonist Yashiro in the early portion of the narrative, and Inden has suggested this as well.[15] In addition, Yomota Inuhiko has noted that Yura has been understood as a "model" for the novel, and the literary critic Inoue Ken has likewise observed that Yura seems to have informed aspects of *The Melancholy of Travel*, adding that Yura influenced Yokomitsu's literary trajectory from early on and became one of the novelist's most ardent supporters.[16] More compelling still are Yura's own writings about *The Melancholy of Travel*, in which he corroborated the argument that he is the model for Yashiro. Yura has written that he became a model (*moderu*) for Yokomitsu's protagonists on several occasions, that he likely served as an inspiration for Yashiro in particular, and that in parts of the novel, he even recognized himself in the character (*kanari watashi ni nitteiru*).[17] He claimed that some passages in *The Melancholy of Travel* were informed by his own lecture notes, which he lent to Yokomitsu during the composition of the novel, and which he claimed sometimes appeared in the text nearly verbatim.[18] It comes as less of a surprise, then, to learn that Yura described *The Melancholy of Travel* as a "novel of ideas" (*shisō shōsetsu*) that took up "the problem of unifying European thought and Japanese thought" (*seiō shisō to Nihon shisō to no tōitsu no mondai*).[19] According to Yura, Yokomitsu took for granted the impossibility of completely resolving the tensions of European and Japanese thought, but as a starting point, he approached the problem by thinking of Yura's own "marriage problem" (*kekkon mondai*) involving a conflict between Shinto and Christianity; in the novel, correspondingly, Yashiro's love for Chizuko is undone by the fact that he identifies with ancient Shinto spirituality whereas she is Catholic and traces her family lineage to a long-dead feudal lord who converted to the foreign faith centuries earlier.[20] As Yura summed up: "Yokomitsu's plan for the novel seems to have been to examine the relationship between Shinto and Christianity, and to investigate the workings of their internal logic side-by-side. That was the motivation behind this novel of ideas, which was his life's work."[21]

Noting Yura's lingering presence in the background of *The Melancholy of Travel* complicates the more intuitive interpretation of the novel as a piece of autobiographical fiction about Yokomitsu's own travels through Europe and Asia and suggests that in addition, it might be read as a novel of ideas more broadly conceived that refracted a range of contemporaneous trends in thought. This is not to deny its autobiographical elements, however. Its first serial installment appeared soon after Yokomitsu himself returned from a six-month trip to Europe in 1936, during which he visited Paris and covered the Berlin Olympics while writing dispatches for two Japanese newspapers, the *Tokyo Nichinichi Shinbun* and the *Osaka Mainichi Shinbun*. Since the novel takes up the experience of young travelers in Europe in the 1930s, it could be read as Yokomitsu's self-reflexive account of his own time abroad, if only because much of the novel is autobiographical, to be sure. But the suggestion that it was imagined in part through the lens of Yura's intellectual journey to work with Cassirer would seem to resonate with some of the deeper substance of *The Melancholy of Travel*. The Olympic games that Yokomitsu was dispatched to cover hardly figure in the novel at all, for example, whereas dense ruminations on symbolic cultural forms East and West, ancient and modern, consistently take center stage in scenes redolent of the intellectual foment associated with Kyoto School thinkers (including Yura) and their European interlocutors (including Cassirer).

More broadly, too, the intellectual historical reverberations that echo throughout *The Melancholy of Travel* confirm the received image of Yokomitsu as more of a philosophically minded writer than a "congenital novelist." Even before Yokomitsu's "novel of ideas" began serialization, Yura himself had already interpreted his literary theory and fiction as a form of philosophical reckoning by other means in *Yokomitsu Riichi no geijutsu shisō* (The Aesthetic Ideas of Yokomitsu Riichi, 1937). In 1935, the philosopher Tosaka Jun wrote that Yokomitsu's penchant for dry theoretical writing made him a kind of "academic" (*akademishan*), adding that "rare have been the novelists in Japan who have taken up difficult philosophical premises [*tetsuri*] to the extent that Yokomitsu has."[22] More recent scholarship has noted Yokomitsu's interest in cosmopolitan "philosophical premises" in particular. Dennis Washburn, for example, has examined Yokomitsu's early career, during which he formed the literary modernist group called the "New Sensationist School" (*Shinkankaku-ha*) with the novelist Kawabata Yasunari in the 1920s. Washburn has observed that "what Yokomitsu longed for was a culture that was at once parochial and universal, which subsumed the West under an all but impossible synthesis of the national and the cosmopolitan. This desire for synthesis is manifested in the formation of his theory of New Sensation [*Shin kankaku*]."[23] In a related vein, the literary scholar Irena Hayter has observed that the modernism of the New Sensationist School was marked by a "deeper continuity with the powerful vitalist ideas of the turn of the [twentieth] century, namely, the urge to dissolve subject-object divisions."[24] According to Hayter, the vitalist "philosophers of life"—including prominently Henri Bergson and his first interpreter in Japan, Nishida himself—inspired Yokomitsu with their skepticism toward the divisions of intellectual inquiry and cultural history, and their alternative premises that held, according to Hayter, that "it was possible to transcend the oppositions of materialism and idealism; [that] all world religions had the same fundamental principles, and [that] Eastern and Western thought could be fused into one."[25]

The link between the cosmopolitan syntheses that Washburn and Hayter have examined in the early period of Yokomitsu's career and the worldliness of form that I argue characterized his later "novel of ideas" comes into clearer focus in considering that the English-language word "cosmopolitanism" can be rendered in Japanese as *sekaishugi*, and that both words inflect the Greek *kosmopolitês*, meaning "citizen of the world [*sekai*]." By the 1930s, Yokomitsu was one among many writers and thinkers who turned to the problems of worldly relation out of the conviction that the world historical bonds linking the citizen-self interpolated within national culture to a worldly whole of the human spirit had begun to deteriorate. It was believed that as a result, the possibility for deep communication across world historical time and space—a communication linking past to present, East to West, language to language—had been interrupted.[26] The question of form presently emerged as a key consideration in literary and philosophical narratives, for what social or collective whole could possibly satisfy the cosmopolitan imagination desirous of deep communicative cohesion? What kind of universal bond could ever prove durable enough to hold together a community that would otherwise be divided by the parochialism that defines all national cultures, and the particularities that mark all local histories? For many, the answer was "a world" (*sekai*): it was "a world" that would include the part within the whole, the subject within the object, the history of the nation within the being of the spirit. In the literary theory of the time, Yokomitsu articulated this synthesis in terms of a "fourth-person perspective," and in the realm of modernist praxis, his "novel of ideas" refracted the philosophical preoccupations of other attempts to reimagine a worldly totality in what was believed to have been the age of its deterioration.

As one part of this larger rumination, the worldly imagining that appeared in *The Melancholy of Travel* materialized within contextual coordinates that were more explicitly articulated in the expository sphere, and in the writings of a circle of "Kyoto School" philosophers in particular. Intellectual historians have amply shown that during the interwar years, it was the Kyoto School thinkers—including Nishida and his students Nishitani Keiji, Tanabe Hajime, and Miki (among others)—who most vigorously mobilized the tools of philosophical inquiry in their efforts to explain the crises of the age in world historical terms. As is well known, one of the most notorious Kyoto meditations appeared during a 1941 roundtable discussion that featured Nishitani, Kōsaka Masaaki, Kōyama Iwao, and Suzuki Shigetaka, and that was subsequently published under the title "Sekaishiteki tachiba to Nihon" (The World Historical Standpoint and Japan). The goal of the discussion was to understand the crises that gripped Japan and East Asia within the context of a world historical conjuncture of maximal proportions, and to narrate a future course of action that would endow imperial Japan with a transformative subjectivity capable of initiating a new stage of world history in the near future. The historian Harry Harootunian, drawing on the writings of the literary critic Mikhail Bakhtin, has understood the broader implications of the discussion in terms of the "answerability" of Kyoto School thought—and the vocation of philosophy itself—to the demands of its own historical present, arguing that insofar as "the determined purpose of the philosophy of world history was the achievement of a new present," it followed that "this project of the present leaned increasingly toward defining Japan's destiny as the subject and substance of the category of world history."[27] Other intellectual historians have also examined how a wide range of Kyoto School thinkers, in various ways, "answered" the questions of their age in world historical terms, at times even calling for the construction of a "New World Order" (*sekai shinchitsujo*) to be initiated through decisive action.[28]

But what, exactly, was the form of the "world" at the center of this discourse, and why was its renewal thought to have been the crux of the crisis in the precarious present? This is a crucial question if we are to understand Yokomitsu's last novel to have been not merely a description of global relations in the international sphere, but a philosophically informed articulation of worldly belonging that materialized in literary aesthetic terms. In this connection, Yura's writings on "worldview" invoked the problem of "worldliness" (*sekaisei* 世界性) and provide clues as to how we might understand the structure of worldly relations per se in this context.[29] In *Minzoku kokka to sekaikan* (The Ethnic State and Worldview, 1943), Yura invoked the German word "Weltanschauung" (worldview) and argued that it meant "to intuit a world" (*sekai o chokkan suru*). He elaborated: "If we scrutinize this notion of 'intuition' [*chokkan*] more deeply, it becomes clear that it does not mean that a subject simply beholds the exterior [*gaimen*] of its other [*tasha*]. Rather, 'intuition' has to do with a much deeper, stronger, and more direct functioning than that. To intuit means to forget the self, and to become one with the other [*ta to gōitsu suru koto*]. It means that subjectivity and objectivity directly merge into one."[30] Yura concluded that a worldview joined self and other through a kind of deep communicative catharsis. As he put it:

> This kind of deep vision is not something that can be seen through the eyes, nor something that can simply be seen through the heart. It is the working of a deeper unity. It is a deeper, stronger working of the self [我] that passes into the world [世界], and that envelopes the world. It is an action. It is a power that holds together form. Which is to say that a worldview [*sekaikan*] is that which *makes* a world, which brings forth a world, which forms a world. The world itself is actually formed from the working of this vision.[31]

Yura's perspective on Weltanschauung seems to have implied that a "world" is a system of relations in which the self interpolated within national culture opens up to what lies beyond it as it gains a deeper perspective into its own connections with ancient pasts and distant others. Read this way, we begin to see that the Kyoto School imagining of worldly relations communed with a much broader philosophical problematic that has been described by Cheah, a theorist of cosmopolitanism who has suggested in another context that the structure of worldly relations might be conceived of as "a limitless field of conflicting forces that are brought into relation and that overlap and flow into each other without return because each force, as part of a world, is necessarily opened up to what lies outside."[32]

Cheah's study of worldly form in literature and philosophy did not reference the Kyoto School confluence, to be sure, but it did work through writings by figures whose ideas powerfully informed the Kyoto imagination, including Kant, Hegel, and Heidegger. As a supplement, then, his analysis helps us to see the structure of worldly relations as a philosophical problem in general, and to begin to consider how its uptake in the Kyoto imagination availed itself to distinctive literary distributions in Yokomitsu's fiction in particular. In his reading of Johann Wolfgang von

Goethe's influential conceptualization of "world literature" (*Weltliteratur*), for example, Cheah observed that "the world in the higher sense is spiritual intercourse, transaction, and exchange aimed at bringing out universal humanity. It does not abolish national differences but takes place and is to be found in the intervals, mediations, passages, and crossings between national borders and boundaries. The world is thus a form of relating, belonging, or being-with."[33] Working from this perspective, Cheah's analysis reminds us that because the form of a "world" is necessarily open-ended, it differs from the form of a "globe," which is a physical object limited by its own finitude and self-enclosure. And whereas worldly relations materialize through "spiritual intercourse" that generates the experience of "being-with," global relations more often relate to the liberal economic imperative of entrepreneurial profit seeking, which generates hierarchies of domination in the international marketplace that are mirrored in the colonial sphere. However extensive and infrastructural these economic relations might seem to be, though, they are always constrained by the fact that they are based on the closed circuits traced by capital circulating within finite geographical space, and by the fact that these circulations have situated Europe at the center of the global marketplace. Making this point, Cheah has written that the enclosure of global capitalism itself "incorporates peoples and populations into the world-system by tethering them to Western modernity's unrelenting march of progress and capitalist time and violently destroying other worlds and their temporalities."[34]

From this perspective, the purportedly universal claims of European liberalism that underwrite the international economic regimes of globalization are, in fact, destructive forces that obscure the particularities of the global periphery in favor of exalting the capitalist center. The phenomenality of "being-with" enabled by worldly relations promises an alternative: in contrast to the hierarchies created by "globalization," worldly belonging opens up to deep communication across deep time in a boundless idiom occasioned by a universal human spirit seeking its own expression. This was the sort of worldly form that Yura seems to have had in mind when he described the essence of "worldview" in the "deeper unity" that melds self and other, subject and object, and that articulates itself as a "power that holds together form," and that even "brings forth a world." And this was the form of a worldly "being-with" that promised the broader Kyoto School imagination an escape from the domination of a Eurocentric era of world history itself, an era that was believed to rest on a false universalism that ironically wrote the global periphery (including East Asia) out of "world history." Drawing these threads together, Harootunian has concluded that "what these [Kyoto School] philosophers sought to envision was a figure of world history that would account for the excluded particularities that had remained shadowed by the universalistic claims projected by imperial domination and colonial oppression. . . . In their time, they were driven to identify a dangerous presence in the present: a deteriorating world situation requiring immediate resolution."[35]

But if we are to read *The Melancholy of Travel* through the prism of worldly belonging, then it must not be forgotten that as the ideas that animated the Kyoto School discourse on "world history" contributed to a wider "revolt against the West," they also articulated a fascist politics in the language of consensual bonding. Yura, for one, cheered the rise of the Nazis in *Hittora to Doitsu minzoku kokka* (Hitler and the Ethnic State of Germany, 1944), which described Hitler in its first sentence as a hero and "the most original genius of modern Germany—nay, the world."[36] More broadly, too, Harootunian and the historian Tetsuo Najita have observed in their reading of the Kyoto School discourse that "a closer examination of this 'philosophy of world history' reveals a thinly disguised justification, written in the language of Hegelian metaphysics, for Japanese aggression and continuing imperialism. In prewar Japan, no group helped defend the state more consistently and enthusiastically than did the philosophers of the Kyoto faction, and none came closer than they did to defining the philosophic contours of Japanese fascism."[37] Whatever the promise of cohesive collectivity may have been within the discursive confines of literary and philosophical texts, it was a promise that supplied the alibi for a normative narrative of empire that was infamously articulated in the philosophically informed imperial propaganda of the age. One of the most prominent examples of this was the government-sponsored tract *Shin Nihon no shisō genri* (Principles of Thought for a New Japan, 1939), which was composed by Miki and other intellectuals in the Shōwa Kenkyūkai (Shōwa Research Association) who served Prime Minister Konoe Fumimaro, and which announced that war with China would hasten the end of a Eurocentric age in world history itself: "Spatially speaking, the world historical significance [*sekaishiteki igi*] of the China Incident is the possibility of unifying the world by first realizing the unity of East Asia. Up to now, the notion of 'World History' itself has in fact referred to nothing more than the cultural history of Europe. It has been something which has been considered only from what might be called a 'Eurocentric' perspective [*Yoroppashugi no tachiba*]."[38] In accounting for the "world historical implications" (*sekaishi ni okeru igi*) of imperial warfare, the authors of *Principles of Thought for a New Japan* argued that overcoming earlier Eurocentrisms through decisive action unifying East Asia would ultimately lead to a more worldly world itself: "If the unification of East Asia is not actualized, then the true unity of the world cannot exist. Thus, the unification of East Asia is not for the purpose of isolating East Asia from the world; quite to the contrary, it is necessary so that the world itself might become truly worldly [*sekai ga shin ni sekaiteki ni naru tame ni*]."[39]

Sketching these expository articulations of worldly imagining sets the stage to inquire after the necessity of literary aesthetic form in the section that follows. For if the stakes of the discourse were already drawn in philosophical and propagandistic writings, what need could there be to study Yokomitsu's literary modernism in this context? What kind of worldly orchestration can a literary text itself perform that expository theory cannot? Posing these questions helps us to see how a noted "novel of ideas" conspired with adjacent intellectual expositions.

The Worldliness of Literary Form

The scholars of world literature Shu-Mei Shih and Cheah have indicated that one way to begin thinking through the questions raised above would be to recall that in *The Human Condition* (1958), the philosopher Hannah Arendt wrote that "because of their outstanding permanence, works of art are the most intensely worldly of all tangible things. . . . Nowhere else does the sheer durability of the world of things appear in such purity and clarity."[40] Arendt made this point in observing that objects made for use—such as furniture—deteriorate in the course of their being used up by the very human beings who create them. In contrast, the art object is durable in its uselessness: it stands as a repository of worldly imaginings because it has no instrumentalist use-value, and therefore shelters outside the arc of creation, utilization, and deterioration that ultimately destroys other objects. Extended to the context of the current analysis, Arendt's insights would suggest that the instrumentalist orientation of wartime propaganda and the argumentative edge of Kyoto School philosophy marked a narrative episteme that categorically differed from the literary aesthetics of Yokomitsu's modernism, whatever their conceptual consanguinity might have been. One of the implications that follows is that compared to the power of the aesthetic imagination to construct a literary narrative of durable worldly implication, the argumentative exposition of Kyoto School philosophers on the topic of "world history" was not necessarily the most potent and affecting articulation of the worldly imagination in wartime Japan—even if (or precisely because) it was the most explicit and purposeful.

Of all aesthetic forms, moreover, the literary in particular has been argued to share a curious affinity with the worldly imagination—an affinity that promises an appealing conduit away from the perishable purposefulness of expository argument. Cheah has written in this connection that the philosopher Martin Heidegger understood poetry to have an indeterminate form akin to worldly relation itself because poetry, in Cheah's paraphrase of Heidegger, "is neither a subject's spiritual product nor a material cause in the objective world. It is instead the power of joining-together."[41] Cheah elaborated that by Heidegger's reckoning, "poetry makes worldliness visible because it has an ontological status similar to that of the world. The world is the total context of meaningfulness that holds us together with other beings at the same time that it is held together by the force of temporalization. Poetry reveals this holding-together because as an expression of the logos, it is itself a meaningful whole."[42] Cheah's reading of Heidegger's writing on poetry led him to conclude that the language of literature in general can perform "a joining of one thing to another" that is reminiscent of the cosmopolitan cohesive of worldliness itself. As he put it: "The meaningful word joins a meaning and a sound, and the fact of discourse joins the speaker and the addressee together in a circle of understandability as parts of a whole that necessarily belong to each other."[43] The literary text, then, forms praxis out of the theory of merging parts and wholes: its words and grammar, sounds and structure, orchestrate a "being-with" meaning in ways that link the private experience of each individual reader to a communal catharsis irreducible to subjective explication.

This is a particularly significant insight in the context of the Kyoto School rumination on "world history" because it suggests that for an imagination tired of the demands of liberal individualism and desirous of collective subjectivity, the act of reading might have offered an experience in which each reader-subject could merge with others in a structure of meaning organized by shared language, grammar, and narrative. Cheah would remind us that in this context, the worldliness of literary form owes not only (nor even primarily) to its descriptive narrations of globalization, and not at all to the international circulation of any particular text that is read in different locations around the globe. Instead, the worldly force of the literary owes to how it balances self and other in relation to an inexhaustible meaning that is ultimately unknowable, yet immanently palpable. As Cheah put it:

> The radical indeterminacy of literature's meaning also means that it exceeds the subject's powers of interpretation. Hence, literature does not merely map the spatialized world and give it value and meaning. Rather, its formal structures enact the opening of a world by the incalculable gift of time. We may therefore speak of the world as having a "literary" structure that is more fundamental, more infrastructural, to adopt Marx's language, than the material reality of economic production.[44]

Cheah elaborated through a reading of Jacques Derrida that these dynamics owe to the "peculiar ontological status" of literature itself, which supplies a structure of meaning that exceeds the subjective intentions of an author and the private experience of any individual reader.[45] He noted that because literature detaches from its "putative source" and endlessly calls forth conjectures about its meaning, "literature exemplifies the undecidability that opens a world."[46] The appeal of literary form to the worldly imagination presently comes into view, for as Cheah has observed, "worldliness is fundamental to literature and even part of its structure. Literature cannot cause or make anything, because its reality is neither spiritual nor material, subjective nor objective. But as the expression of the total meaningfulness of the logos or the setting up of a world, literature uncovers the world and opens up other possible worlds."[47]

To be sure, Cheah's analysis organized in relation to contemporary postcolonial fiction, and remarked on the vocation of worldly literature in postcolonial contexts to "play an important role in announcing the advent of new collective subjects and giving public phenomenality to their ongoing attempts to remake the world."[48] My own analysis, in contrast, revolves around the aggressive politics that materialized in Japan's imperial age. But still, Cheah's reflections on the worldliness of literary form can open analytical possibilities for understanding the nexus of fiction and philosophy in the interwar years because it, too, was a time that a range of writers and thinkers believed to have been riven by world historical confusion, and in need of fresh literary forms "announcing the advent of new collective subjects" joining part to whole.

In the essay "Situation of the Writer in 1947," for example, the French philosopher and literary writer Jean-Paul Sartre (1905–80) wrote that the task of the novelist in the global 1930s had been "to create a literature which unites and reconciles the metaphysical absolute and the relativity of the historical fact, and which I shall call, for want of a better name, the literature of great circumstances."[49] Sartre reflected on the crux of this "literature of great circumstances" with reference to the novelist's role in merging self and world within the peculiar historical "situation" of the age:

> From 1930 on, the world depression, the coming of Nazism, and the events in China opened our eyes. It seemed as if the ground were going to fall from under us, and suddenly, *for us too*, the great historical juggling began. . . . And our life as an individual which had seemed to depend upon our efforts, our virtues, and our faults, on our good and bad luck, on the good and bad will of a very small number of people, seemed governed down to its minutest details by obscure and collective forces, and its most private circumstances seemed to reflect the state of the whole world. All at once we felt ourselves abruptly *situated*.[50]

For Sartre, then, the "situation of the writer" in the global 1930s necessitated a literary perspective that would dissolve the "most private circumstances" of the individual into the collective "state of the whole world"—a dissolving that Yokomitsu also envisioned in the form of what he had called "fourth-person perspective." In this context, *The Melancholy of Travel* could be read as Yokomitsu's contribution to what Sartre called the "literature of great circumstances" insofar as it was a novel that attempted to perform the "great historical juggling" that would hold together its own "situated" position with the world historical "situation" of the 1930s. In so doing, Yokomitsu's "novel of ideas" also contributed a literary perspective on the problematic of "answerability" that Harootunian has examined in his consideration of the Kyoto School discourse on "world history"—a problematic by which the philosophical imagination took up a dialogue with the most urgent crises of its historical present.

In linking the intellectual history that revolved around the questions of world history and worldly relations to a close reading of passages from the novel itself, one of the first questions to ask is what kind of a world does the novel hold together. Most obviously, *The Melancholy of Travel* describes Yashiro's movements around the globe: it traces his voyage by ship from Japan to Europe, which takes him through the Indian Ocean and the Suez Canal to the port of Marseilles; it then describes his urban ambulations in Paris and his excursion to the Alps region of Tyrol before finally narrating his return to Japan overland by rail, moving through Berlin, the Soviet Union, and Manchuria, ultimately arriving in Tokyo. These movements characterize the broad structure of *The Melancholy of Travel*, and might seem to suggest that the novel is an allegory for a generation of cosmopolitan Japanese thinkers who tired of Anglo-European influence and "returned to Japan" (*Nihon e no kaiki*) seeking refuge from the hybridity of the globalized international sphere in the warmth and wholeness of an imagined native place. While this is no doubt part of the story, my own approach to the text proceeds from the premise that its worldly dynamics exceeded these global dimensions. Drawing on Cheah's perspective, I would argue that insofar as the physical "return to Japan" narrated by the novel is premised on a "return" marked by movements across the Earth's surface, it is a "return" that is circumscribed within the closed complex of globality. It follows that reading strategies that focus on the global scale of the novel—however maximal that scale might seem to be—run the risk of constraining the range of imaginable relations within the text to a scope that is necessarily bounded by geographical finitude, and the binaries of "East" and "West," national self and foreign other, which are interpolated within that finitude.[51]

To open the novel up more radically, I refocus attention on its worldly (rather than global) dynamics, and consider how it materializes the nexus of text and world in more open-ended terms than the closed circuits of global circulation could ever allow. This approach remembers that in positing a "world" as a phenomenality of interrelation—"a form of relating, belonging, or being-with"—Cheah elaborated that if we are to read the worldliness of literature, "what is at stake is not merely the inclusion of the greatest possible number of human beings and the maximal increase of the range of circulation of peoples and products so that it spans the entire globe but the manner of inclusion and the kind of whole that is created. As the greatest possible whole of existence, a world must be structurally open. Better yet, it must be the endless process of opening itself."[52] Drawing on Cheah's analysis, my reading of *The Melancholy of Travel* aims to account for "the manner of inclusion" and "the kind of whole that is created," which allows for a phenomenality of "being-with" to emerge in the novel. Beyond the global circulations of people and ideas that are described in the text, what is the substance of worldly bonds that brings the vast concatenations of cultural historical forms that the novel narrates into a world of concordant meaning? This question intertwines with the related question of how the novel opens up to what lies beyond itself through aesthetic and intellectual resonances with adjacent texts. As I examine the worldly forms of "being-with" that appear within Yokomitsu's "novel of ideas," then, I also ask: How does the novel itself remain "structurally open" to contemporaneous imaginings of a "worldly world" that appeared in the domains of philosophy and literature, both in Japan and beyond?

One crucial consideration in responding to these questions is the matter of time, and how the shared time of contemporaneity collects a worldly form of "being-with" within the text. We begin to see the worldliness of the novel in the temporal terms of unfolding by examining how Yokomitsu juggled the tensions of contingent historical time and determinate narrative form that drew taut as the serialization of *The Melancholy of Travel* progressed. The novel courses over more than nine hundred pages in Yokomitsu's *zenshū* (complete works), but it originally appeared in pieces that were anything but complete: it first emerged as a series of textual fragments scattered across newspapers (*Tokyo Nichi Nichi Shinbun* and *Osaka Mainichi Shinbun*), literary journals (*Bungei Shunjū* and *Bungakkai*), and stand-alone volumes over the course of a tumultuous decade (1937–46) that witnessed the climax and collapse of the Japanese empire. The first installment of the novel was published in April 1937, and the last appeared in April 1946 as a short piece released under a separate title. In between, there were gaps in serialization, the longest of which stretched to almost two years. In addition to its serialization in periodicals, bound editions (*tankōbon*) of sections of the novel were released intermittently, too, the first appearing in June 1940. It seems that Yokomitsu may have considered abandoning the novel during the lengthy course of its publication; it also seems that he had plans to continue it at the time of his death, and that some of the loose ends in the last installments—such as Kuji's jarring reappearance after a long absence—were in fact parts of a planned narrative trajectory that was never realized.[53] *The Melancholy of Travel* is an unfinished novel, but even the author's own inability to complete it did not mark the end of its convulsions. The scholar Toeda Hirokazu has observed that sensitive passages from the wartime version of the text were rewritten in a censored Occupation-era version of the novel with alternatives more friendly to Pax Americana sensibilities.[54] These so-called postwar versions of the text (*sengoban*) were released in 1946.[55]

The narrative chronology of the story itself, however, occupies a much shorter timeline than does the novel's nearly decade-long serialization. The novel opens in Paris just before Easter 1936 and ends less than two years later in Tokyo in early fall 1937.[56] This tells us that the novel narrates the contingencies of a cataclysmic age with a future that revealed itself to Yokomitsu and his readers over the course of the novel's lengthy serialization from 1937 to 1946, but not to his fictional characters, whose lives in Paris and Tokyo (mostly) are narrated over a chronology lasting less than two years during 1936 and 1937. This is not to say that the time narrated by the novel was peaceful. Among other flash points, the early stages of the Second Sino-Japanese War leave their traces on the narrative. Also apparent are the conflicts surrounding the rise and brief efflorescence of the antifascist Front Populaire in France, a leftist coalition movement that culminated in the 1936 election of socialist prime minister Léon Blum, a complex figure whom the historian Tony Judt has described as a distinctive, controversial, and today "half-forgotten" leader of that age.[57] But the Japanese bombing of Pearl Harbor in 1941, the violence of the Pacific War between Japan and the United States, and the atomic bombings of Hiroshima and Nagasaki in 1945—not to mention the French surrender to Nazi Germany in 1940 following the fall of the short-lived Front Populaire—all remain deferred in *The Melancholy of Travel.*

In this sense, Yokomitsu's historical fiction engages complexities of narrative and time redolent of those that also animated Thomas Mann's *The Magic Mountain* (1924), a "novel of ideas" set just before the outbreak of what would become known as World War I. In the Foreword to *The Magic Mountain*, Mann remarked in terms that might be extended to a reading of *The Melancholy of Travel* that "stories, as histories, must be past":

> But the problem with our story, as also with many people nowadays and, indeed, not the least with those who tell stories, is this: it is much older than its years, its datedness is not to be measured in days, nor the burden of age weighing upon it to be counted by orbits around the sun; in a word, it does not actually owe its pastness to *time*. . . .
>
> But let us not intentionally obscure a clear state of affairs: the extraordinary pastness of our story results from its having taken place *before* a certain turning point, on the far side of a rift that has cut deeply through our lives and consciousness. It takes place, or, to avoid any present tense whatever, it took place back then, long ago, in the old days of the world before the Great War, with whose beginning so many things began whose beginnings, it seems, have not yet ceased.[58]

For Yokomitsu, narrating time "*before* a certain turning point, on the far side of a rift," would have been no small task, considering that *The Melancholy of Travel* was published in the same periodicals that were also reporting the linear progress of homogenous empty time in the form of current events appearing in daily, weekly, and monthly intervals. In moments of greatest difference, the contradictions between history and fiction dripped with a grim irony: at the end of the novel, for example, prospects for the "New Order" in East Asia shine bright in the world of the storydwellers, but they had long since died in the world of the storyteller, Yokomitsu, when he published the last serial in 1946.

These sorts of discontinuities mark the fissures of nonsynchronous time opened up by the unfolding of the novel itself within its own historical *situation* (in Sartre's sense of the term). They remind us that the world of meaning held together by *The Melancholy of Travel* involved not only the finite global spaces of Europe and Asia, but also the open-ended time of the world historical present. This is to say that part of the paradox of the novel is that while its form inevitably gave structure to the contingent historical present that it narrated, the text also communed with the perceived open-endedness of a time when "so many things began whose beginnings, it [seemed], [had] not yet ceased" during the lengthy course of the novel's serialization. The competing forms of time and narrative conspire to convey the experience of the historical present as something that, in the words of the literary scholar Lauren Berlant, "is perceived, first, affectively: the present is what makes itself present to us before it becomes anything else, such as an orchestrated collective event or an epoch on which we can look back."[59] In this connection, the resonances between what Sartre called the contingent "situation of the writer" and the affective experience of the present come into focus, for as Berlant has observed, "a situation is a state of things in which *something* that will perhaps matter is unfolding amid the usual activity of life."[60]

One early scene in *The Melancholy of Travel* gives a sense of how the dynamics of time and narrative, historical situation and fictional representation, collide and collude in the novel. It features the Japanese expatriates Kuji and Chizuko dining at a tranquil Paris café. Kuji has just arrived carrying two newspapers:

> "Oh my" he whispered, and craned his neck closer to the page as he began to read the top story. Printed boldly on the front page of the newspaper was the headline: "China and Japan Go To War."
>
> "China and Japan are at war in Mongolia and Guangdong," Kuji said to Chizuko. "The reports may be overblown, but even so, never before has this sort of thing been frontpage news."
>
> Kuji looked at the other newspaper, and it, too, reported the Sino-Japanese War on the front page. They delved into the news stories. Up to this point, Kuji and Chizuko had seen headlines about the escalating tensions between Japan and China almost daily, but those incidents had always been treated as peripheral events, and given only short shrift in the press. Kuji and Chizuko had gotten used to articles full of false information and conjecture. But the fact that two newspapers had elevated the story from the margins to the boldface type of the front page suggested that even if these incidents were being exaggerated, there was still something to the reports.[61]

The literary critic Mary Favret has observed that in contexts such as these, when the unresolved experience of ongoing warfare is distributed by the mediating force of newsprint across great geographical distances, the rendering of historical time itself can shift from the vocation of the scholarly historian to that of the literary writer. Favret made this argument in considering how the unknowability of mediated wartime raises questions that cannot be answered except by those looking back: Who will prevail? When will the time of war end? What will happen next? These unanswerable questions structure an affective experience that can survive only until it is destroyed by the certitude of retrospective explication. But as long as it lingers, the unknowability of wartime gives form to an open-ended experience that affords tremendously extensive relations to materialize in the novel. It is an experience that ripples through affective flows collecting even those far removed from battlefield violence—such as Kuji and Chizuko reading the news at a Paris café—and encompassing events with implications extending in different ideological directions at the same time—such as the rise of the Right responsible for the 2/26 Incident in Tokyo and the promise of the Left that fueled the then-ascendant Front Populaire in Paris.

Part of the worldly structure of *The Melancholy of Travel*, then, owes to its holding together of time in a way that differs from more conventional modes of historical periodization. Favret has explained in this regard that insofar as the time of war is a kind of affective experience, it "often eludes the usual models for organizing time such as linearity, punctuality, and periodicity; it eludes as well the usual models for organizing history. If we take wartime less as an object of cognition bounded by dates—a period—and more as an affecting experience which resonates beyond the here and now, then wartime literature becomes an attempt to trace and give shape to such affect, to register its wayward power."[62] Rather than reckoning with contemporary history in terms of foregone conclusions that play out on a timeline capped by an ending that is always pending, then, historical fiction that "traces" the undulating affect of wartime holds together an open-ended world of relations that would otherwise be closed off by the empty homogenous time of clocks and calendars. This helps us to see how narrations of "war at a distance" in particular enact a continual opening up of worldly affect when, to borrow Favret's words, they "shy away from the spectacular and sublime effects usually associated with the representation of war, inclining toward the unconsidered or commonplace. . . . In not calling attention to themselves, such aesthetic strategies are nonetheless—and maybe all the more—

affecting, as they glide into the rhythms of ordinary life."[63] The rhythms of ordinary life in the unresolved historical present are what reverberate in the passage above featuring Kuji and Chizuko, in which we witness, in Favret's words, "a dislocation of the bounded terrain usually associated with war, and the extension of war into a realm without clear limits."[64]

Situated within this sort of borderless "affective zone," Yokomitsu's novel renders a world of reverberations that resonate across both time and space. Some of the most potent of these reverberations gather as characters contemplate the particularity of aesthetic objects in the unfinished time of world historical crisis. One example of this unfolds in the course of a narrative sequence moving from Yashiro's arrival in France at the beginning of the novel to his visit to the Tyrol mountains partway through his sojourn abroad. His first encounter with European art on arriving in Marseilles is one of the most provocative scenes in the novel. Glimpsing a sculpture of Christ's corpse, Yashiro is shocked by the verisimilitude of the gruesome image, and specifically with the mimetic "sensation of the real thing" (*jitsubutsu sono mama no kankaku*) that it conjures. His shock, though, leads him to a strange epiphany. As he contemplates the sculpture, he comes to sense that it reveals that even in Europe there was once such a barbarous age, and that it was this barbarism, moreover, that produced the drive for realistic clarity and explicit representation embodied in the sculpture. "Such was the psychology of realism from which this civilization was no doubt born and raised," Yashiro comes to believe. He then takes this meditation one step further: "Realism killed Christ," Yashiro thinks to himself, sensing that he has just glimpsed one of the "secrets of Europe." He then reunites with Chizuko and Kuji, and together they gaze out at the French landscape. It is the "actual thing" (*jitsubutsu*) that they had seen so many times represented in the paintings of Cézanne while still in Japan: "The actual thing [*jitsubutsu*] that had established the conceptualization [*kannenka*] of painting itself was right there."[65]

This scene is organized as an amalgamation of seemingly unrelated images (Christ's gruesome corpse, the placid French landscape) and inexplicable epiphanies ("Realism killed Christ," glimpsing one of the "secrets of Europe"). The disjointed style of the passage evokes (without resolving) the cognitive tension that results from Yashiro's confrontation with an alienating representational scheme. For Yashiro, that is, the "psychology of realism" amounts to a pathological drive for clarity and need for transparent explication. It might be said that in this sense, the scene implies that "realism" itself has a kind of "global" form, so to speak, and one that, however internationally translatable, nevertheless relies on the concrete closures of its own explanatory episteme, which cut humanity off from the open-ended unfolding of worldly phenomenality by anchoring representation to a real and inarguable object (*jitsubutsu*). Yashiro's horrified response to the "realistic" sculpture of Christ's corpse brings these threads together, revealing that he views the transfiguring of reality into the artistic concept of "realism" to be the sanction of grotesque literalizations that denature aesthetic experience: "Realism killed Christ" by barbarically enclosing the sensation of divine transcendence within an explicit image.[66]

One irony, though, is that this critique of heavy-handed realism in art is expressed in Yokomitsu's own heavy-handed style. And in this sense, Yashiro's cerebral encounter with the sculpture reminds us that this is a "novel of ideas," that "slightly monstrous" style of storytelling in which analytical turns of mind often take center stage. To be sure, this is not to say that the recuperative powers of the aesthetic are absent from Yashiro's experience altogether. In fact, Yashiro's later trip to the Alps region of Tyrol provides a companion scene suggesting that the root of his aesthetic alienation in Marseilles lies not only in his self-declared estrangement from an alien culture—as if Europe alone were the crux of the problem—but also in his growing awareness that the self-enclosed globality of the "realist" logos had suffocated the open-ended enchantment of a worldly pathos. Read this way, Yokomitsu's logos-driven novel of ideas struggles against itself through its engagement with an aesthetic pathos at the edges of its own narrative structure. These dynamics come into clearer view in recalling that in another context, Ngai observed that the very premise of aesthetic catharsis in a novel of ideas might seem to be out of place, at least insofar as any outpouring of pathos sharply contrasts with the logos-oriented narratives that novels of ideas build up around their more tightly structured presentations of thought (and sometimes canned thought at that); but on a deeper level, Ngai argued, the apparent paradox is resolved in realizing that structurally, the novel of ideas logically requires magical eruptions and cathartic outpourings to alleviate the strained intellectual tensions that its own overtaxed narrative order creates.[67] In the context of Yokomitsu's novel in particular, this helps us to see the narrative sequence in which Yashiro moves from the tense politics and intellectual life of Paris toward the magic of the mountains as a coherent "novel of ideas" progression, rather than as stand-alone scenes without any meaningful relation.

After traveling from Marseilles to Paris, and dueling in a series of monotonous intellectual debates with Kuji, Yashiro first becomes excited about his trip to Tyrol by the prospect of abandoning his own native language:

> The mountainous region straddling the borders of Austria, Germany, Italy, and Switzerland is called Tyrol, and Yashiro's trip there was the first time that he had completely left the company of his fellow Japanese and been alone since he departed Tokyo. In this region, the language Yashiro knew was practically useless. He fully imbibed the pleasure of true solitude, never having realized what a breathless joy it could be to glimpse not a single Japanese face nor be able to use language at all. Could there really be such pleasures in the world? Every time he looked out of the train window, he felt his heart brighten as if roused by a melody. His body, too, felt as if it were being washed by ceaseless waves of pristine water. From time to time, a lake would appear in the forest before disappearing again. But never once did he think to consult a map.[68]

Leaving behind language and the society of those who use it becomes a symbolic ablution for Yashiro in this scene, one that washes him clean of the contextual coordinates enforced by the cartography of the intellectual mind. As a result, Yashiro finds that the enclosures of "realism" no longer restrict the affective resonances of experience within the received categories of an explanatory logos. Instead, sensation (*kankaku*) is allowed to flow beyond the confines of concepts (*kannen*), and he rejoices at the prospect of accessing a feeling for which he knows no interpretive grammar.

It follows that Yashiro's trip to Tyrol is one of the high points of the entire novel. It unfolds within an enchanted land of immediate sensory experience redolent of the atmosphere conjured by Mann's *The Magic Mountain*, in which Hans Castorp, "an ordinary young man," leaves behind Hamburg and journeys to Davos in the Swiss Alps, not far from where Yashiro finds himself in *The Melancholy of Travel.* The scholar Peter Gordon noted in his intellectual history of the 1929 Cassirer-Heidegger debate in Davos that the spa town "enjoyed a symbolic status in the European cultural imagination as a theater for events of world-historical importance," long having hosted intellectuals, artists, and writers.[69] A little more than a decade before Yokomitsu's novel began serialization, Mann's classic "novel of ideas" described Castorp's travel to the region as a movement through space that has the effect of a movement through time and leads to forgetting:

> Two days of travel separate this young man (and young he is, with few firm roots in life) from his everyday world, especially from what he called his duties, interests, worries, and prospects—separate him far more than he had dreamed possible as he rode to the station in a hansom cab. Space, as it rolls and tumbles away between him and his native soil, proves to have powers normally ascribed only to time; from hour to hour, space brings about changes very like those time produces, yet surpassing them in certain ways. Space, like time, gives birth to forgetfulness, but does so by removing an individual from all relationships and placing him in a free and pristine state—indeed, in but a moment it can turn a pedant and philistine into something like a vagabond. Time, they say, is water from the river Lethe, but alien air is a similar drink; and if its effects are less profound, it works all the more quickly.[70]

In *The Melancholy of Travel*, too, readers follow Yashiro's passage into the realm of "a free and pristine state" that is accessible only through a form of forgetting that feels like a religious ablution, "as if his body were continually being washed by pure water." To borrow Mann's words, it might be said that "alien air" has the effect of time on Yashiro, too, allowing him to forget his intellectual position within the "novel of ideas," and turning "the pedant and philistine into something like a vagabond."

After Chizuko joins him, they travel together into the mountains and prepare to spend the night in a small chalet. As the sun goes down, they glimpse a herder and his flock of sheep pass through a meadow below:

> The evening sun streamed beams of light through the breaks in the clouds. Just as Yashiro and Chizuko had nearly forgotten about the sheep, they

heard what sounded like frogs far off in the distance. But as the sound continued, they realized it was not frogs they were hearing, but the shepherd's song of Tyrol [*Chiroru no uta*] summoning the sheep in the pasture.

"There it is," Chizuko said as she grasped Yashiro by the arm. The song of Tyrol came through in a well-worn, melancholic voice. Within the steady rhythm of "koro koro koro," the sounds of "ruku ruku ruku" gradually came through clearly, too. It was a shepherd's voice to be sure, one polished by the clouds and ice.

Drawn by the song, the sheep's bells began to ring forth as they gradually gathered from all directions, coming together in the valley below. At first, the sheep appeared like a mix of white clouds, but as thousands of them merged, they came to resemble a river that had overrun its banks, filling the valley below as they flowed through it.

Yashiro felt his chest turn cold and empty. The glimmer of sunset glistened off the mountain peaks. Below, the sound of the ringing bells of the sheep mixed together, echoing off the valley walls, multiplying in force, swirling through the air like a rising swarm of mosquitoes. In the midst of it all, the shepherd's song of Tyrol formed a main melody calling together the herd of sheep.

"ruku ruku ruku ruku, ru ru ru ru ru ru—ruku ruku ruku ruku, ru ru ru ru ru ru—"

"It's like I'm seeing God," Chizuko said quietly and looked down below absent-mindedly.[71]

Sensory experience becomes spiritual transcendence for Chizuko in this scene in a way that sharply contrasts with Yashiro's aesthetic alienation in Marseilles. In a foil to the realism that Yashiro believed had "killed Christ," this passage revolves around the uncontained epiphany conjured by sounds without semantic content ("ruku," "ruru"), sensory satisfaction liberated from the tyranny of concepts, and a silent intellectual void of "absent-mindedness" (*bon'yari hōshin*).

By subordinating rational clarity to the immediacy of the senses, the magic of the mountains becomes the antidote to the logical transparency sanctioned by the "psychology of realism." As Chizuko and Yashiro watch the sheep pass through the meadow below, finally vanishing from sight, "they looked at each other for the first time, but neither said anything. In the vacant pasture below, darkness flowed in place of the sheep."[72] After the enveloping sound of the sheep's bells and the shepherd's song melts into a vision of God and then quietly subsides, the image of darkness flowing where the sheep once roamed does not filter through any subjective perspective. Yashiro and Chizuko remain silent in a "free and pristine state," and whether or not they see it or know it, the unfolding of the narrative itself renders a flowing darkness that becomes the sensory inversion of the now-absent white stream of sheep. In scenes like this, the senses become a middle ground where otherwise implacable antinomies—nature and culture, subject and object, East and West, the novel and ideas—relate to one another through an aesthetic energy. As a worldly holding together of meaning emerges in language that renders the phenomenality of "being-with" the other, we begin to see (as Ngai has argued) how this sort of magical catharsis emerges from the tense structure of the novel of ideas itself.

Taken this way, the Tyrol scenes might seem to glimmer with a cosmopolitan humanism released from the nationalistic rhetoric often associated with 1930s Japan in general, and with Yashiro's statements throughout the novel in particular. But one must be cautious. To the extent that Yashiro's Tyrol excursion promises a form of pure aesthetic liberation from the strictures of politics and thought, it could be counted among the many "fascist moments" that Alan Tansman has identified in the literary writings of 1930s Japan.[73] On this score, too, Yashiro's transcendent experience in Tyrol resonates with aspects of the roughly contemporaneous novel *Yukiguni* (Snow Country, 1935–48), which was written by Yokomitsu's New Sensationist collaborator Kawabata Yasunari. In Yokomitsu's text, the affecting force of rejuvenated (and rejuvenating) language connecting self and world washes over the reader only all the more forcefully because its poetics stand out in this "novel of ideas." Long stretches of the first half of the novel are given to the development of a tedious dialogue between Yashiro and Kuji that revolves around the question of if and how the cultural histories of Europe and Asia might be braided together into a cosmopolitan whole. Within this schematic, much of the narrative feels predictable: Kuji advocates for a progressive European perspective, Yashiro for the spiritualist Japanese alternative, and their rivalry for Chizuko's favor comes to symbolize the ideological conflict that their debates speechify. Their physical travels from Asia to Europe and back again inevitably symbolize this conflict, too, becoming, in the words of Lippit, the "physical embodiment of a specific psychological and ideological experience of early-twentieth-century intellectuals."[74] This claustrophobic narrative structure is relieved by the Tyrol scene. In a logos-centered novel full of ideas and arguments, the pathos of sounds that say nothing—"ruku ruku"—comes to mean everything.

As the narrative shifts from France to Japan, though, and narrows its focus around Yashiro's meditations on Japanese cultural history, how can it continue to conspire with a wider worldly imagination, and breathe with something larger than its own narrative confines? One way of beginning to answer this question is to read the latter half of the novel through the widely elaborated philosophical premise that authentic cultural particularity and world historical universality each require the other. The scholar Travis Workman has elucidated aspects of this perspective in his reading of the Kyoto philosopher (and mentor to Yura) Tanabe Hajime, showing how the dialectics of "expression" materialized an imperial politics that mixed otherwise irreconcilable opposites. Workman noted that "in the period of the discourses of the world-historical nation-state in the late Japanese empire, expression, which was also anthropologically defined in terms of national language and national culture, was understood as the cultural mediation through which identity and nonidentity, the positive and the negative, the present and the past, and space and time could be united."[75] Elsewhere, Workman's reading of Yokomitsu's interwar writings suggested that in an age in which philosophers came to view the Japanese nation-state as an expressive totality within world history itself, Yokomitsu envisioned in literature a resonant synthesis that culminated in a fascist aesthetic as it "eventually arrived at a new organic view of the social totality in which colonizer and colonized, human and machine, and the nation-state and its internal differences were all unified through an embrace of national culture, national language, and collective death," as Workman put it.[76] Drawing these insights into dialogue with Yokomitsu's magnum opus, we begin to see how the latter portion of *The Melancholy of Travel* presents a meditation on native cultural historical forms that both demand and dissolve the conditions of their own possibility, at once anchoring themselves to time and place, blood and soil, while also joining a cosmic pantheon of other situated expressions, and collectively positing the national cultural history of Japan as an expressive totality of world historical implication.

Some of the philosophical stakes of this project were earlier developed by another of Yura's mentors, the German philosopher Ernst Cassirer. Yura collaborated with Cassirer from 1928 to 1931, and more generally, Cassirer was among the influential European intellectuals whose texts were read by Nishida and his students in Kyoto.[77] To be sure, this is not to suggest that Cassirer was politically aligned with Yura, nor that he was ideologically sympathetic to the fascist implications of Kyoto School thought; he was not. But it is to remember that in *The Philosophy of Symbolic Forms*, vol. 1, *Language* (1923), he wrote that art and cognition, myth and religion, "all live in particular image-worlds," adding that these were worlds of symbolic forms that, despite the specificity of their individual articulations, were "not different modes in which an independent reality manifests itself to the human spirit but roads by which the spirit proceeds towards its objectivization, i.e., its self-revelation. If we consider art and language, myth and cognition in this light, they present a common problem which opens up new access to a universal philosophy of the cultural sciences."[78] Working from this premise, Cassirer described the task of the philosopher in terms of devising the proper narrative "standpoint"—or what in the Kyoto School discourse on world history would be called *tachiba*. He wrote that "the ultimate decision seems to rest with philosophy alone, as the supreme authority and repository of unity," while also admonishing against dogmatic perspectives that "cut themselves off from particular aspects of cultural life and the concrete totality of its forms":[79]

> Philosophical thought might avoid this danger of occlusion only if it could find a standpoint situated above all these forms and yet not merely outside them: a standpoint which would make it possible to encompass the whole of them in one view, which would seek to penetrate nothing other than the purely immanent relation of all these forms to one another, and not their relation to any external, "transcendent" being or principle. Then we could have a systematic philosophy of human culture in which each particular form would take its meaning solely from the *place* in which it stands, a system in which the content and significance of each form would be characterized by the richness and specific quality of the relations and concatenations in which it stands with other spiritual energies and ultimately with totality.[80]

As a literary writer composing a novel of ideas, Yokomitsu implicitly shifted the method for achieving the synthesis Cassirer described above from philosophy to fiction. But in the same spirit, it might be said that in composing *The Melancholy of Travel*, Yokomitsu, like Cassirer, envisioned a "standpoint situated above all [cultural] forms and yet not merely outside them," a "standpoint" that could articulate the distinctive "*place*" of any cultural form by limning the "relations and concatenations in which it stands with other spiritual energies and ultimately with totality."

Taken this way, the latter portions of *The Melancholy of Travel* might be read not only as a "return to Japan" in the nationalist sense of a retreat into origins, but also as an exploration of the worldliness of Japanese cultural history itself from ancient times to modern. This was an exploration that, however fraught with paradox, might be said to have articulated some of the untranslatable aspects of Japanese cultural history—from the performance of Shinto rituals to the sounds of the Japanese language itself—into a wider world of situated meaning where they might take their "*place*" alongside "other spiritual energies and ultimately with totality." In suggesting this perspective, I do not forget that the scholar of comparative literature Emily Apter has warned of the tensions that draw taut as the immense scales of meaning implied by the rubric of "world literature" enter into conflict with the untranslatable particularity of language and literature.[81] These tensions layer the latter portion of Yokomitsu's novel, too, but as they do, they reveal that part of the Kyoto School meditation on world history required a series of scalar shifts from the universal to the particular all along. Far from maintaining a contradiction between native culture and worldly relations, then, *The Melancholy of Travel* might be read as an attempt to reconcile the problems of untranslatability with the world historical imagination. And in the context of empire, the stakes of this reconciliation were intense, for without it, there would be no way to cast Japanese cultural history as the rightful subject of world historical progress per se.

These threads come together as Yashiro returns to Japan at the beginning of part 3. It is late summer 1936: his train from Berlin has traversed Siberia and finally approaches the Manchurian border, which he understands to be the frontier gateway to his homeland. Serialization of part 3 began in 1942; parts 4 and 5 subsequently appeared by 1945, and what would be the last installment of *The Melancholy of Travel* appeared as a stand-alone short story titled "Meibin" (Plum Vase) in 1946. The publishing timeline of the latter half of *The Melancholy of Travel*, then, ranges from a moment when Japanese imperial influence was at its apex, around 1942, to a moment when the tables of domination had been turned and Japan came under American occupation in the postwar period. But with that said, it must not be forgotten that the narrative that emerges in parts 3, 4, and 5 and "Meibin" narrates events set in 1936 and 1937. As the narrative of *The Melancholy of Travel* unfolds, then, it treats the mid-1930s from an ever-greater historical remove.

This is to say that installments in the latter half of the novel that ponder the conflict between China and Japan from the safety of Yashiro's largely uninterrupted daily life, and that unfold during Blum's brief tenure as prime minister during the apex of influence for the Front Populaire, were in fact serialized as Yokomitsu lived through the catastrophes of the Pacific War, and after Nazi Germany had occupied France. In this light, part of the narrative work that the latter half of *The Melancholy of Travel* performs is keeping the lived experience of the storyteller from intruding into the imaginations of the storydwellers. In another context, the literary scholar Michael André Bernstein has pointed out that novelist Robert Musil (1880–1942) faced much the same narrative conundrum in his "novel of ideas," *The Man without Qualities*, an unfinished historical fiction set on the eve of what would become known as World War I. Bernstein has observed that the novel looks back at a world whose imminent demise is a foregone conclusion for Musil's readers: it begins in August 1913, one year before the outbreak of war, as its protagonist Ulrich works with others in planning an elaborate celebration set for 1918 that will commemorate the seventieth anniversary of Emperor Franz Joseph's coronation; but in reality, Joseph would die in 1916, and his empire would be replaced with a republic by 1918. Musil started writing *The Man without Qualities* in the 1920s, and its first pieces appeared in print in 1931.

As Bernstein has summed up: "Musil's readers know from the outset that the political and social world the novel describes has very little time left before perishing in the conflagration of war."[82] But this did not stop Musil from writing about it in an open-ended novel of ideas that occupied him for the last two decades of his life, more or less, and that, although left incomplete at the time of his death, still stretches to more than 1,100 pages in Sophie Wilkins and Burton Pike's English translation (1996)—a count that does not include hundreds of pages of "posthumous papers." Bernstein lauded Musil's novel as a model of multidirectional narrative because it looks back on a moment more often narrated in relation to a sense-making endpoint—the assassination of Archduke Ferdinand and the subsequent chain of events that led to World War I—and supplies it with a narrative structure that allows readers to feel the unresolved affect of its historical present.

The scene on Yashiro's railcar traveling through Siberia toward the Manchurian border at the beginning of part 3 suggests that *The Melancholy of Travel* strives for a similar sense of historical contingency as it narrates a moment that Yokomitsu would have known, looking back, was on the cusp of catastrophic conflict, but that his novel, as a piece of historical fiction, imagined in terms of historical indeterminacy. Alongside Yashiro in the railcar are a French antiques dealer traveling from Paris to Beijing, two Nazi officials transiting from Berlin to Tokyo, a Chinese young adult of around twenty years of age, and a French woman—all of whom gather to banter amicably in the hallway outside Yashiro's room. An American newlywed couple is also aboard, but they keep to themselves.[83] The geopolitics of the global 1930s figure in this scene, to be sure, but they are laminated by the prosaics of everyday life: the strengthening alliance between Germany and Japan explains why Nazi officials would be traveling to Tokyo, for example, but in this moment, on this railcar, *The Melancholy of Travel* evokes a sense of time unburdened by what later readers would know were its own foregone conclusions.

After Yashiro returns to Tokyo, the rest of the novel dwells primarily on his conflicted attempts to achieve some measure of emotional and spiritual well-being. This proves to be no simple task. Without any direction in life or articulated ambition, he becomes something of a "man without qualities" himself, spending much of his time idly submerged in extended periods of pensive isolation. His mind is at times nurtured by the familiarity of home, but brief moments of catharsis appear only intermittently between much longer spells of formless desolation. The threat of world war in the age of world historical crisis flits through his mind, but it is not Yashiro's most pressing worry. He is more concerned with being condemned by the spirits of his long-dead ancestors, who were overcome centuries ago by a feudal lord in Kyushu who had converted to Christianity, and who subsequently routed Yashiro's paternal relatives with guns obtained from Europeans trading in the area. Yashiro fears that his ancestors will curse him for falling in love with Chizuko, a practicing Catholic whose faith in a foreign god aligns her in Yashiro's mind with the Europeans responsible for his own family's demise centuries ago. The existential crisis that ensues might well be regarded as the mainline narrative of the novel from at least the beginning of part 3 onward.

The muddled narrative atmosphere in the latter half of the novel occasions—and is occasioned by—a series of Yashiro's pensive dilations. Lippit has described how some of these dilations emerge during a narrative sequence in which Yashiro travels to the ancestral home of his father in Kyushu after his father dies. He observed that the father figure had learned from the writings of Fukuzawa Yukichi and symbolizes in the novel a Meiji mind that accumulated knowledge from abroad—so much so, in fact, that Lippit wrote that aspects of Yashiro's journey to Kyushu following his father's death function as a "symbolic repetition of his voyage to Europe."[84] But another journey in the second half of the novel traces other sources of Yashiro's genealogy, and it takes him to the region in which his mother was born and brought up (*furusato*). It is an area apart. The town he visits is nestled in the Tōhoku region, ten hours by train from Tokyo. Yashiro observes that "in its customs and temper, it was among those rare places in Japan that had taken on almost no influence from the West."[85] Surveying the landscape, he recalls lines composed centuries earlier by the traveling poet Matsuo Bashō, who, on gazing at the mountains of northern Japan, had written: "Never shall I lose the soul of the mountain man." Yashiro's thoughts then turn to his father, who pursued the liberal dream of universal civilization. Gazing on a train tunnel cutting through the mountains, Yashiro recalls his father telling stories of digging tunnels himself. He would rise at night, unable to sleep, gripped with excitement to see the train pull through safely. Again, the words of Bashō: "Never shall I lose the soul of the mountain man."

The repeated reference to Bashō reminds us that Yokomitsu seems to have felt a kindred spirit with the poet. In fact, Bashō is said to have been related to Yokomitsu himself by blood, and in the scene above, the poet appears as an almost spiritual figure hovering over Yashiro's bloodlines, too, as if part of his lineage.[86] In this context, the "soul of the mountain man" would appear to be something untranslatable because it emerges from the unique mix of blood and soil that makes up Yashiro's inheritance. It is the opposite of the easily translatable ideas of Scottish Enlightenment thought and European liberalism that Fukuzawa is known for disseminating in Meiji Japan in the name of "civilization and enlightenment" (*bunmei kaika*): whereas the exchange economy of translatable information allowed Fukuzawa's prose to interpolate Meiji Japan within a global system full of foreign nations, the language of Bashō's poetry, in contrast, promised the worldly enchantment of "being-with" kin that can only emerge from the irreversible conditions of natality.

The untranslatable authenticity of blood and soil that shadows Yashiro's birth is the origin of "soul" (*kokoro*), then. But it is a "soul" that takes its place in the cosmos, an ethereal realm of world historical forms that paradoxically owe their consanguinity to their untranslatability. As Yashiro's meditations on ancient Japan and the modern world continue in the latter portion of *The Melancholy of Travel*, unexpected convergences between scientific knowledge and aesthetic experience, religious ritual and modern rationality, continue to inform his vision of a cosmic totality beyond the one-to-one correspondences of exchange, influence, and translation. In one case, Yashiro elaborates on the intellectual implications of ancient Shinto rituals. When he is asked if geometry existed in ancient Japan, he responds that it did, and as an example, he observes that Shinto shrines feature folded white paper offerings as objects of worship. Yashiro explains that these white strips of paper could be cut and folded in geometric patterns, and that this expression of the geometric imagination was also a form of prayer in ancient Japan. "This tells us that the central idea of our nation [*kuni*] is a belief in the beauty of the cosmos [*uchū*]," he says. With reference to *Kojiki* (Record of Ancient Matters, 712), he concludes by suggesting that his own appeals to the national community (*kokka*) are actually a way of talking about the cosmos "our ancestors imagined" in the translated language (*hon'yakugo de*) of "the nation" (*kokka*).[87]

This account of past and present, nation and world, posits a cosmos that cradles the particularity of Japanese cultural history within the universality of a poetic ether. The allusion to *Kojiki,* a creation story connecting the Japanese islands, imperial line, and language to the gods (*kami*), seems to suggest that the link between the parochial and the cosmopolitan materializes in Yashiro's imagination in the form of something akin to what Cheah has called "deep communication" across "deep time." In the course of reading allusions to Rainer Maria Rilke's *Duino*

Elegies (*Duineser Elegien*, 1923) in Amitav Ghosh's novel *The Hungry Tide* (2004), Cheah observed that whereas "shallow communication" can easily be translated because it "conveys mere information," the literary intertextuality of Ghosh's novel conveys "deep communication [that] is not about determining semantic content."[88] Beyond factual information, "deep communication" "elicits a richer evocative 'knowledge,' the constitutive imbrication of words in the larger web of relations that make them meaningful."[89] In making this claim, Cheah argued that "literature is better able to portray and enact deep communication than conceptual knowledge and information because it is an intertextually constituted linguistic artefact."[90] In *The Melancholy of Travel*, too, Yashiro senses the "deep communication" between ancient Shinto ritual and geometry which echoes across the "deep time" of world history in the forms (rather than the content) of spiritual ritual and secular knowledge.

But with that said, Yashiro also suggests that other possibilities for "deep communication" across "deep time" have been corrupted by "the language of translation" (*hon'yakugo*), which replaces the poetic form of the cosmos with the prosaic content of the nation. In this sense, "the language of translation" is the useful and purposeful language of an information economy of circular reference in which all content is ultimately exchangeable, and all semantics have commensurable equivalents. This is to say that the "language of translation" as Yashiro understands it is defined by the same semiotic enclosures and representational finitude as the mimetic realisms that he believed had "killed Christ." In contrast, the language of deep communication unconceals the truth of worldly "being-with" in the deep time of being itself. Yokomitsu's novel senses that the mythical time of *Kojiki*, which draws humanity into communion with the gods (*kami*), is contemporaneous with a modern world in which Euclidean geometry is enriched by the religious ritual of ancient Shinto, as Yashiro explained. None of these relations require any "translation" into commensurable language forms (*hon'yakugo*); instead, their concordance emanates from a "deep communication" across "deep time."

As *The Melancholy of Travel* envisions a consensual cohesion among the vastly disparate forms appearing in all cultural histories, though, it does so with an awareness of the violent beauty of an overwhelming cosmic embrace. In one of the most troubling confluences of East and West, ancient and modern, that appears in the latter half of *The Melancholy of*

Travel, Yashiro converses with Chizuko and compares the shape of the Nazi swastika to the sound of *kotodama*, the magical words believed to be imbued with ritualistic efficacy that are often associated with the poetry of *Kojiki* and *Man'yōshū* (Collection of Ten-Thousand Leaves, c. 759).[91] Their conversation begins when Chizuko asks Yashiro if modern man will ever feel satisfaction (*kindaijin ga manzoku dekiru mono desuka ne*), to which Yashiro responds, "No, there is no happiness [*kofuku*] worthy of the name 'satisfaction' for modern man." The problem, Yashiro explains, is that modern man lives in a moment of world history that is riven by a profound schism. He says that in ancient times, Greek and Japanese civilizations developed as parallel cultural universes: Greek civilization was founded on the geometric form of the three-pointed triangle, whereas Japanese civilization was founded on the three vowel sounds *i*, *u*, and *e*. If the forms of Greek geometry and the sounds of Japanese language could be merged, perhaps then, Yashiro wonders aloud, modern man would know satisfaction. He then concludes cryptically: "The form of the swastika [*gyaku manji*] on the Nazi flag resembles the basic form of Japanese *kotodama*. Whether or not the Germans realize that their flag is the geometric rendering of what is understood in Japan as an ebullient life force [*seimeiryoku to iu mono no hirogari*] I cannot say, and I suppose that the Nazis have their own reasons for using the symbol."[92]

Yashiro's brief comments on sound and symbol in the civilization histories of Europe and Japan render in more explicit terms the politics that lurk in the cosmopolitan confluences that appear throughout the novel. Some of these convergences appear to be innocent-enough evocations of a modernist inclination to see connections among vastly disparate cultural phenomena; but in Yashiro's discussion of the Nazi swastika and *kotodama*, something more sinister comes to the fore. He suggests that an alliance of Axis regimes East and West will lead modern man (*kindaijin*) to a kind of otherwise inaccessible feeling of "satisfaction" by overcoming the binary oppositions that separate Europe and Japan, symbol and sound, image and word. He prophesies the blending of these and other categories of expression into a cathartic cultural whole, the form and feeling of which he codes as part swastika logos, part *kotodama* pathos. To be sure, this startling vision appears in a minor scene: it flits through a conversation and then recedes from view, overwritten by the prosaic concerns of daily life. But even if only faintly, Yashiro's cryptic comments suggest the possibility of a cultural community of the future in which modern man will learn the satisfaction that he and Chizuko experienced in the mountains of Tyrol by coming into contact with an untranslatable pathos confessed by an irreducible logos.

This resonates what Miki and his Shōwa Kenkyūkai colleagues had in mind when they called for the establishment of a colonial culture grounded in the principle of *kyōdōshugi* (collectivism). And these threads directly entwine at the end of the novel.

A Future in the Past

At a Hibiya Park rally in the last installment of *The Melancholy of Travel*, the haiku poet Tōno gives a speech called "Shin chitsujo" (The New Order). The crux of his message is that the world is in tumult and that everyone lives with fear and anxiety (*urei*); the solution, he avers, is the creation of a "New Order" that will bring calm, and he exhorts literature, philosophy, religion, even a new kind of affection (*aijō*) to all move toward this goal.[93] Some believe that Yokomitsu had plans to continue the novel from here. Yura has written that Yokomitsu had intended for Yashiro to be conscripted to fight on a distant battlefield, and that the letters exchanged between him and Chizuko in a planned but never finished continuation of the narrative were to evoke the pathos of the age.[94] In another account, the literary critic Mogi Masao has written that Yokomitsu had planned for Yashiro to die in the war for empire and for Kuji to fall in love with and marry Chizuko.[95] Aspects of the existing narrative would seem to support Yura's and Mogi's accounts: most obviously, Kuji's bizarre resurfacing in the final installments after having long been absent from the story hints that perhaps Yokomitsu had intended for him to become a central figure in a continuation of *The Melancholy of Travel* that was ultimately never written. If so, then like Hans Castorp in Mann's *The Magic Mountain*, Yashiro might well have been destined for a battlefield death in a narrative trajectory faintly perceptible just beyond the borders of the text itself. But when Yokomitsu himself died on December 30, 1947, he left his magnum opus unfinished.

The most distinctive aspect of the last installment of the novel is the title of Tōno's speech. The "New Order" he discusses was in fact most notably theorized by Miki and his colleagues in the Shōwa Kenkyūkai, a "brain trust" in the service of Prime Minister Konoe Fumimaro. One of the most important tasks of the Shōwa Kenkyūkai was to formulate an official policy for seizing the war with China (the "China Incident," or *shina jihen*, as it was euphemistically known) as an opportunity to begin establishing an economically robust, culturally cohesive regional bloc in East Asia. The historian Lewis Harrington has pointed out that the Shōwa Kenkyūkai described its raison d'être in 1936 as the development of a comprehensive plan for "mobilization of the experience and intelligence of the entire nation," adding that "since the cornerstone of this mobilization requires complete agreement on national intentions among all sections of Japan's society—among the bureaucrats, military, businessmen, scholars, and social critics, etc.—there is a pressing need for the formation of a research organization which will undertake the task of formulating a proper national policy. For this reason, we have organized the Shōwa Kenkyūkai."[96] Drawing on the narrative of a new colonial modernity that Miki and his colleagues soon developed, Konoe declared the beginning of a "New Order in Greater East Asia" (*tōa shin chitsujo*) on November 3, 1938; it would later be rebranded "The Greater East Asian Co-prosperity Sphere" (*dai tōa kyōeiken*).

As the writing of *The Melancholy of Travel* ended in 1946 with an elegy to the dead dream of the "New Order in Greater East Asia," it linked the worldly desire for collectivity to the more sinister politics that intellectual historians have associated with the cosmopolitan thought of the age. In this connection, the scholar John Namjun Kim has observed that Miki's writings on "cooperativism" (*kyōdōshugi*) attest to the fact that Japanese imperialism was fueled in part by philosophically informed dreams of freedom and inclusion, which implicitly justified colonial violence in the name of what Kim has called "imperial cosmopolitanism."[97] Kim also discussed the writings of Tanabe Hajime, a philosopher who was one of Miki's Kyoto School mentors and who, as the intellectual historian Naoki Sakai has also elaborated, contributed to a vision of imperial culture as a form of cosmopolitan praxis rather than as a rigidly nationalistic form of dominance.[98] Writing at a time (1982) when few scholars in the Anglophone academy favored the term "fascism" in their descriptions of the culture and politics of 1930s Japan, the historian William Miles Fletcher provided a sustained analysis of how Miki and the Shōwa Kenkyūkai resembled their fascist counterparts in Europe.[99] More recently, Harootunian has described Miki's philosophical project in particular as fascistic, concluding that Miki "often sought to distance himself from historic fascisms even as his analysis of Japan's modernity and his defense of imperialism led him to imagine an order that was just as fascistic, inasmuch as it sought to salvage capitalism and the folk which had been estranged from it in its original form as an organic community. A 'modern gemeinschaft' propelled by technological rationality and an organicist folk cooperativeness was simply another name for fascist political totalism."[100]

In making this claim, Harootunian noted that *The Melancholy of Travel* might be counted as the aesthetic expression most strongly redolent of Miki's *Theory of Imagination*, an extensive philosophical meditation on cultural forms begun at around the time Miki led the Culture Bureau of the Shōwa Kenkyūkai. The comparison seems to have been suggested (at least in part) by their capacious ranges: writing in terms reminiscent of Yokomitsu's discourse on a "fourth person" synthesis, for example, Miki said in the 1943 preface to his *Theory of Imagination* that for more than a decade, he had been fascinated with the basic question of how cultural forms synthesize "the subjective and the objective, the rational and the irrational, the intellectual and the emotional. I have formulated this problem as a question of the unity of logos [*rogosu*] and pathos [*patosu*]. My main task has been to analyze how the elements of logos and pathos coexist in all things historical [*subete no rekishiteki na mono*], and to consider the dialectical unity among these elements."[101] Harootunian described Miki's exploration of this synthesis as an "intellectual adventure [that] visited all of the major venues: neo-Kantianism, phenomenology, existentialism, Marxism, pragmatism, and their variants and hybrids," adding that this "adventure" "attempted to bring the vast diversity of ideas into concourse with each other, almost as if this immense orchestrating itself possessed the power of an amulet."[102] The same could be said of Yokomitsu's *The Melancholy of Travel*, a "novel of ideas" that attempted a holding-together of meaning so extensive as to move literary history itself into the new age of "fourth person perspective."

Remarking on these parallels, Harootunian has observed that "in many ways, Miki was the consummate modernist thinker and resembled in philosophy and thought the writer Yokomitsu Riichi whose own career traversed a dizzying course of literary innovations, only to exhaust himself in the end."[103]

This chapter has drawn on these resemblances, too, aiming to show that the worldly rumination in interwar Japan articulated itself in rhetorical registers ranging from imperial propaganda and elite philosophy to avant-garde literary modernism. Glimpsed through this lens, Yokomitsu's literary imagination appears to take shape through a series of engagements that were uncontained by the boundaries often ascribed to literary history. In fact, the wayward movements of Yokomitsu's curiosity recall something of Huxley's description of the literary mind of Philip Quarles in his novel of ideas *Point Counter Point*:

> The amoeba, when it finds a prey, flows round it, incorporates it, and oozes on. There was something amoeboid about Philip Quarles's mind. It was like a sea of spiritual protoplasm, capable of flowing in all directions, of engulfing every object in its path, of trickling into every crevice, of filling every mould, and, having engulfed, having filled, of flowing on toward other obstacles, other receptacles, leaving the first empty and dry. At different times in his life and even at the same moment he had filled the most various moulds. He had been a cynic and also a mystic, a humanitarian and also a contemptuous misanthrope; he had tried to live the life of detached and stoical reason and another time he had aspired to the unreasonableness of natural and uncivilized existence. The choice of moulds depended at any given moment on the books he was reading, the people he associated with.[104]

Or put differently: on the books, people, and ideas with which he conspired. In all cases, the thing that mattered most was the movement these moments of breathing together propelled. As Huxley had it:

> The essential character of the self consisted precisely in that liquid and undeformable ubiquity; in that capacity to espouse all contours and yet remain unfixed in any form; to take, and with an equal facility efface, impressions. To such moulds as his spirit might from time to time occupy, to

> such hard and burning obstacles as it might flow round, submerge, and, itself cold, penetrate to the fiery heart of, no permanent loyalty was owing. The moulds were emptied as easily as they had been filled, the obstacles were passed by. But the essential liquidness that flowed where it would, the cool indifferent flux of intellectual curiosity—that persisted and to that his loyalty was due.[105]

Huxley's description of the amoeba-like movements of the literary mind contrasts with Musil's description of tyrannical philosophers in times of crisis. Musil wrote in *The Man without Qualities* that "philosophers are despots who have no armies to command, so they subject the world to their tyranny by locking it up in a system of thought. This apparently also accounts for the presence of great philosophers in times of great tyrants."[106] Drawing on these perspectives, we begin to see that while it might be tempting to conclude that Tōno's speech at the end of *The Melancholy of Travel* indicates that the ultimate destination of Yokomitsu's literary modernism dissolved into the political climax of Miki's philosophical itinerary, it is also true that the allusion to the "New Order" at the end of the novel discloses the world of difference separating Yokomitsu's literary project from Miki's Shōwa Kenkyūkai prescriptions for colonial culture. After all, Yokomitsu's "novel of ideas" was "useless" in Arendt's sense of the word: it promised no instrumentalist "effect" because it was a work of literary art with no objective meaning to which any subjective interpretation could ever aspire. In contrast, Miki's participation in the Shōwa Kenkyūkai articulated his belief that philosophical rumination on the question of "world history" must lead to decisive action through the institution of the wartime state. Over time, the purposefulness of Miki's and other intellectuals' propagandistic prose diminished as their normative narrative of empire failed.[107]

My analysis has tried to show that in contrast, Yokomitsu's last novel did not terminate with "success" or "failure" in quite the same way, and that this was so because literary writing (unlike the philosophically informed propaganda of the Shōwa Kenkyūkai) never promises to be a cause that leads to any useful effect. However paradoxically, it was this ambiguous ontology of the literary that availed Yokomtisu's last novel to the cosmopolitan imagining of worldly relations. Drawing on Cheah, I conclude that because the literary is neither fully materialist nor completely spiritualist, and because it is neither a conduit to objective meaning nor a merely subjective form of personal experience, it was the literary itself that was uniquely positioned to dissolve the cosmopolitan synthesis articulated by Kyoto School expositions into a "useless" aesthetic form less tightly constrained by the perishable purposefulness that welled up within the temporal tectonics of its own precarious present. Noting this is not to imply that the novel was more "innocent" than other writings, nor to forget that after the war, Yokomitsu himself was counted among the many writers bearing "war responsibility" for his contributions to the wartime zeitgeist, and that his reputation has suffered as a result of the damning charge of "complicity."[108] But I close this analysis by observing that his deepest "complicity" arose not from any explicit statements he made, nor from the moments of clear-cut imperial exhortation in his writings. Rather, the deeper politics emerged from the relations examined in this chapter, relations by which his last novel conspired with the cosmopolitan dream of worldly relation without constraining that dream within the discursive boundaries of any purposeful expository idiom.

The next chapter complicates this picture by turning to leftist writers and thinkers who countered the elegant purposelessness and worldly abstraction of literary aesthetics by recuperating the social utility and meaning-in-context of everyday utterances.

CHAPTER 3

Overcome by the Literary

Nakano Shigeharu, Tosaka Jun, and the Prosaic Politics of the Left

Aristotle wrote *Poetics*. But no one has ever written *Prosaics*.
—Satō Haruo, "The Origins of the Spirit of Prose"[1]

In *Problems of Dostoevsky's Poetics*, the noted literary theorist Mikhail Bakhtin observed that the way language strikes the ear in everyday life is one of the most potent inspirations of the literary imagination. His point was that the aesthetic experiences afforded by the prose form of the novel are not unrelated to the most pragmatic utilizations of language in contexts with no aesthetic pretenses whatsoever, with the larger implication that the imagined barrier separating "real life" from literary art is a stultifying contrivance. As a corrective, Bakhtin argued that the utilitarian articulations that permeate the most mundane moments of everyday social interaction in fact take the form of a nuanced dialogue that is too often overlooked because it is commonplace, and therefore appears to be the opposite of artistic. The prose writer recuperates its import by listening to its voices:

> For the prose artist the world is full of other people's words, among which he must orient himself and whose speech characteristics he must be able to perceive with a very keen ear. He must introduce them into the plane of his own discourse, but in such a way that this plane is not destroyed. He works with a very rich verbal palette, and he works exceptionally well with it.
>
> And we, when perceiving prose, orient ourselves very subtly among all the types and varieties of discourse analyzed above. Moreover, in real life

> as well we very keenly and subtly hear all these nuances in the speech of people surrounding us, and we ourselves work very skillfully with all these colors of the verbal palette. We very sensitively catch the smallest shift in intonation, the slightest interruption of voices in anything of importance to us in another person's practical everyday discourse. All those verbal sideward glances, reservations, loopholes, hints, thrusts do not slip past our ear, are not foreign to our own lips. All the more astonishing, then, that up to now all this has found no precise theoretical cognizance, nor the assessment it deserves![2]

It is almost as if for Bakhtin, the novelist breathes with everyday life, taking in its vernacular voices and exhaling them back out again in the form of a textual art that evokes the unfinished aspect of contemporary history itself.

Without any apparent knowledge of Bakhtin, writers and thinkers on the left in wartime Japan sensed that these were the sorts of rhythmic affordances of an everyday idiom that was fast being overwritten by the *kokutai* jargon of national identity examined in chapter 1, and by the philosophical abstractions examined in chapter 2. As they saw it, the crisis of representation of their time originated with the dissolution of the indexical bonds by which everyday language connected literary representation to contemporary social history—a dissolution that they believed to have been occasioned by the mutually accelerating forces of print media censorship, state-issued propaganda, literary romanticism, philosophical jargon, and nativist mythology. In response, they conspired to resist the trends of a time that they believed to have been intoxicated by an excess of literary thinking. They limned the limits of the literary by stepping outside of what they viewed as the internally bounded regime of literary aesthetics altogether, and searched for fresh inspiration in the nonaesthetic elements of socially contextualized everyday discourse.

One of the most legible loci in which these concerns collected in wartime Japan was under the banner of the "spirit of prose" (*sanbun seishin*). The scholar of Japanese literature Richard Torrance has examined how the "spirit of prose" came to signify a resistance that galvanized in a coterie gathered around *The People's Library* (*Jinmin bunko*), a leftist literary journal that published from 1936 to 1938, and that advocated for "the spirit of prose" in opposition to the poetics of violence and death championed by novelist Yasuda Yojūrō and the Nihon Roman-ha (Japan Romantic School).[3] Torrance has shown that in forging this resistance, *The People's Library* circle moved beyond some of the more doctrinaire preoccupations of the earlier proletarian arts movements with which many of its contributors had been involved, and discovered formal possibilities for devising a new leftist literary politics in the writings of popular Tokugawa period writer Ihara Saikaku (1642–93) and in the novels of their contemporary Tokuda Shūsei (1871–1943)—neither of whom was a proletarian writer, but both of whom, it was believed, had rendered the granular details of everyday life in prosaic dialogue with the open-ended time of contemporary history. Working from this perspective, writers associated with *The People's Library* waged what Torrance has called "Japan's most articulate, organized, and popular literary opposition to fascism."[4]

This chapter maps some of the more extensive literary and philosophical coordinates of this discourse as it charts a course through the high point of the proletarian arts era in the late 1920s to the subsequent consolidation of the "spirit of prose" resistance in the mid-1930s. My interpretive trajectory then continues beyond the police crackdown on leftists that all but eliminated the possibility for open resistance by the late 1930s, and examines how some of the submerged implications of the earlier discourse came into fuller articulation during the Occupation era (1945–52). Reading through this transwar chronology, I aim to show how a wide range of writers and thinkers who were harshly policed throughout the period did, in fact, advance a collective rumination that was larger in implication than the sum of its widely dispersed parts.[5] In making this point, I will argue that studying the literary Left in transwar Japan can expand and politicize the conversation around what has been called "prosaics"—a keyword that I adapt from the analysis of the literary scholars Gary Saul Morson and Caryl Emerson, who claimed in their study of Bakhtin's life and thought to have coined the neologism. They wrote that "prosaics" "encompasses two related, but distinct, concepts": first, "a theory of literature that privileges prose in general and the novel in particular over the poetic genres," and second, something "far broader than [a] theory of literature: it is a form of thinking that presumes the importance of the everyday, the ordinary, the 'prosaic.'"[6] I will focus on the second of these "concepts" in particular, and connect the problem of prosaics to a broader dialogue about the social life of everyday language that signifies within the open-ended time of its contextualized usage.[7] This leads me to link together writings scattered across the registers of philosophical contemplation, proletarian poetry, and literary criticism, and to see them as parts of an implicitly networked dialogue among contemporaries which might otherwise be obscured by its own polyphony.

In turn, this approach overlays the transwar chronology outlined above with a conceptual narrative that begins with the theorization of authoritarian poetics, then moves on to the realm of prosaic literary practice, and finally culminates by considering how the register of literary criticism materializes in between those of theory and practice. The first section of this chapter reads the Marxist philosopher Tosaka Jun's insights into language politics alongside those of other theorists in the global 1930s. The next section then connects aspects of this intellectual history to the literary realm as it performs close readings of the prosaic practice that Nakano Shigeharu formulated as a literary writer himself. In the last section, I consider how Nakano, as a literary critic, elucidated some of the *faux amis* (false friends) of the prosaic persuasion in the form of seemingly related techniques appearing in Japanese literary history that had in fact developed along more right-leaning trajectories tethered to institutional authority. In positing this group of leftist writings as part of a coherent conversation about the problems of prosaics, I am mindful that the perspectives examined in this chapter originally appeared in considerable dispersion, rather than in synchronous dialogue with one another: Nakano and Tosaka had little to do with *The People's Library*, for example, and little to do personally even with one another, in fact. But the wager of this analysis is that if we are to read the literary history of a leftist language politics that was policed at times to the point of being all but obliterated, one interpretive strategy might be to embrace an approach that is undaunted by the dispersion of sometimes only implicit links among writings and writers. The payoff of this approach is a better understanding of how these links in fact outline a continuum of theory and practice in a network of writings that conspired within what might be called the "prosaic imagination" of transwar Japan.

Tosaka Jun and the Jargon of Japanese Fascism

Perhaps the most likely way to read Nakano and Tosaka together would be to compare their interpretations of (and contributions to) Marxist thought. But the problem of prosaic everyday language at the center of this chapter is not an inevitably Marxist, proletarian, or revolutionary premise. In fact, Morson and Emerson downplayed the politics of Bakhtin's writings on the topic: while acknowledging that his perspective developed in part through his dialogue with Marxist interlocutors (including V. N. Volosinov), they held that his understanding ultimately remained "sociological without being Marxist."[8] Elsewhere, the literary scholars Michael Lucey and Tom McEnaney have more recently explored the dialogues connecting literary texts to the semiotics of "language-in-use" in contexts far removed from the sort of tense political situation that the subjects of this chapter engaged. They began by observing that "literary critics and theorists often shy away from talking about writers and readers as people who put language to use," noting in particular a scholarly inclination to avoid "turning a literary artifact into mere data or information, or making it part of an exchange of language that is not exclusively aesthetic in nature."[9] In response, Lucey and McEnaney drew on the insights of Bakhtin and others in pointing to how the literary imagination is informed by some of the same sociolinguistic cues that also arrest the nonaesthetic attention of the linguistic anthropologist. As they put it, "Linguistic anthropologists, like many novelists and other writers, are interested in what could be called 'the social life of language,' in how culture happens when humans use language to interact, in how the social world's existence is maintained through multifarious particular acts of language use. To notice this requires listening to language in certain ways."[10] The acoustic imperative of this perspective informed an approach to literary texts premised on the rhythms of "language-in-use" that make text into "the dynamic product of an interactive process," rather than a "stable object."[11] Lucey and McEnaney's consideration of Marcel Proust's legendary prose in particular underscored their argument that "even the most literary of artifacts can be considered from this point of view."[12]

In showing how the nonliterary perspective of linguistic anthropology can link the forms of literary art to the nonliterary realm of everyday language-in-use, Lucey and McEnaney revealed that the sociolinguistic imperative of literary language materializes in a wide range of contexts. But in 1930s Japan, "the social life of language" that they described became a battleground for many writers and thinkers with Marxist commitments in particular, who came to believe that theirs was an age of altogether too much literary and aesthetic thinking, feeling, and imagining. Tosaka was one of the most articulate among them. Born in 1900, he rose to prominence in the early 1930s as the leader of the Yuibutsuron Kenkyūkai (Society for Materialist Research), a group whose eponymous journal proved to be a force in disseminating the increasingly suppressed methods of materialist social critique. His argument that the cultural political phenomena of 1930s Japan were inflections of a global tendency toward fascism remains one of the most penetrating insights into Japanese modernity from the period, and his drive to understand the workings of modern politics through the forms of mass culture put him into implicit conversation with contemporaries in the Frankfurt School writing on the same problems.[13] Tosaka trained as a philosopher, but his writings ranged over topics from journalism to ideology, mass media to literature. This led the noted scholar Yoshimi Shunya to count him among the intellectual pioneers who established the foundation of what is now known as "cultural studies" (*karuchuraru sutadiizu*) in Japan.[14]

Undergirding Tosaka's wide-ranging interests was the conviction that the true stakes of philosophical thinking (*tetsugaku*) originated in the unresolved conflicts of everyday life, rather than in elite and complete canons of knowledge handed down from the past. In this connection, the film and media studies scholar Yuriko Furuhata has observed Tosaka's "critique of the institutionalized discipline of philosophy" in particular. "Writing in the 1930s against the rise of fascism in Japan," Furuhata noted, Tosaka "fervently argues that the discipline of philosophy must begin to integrate the critical perspective of journalism, an antidote to philosophers' tendency to avert their gaze from the current political situation and retreat into the safe haven of ideational abstraction."[15] The scholar Fabian Schäfer has also remarked on Tosaka's understanding that "the most important feature of journalism lies in its actuality and the critique of the everyday," with the implication that the most urgent philosophy engages contemporary social problems with journalistic timeliness, and avoids the hermetic world of academicism.[16]

Tosaka's career came to embody these ideals. He was trained in philosophy at Kyoto Imperial University by Nishida Kitarō and Tanabe Hajime, two of the leading figures of the Kyoto School examined in chapter 2. But he later distanced himself from his own academic lineage by criticizing the calcification of intellectual work itself into narrow professional cliques (*gaku-ha*). In fact, it was Tosaka himself who coined the now-familiar appellation "Kyoto School philosophy," and he meant it as a critique of his former Kyoto colleagues and mentors, who he believed had abandoned the material ground of lived experience in favor of what he viewed as idealistic meditations on religious consciousness and phenomenology. For almost his entire career, Tosaka was without the privileges conferred by a professorship in the academy, and although he was among the most prominent Marxist intellectuals of his generation in Japan, he never joined the Japanese Communist Party (JCP). He forged his critiques of modern cultural politics as a kind of outsider whose own career as a journalist, editor, and, in the end, outlaw intellectual became the practice of one of the most fundamental convictions of his thought—namely, that the locus of philosophical activity must be the everyday realm governed by the contingent time of the historical present. He would give his life for this purpose, dying in prison as an unapologetic political prisoner on August 9, 1945—the same day, in fact, that the United States dropped the atomic bomb on Nagasaki, effectively ending the reign of the regime that put him to death.[17]

Tosaka is best remembered today for arguing that fascism in 1930s Japan was an expansive ideological force, rather than a narrow, institutionally contained politics. The historian Reto Hofmann has paraphrased his perspective in writing that "for Tosaka, fascism went beyond the economic and political domains. Fascism did not only take over political institutions in a barely perceptible manner; its capacity to work at the level of people's common sense also meant that it crept into a nation's culture. In this sense, the sophistication of Tosaka's analysis lies in his explanation of the insidiousness of fascism."[18] Needless to say, Tosaka's critique broadly (if only implicitly) affiliated his perspective with the antifascist politics of *The People's Library* that Torrance has described. But the confluence of intellectual and literary sensibilities fueling the resistance comes to the fore in more precise terms in considering that Tosaka shared with the "spirit of prose" writers the conviction that mythical poetic language had become one conduit by which the form of fascist politics insinuated itself into a language landscape that had been drained of prosaic everyday values. The semiotic focus of their cumulative critique implied that fascist ideology in the global 1930s articulated itself on the more "insidious" plane of what Gilles Deleuze and Félix Guattari have called the "micropolitical" level. In this connection, Harry Harootunian has argued that insofar as fascism in Japan was something more extensive and nebulous than a state-centered political authoritarianism or self-declaring movement, we should remember that "DeLeuze and Guattari put it best when they equated fascism with a micropolitics and located its force in a form of molecularity."[19] From this perspective, the overarching, "macropolitical" structures of fascism manifested in an authoritarian regime are only the more visible expressions of ideologically charged sentiments circulating more extensively on the smaller scale of seemingly minor or even apolitical phenomena. That is why Deleuze and Guattari argued that "what makes fascism dangerous is its molecular or micropolitical power, for it is a mass movement: a cancerous body rather than a totalitarian organism."[20] And as a matter of language politics in particular, this perspective located the fascist form within semiotic regimes originating within the body politic itself, rather than only or primarily in the ideologies announced officially by the state.[21]

Taken a step further, this meant that fascist language extended far beyond words and arguments that explicitly communicated content amenable to a fascist perspective per se. From the micropolitical perspective, the fascist function also articulated itself through the nonsemantic workings of closed and complete language that mimicked the politics of binding in the microcosms of its own forms. The prosaic imagination took up this micropolitical perspective because it illuminated how the nuts and bolts of language could emanate subtle sinusoidal rhythms of political feeling that often went unnoticed on the level of isolated articulations, but that, in their more extensive "molecular" agglutinations, produced (and were produced by) poetic words and grammar combining throughout the language landscape to form a "cancerous" concatenation.[22] The semiotic imperative of this perspective reflected the broader premise stated in V. N. Volosinov's *Marxism and the Philosophy of Language* (1929) that "everything ideological possesses *meaning*: it represents, depicts, or stands for something lying outside itself. In other words, it is a *sign*. *Without signs there is no ideology.*"[23] In forging an allied critique, Tosaka and the "spirit of prose" writers seem to have sensed a growing division between the signs of what their contemporary Bakhtin would call "poetic" and "prosaic" language politics. This connection is only implicit, though, for Bakhtin himself labored largely in obscurity through the 1930s and beyond, and his texts would not have been known to his Japanese counterparts.

But nevertheless, at around the time that the "spirit of prose" resistance took shape in Japan, Bakhtin wrote in what would become an iconic essay, "Discourse in the Novel" (1935), that prosaic language is the heteroglossic language of everyday life in which the vernaculars of all social strata talk to each other in an almost musical conversation. One of the most important implications of this formulation was that the prosaic writer does not create or control language completely, but only animates the already existing languages and social speech genres of his moment in time. As Bakhtin put it, the prose writer "does not speak in a given language (from which he distances himself to a greater or lesser degree), but he speaks, as it were, *through* language, a language that has somehow more or less materialized, become objectivized, that he merely ventriloquates."[24] As this happens, the prosaic writer "welcomes the heteroglossia and language diversity of the literary and extraliterary language into his own work not only not weakening them but even intensifying them (for he interacts with their particular self-consciousness)."[25] From this perspective, it might be said that the prosaic literary imagination sets aside the romantic image of the inspired literary author who invents an entirely original expressive idiom autonomously. Rather than "creating" a language and dominating it with complete control, the prosaic writer converses with the extraliterary linguistic diversity of contemporary history in order to composite various verbal threads into a textured textual weave. This suggests that in contrast to belletristic notions of the creative writer as an isolated individual who brings forth a self-contained form of beauty through his own inimitable powers of imagination, the prosaic mind envisioned the writer as one who converses with (rather than controls) the structures of an everyday language idiom already familiar to all.

This helps us to see the political implications of Bakhtin's critique of "poetic" language, too. He argued that in contrast to prosaic language, "poetic" language is univocal and hermetic, a language conjured in isolation from the conflicts of history and society in which the poet actually lives and breathes. And for this reason, Bakhtin reasoned, poetic language is a contrivance: It is a language with no organic bond to a social world beyond its own forms, and its semiotics bear no trace of indexical relation to their own moment in history. What poetic language expresses is an imaginary self existing purely in its own formal containment, a self unmediated by the contingency of historical time and contemporaneous social life.[26] This extreme degree of isolation allows the poet to create, control, and possess his language in ways the prosaic writer could never imagine: As Bakhtin put it, "the language of the poet is *his* language, he is utterly immersed in it, inseparable from it, he makes use of each form, each word, each expression according to its unmediated power to assign meaning (as it were, 'without quotation marks'), that is, as a pure and direct expression of his own intention."[27] For the contrived control of the poet to materialize, though, almost everything else has to be shut out.[28] Bakhtin wrote that "any sense of the boundedness, the historicity, the social determination and specificity of one's own language is alien to poetic style, and therefore a critical qualified relationship to one's own language (as merely one of many languages in a heteroglot world) is foreign to poetic style."[29] In making this point, Bakhtin implied that the beauty of poetic language requires a kind of silence because its first condition of possibility is the erasure of social and historical cacophony that would otherwise mediate its signs. It rings clear because it mutes everything else in its vicinity.

Without having read Bakhtin, writers in 1920s and 1930s Japan sensed the tension between the regimes of poetic and prosaic language in something like these terms, too. In an essay titled "Sanbun seishin no hassei" (The Origins of the Spirit of Prose, 1924), for example, the writer Satō Haruo continued Hirotsu Kazuo's advocacy for the "prosaic arts" (*sanbun geijutsu*) as he defined the opposition between poetics and prosaics in ways that implicitly resonated with aspects of Bakhtin's critiques to come roughly a decade later. Satō wrote that "poetic spirit" (*shiteki seishin*) revolves around "orderly balance" (*chitsujo aru kinkō*), "harmony" (*chōwa*), and "unity" (*tōitsu*), adding that the lifeblood of poetry (*shi no seimei*) is a beauty that arises when the poet controls the world of chaos and cacophony (*konton no sekai*), bringing unity, harmony and even purification.[30] He argued that "the poetic [*shiteki to iu koto*], however else it might be interpreted, can, in the broad sense, be nothing other than the joy [*yorokobi*] that comes from the beauty of harmonious unity. In this sense, poetry resembles religious faith [*shūkyōteki na shinkō*]."[31] He claimed that "the spirit of prose is diametrically opposed to the spirit of poetry" because the prosaic imagination embraces the "unsystematic" (*muchitsujo*), "ununified" (*mutōitsu*), and "disharmonious" (*muchōwa*), "for in the chaos and cacophony (*konton*) of the world we discover beauty."[32] Broadly construed, these descriptions of prosaic language imply that "the spirit of prose" signified a literary activation of the notion of "everydayness" (*nichijōsei*) that Tosaka philosophically conceptualized in the 1930s. And by bringing these literary and intellectual threads together, we begin to see that while Tosaka had little personal contact with the central figures behind *The People's Library*, he implicitly affiliated with them through the shared premise that literary prosaics originated in everyday language that was, to borrow Bakhtin's expression, "born in a zone of contact with unresolved contemporaneity."[33]

For these writers and thinkers on the left, though, the problem in the global 1930s was that poetics was erasing prosaics altogether. The scholar of Japanese literature and fascism Alan Tansman has examined this process in depth, revealing how Japanese fascism operated partly through poetic language that agglutinated in what he called "fascist moments," which relieved readers of the inclination to intellectual analysis and delivered them to a more pristine, even mythic space beyond time.[34] Needless to say, these "fascist moments" were the antithesis of the prosaic preoccupation with the everyday time of "unresolved contemporaneity." Their effects amplified within what Tansman has described as a "representational vacuum," a contrived semiotic field in which censoring authorities emptied out the language landscape of what they deemed to have been dangerous political registers and expressive styles, while at the same time promoting alternatives that were believed to have been more amenable to state control.[35] Connecting Tansman's argument to the discussion above, it might be said that inasmuch as the "representational vacuum" cleared by censorship and filled by the romantic imagination harbored the alluring signs of harmonious consensus after first creating a kind of semiotic silence, it materialized something akin to the poetic authoritarianism that Bakhtin also critiqued at around this time.

In interwar Japan, furthermore, Tosaka shared the conviction with the *People's Library* coterie that this sort of an authoritarian poetics was threatening to silence the extraliterary languages of everyday prosaics. He sensed that the combined forces of literary romanticism, censorship of print media, and state-issued propaganda had conspired to flatten the varied vernaculars of stratified social registers into a placid poetic aesthetic. This transformed the communicative sphere of wartime Japan into a closed circuit in which empty literary signs could refer only to each other in a homogenous poetic register with no form of social or historical indexicality. Tosaka referred to this poetic saturation with the coinage "literaturism" (*bungakushugi*), a term that he used to describe the process by which the belletristic imagination territorialized formerly extraliterary registers.[36] In *Nihon ideorogii ron* (The Japanese Ideology, 1935), he defined "literaturism" as a special interpretive method that linked literary images to other literary images, and in so doing, replaced the meaningful organization of actual philosophical categories based on what he called the actual order of things (*genjitsu no chitsujo*) with a merely literary logic as stable and self-contained as the closed and complete conjuration of a literary narrative.[37] In critiquing the empty formalisms produced by this sort of literary aestheticism, Tosaka identified something akin to the "scandalous [inversion of] the order of things" that the Marxist philosopher Louis Althusser discovered in the rote religious imperative to "kneel down, move your lips in prayer, and you will believe."[38] For like Althusser, Tosaka sensed that when the isolated forms of merely literary words gave rise to ecstatic epiphanies loosed from the material ground of dialogic discourse, prosaics became impossible. In its place, the autonomous poetic utterance alone remained, an alluring conjuration signifying a world of meaning (*imi no sekai*) all its own.

Harootunian has pointed out that Tosaka believed this process of transmuting the contingency of historical experience indexed by prosaic language into the stability of poetic signs to have been most clearly in evidence in the ways that some intellectuals tried to understand the modern world through the methods of hermeneutics and philology.[39] The two were linked: "As a method," Harootunian has written in his reading of Tosaka's critique, "hermeneutics was based on a depth analysis, and was driven by the ceaseless search for truth beneath the surface of things; its aim was to reach an essence and the place of the spirit. It relied upon philology, which drew its force from examining etymologies of words in dead languages and performing textual interpretations of documents, 'masquerading as a philosophic concept.'"[40] Tosaka allowed that philology might elucidate the meaning of a word embedded in the fixed context of an ancient text, but as Harootunian has observed, drawing a line between Tosaka's critique and those of Volosinov and Bakhtin, Tosaka feared that trying to understand the more contingent problems of an evolving modernity through formal analyses of isolated native words could only lead to a circular ethnocentrism.[41] This was so, Tosaka argued, because philological fetishes divorced language from life and transformed the parochial signifying range of Japanese *kotoba* into a universalized philosophical jargon. In this regard, Tosaka implicitly concurred with Volosinov's insight that philology treated the word as a "defunct, monologic utterance" and an "isolated monument." In *Marxism and the Philosophy of Language*, Volosinov observed that "guided by philological need, linguistics has always taken as its point of departure the finished monologic utterance—the ancient written monument, considering it the ultimate realium," but he added that by understanding language as a group of complete, self-identical forms (or "monuments"), "the philologist-linguist tears the monument out of that real domain and views it as if it were a self-sufficient, isolated entity."[42] Without any apparent knowledge of Volosinov's thesis, Tosaka recognized in 1930s Japan that as the literaturistic imagination drew on the methods of philological hermeneutics, it repressed the unevenness of an unresolved modernity by representing modern life itself as if it were as stable as the grammar of an ancient text.

The result was that the surface of virtually any native word could be plumbed for conceptual implication and endowed with philosophical depth.[43] At an extreme, this meant that the Japanese language itself could be believed to hold together an exclusive philosophical system within its own philological forms. This came out in Tosaka's reading of eminent philosopher Watsuji Tetsurō's (1889–1960) *Ningen no gaku toshite no rinrigaku* (Humanity and Ethics, 1934), which offered one of the best examples of how he understood philology to authorize specious philosophies of Japanese superiority.[44] In one case, Tosaka rejected Watsuji's claim that the Japanese word for "ethics," *rinri* (倫理), implied that Japanese people possessed an intuitive sense of collectivity (*kyōdōtai*), and criticized the larger implication of Watsuji's methods, which he believed gave the impression that Japanese society was exemplary and even possessed a peerless *kokutai*.[45] Tosaka elaborated on what he understood to have been the inherent ethnocentrism of Watsuji's philological formalism, claiming that it inevitably gave the impression that the Japanese themselves embodied the ideals of abstract philosophical concepts, including "ethics," "humanity," and "being":

> Textual interpretations based on words always place the thing being interpreted within the confines of a national language [*kokugo*]. The Japanese words for "ethics" [*rinri*], "humanity" [*ningen*], and "being" [*sonzai*] all exemplify this. It follows that not only will the things called "ethics," "humanity," and "being" be interpreted only as they occur in Japan, but it also becomes inevitable that the Japanese instances of these things will become the standards for interpretation. This is because although things like "ethics," "humanity," and "being" can be understood in global terms, when the global and the Japanese senses of these terms must be negotiated, philological interpretation will of course always figure the Japanese side as the most central.[46]

Tosaka argued that the result was normative logic (*norumaru na rojikku*) by which language guided thought rather than the reverse, yielding a philologically grounded but philosophically unfounded theory of Japanese superiority. In making this claim, Tosaka explained how the closed and complete language of an empty poetic formalism threatened to replace the unresolved urgency of true philosophical insight.

Worse yet, the politics of binding that Tosaka believed to cohere within philological philosophy were not limited to the realm of wartime Japanese thought. As Furuhata has pointed out, Tosaka's critique of philology also extended to Heidegger's phenomenology, which Tosaka responded to by writing, "Of course nothing is wrong with the existence of philology as a discipline, but the *actuality* of the present world cannot become an object of philological inquiries."[47] In Furuhata's paraphrase, Tosaka's point was that "neither phenomenology nor philology offers a philosophical mode of critique that allows political engagement with present-day reality."[48] This brings us closer to seeing how Tosaka's critique of Watsuji and Heidegger implicitly affiliated with elements of Theodor Adorno's better-known critique in *The Jargon of Authenticity* (1964), which might be said to have examined the anti-actual "poetics" of Heidegger's philosophy. Adorno argued that Heidegger's writings on phenomenology and ontology in the 1920s and 1930s had emptied out language of everyday values and transformed mundane words into a magical "jargon of authenticity" imbued with a poetic aura as captivating as it was chimerical:

> The fact that the words of the jargon sound as if they said something higher than what they mean suggests the term "aura." It is hardly an accident that [Walter] Benjamin introduced the term at the same moment when, according to his own theory, what he understood by "aura" became impossible to experience. As words that are sacred without sacred content, as frozen emanations, the terms of the jargon of authenticity are products of the disintegration of the aura.[49]

Working from a similar premise, Tosaka believed that Watsuji's fetishization of native *kotoba* had conjured the impossible fantasy of a closed and complete philosophy existing exclusively within the forms of the Japanese language. As the jargon of Japanese fascism contrived to convey the aura of native philosophy in "words that are sacred without sacred content," it supplied the narrative structure for a poetic desire to link the mythic past to an imagined future through an imperishable grammar as calcified as that of a dead language.

By unmasking this micropolitical accumulation in language, Tosaka's critique of Watsuji identified the fascist function in the same ruse that Adorno critiqued in the context of Heidegger's philosophy:

> When [the jargon] dresses empirical words with aura, it exaggerates general concepts and ideas of philosophy—as for instance the concept of being—so grossly that their conceptual essence, the mediation through the thinking subject, disappears completely under the varnish. Then these terms lure us on as if they were the most concrete terms. Transcendence and concretion scintillate. Ambiguity is the medium of an attitude toward language which is damned by its favorite philosophy.[50]

Working from a similar premise, Bakhtin argued in the middle 1930s that when we take "language not as a system of abstract grammatical categories, but rather language conceived as ideologically saturated, language as a world view," we begin to see that "a unitary language gives expression to forces working toward concrete verbal and ideological unification and centralization, which develop in vital connection with the processes of sociopolitical and cultural centralization."[51] This is why Bakhtin concluded that "the language of poetic genres, when they approach their stylistic limit, often becomes authoritarian, dogmatic and conservative, sealing itself off from the influence of extraliterary social dialects."[52] For Tosaka, too, language entered into the service of authoritarian politics as it accelerated a whirling confluence that produced (and reflected) the desire to commune with the poetic aura of whole language in the age of its perceived dissolution into meaningless fragments. In formulating this critique in 1930s Japan, he discerned in the moment what Adorno would sum up, looking back: "Prior to any consideration of particular content, this language molds thought. . . . Fascism was not simply a conspiracy—although it was that—but it was something that came to life in the course of a powerful social development. Language provides it with a refuge. Within this refuge a smoldering evil expresses itself as though it were salvation."[53]

Nakano Shigeharu and Prosaic Praxis

Although Tosaka has rarely been read in dialogue with his contemporaries in the literary world, my attempt to affiliate them revolves around the observation that the writers who promoted "the spirit of prose" in 1930s Japan conspired in opposition to the same poetics of Japanese fascism that he was then critiquing in expository terms. As an alternative to limitless decontextualization, moreover, the "spirit of prose" writers advocated for a more sociohistorically circumscribed language that would breathe with the unresolved conflicts of everyday life, and this, too, drew them into league with the broad dynamics of Tosaka's perspective on language politics, even if they were never in actual dialogue with one another per se. In this connection, Torrance has observed that at around the time that Takeda Rintarō organized *The People's Library* in 1936, he announced in another literary journal that "our primary obligation is to take action in opposition [to fascism]."[54] It followed that the literary group that formed around *The People's Library* exalted "the spirit of prose" that had been alive in earlier literary realisms, but that had been denigrated by their contemporaries who shared the romantic poetic sensibilities championed by the then-ascendant Nihon Roman-ha.[55] For both Tosaka and the *People's Library* coterie, then, prosaics became the semiotic solution to the crisis of representation in 1930s Japan.

The broad premise of a leftist prosaics articulated itself in a wide range of narrative formats, some more often noted than others. As discussed above, Furuhata has explained part of Tosaka's philosophical project in terms of "a strong emphasis on philosophy's need to be 'actual' and relevant to the present," with the implication that philosophy itself might be reconfigured "as a practice of *timely criticism situated in the present.*"[56] These prosaic implications for philosophical rumination reverberate with the concern for actuality and timeliness that has appeared in aesthetic contexts, too, as Furuhata's own discussion of "cinema of actuality" in 1960s and 1970s Japan has demonstrated. In the literary realm, the novel became the focus of the most prominent reflections on literary prosaics, whether in Bakhtin's iconic critiques or in the "spirit of prose" discourse in Japan to which Satō Haruo, Hirotsu Kazuo, Aono Suekichi, and others contributed. But in addition to the distributions of prosaic sensibility into reckonings with the problems and possibilities of philosophy, cinema, and the novel, consideration of prosaic possibilities in the less likely realm of poetry also appeared. Needless to say, a prosaic poetry would seem to present a contradiction in terms, but as the literary critic Kamiya Tadataka has argued, it should be recalled that the writers who collected around *The People's Library* understood "the spirit of prose" not only as a simple matter of genre, but also as a larger matter related to the spirit of the writer himself (*sakka no seishin*).[57] From this perspective, the prosaic preoccupation with actuality and timeliness could, at least in theory, figure in a poetry beholden to the unresolved experience of everyday life. This was suggested by Moriyama Kei, who is quoted by Kamiya as having written in 1939 that "the spirit of prose and the spirit of poetry are not at all opposed to one another. The opposition is between the spirit of prose and the spirit of *belles lettres* [*bibun seishin*]."[58]

In Japanese literary history, the realm of the everyday has long inspired the imagination of poets: the Edo-period *haikai* of Matsuo Bashō and the transcriptive realism of Masaoka Shiki's Meiji-period *shasei* come first to mind. And they were remembered by the most prominent writer to discuss the place of poets in the prose tradition of modern Japan: Akutagawa Ryūnosuke. In the iconic essay "Bungeiteki na, amari ni bungeiteki na" (Literary, All Too Literary, 1927), a fragmentary evocation of Japanese literary history, he reflected on "our prose" (*bokura no sanbun*) in Japan, declaring that he would "include consideration of the power that poets [*shijin*] have imparted to our prose."[59] Akutagawa discussed "the prose of poets" (*shijintachi no sanbun*) with reference to Bashō, and counted the more recent contributions to the literary prosaics of modern Japan made by poets Masaoka Shiki, Kinoshita Mokutarō, and Kitahara Hakushū. In particular, Akutagawa emphasized the link between the prosaic rendering of everyday life and the literary techniques that Shiki had developed under the banner of *shasei*, a method sometimes translated as "sketching from life." But with that said, Akutagawa was far from thorough in developing the link between these late-Meiji poets who developed the *shasei* techniques of realist transcription and the prose tradition of modern Japan, and in this sense, his essay presents less a theory or even an argument than the beginning of an interpretive rumination that he himself never came close to completing. What Akutagawa's essay carried forward, then, was an interpretive affordance: it offered the opportunity to think through the problem of literary prosaics in the less obvious context of poetry that engages everyday life.[60]

One way of developing the interpretive affordance that "Literary, All Too Literary" opened up would be to recall that by the time Akutagawa discussed poets' contributions to "our prose" tradition in the 1920s, the *shasei* realisms of the late Meiji years had faded from the Japanese literary mainstream, and that in their place, a new generation of prosaic writers had appeared under the banner of proletarian literature. In general, these proletarian writers shared with the Meiji realists a commitment to the transcriptive rendering of everyday life, but they differed from the earlier generation in that they attempted to connect the methods of literary realism to a revolutionary leftist politics in the age of global capitalist crisis. In a section of "Literary, All Too Literary" titled "Puroretaria bungei" (Proletarian Literature), Akutagawa considered the possibility that proletarian writers in 1920s Japan composing "poetry on life" (*seikatsu no shi*) might continue to develop and refine the techniques of literary prosaics that had earlier been devised by Meiji period *shasei* poets. The Marxist literary critic Odagiri Hideo has pointed out that although Akutagawa recognized the necessity of socialist critique as an intellectual proposition (*shisōteki ni wa*) late in his life, he only came to believe in the possibility of proletarian literary art (*puroretaria geijutsu to iu mono ga ariuru*) after he read the fresh language of a young writer who was only just beginning his career as a poet and critic: Nakano Shigeharu.[61] The literary scholar Takeuchi Emiko has noted that Akutagawa conveyed his fascination with Nakano's writing in a 1926 letter to their mutual acquaintance, the poet Murō Saisei, in which Akutagawa said that he had read most of Nakano's poems and had found them to be full of vitality.[62] In June 1927, Akutagawa invited Nakano to his home and expressed his hope that the young activist-poet would not abandon literary writing as his involvement in the bourgeoning proletarian movement deepened; Nakano assured Akutagawa that his political convictions would never overwrite his literary ambitions. Weeks later, Akutagawa died by his own hand.[63]

Akutagawa's encounter with Nakano reveals the perceived possibility that more sophisticated expressions of the proletarian persuasion that gained steam in the late 1920s could take up elements of a prosaic interest in everyday life, even (or especially) as it imbued literary prosaics with an avowedly leftist politics in the age of capitalist catastrophe. To be sure, this was a promise whose aesthetic potential often went unfulfilled: to take one example of how leftist writers have been critiqued from within their own ranks, it might be remembered that the writer and critic Aono Suekichi—who had himself been involved in the proletarian arts movement and *The People's Library*—suggested in an essay titled "Sanbun seishin no mondai" (On the Spirit of Prose, 1940) that the rise of leftist literature in the 1920s had led to the overemphasis of socially and politically relevant "material" (*sozai*) at the expense of more literarily sophisticated techniques.[64] But Nakano would seem to have been a case apart, if only because Akutagawa's premonition that his proletarian poetry would transcend the category of "proletarian art" and commune with the more mainstream appeal of prosaic literary realism has proven prescient. After all, literary critics on opposite ends of the political spectrum have found in Nakano's writing a moving language of everyday life with implications that go far beyond any conventional proletarian problematic. In *Shōwa no bunjin* (The Literati of the Shōwa Period, 1989), for example, the right-leaning critic Etō Jun recalled being shocked by how overwhelmed he became while reading Nakano's poem "Ame no furu Shinagawa Eki" (Shinagawa Station in the Rain, 1929) in his university course on modern Japanese poetry. He claimed that his reaction to the poem had nothing to do with the ideology of the Japanese proletariat; instead, it was the "radical melody" (*radikaru na senritsu*) of Nakano's language that moved him, layering the desolation of his own daily commute through Shinagawa Station with the affecting resonance of a literary vision.[65] Responding to Etō, Odagiri argued that the leftist politics and the literary aesthetics of the poem are inseparable, and he blamed what he viewed as Etō's misreadings in part on what he called Etō's literary and intellectual conservatism (*bungakutekina hoshushugi to shisōtekina hoshushugi*).[66] Moving closer to the political content of the poems, Miriam Silverberg showed in *Changing Song: The Marxist Manifestoes of Nakano Shigeharu* (1990) how Nakano's verse articulated canonical Marxist theses in a Japanese literary idiom.[67]

My own reading of Nakano's poetry enters into this conversation by advancing the perspective that we might draw form and content together by reading his writings through the problematic of prosaics introduced above. To be sure, this is not to suggest that his poems were originally written under the banner of the "spirit of prose," nor that they were self-consciously composed by Nakano himself in pursuit of an already-articulated theory of prosaics; they were not. The point, rather, is to show that even in the realm of poetry that did not explicitly identify itself under the sign of "prosaics," it might still be true that the aesthetic and political affordances of what I have been calling "prosaic" language animated (and were animated by) the leftist politics of one of the most celebrated Marxist writers of the age. From this vantage point, we begin to see that the politics of the poems owed not only to how their avowed content resonated with the theses of an extrinsic Marxist discourse, nor exclusively to their position within the literary history of proletarian arts movements in Japan, but also emanated from the very forms of dialogic language in which the poems themselves materialized.

These dynamics came through most clearly in Nakano's poems that addressed instances of reading, writing, and speaking in particular, especially in contexts involving the genres of expression that had been institutionalized by the mass media form of newspaper journalism. In these writings we find a literary imagination invested in something akin to what Lucey and McEnaney called "literary fieldwork," or the processes by which narrators within text excavate the social and historical sediments of contextualized utterances by digging through the surface level of semantics to reveal how specific moments of language-in-use produce (and are produced by) the deeper social architectures giving shape to social life.[68] To see and hear these dynamics in everyday language requires a form of "literary fieldwork" on the part of the reader-interpreter, too, or a hermeneutic by which we "tune in to words and meanings perhaps previously invisible or inaudible without these methods," as Lucey and McEnaney had it.[69] What this approach reveals in Nakano's poems in particular is that when they take up the endlessly recyclable forms of seemingly banal language—such as newspaper formulae, daily greetings and goodbyes, and declarative copulas (*de aru* and *darō*), for example—they do not understand the meaning of these nonaesthetic utterances in terms of a kind of semantic freight or representational content alone. In addition, and more importantly, Nakano's poems perform a kind of literary fieldwork that elucidates how the implications of even (or especially) familiar expressions are actively produced in the course of their being used in various contexts. What is at stake, his poems tell us, are the interactions among the surfaces of verbal signs that are imbued with deep social meaning in the everyday acts of reading, writing, and speaking.[70]

Nakano's early poem "Shinnin taishi chakukyō no zu" (The Picture of the Newly Appointed Ambassador Arriving in Tokyo, 1926) offers one example of how these threads come together:

The Picture of the Newly Appointed Ambassador Arriving in Tokyo

The photo of that man appeared in a hundred newspapers this morning
Accompanied by his wife and daughter
Surrounded by police and petty officials

I wonder what he's got it in mind to do
I bet he's got it in mind to tell some lies
I bet he's here again to tell some more lies
I wonder who he's lying for
I wonder how those lies will come through
I wonder what kind of a ring those lies will have when we hear them

The photo of that man
Surrounded by his wife, daughter, police and petty officials
At once appeared in a hundred newspapers this morning[71]

The prosaic imagination alive in this poem revolves around newspaper journalism and the reading practices that its combinations of text and image afford. In one sense, the poem resonates with Tosaka's observation that *jour*nal*ism* is supposed to articulate the "ism" of the "day" (*jour*): as he put it in *The Japanese Ideology*, "journalism, as the very word itself implies [*kotoba dōri*], is an 'ism' [*shugi*] founded on actual daily life, and it is therefore based on the principles of everydayness [*nichijōsei*]."[72] The connection between Nakano's rendering of prosaic literary language and journalism comes into clearer view still in recalling that Furuhata has observed that journalism has been said to convey the "sensation of actuality" in the form of newsworthy timeliness mixing with the simultaneity of mass readerly reception in the unresolved time of an everyday "now." Drawing on elements of Tosaka's critique of newspaper journalism and Gabriel Tarde's perspective on crowd psychology, Furuhata has considered how the "sensation of actuality" conjured by the newspaper "depends closely on its relation to journalistic periodicity"—that is, on the sense of time implied by regular daily installments that are collectively consumed.[73] In this view, journalism is powered by a semiotic process that produces the spectacle of novelty at the same time that it consigns that novelty to almost immediately dated obsolescence. The urgency of journalistic narrative is only imaginable in the perishable time of the impermanent present, then, for the novelty of newsworthy information expires in the very moment of everyday reading that it compels.[74]

Situated within this everyday time of journalistic reading, the markings of newsworthiness leave their extraliterary inscriptions on Nakano's poem unmistakably. Most notably, the dense title "Shinnin taishi chakukyō no zu" (新任大使着京の図) mimics the terse style of newspaper captions, as Silverberg has pointed out in her reading of the poem.[75] In addition, the first and last three lines of the poem repeat almost all of the same vocabulary making all of the same declarative statements, and their common constructions evoke the mechanical reproducibility of "a hundred newspapers" published "at once." The premise of the poem, then, is that within the bounded world of journalistic narrative, familiar formal features conspire to recruit the reader-subject into a language landscape full of genre-bound structures (headlines, articles, captions, photographs) that are daily reproduced by the corporate press in the form of a ready-to-read commodity.

The repetitions of these familiar features in Nakano's poem remind us that the prosaic ideal of actuality that is promised by journalism in theory is always mediated by the necessary artifice required to produce journalistic narratives in practice. In dialogue with Jacques Derrida's writing on the portmanteau "artifactuality," Furuhata observed that "the term *artifice* here does not necessarily imply deception, but it points to the constructed nature of actuality. The sensation of actuality that the media generates daily relies heavily on the process of fabrication, and there is indeed no actuality apart from this artifice."[76] In 1930s Japan, Tosaka argued that the ideal of everyday actuality in *jour*nal*ism* always existed in uneasy tension with the artificiality of the ready-to-read commodity of the newspaper. He observed that whatever its everyday possibilities might be in theory, the practice of journalism had more often been beholden to the interests of capital and subject to the distortions of mass mediation. For this reason, Tosaka argued, journalistic language should be understood in terms of a "regime of news media representation" (*hyōgen hōdō genshō*), rather than assumed to be a neutral transcriptive realism to be trusted implicitly.[77] This corroborates Silverberg's reading of Nakano's poem, which focused on its depiction of the journalistic usage of photography. Silverberg argued that the poem suggested that "newspapers actually isolate the reader from understanding, and the form of the message is as responsible as its content for this abuse of truth."[78]

Once we understand that the affordances of newspaper journalism run the gamut from everyday actuality to commodified artificiality, we begin to see that Nakano's poem is a meditation on how the seemingly mundane act of reading the newspaper in fact volatilizes a confrontation between the semiotic regimes at those two poles of representation. In this connection, it is telling that the poem describes the photograph of a foreign ambassador arriving in Tokyo because the political pageantry of the staged event is formally congruent to the ready-made language of newspaper poetics. It might even be said that Nakano's reader is engaging the idea articulated by the scholar of anthropology and linguistics Michael Silverstein that "'politics' *is* 'poetics'" in the sense that "political events, that is, events that can by analyzed in relation to a political order, reach whatever effectiveness they have only in a semiotic—a sign-mediated—order or they don't reach any effectiveness at all qua sociocultural fact."[79] Silverstein would remind us that insofar as the realm of the political is an irreducibly semiotic sphere, the print medium of the newspaper in particular plays a central role in signaling the constructs of a political "message" or "brand," and in circulating "the complex *son et lumière* of occasion, of staged governmental ritual, designed and carried off just so."[80] In addition, Nakano's rendering of the newspaper-reading subject indicts the role of corporate newsprint in the process of ideological "interpolation," as Althusser's critique would have had it. And as the poem positions the act of reading at the threshold of this interpolation, it implicitly considers the homogenizing effects of modern mass culture that would later be critiqued in Max Horkheimer and Theodor Adorno's iconic essay "The Culture Industry: Enlightenment as Mass Deception" (1944).[81]

But although Nakano's poem reminds us of these better-known critiques of modern mass media and the poetics of politics, it also elaborates their premises in literary terms with its own prosaic preoccupations. Theorists' critiques help us to see that the poem begins and ends with a unidirectional articulation of political poetics that neatly packages information for the properly interpolated reader's easy consumption, but the appearance of the speculative copula *darō* (translated above as "I wonder" and "I bet") six times in the six middle lines signals the disruptive appearance of a skeptical readerly imagination not so easily "interpolated" at all. In Nakano's poem, *darō* is a social index that indicates a first-person reader who filters the seemingly transparent declaratives of newspaper poetics through the prosaics of the speculative tense, reacting against the regime of linear "interpolation," and gumming up the mechanical reproduction of the ever-same language articulating the ever-new events of the day. In the process, the stable text-as-object (newspaper) becomes an occasion for an interactive dialogue that moves in two directions: the text of the newspaper speaks to the reader, and the reader speaks back.

The indexical relevance of *darō* is further in evidence in considering that its appearance coincides in the middle six lines of the poem with the disappearance of the stable nouns that characterize the first and last three lines ("man," "picture," "newspaper," "wife" "daughter," "police," "officials"). They get washed out by a skeptical imagination that dissolves these nominal declaratives into probing speculations: "What does he have it *in mind to do*" (*nani o suru ki de kare wa iru darō*); "He *probably* has it *in mind* to tell some lies" (*osoraku uso o tsuku ki de iru darō*). By replacing the solid nouns that appear in the first and last three lines of the poem with the more liquid grammar of guile (気; *ki*), the middle six lines render the smooth language of corporate journalism sticky with the residue of interruptive speculation. With this, a double-voiced narrative coalesces that balances political poetics and readerly prosaics in ways that unravel the monologic genre forms of newsprint. As a result, the otherwise automatic mechanisms of readerly interpolation break down, and the prosaic imagination begins to remap the semiotic terrain of politics itself outside the strictures of contrived newspaper poetics.

In this light, we begin to see how Nakano understood the act of reading to inform the act of resistance. He developed this perspective in the poem "Shinbun o tsukuru hitobito ni" (To the People Who Make the Newspapers, 1927):

To the People Who Make the Newspapers

All of you, journalists
All of you, who make the newspapers
All of you, who write articles with your own hands
Who assemble them
Who print them
Who deliver them
All of you
Who stuff people's eyes with spectacular incidents and bloody ones, too
Who sear and scorch people's hearts
With shame and anger and all things insufferable
All of you who make the newspapers
We are waiting[82]

Whereas "The Picture of the Newly Appointed Ambassador Arriving in Tokyo" staged an internal monologue in the mind of a reader encountering the repetitive, declarative style of newspaper language, the portion of the poem above takes the form of an indictment in which the reader directs language back "to the people who make the newspapers" (*shinbun o tsukuru hitobito ni*). The orderly syntax of the first seven lines narrates production roles separated by the divisions of labor, and the mechanical repetition of *hitotachi* (signifying all of those "who . . .") identifies adversaries eight times, building tension through the staccato sounds of three hard consonants—*to*, *ta*, and *chi*. These rhythmic repetitions of sound evoke the mechanical labor of the printing press itself, and syncopate Nakano's narration of the process by which its machinery alienates the prosaic language of the present into the composited form of journalistic poetics. Reading to the beat, we realize that the poem guides our attention through a kind of supply chain that produces poetic artificiality: journalists first package a lived event into an article "with [their] own hands," after which several articles are "assembled" on the page, printed, and delivered in the ready-made form of the newspaper. At every stage, the actuality of lived experience is abstracted into artificiality through a process of centripetal consolidation culminating in the commodity form of the newspaper itself.

In this regard, Nakano's prosaic verse anticipates Tosaka's argument that although corporate journalism purports to transparently transcribe the lived experience of contemporary history, what it in fact offers is a specious realism that promises mimetic fidelity, but more often functions through a regime of representation that (re)produces a constrained jargon that is ironically incapable of the most meaningful indexicality. With that said, though, "To the People Who Make the Newspapers," like "The Picture of the Newly Appointed Ambassador Arriving in Tokyo," also suggested that the prosaic literary imagination could devise what Horkheimer and Adorno called the "machinery of rejoinder" in the age of mass media. After all, the speaker of "The Picture of the Newly Appointed Ambassador Arriving in Tokyo" resists the abstraction of language by transforming newspaper declaratives into subjective speculative forms (*darō*), and the speaker of "To the People Who Make the Newspapers" writes back against the assault of journalistic language, returning fire, so to speak. The first several lines of "To the People Who Make the Newspapers" unmask how journalism extracts novelty and spectacle from daily life, packaging and delivering them to a docile reader-receiver, but Nakano's speaker then confronts the anonymous producers of newspapers in rapid-fire statements that expose the artifice of journalistic language itself. Nakano's subject speaks in a militant, confrontational voice that dialogizes what is conventionally a unidirectional flow of communication, devising a "machinery of rejoinder" with the simple statement "We are waiting" (*matteiru no da oretachi wa*).

The next section of "To the People Who Make the Newspapers" makes clear that the language Nakano's subject is "waiting" for is a prosaic language organic to everyday life:

We are waiting
For accurate reports and for reports without fabrications
Without deference to anyone
Without fear of anything
For reports of reality just as it is
For the first such report
For the raw report whose warmth we will feel in the palm of our hand
We will be the first to recognize it
For the report that spurs us into action right away
It will be you who hand it to us
For a report that will make us grateful to all of you
O, people who make the newspapers
All of you[83]

In contrast to the abstraction of daily life that frustrated Nakano's newspaper-reading subject in other poems, a prosaic journalism of the present is described above in terms of a "raw report," or *nama no hōdō.* The modifier *nama* denotes something unadulterated and unabstracted, and these qualities contrast with the centripetal movement away from lived experience that the roll-call indictment at the beginning of the poem narrated. Nakano's notion of *nama* language came through more explicitly in his reading of Akutagawa's writings on the anonymous ancient folktales (*setsuwa*) found in the twelfth-century collection *Konjaku monogatarishū* (Collection of Tales from Times Now Past). He observed that Akutagawa had described these tales in terms of a "beautiful rawness" (*utsukushii namanamashisa*) and argued that this "rawness" (*namanamashisa*)—whether truly "beautiful" or not—was their "artistic lifeblood" (*geijutsuteki seimei*). Nakano excerpted writings in which Akutagawa associated this rawness with a sense of "brutality" (*yasei*) and what he claimed had appeared in its time to have been a savage element (*yaban*) far removed from refined courtly notions of elegant beauty (*yūbi*).[84] But with that said, Nakano also countered that Akutagawa had never noticed how his own thinking set up a false binary that opposed the rawness of the folktales to the aesthetics of art, and suggested that for this reason, Akutagawa had overlooked how *Konjaku* could in fact be read as part of what Nakano called the "necessary path of development of beauty itself" (*bi no hitsuzenteki na hatten no michi*), rather than its radical other.[85] This helps us to see that in the context of Nakano's poem excerpted above, *nama* is a marked term coding a desire to undo the abstractions that resulted not only from the commodity form of the newspaper, but from aristocratic notions of elegance and modern practices of belletrism, too. In contrast, the spontaneity of *nama* language afforded an intuitive bond between art and life—a "warmth we will feel in the palms of our hands"—forged through everyday language "just as it is" (*sono mama*).

In a later essay, "Nechi nechi shita susumikata no hitsuyō" (The Necessity of Proceeding in a Sticky Way, 1939), Nakano described this sort of language rooted in the cacophony of daily life as "sticky" (*nechi nechi*) because it clung to the social and historical indices of its moment of contextualized usage. He explained that this sticky indexicality distinguished everyday language from the clean, "ready-made language" (*dekiai no kotoba*) of nationalist slogans. But by the 1930s, Nakano feared that the language landscape was fast being cleansed of its social "stickiness" by the regime of wartime censorship, which polished the language of print media in particular to a metallic shine. The scholar of comparative literature and censorship in modern Japan Jonathan Abel has pointed out that for Nakano, this sort of censorship left its mark in the "compensatory overuse of circumlocutory writing (metaphor, innuendo, euphemism, and redaction)" that it coerced.[86] Abel noted that Nakano referred to this coerced language as "the language of slaves" (*dorei no kotoba*), signaling that he believed that the imprisonment of language under the regime of censorship yoked the micropolitics of the printed word to authoritarian control.[87] In this context, language did the work of the authorities for them, and this is why Nakano believed that the only real referent indexed by clean journalistic language washed of its social "stickiness" was the authoritarian poetics of the police.

Against the backdrop of these expository writings, we begin to see that the *nama no hōdō*, or "raw report," to which Nakano's poetry alluded was an indication of his yearning for a revolutionary rupture in the "ready-made language" of "slaves." A vision of that raw language appeared in Nakano's 1927 poem "Kisha: San" (Train: Part Three). Although "Kisha: San" was originally published as part of a trilogy, part three stands on its own as the prototype of a new language rooted in the actual social intercourse of daily life. In the first stanza, factory girls return home from the city to rural Toyama for the New Year's holiday:

> Sayonara sayonara sayonara sayonara
> Sayōnara sayōnara sayōnara sayōnara
> We witnessed it
> A hundred factory girls off boarding
> And a thousand more continuing on[88]

The repetition of *sayonara* and *sayōnara* suggests how the poem establishes a communicative frame rooted in the social transactions of daily life.[89] The elongated vowel that distinguishes *sayōnara* from *sayonara* denotes a difference in intonation that indexes the spontaneity of "raw" (*nama*) discourse in a living language. The implications of this indexing come through in remembering that at around the time that Nakano wrote this poem, his Soviet contemporary Volosinov observed that different intonations suggest how the same verbal form "may, of course, be pronounced in an enormous variety of intonations in keeping with the wide diversity of situations and moods that occur in life."[90] And insofar as Nakano's elongated vowel rendered the acoustic element of these verbal forms, it indicated how the meaning of speech is an "*effect of interaction between speaker and listener produced via the material of a particular sound complex*," as Volosinov put it.[91]

The last portion of "Train: Part Three" suggested that the poem as a whole might be read as a meditation on the social origins of the simple utterances *sayonara* and *sayōnara*:

> Sayonara sayonara sayonara sayonara
> Sayōnara sayōnara sayōnara sayōnara
> That was Etchū
> Atop the windswept dirt platform of that tiny train station
> The girls, their parents, and siblings comforted each other
> The parting words of those getting off and those riding on
> Of the girls who would be bought next time by different factories
> Of the spinning mill factory girls who would likely never meet again
> The chorus of their thousand voices
> Danced upward in the sky of ever falling snow[92]

The "chorus of [the factory girls'] thousand voices" produces in the poem only the words *sayonara* and *sayōnara*. But the final section of "Kisha: San" suggests that *sayonara* and *sayōnara* are more than words; they are also metonyms for a language saturated with the inscriptions of everydayness (*nichijōsei*). "Kisha: San" dilates on the material and social circumstances of the factory girls' utterances, indicating that the value of *sayonara* and *sayōnara* circulates within the unique confluence of sociohistorical forces out of which these words appear. In this regard, *sayonara* and *sayōnara* heuristically evoke the possibility of a raw prosaic language, one that figures meaning as the product of the dialogical intercourse between recyclable verbal structures and the shared social circumstances of the communicative event. These ideas are given their fullest literary expression in the last lines of "Kisha: San": as the words of "the chorus of their thousand voices / danced upward in the sky of ever falling snow," the poem closes with the image of the utterance emanating from the social ground.

Faux Amis

In 1929, Volosinov wrote in *Marxism and the Philosophy of Language* that "*without signs there is no ideology.*"[93] Adorno would later elaborate the link between signs and ideology when he reflected on the aura of phenomenological philosophy in *The Jargon of Authenticity*, concluding that "this language molds thought." From their perspective, ideas do not simply give rise to language that expresses thought; rather, ideological consciousness itself is produced by a normative semiotic force, as Volosinov explained:

> Consciousness takes shape and being in the material of signs created by an organized group in the process of its social intercourse. The individual consciousness is nurtured on signs; it derives its growth from them; it reflects their logic and laws. The logic of consciousness is the logic of ideological communication, of the semiotic interaction of a social group. If we deprive consciousness of its semiotic, ideological content, it would have absolutely nothing left. Consciousness can harbor only in the image, the word, the meaningful gesture, and so forth.[94]

Drawing on Volosinov's perspective, it might be said that the proletarian arts movements with which Nakano identified when he wrote the poems above aimed to recalibrate how the popular consciousness "harbored" in "the image, the word, the meaningful gesture" by rewriting the semiotics of the language landscape in a more prosaic idiom.

But in the early 1930s, the proletarian arts movements that had framed the appearance of Nakano's poetry were largely destroyed by escalating enforcement of the Peace Preservation Law (1925), which allowed for the arrest and imprisonment of suspected communists, socialists, proletarian activists, and others deemed a threat to the state. The police crackdown on the Left led to the death of the famed proletarian novelist Kobayashi Takiji, who was killed by Tokyo police while incarcerated in 1933. It also coerced leaders of the Japanese Communist Party Sano Manabu and Nabeyama Sadachika to change course in the same year, renouncing their party affiliations under the duress of incarceration. These high-profile incidents were the more visible expressions of an expansive suppression that led the number of arrests of suspected leftists to balloon (by one estimate) from 6,124 in 1930 and 10,422 in 1931 to approximately 18,000 in 1933.[95] Nakano himself counted among these arrests: he was imprisoned on account of his Communist connections in 1932, and during his stint behind bars, illness, malnutrition, and police abuse combined to imperil his life. He was freed in 1934, but only after he joined the thousands of other leftists who won release from prison by officially renouncing any Communist Party ties and antiestablishment politics through a process of so-called ideological conversion (*tenkō*).

These were the pressures leftists faced at around the time *The People's Library* coterie championed "the spirit of prose" as their rallying cry of resistance. Torrance has pointed out that this group gathered in the mid-1930s as a kind of patchwork resistance formed from what one among its number called the "leftist survivors" fortunate enough to have escaped the purges of the early 1930s with their lives.[96] According to Torrance, "almost all of the fifty or so contributors were leftists who had been arrested for their political activities."[97] Their journal officially aligned with the International Popular Front against Fascism in 1936, but it did not survive for long. In January 1938 *The People's Library* was outlawed, ending its two-year run as a prominent venue of literary resistance. In the same month, Tosaka and Nakano were both banned from writing, again under the expansive provisions of the Peace Preservation Law. Essays on "the spirit of prose" still continued to appear: Hirotsu Kazuo's "Sanbun geijutsu shomondai" (Various Problems of the Prosaic Arts, 1939) and Aono Suekichi's "Sanbun seishin" (The Spirit of Prose, 1940) joined other essays and published "dialogues" (*taidan*) that discussed "the spirit of prose" in the years after authorities shut down *The People's Library*. But overwhelmingly, the bans issued in January 1938 signaled a dramatic rise in hostilities directed at the Left that moved the wartime "spirit of prose" resistance—already a compromised reconfiguration of agitators from earlier proletarian arts movements going back to the 1920s—into its last throes. The fate of the journal was typical of a much more extensive suppression that impacted almost every leftist of the era. Tosaka would die in prison in 1945 without ever having published another word, and although Nakano would be allowed to publish again after two years, in 1940, he did so facing ever-greater scrutiny from the censors, and the looming threat of another perilous imprisonment.

It was in this context that Nakano wrote extensively about two right-leaning writers who had risen to prominence in the late Meiji years: Mori Ōgai (1862–1922) and Saitō Mokichi (1882–1953). Nakano's writings on these figures stand out because Ōgai and Mokichi aligned with institutional authorities who were obviously opposed to the revolutionary politics that Nakano himself advocated, and at whose hands he had himself suffered as a political prisoner. Ōgai was a military man, physician, novelist, and biographer; Mokichi was a noted poet who is remembered (among other things) for his nationalistic war poetry. In the 1940s, Nakano began work on what would become book-length volumes of essays on each writer—*Saitō Mokichi nōto* (Notes on Saitō Mokichi, 1940–1941) and *Ōgai: Sono sokumen* (Ōgai: A Profile, 1940–1952). To be sure, these texts do not seem to bear any obvious resemblance to the "spirit of prose" persuasion. By the time Nakano began writing them in the early 1940s, after all, *The People's Library* was already a thing of the past, and the premise of a leftist literary resistance that it had embraced had largely been stamped out. But my interest in these and others of Nakano's critical writings has to do not only with the content of their claims, but also with their form, and specifically, with the fact that they materialized in the realm of criticism—a realm in between those of theory and practice outlined above.

Chronologically removed from the earlier days of proletarian activism in the late 1920s and the reconstituted struggle of the "spirit of prose" resistance in the mid-1930s, moreover, Nakano's criticism of the 1940s and 1950s offers a glimpse of one transwar trajectory traveled by the prosaic imagination from the late stages of the Pacific War that ultimately ended the Japanese empire in 1945 to the early years of the midcentury era to which I turn in the next portion of this study. As I make this transition, the light shed by the in-between register of Nakano's criticism helps us to see a set of in-between relationships by which the prosaic imagination in transwar Japan engaged with what might be called its *faux amis*, or "false friends," in Japanese literary and cultural history. By this I mean that in the context of the networked affiliations of the prosaic imagination examined here, Nakano's expository criticism constitutes a revealing interpretive vector extending in the direction of representational possibilities that at first seem to imply something akin to the prosaic premise, but that on closer inspection are revealed to proceed along different—and even contradictory—lines. Reading between literature and history, his most important conclusion as a critic would be that although the arrival of Occupation-era liberalism after 1945 promised a new age of democracy and freedom, it ironically produced a poetics of its own that Nakano would have counted among the *faux amis* of the prosaic imagination. In making this critique, Nakano becomes a reader himself akin to the newspaper-reading subject that his own poetry had dramatized years earlier: a reader holding onto everyday usages against the conditions of possibility for their poetic obliteration.

One way to glimpse the literary imagination alive in Nakano's critique of postwar poetics is to first turn to his criticism of the great Meiji writer Mori Ōgai. Although Ōgai would seem to have little to do with the politics of postwar Japan, Nakano's approach to his writings reveals how a subtly attuned reader could meticulously work through the style of seemingly prosaic language to expose its *faux amis* in the form of an authoritarian poetics hidden beneath the surface. This would be the same critical inclination that would guide Nakano's Occupation-era critique of the early postwar literary imagination and language. But given that the first essays in *Ōgai* were composed in the early 1940s, under the wartime regime, it might seem that his interest in Ōgai marked a conciliatory move from a leftist who, fearful of another imprisonment and operating under the yoke of an extensive censoring regime, accommodated his adversaries by turning to a "safe" subject friendly to establishment authority. While this may be part of the story, it does not fully explain Nakano's extensive writings on Ōgai, if only for the simple reason that Nakano continued to write about (and praise) Ōgai even long after the war. In 1957, for example, Nakano concluded the preface to a volume he edited, *Mori Ōgai kenkyū* (Studies of Mori Ōgai), by writing that when he read Ōgai, and when he learned about Ōgai's life, the feeling conveyed was a feeling of intense ascetic devotion, adding that it gave him the chills.[98] This reminds us that although Nakano would at other times disparage Ōgai, there were moments of readerly sympathy, too. The attraction might have been due to the fact that some of Ōgai's texts revealed literary techniques that affectingly rendered a sense of factuality and actuality with the bare minimum of aesthetic embellishment. As a novelist, after all, Ōgai was not a romantic known for his poetic flights into atmospheric fancy, but more the opposite: an austere writer whose career trajectory tended away from aesthetic artifice and toward the lure of unvarnished historical fact. In this sense, Ōgai was another writer who sensed the limits of the literary.

Late in his career, in the 1910s, Ōgai largely abandoned the artistic façade of literary fiction (*shōsetsu*) in favor of meticulously researched historical-biographical writings (*shiden*) that related the minute details of Tokugawa-period physician-scholars' lives. The best known of these is *Shibue Chūsai* (1916).[99] The scholar of Japanese literature Marvin Marcus has described this project as an adventure in "the literature of fact," observing that "if one were to elect the most salient characteristic of Ōgai's *shiden*, it would be the narration of historical fact—*shijitsu*. Ōgai positively embraced the factual."[100] The premise of actuality at the heart of these historical writings comes through in recalling that Ōgai himself explained aspects of his method in the expository piece "Rekishi sono mama to rekishi banare" (History As It Is and History Abandoned, 1915), writing: "In studying historical records [*shiryō*], I came to revere the reality [*shizen*] that was evidenced in them. Any wanton change seemed distasteful to me. This is one of my motives."[101] Read alongside Nakano's own writings, Ōgai's desire to represent historical "reality" (*shizen*) "just as it is" (*sono mama*) by presenting the language and voices of authentic historical records (*shiryō*) without "any wanton change" recalls the austere beauty of *nama* (raw) language which also attracted Nakano's attention.

We glean a deeper sense of the *nama* element of actuality central to Ōgai's "literature of fact" in remembering that Marcus has suggested that the "earliest precursor" to the author's turn to historical biography (*shiden*) might have been the minor work "Hatori Chihiro" (1912), a short text that Nakano admired.[102] In this piece, Ōgai briefly introduces a letter he received from an aspiring medical student, Hatori, who had written to Ōgai in the hopes of studying medicine with him. The bulk of the text, though, is given to Ōgai's transcription of the young student's epistle itself, which is offered to the reader "just as it is" (*sono mama*), without any apparent adulteration. Part of the force of the letter is accounted for by the fact that Ōgai's expository preface reveals that Hatori died of illness at the age of twenty-four, before completing his studies. "Much taken with this fine young man whose life was tragically cut short," Marcus summed up, "the author [Ōgai] lent his own imprimatur to the memorialization of an obscure but exemplary life."[103] In this sense, it might be said that Hatori was a "paragon of the ordinary," to borrow Marcus's turn of phrase.

In the late 1950s, Nakano remarked on the way "Hatori Chihiro" mixed the narrative voice of the author (Ōgai) with the extraliterary voice of someone else (Hatori), giving form to a double-voiced text irreducible to any single subject.[104] His reading of Ōgai's language revealed that its effect had to do not only with the material it described—its content—but with how the author combined literary sensibilities and extraliterary material to articulate the pathos of death in simple words. For example, when Ōgai wrote "Hatori Chihiro is a real person [*jitsuzon no jinbutsu de aru*]. But strangely, I must now say that he was a real person [*ima de wa jitsuzon no jinbutsu de atta to iwanakute wa naranai*]," Nakano pointed out that Hatori's death is reported without the word for "death" itself ever being used.[105] He described Ōgai's resolute prose style (*bunshō*) in terms of an "austere beauty" (*kibishii utsukushisa*).[106] This element of Ōgai's style seems to have gripped Nakano in particular, and he suggested that to bring it out, readers should move over the text gently, noticing how the small details of its verbs and nouns amalgamate into a prose grammar.[107] Nakano strikes an appreciative tone here, revealing how he savored the grammatical structures of Ōgai's meticulous writing by embracing the precision of language shorn of all excess. But he also observed that trapped within its own formal containment, Ōgai's style was so precise that it led to nowhere other than its own completion. "With all this said, though, it is better not to try and imitate this prose style [*bunshō*]," Nakano wrote. "Ōgai brought his style to its full achievement, but there is nowhere to go from there. It is perfect [*kanpeki*], but at the same time, it culminates in its own dead end [*ikidomari*]."[108] Nakano implied that as Ōgai's prose articulated its own formal apex, it became "perfect" in both the stylistic sense of unsurpassed and in the grammatical sense of fully completed. This would not have been a good thing by prosaic standards, according to which only an authoritarian poetics could ever achieve its own perfection.

This helps us to see why Nakano's reading of Ōgai mixed reverence and rejection. On the one hand, he recognized that Ōgai's influence on Japanese literary modernity had been incalculable, and that the prose of unvarnished writings like "Hatori Chihiro" could move readers with their austere aesthetic of ordinary actuality. But on the other hand, Nakano also sensed that the trail blazed by Ōgai could only lead to the writings Ōgai himself had already composed, particularly in the biographical and historical writings (*shiden*) of his later career. There was no lineage, and there were no epigones, for Ōgai's style culminated in its own completion—or, as Nakano had it, in its own "dead end."[109] In this sense, Ōgai's style would have lacked what Morson and Emerson, in their study of Bakhtin, elucidated under the term "unfinalizeability," or the quality of prosaics by which it becomes an inexhaustible process of everyday language that is never able to complete itself.[110] This may well have been why Nakano argued in 1950 that Ōgai's writing in fact contradicted the basic premises of the "spirit of prose" (*sanbun seishin*) movement that Hirotsu Kazuo and others articulated:

> If we look back on the work of Ōgai, we notice that the Japanese language [*Nihongo*] in Ōgai's literature is certainly not of the sort that would have moved our language in the direction of modernization [*kindaika*]. In particular, the biographies of his late years—although peerless and brilliant—are not modern or familiar on the level of language [*kotoba*] and the sort of feeling [*kokoromochi*] that the language conduces; indeed, they are reactionary and overwhelmingly hermetic.
>
> I believe that it is here that we can clearly recognize how the direction implied by Ōgai's literature conflicted with those that came later, such as

"prose" and "the spirit of prose" first championed by Hirotsu Kazuo, and with the direction of the modern itself and of the people more generally.[111]

Although Nakano engaged the aesthetics of Ōgai's language in his reading of "Hatori Chihiro," he never forgot that Ōgai represented a conservative establishment opposed to the revolutionary politics that leftist writers like himself agitated. Nakano discussed politics explicitly in an essay examining the places of Ōgai and Natsume Sōseki in the development of modern Japanese literature, noting their contributions while also asking if they had played their roles with a progressive implication (*shinpōteki na imi*) or with a conservative (*hoshuteki*) orientation. "Their roles moved in the conservative direction," he concluded, later adding: "In Ōgai's case, he even became a reactionary late in life."[112] Elsewhere, Nakano's critique of Ōgai's politics came out in harsher terms. In his most vitriolic condemnation, he wrote that Ōgai was the most exalted ideologue of the traditional hegemony in Japan (*Nihon no furui shihai seiryoku*), adding that for this reason, "we must recognize that Ōgai is the greatest enemy of the Japanese people and of Japanese literature."[113]

These writings on Ōgai reveal that within the in-between realm of criticism, Nakano himself became the sort of reader that his own proletarian poetry had dramatized years earlier, in the poems examined above: a reader sensitive to the undulations of language as a matter of form, and one who understood that even everyday content and seemingly simple prose could be coopted and degraded within the semiotic force fields of political mediation. Perhaps the greatest praise for this sort of readerly imagination is that it constituted a kind of "resistance" that untied the knots that had been bound up in the age of authoritarian myth-making. And "resistance" was how the Japanese philosopher Takeuchi Yoshimi read Nakano's *Notes on Saitō Mokichi*. The background of Takeuchi's comments was that Mokichi had been a noted poet who, during the war years, gave voice to visions of imperial purpose in the idiom of modern and classical Japanese poetry. In 1937, he edited a collection of *Man'yōshū* poems paired with his own exegeses (*kaisetsu*), published it under the title *Man'yō shūka* (The Best Poems of *Man'yōshū*), and distributed it in the hopes that it would edify others during the war years. In noting that this collection is said to have been carried into battle by thousands of soldiers, the scholar Amy Heinrich wrote: "Mokichi's support [of the war effort] was not merely a matter of course; it was enthusiastic: war stirred his blood. He was a patriot in the Meiji mold, and firmly believed it his duty to follow, and not to question, the Emperor and through him the nation."[114]

Nakano's *Notes on Saitō Mokichi* appeared in the early 1940s, and in the 1957 essay "Kindai chōkoku" (Overcoming Modernity), Takeuchi noted that this piece of literary criticism "is regarded as one of the primary texts of wartime resistance [*daiichi no teikōsho*]."[115] Takeuchi did not elaborate on this point in great detail, but from context, it seems that he believed that Nakano's study of Mokichi's poetry achieved the highest ideal of resistance writing not because it polemically attacked the poet-nationalist, but because it meticulously worked through the formal qualities of wartime language on their own terms. As Takeuchi put it:

> To negate war poetry because it is war poetry is to negate the people's lives. The moment of resistance emerges when one decides to change the very nature of the war by accepting war poetry as such but then criticizing both its dependence on the old notions of war and its misunderstanding of the nature of the war being fought (which is not that of imperialist war). This helps create a war poetry that is appropriate to the total war. Scribbling "Oppose the war of invasion!" on bathroom walls or popularizing such *witticisms* as "Down with British Planes/Hideki!" is not resistance but the dissolution thereof. It is dragging thought down to its most pedestrian level.[116]

Takeuchi made these comments in response to a key passage in *Notes on Saitō Mokichi* in which Nakano discussed the nature of total war and its demands on language:

> In the context of world history, Japan today possesses the greatest originality in terms of its abilities and activity. War itself has also become much more massive and complex. "Military depth" has shifted from the battlefield to international relations, the vanguard and rear are now inseparable, and fighting against enemy "plots" has become an everyday task for people at the home front.
>
> If Itō Sachio's Russo-Japanese War poetry or Saitō Mokichi's poem "My Elder Brother at the Front" [Senjō no ani] still reverberate as narratives today, then that tells us that the present war is so massive and complex as

> to be only partly visible in prose—hence, it requires a far higher poetic form and unity. Perhaps this explains the current (1941) national outpourings of war poetry. In light of the several collections on the China Incident, those on bereaved families, and the war poems of the *tanka* poets, it seems that the war is capable of summoning up the people's poetic voice on a national scale.[117]

By this reckoning, total war required total language—a poetics, in other words, that is self-completing and self-contained, rather than an unfinalizable prosaics distributed across social registers and stratified into constituent parts that never sum. That is why *Notes on Saitō Mokichi* declared that "the present war is too massive and complex to become visible piece by piece in prose [*bubunteki ni wa sanbunteki ni mieru made ni*]—hence, it requires a far higher poetic form and unity [*haruka ni takai shiteki kōsō, tōitsu*]." Takeuchi reminds us that the poetics of total war could best be described—indeed, could only be recognized as poetics in the first place—by the literary imagination of a prosaic writer like Nakano, an outsider to the world of belles lettres who nevertheless allowed himself to feel the aesthetic thrall of literary writings composed by his political adversaries, including Mokichi and Ōgai. It might be said, then, that one of the last wartime articulations of the literary resistance premised on "the spirit of prose" came in a book of literary criticism that reckoned with the politics of wartime language as a matter of form.

Occupation-Era Afterlives of the Prosaic Imagination

One of the unanticipated developments that confronted the prosaic imagination in transwar Japan was that its resistance to authoritarian discourses remained an urgent cause even after the fall of the wartime regime against which it had originally organized. In the early postwar period, Nakano breathed with the earlier ideals of a leftist language politics by continuing a fight which, for him, stretched back to the proletarian arts movements of the 1920s. But in drawing breath with the memory of that past, he also confronted new adversaries who appeared for the first time during the postwar period.

As the wartime regime fell and the era of Occupation (1945–52) dawned, the promise of democratic politics might have seemed to imply a more polyphonous public sphere, one less constrained by the authority consolidated in the state, and more open to the popular discourse of civil society. But this perceived promise of the age was broken in Nakano's view: he came to sense that the postwar pacifism of Occupation-era Japan had begun to play the role of *faux ami* by promising greater freedom of expression in the new liberal age while in fact creating its own historical poetics that coerced the forgetting of the wartime past in the name of an exalted future. Within the contextual coordinates of this study as a whole, moreover, Nakano's postwar perspective wraps up my consideration of the prosaic persuasion at the same time that it also opens up to the latter portion of my narrative, which takes up the literary dynamics of the midcentury years, and beyond. The bulk of that analysis appears in chapter 4 and the epilogue, but as I move from the politics of the war years to the postwar period that followed, I begin by observing that the momentum created by the "spirit of prose" resistance that cast its roots much earlier, in the 1920s proletarian movements, ended by engaging the language politics of Occupation-era liberalism.

Soon after the Japanese surrender to the United States in August 1945, a conflict over the question of war responsibility raged among literary writers and cultural critics in Japan. Nakano played a key role in these conversations. Beginning in 1946, he led the Shin Nihon Bungakukai (New Japanese Literary Association), a group of writers and thinkers who operated with the sanction of the Japanese Communist Party (JCP). By this time, too, he had become an elected member of the National Diet representing the JCP. In the debates surrounding the volatile question of literature and politics (*seiji to bungaku ronsō*), Nakano implicitly advocated for a prosaic interpretation of the granular politics and stratified experience of a lived past, rather than a poetic view of the war years that totalized history into a single experience.[118] Along these lines, too, Nakano argued that Occupation-era censorship in the name of liberal democracy had accelerated the poetic fantasies of postwar Japan in a new language of peace. He believed that banning earlier writings that bore the inscriptions of wartime ideology had the effect of concealing the crimes committed in the name of the defeated regime. In particular, he noted that removing offensive wartime texts from postwar circulation in fact amounted to a censorship practice that emptied out the postwar language landscape of prosaic possibilities for remembering the causes of the war itself: he believed that as inoffensive texts circulated freely in the absence of their more problematic others, a policed postwar literary field conjured a placid image of the past in ways that ironically replicated the poetic tendency of the "representational vacuum" created by the wartime authorities themselves.[119] In "Hihyō no ningensei II: Bungaku handō no mondai nado" (The Humanity of Criticism II: On the Literary Reaction, et Cetera, 1947), Nakano wrote that "reactionaries in the field of literature conspicuously rely on the very palpable spiritual weakness of our ethnic nation resulting from the war," explaining that this tendency "appears in the form of propaganda to forget the war. This is characterized by the obliteration of memory: of the causes of the war, how it was conducted, of its direct influence on individuals."[120] He elaborated that the sanitizing effect of literary forgetting "appears in the form of literature that attempts to arrest the spirit of the people in a condition of impoverishment and disruption. It emerges as a literature of ineffectual grumblings, an ahistorical fantasy of the restoration of prewar 'peace' and 'stability.'"[121]

But at bottom, Nakano sensed that the literary poetics of war forgetting were motivated by a "conservative liberalism" that ironically concealed the true origins of the war itself:

> This literature is bolstered by a theory of conservative liberalism and capitalist democracy that claims to be a sheltering of humanity. It hoists a banner of freedom from the Left and Right, freedom from capitalist and labor class, freedom from the reactionary government and reactionary common people and under that banner it asserts the freedom to destroy the concrete accomplishments of the working people [*kinmu jinmin*], the freedom to sabotage them. . . . It hails an individualism that shuns the reconstruction of the ethnic nation as the true humanism. However, a pragmatic criticism of totalitarianism or fascism could not be borne out of the opposition from this sort of individualism.
>
> Any critique of totalitarianism or fascism cannot ignore the fact that both derived from the historical trajectory of capitalism. Liberalism and individualism had long been the vanguard of "capital" in its struggle against

> "the feudal" and "the despotic." Now, they have emerged to hinder the historical process, willfully resisting the ethnic nation's democratic achievements that are inevitable to the historical unfolding of capital. Once vanguard, now rearguard: this is the historical nature of the individualism and liberalism we face today.
>
> Thus, individualism and liberalism aim, consciously or unconsciously, to liberate the organizers and abettors of the war of aggression—a necessary end product of capitalism—from substantive criticism of their totalitarianism and aggressive militarism.[122]

One of the unexpected consequences of the Occupation-era politics that Nakano describes above was that it reinvigorated the "spirit of prose" resistance that first cast its roots in the 1920s and gained steam in the 1930s.

In the postwar context, Nakano gathered together a group of his own essays from the 1930s and re-released them in a bound volume in 1947. He noted in the preface to the volume that although looking back, the war years might seem to have interrupted modern Japanese literary history, "it must never be forgotten that in history, and for those who were there, there was no such thing as an interruption, for an absolute blank space would have been absolutely impossible."[123] He offered the re-release of his own wartime writings as a testament to the specificity of his own ideas within that earlier time. Hirotsu Kazuo, an early articulator of what would become known as the "spirit of prose" ideal, was another writer who cautioned against the common assumption that just because the wartime regime had fallen, the politics of prose no longer mattered. In 1948, he joined Nakano in re-releasing some of his own wartime writings in protest of Occupation-era forgetting. In a brief essay appended to these earlier essays on "the spirit of prose," Hirotsu wrote that he felt that the "spirit of prose" that he had earlier described during the war years—"a time when the advances of fascism [*fassho*] were intensifying right before our very eyes"—had become only all the more important in the midst of what he called the "present postwar confusion" (*ima no sengo no konran*): "For this reason," he wrote, "I believe that the reprinting of these essays [on 'the spirit of prose'] matters today."[124] Hirotsu's statement suggests a sad irony for the "spirit of prose" writers: although they had waged what Torrance called the best-organized and most articulate literary resistance against fascist politics in the 1930s, the fall of the wartime regime in 1945 did not eliminate the tensions out of which their resistance had earlier emerged, but only layered the politics of prose that they had earlier championed with renewed urgency.

The stakes of the "spirit of prose" in Occupation-era Japan come to the fore only more clearly in considering that Tosaka's lucid wartime critique of language, culture, and ideology became one notable casualty of the influx of liberal pacifism after 1945. The editors of *Tosaka Jun: A Critical Reader* (2013) have noted that "in the case of the immediate postwar world Tosaka's critique was marginalized, indeed completely ignored, by the nation-bound thinking on both left and right."[125] Harootunian has also remarked on Tosaka's postwar obscurity, attributing it in part to the fact that he had located fascism and liberalism in cooperative, mutually accelerating relation to one another, which flew in the face of the liberal democratic interests of the American Occupation and the Pax Americana temper of the times. According to this perspective, Tosaka's wartime critique was dismissed or ignored in favor of a perspective insisting that Japan's "dark valley" during the war years had been preceded by eras of more responsible Meiji liberalism and enlightened Taisho democracy, more wholesome persuasions to which a rehabilitated postwar Japan could return. Harootunian has written that in this context, Tosaka's wartime perspective on the liberalism-fascism link in the 1930s had to be obscured by postwar analysts who explained away the wartime ideology as an anomalous element of Japan's national history. In making this claim, Harootunian has observed that

> it is possible to say that the absence of [Tosaka's] critique in [postwar] discussions attests to a powerful forgetfulness among survivors of those years and, perhaps, a loss around which they were able to organize their own discourse. Above all else, recognition of the ground he had already covered would have made the postwar debate appear not so much as the completion of unfinished business (which his discourse had already completed) but risk looking like a repetition of precisely the liberal common sense that offered a space for fascism to gather.[126]

However paradoxically, though, the connections between Tosaka and Nakano might have become clearest in this Occupation-era force field of forgetting. The literary critic Lin Shukumi has claimed that the Occupation-era resistance that Nakano waged in "The Humanity of Criticism" implicitly continued Tosaka's earlier "fight against 'literary liberalism'" (*'bungakuteki jiyūshugi' to no tatakai*) after Tosaka's death. Lin alluded to writings in which Tosaka had used the phrase "literary liberalism" in the 1930s to indicate how the liberal ideals of freedom and progress had articulated themselves in a poetic language that overwrote the actual politics of everyday experience. Drawing on these texts, Lin has contended that in "The Humanity of Criticism," Nakano continued Tosaka's fight against liberal poetics into the postwar years by demanding a prosaic reckoning with war memory and responsibility.[127] In this sense, the Occupation years supplied a kind of coda to the leftist literary affiliations that I have analyzed here, one that conveyed the resonances of Tosaka's earlier critique into a new idiom that he himself did not live to see. In examining the resonances between these two figures, Lin wrote of her own method that it positioned Nakano and Tosaka as if they were two mirrors facing each other (*awase kagami*), such that the intellectual historical implications of Nakano's writings are reflected in Tosaka's texts, just as the literary implications of Tosaka's writings are reflected in Nakano's writing.[128]

More broadly, Lin reminds us that the implications of Nakano's and Tosaka's writings were not contained by the wartime crises to which the "spirit of prose" resistance originally responded. With this in mind, chapter 4 aims to show how aspects of their critique of liberal thought and literary form in fact came to reverberate with an unlikely case study from midcentury America: Edwin McClellan's 1957 translation of Natsume Sōseki's classic novel *Kokoro* (1914).

CHAPTER 4

The Fiction of the Free Market

Natsume Sōseki's *Kokoro* and the Neoliberal Imagination in Midcentury America

When words lose their meaning people will lose their liberty.
—Confucius (as quoted in modified translation by Friedrich Hayek in a chapter of *The Fatal Conceit: The Errors of Socialism* (1988) titled "Our Poisoned Language")[1]

Insofar as the crises of wartime Japan fueled the connections between literature and thought examined in the previous chapters, the collapse of the Japanese empire in 1945 might seem to indicate an inarguable endpoint separating their world from ours today. While acknowledging that in some ways, of course, it does, this chapter sets out to complicate the sense of an ending in 1945 by taking up another intellectual formation that first gathered in the war years, during the same time of crisis that the previous chapters examined. The difference is that its course would unfold primarily in the postwar period, over a *longue durée* spanning the decades after the wartime regimes in Italy, Germany, and Japan had fallen. It was controversial even among its own advocates, and always difficult to define precisely. Its development was riven with discontinuities, self-contradictions, and ironies, all of which have complicated the study of its origins and orientation. Some have denied its existence entirely, while others have argued that it is the governing logic of our global age today.[2] Wading into these waters, I begin by observing that for a time early on in its intellectual history, it occasionally referred to itself by the name of "neoliberalism."

This chapter continues my analysis of literature and thought in confluence and conflict by examining the conditions of possibility during the midcentury years that allowed a Japanese novel to pass through the prism of the nascent neoliberal imagination. As I move the narrative developed in the wartime contexts of the earlier chapters into the midcentury idiom examined here, I aim to bridge the "prewar" / "postwar" divide by observing that the movement to rehabilitate market-oriented thinking and right-leaning liberal sentiments that is sometimes referred to under the label of "neoliberalism" was one of the most influential responses to the crisis of modernity that reached fever pitch during the war years. Among a great many other things, midcentury neoliberalism originally organized around what its advocates understood to be an antifascist persuasion, one that posited the origins of civilized freedom in the self-directed but rule-bound marketplace competition among entrepreneurial individuals, and that understood economic notions of liberty to be an alternative to the wartime impulse to forge solidarity between the state and "the people" through mythologies of blood and soil. This becomes clearer in remembering that in the transatlantic context, the term "neoliberalism" itself seems to have come into at least limited currency at the Colloque Walter Lippmann, a 1938 Paris gathering of intellectuals who met to discuss the threats to liberty that were then engulfing wartime Europe. Fifteen of the figures who met in Paris in 1938 would later reconvene in 1947 to resume discussion on the future of liberalism in the age following the demise of the older laissez-faire ideal in the time of the Great Depression and the rise of collectivisms in Nazi Germany, fascist Italy, and Stalinist Soviet Union.[3] Led by the Austrian economist Friedrich Hayek, their circle would become known as the Mont Pèlerin Society, and it has been identified by economic historians as the most important incubator of neoliberal thought in the midcentury years.[4]

All of this is well known from several recent studies. But since these studies have tended to narrate the intellectual history of "neoliberalism" in terms of figures and formations located in the transatlantic world, they seem to tell a story with no concrete connection to the history of literature and thought in modern Japan that is at the heart of this study. My point of departure, though, is that a Japanese novel did in fact intersect with the development of neoliberal thought in the midcentury years, and in ways, I will argue, that open up aesthetic possibilities for interpreting what is otherwise an expository discourse. To show how, this chapter reads the dynamics of the midcentury neoliberal persuasion through an unlikely but revealing case study: Edwin McClellan's 1957 English-language translation of Natsume Sōseki's 1914 novel *Kokoro*. McClellan was born in Japan to a Japanese mother and a Scottish father, and he counted English and Japanese as native languages. His *Kokoro* translation is a masterpiece that has long been celebrated in the field of "Japan studies," but it was originally conceived and received in a different context: on the Committee on Social Thought at the University of Chicago, where it served as a companion to the dissertation about Sōseki that McClellan completed under the tutelage of Hayek, the Austrian economist whose influence has been cited at the origins of "neoliberalism."[5] By reconnecting the translation to its original context of reception, this chapter brings together economic and aesthetic forms of imagination in the midcentury years to tell the unlikely story of how a Japanese novel conspired with the neoliberal imagination in its moment of becoming.

Within the scope of this study as a whole, moreover, this chapter transitions my narrative away from the wartime context in Japan that I examined in the earlier chapters, and toward global trends that emerged during the midcentury years. I will argue that reading the translation of *Kokoro* in midcentury America opens up a unique perspective not only on the foreign reception of Japanese literature, but also on the rehabilitation of liberal sentiments that figured prominently in the rise of the economic during the postwar decades more generally. In the years after *Kokoro* was warmly received in the liberal imagination of 1950s Chicago, postwar Japan would be hailed as one of the most outstanding examples of a liberal democracy and capitalist economy to have ever developed outside the transatlantic world. To be sure, Japan's postwar economic miracle has usually been explained with reference to the leadership roles of planners and bureaucrats, not neoliberals.[6] Rather than Hayek, it was John Maynard Keynes whose ideas figured prominently, leading the historian Scott O'Bryan to observe that "many, in fact, came to call the period from the end of the [1940s] into the early part of the 1950s the 'Golden Age' of Keynesian research in Japan."[7] But over the longer run, the ideas often associated with Hayek and his circle would become a global sensation. The historian of economic thought Angus Burgin has observed in his study of North Atlantic trends that "advocacy of free markets entered a period of reconsideration and retrenchment during the Great Depression, but it by no means arrived at an 'end.' Instead, the story of the half century after the onset of economic crisis is in part one of its triumphant return."[8] Burgin noted that by the 1980s, in fact, "Keynesianism, rather than laissez-faire, had come to seem a relic of a rapidly receding economic world."[9]

Within this global context, we notice that Hayek himself read *Kokoro* near the beginning of what would become a years-long interest in Japan. In 1971, in fact, he wrote in correspondence to McClellan that he envied McClellan's "forthcoming visit to Japan—the four visits we paid to that country during the last seven years were immensely enjoyable."[10] Hayek's itineraries in Japan included meetings with government officials, business leaders, and academics. Correspondence suggests that some of Hayek's interlocutors in Japan were drawn to his liberal message because they believed that it would provide a bulwark against the rise of leftist sentiments that were then fueling waves of student protest and citizen activism around the time of the contentious US-Japan Mutual Security Treaty (*Anpo*) in 1960.[11] In addition, the recent experience and possible return of Japan's own wartime militarism signaled a threat from the Right for some of Hayek's Japanese counterparts, who hoped that a postwar culture of liberal enterprise and private freedom would counter what they viewed as a Japanese tendency toward totalitarianism.[12] These threads came together in a letter Hayek received from Tanaka Seigen, who wrote in 1963 saying that he would dedicate his life to fighting against communism and fascism, and for the cause of neoliberalism and the Mont Pèlerin Society.[13]

Building on these connections, the task of this chapter is to link Hayek's vision of liberal rehabilitation in the global context of the midcentury years to the aesthetic experience afforded by McClellan's 1957 translation of *Kokoro*. Interpretive hurdles immediately appear, however, the first of which is that while the archive remembers the facts of Hayek's visits to Japan described above, the literary connections bonding McClellan, *Kokoro*, and neoliberal thought have today been mostly forgotten. This suggests that the subjects of this chapter represent another confluence of literature and thought that once wove itself together within the contingencies of its own perishable present, only to subsequently unravel to the point that its constituent threads might now seem to have had little to do with one another all along. For one thing, McClellan largely left the realm of political thought behind as he went on to become an influential figure in the then-emerging field of "Japan studies" during his career as a scholar of literature at the University of Chicago and Yale University. His translation has long been required reading for students of Japan in the Anglophone academy, but in many Japan studies contexts, it has been read in relation to narratives of Japanese history and culture. This tells us that the sign of national culture has sometimes overwritten the more cosmopolitan conjuncture of intellectual history within which the translation was originally produced. And even as a matter of intellectual history, that conjuncture is harder to see today because McClellan's two graduate advisers—the prominent conservative Russell Kirk (1918–1994) and the neoliberal economist Hayek—had a noted falling out that makes it seem unlikely that a student of one would go on to work with the other, or that there was ever a common thread linking all three of them to each other—much less to Sōseki—at all.

But this chapter remembers that McClellan actually completed the *Kokoro* translation as a labor of love in a "previous life," so to speak, while he was still one of Hayek's graduate student advisees on the Committee on Social Thought at Chicago. He prepared the translation as a companion to his dissertation on Sōseki, but the starting point for my analysis is that at that time, he was more of an insider to a segment of the academy studying the intellectual history of liberalism than he was to the academic field of Japan studies we know today—which, after all, did not even exist when he translated *Kokoro*. The distance separating the translation from Japan studies is indicated by the fact that Hayek himself described McClellan in a 1956 letter of recommendation as a kind of political scientist: "He is of half Scottish and half Japanese descent and after getting his first degree at St. Andrews (Scotland) is now a permanent resident of this country. He is an unusually cultivated man of wide interests and is now employing his good background in economic and political science for a study of certain very important intellectual trends in Japan—an aspect of the influence of Western ideas on the political developments in that country."[14]

The context of McClellan's collaboration with Hayek came through even more clearly in a letter Hayek wrote to R. C. Cornuelle of the William Volker Fund in 1954. Burgin has pointed out that the Volker Fund became a supporter of Hayek's brand of economic freedom, and Hayek's 1954 correspondence with the fund revolved around the distribution of two Volker Fellowships in the amount of $2,500 each, one of which had been awarded to support McClellan's graduate work with Hayek at Chicago.[15] In the letter, Hayek lamented that there were not more outstanding candidates for the fellowship such as McClellan and another awardee, even going so far as to note McClellan's potential to contribute to American "Far Eastern Policy":

> While I am quite pleased with the two candidates to whom we awarded fellowships, I am again very disappointed with the applications which we received. These two were indeed the only two worth serious consideration. They are both foreigners resident in this country. Mr. McClellan is half Scottish and half Japanese, an intelligent and pleasant young man who for a year has been working with Russell Kirk at Michigan State and has now a rather interesting project which fits in well since I have also an extremely intelligent Chinese who is doing under my supervision a parallel study of the influence of Western Civilisation on the Chinese tradition. Both are of some significance for the understanding of why the attempt to bring Western Civilization [to] oriental people so frequently disposes them to turn to communism and may, I hope, in the long run have some influence of the Far Eastern Policy of this country.[16]

In looking back on the translation years later, McClellan, too, would remember that it was conceived and received outside the field of Japan studies. He remarked in a 1998 lecture that he was not trained as a scholar of Japan or Japanese literature at the time he rendered *Kokoro* into literary English as a graduate student at Chicago:

> My education itself had very little to do with this [Sōseki and Japanese literature] because I went to a Scottish university [St. Andrews], which was the birthplace of the Scottish reformation, and my special subject was the Scottish reformation. And then when I went to study with Hayek and David Grene, what was I doing? I was reading Tocqueville.
>
> So my choice to do Sōseki finally or, rather, translate *Kokoro* was, in a sense, an attempt to persuade two men whom I really thought very highly of, who knew nothing about Japanese literature, to persuade them to

> accept the next step in what I wanted, which was to write about Sōseki. And if they were going to say yes they would have to be shown a novel by Sōseki which I thought might have a chance of touching them.[17]

Ironically, then, the translation that would come to be viewed as a kind of foundation of Japan studies in the American academy originally had nothing to do with Japan studies at all, and was, in fact, first read within a liberal imagination that organized in closer relation to what it believed were globally relevant social scientific, economic, and philosophical forms of knowledge. The crux of the matter presently comes into view: What was it about *Kokoro* that made it the novel of modern Japan with the best chance of "touching" Hayek and the neoliberal imagination at midcentury Chicago? This chapter tries to answer that question by reconstructing elements of the intellectual historical idiom in which the translation originally breathed with segments of the midcentury American Right.

Imagining the Imagination of a "Truly Liberal Radicalism"

Some scholarship on midcentury Japan has read the intellectual and political dynamics of the period through the lens of "democracy," placing emphasis on its prospects and paradoxes after the fall of the wartime regime in 1945. In one intellectual portrait, the historian Adam Bronson explored how a group of intellectuals that included the noted liberal thinker Maruyama Masao formed the "Science of Thought" (*Shisō no kagaku*) circle in postwar Japan and tried to transmit the ideals of democracy to a mass audience.[18] In another recent study, the historian Jennifer Miller raised the related problem of "anticommunism" in order to specify the Cold War constraints placed on democratic freedoms in early postwar Japan, and beyond. She explained that although "the experience of depression and war fostered a belief that subversive ideas and ideologies posed a fundamental threat to democracy," it was also true that the democratic mandates of free speech, a free press, and open elections left democratic societies particularly vulnerable to "demagogic promises of false glory" that were believed to come "from fascists, militarists, and communists alike."[19] Aspects of the Cold War debates about democracy and anticommunism appeared in the realms of literature, criticism, and the arts, too, as the scholars Michael Bourdaghs and Justin Jesty have shown in their respective studies.[20]

Against this backdrop, my use of the term "neoliberalism" might be jarring. For one thing, the prominent theorist David Harvey and other analysts have described neoliberalism as a politics that fully emerged only later, in the 1970s, more or less.[21] And even though intellectuals used the term themselves much earlier than that, and even though no less a thinker than Michel Foucault had already theorized "neoliberalism" in intellectual historical terms with reference to Hayek by the end of the 1970s, it is still true that "neoliberalism" remains a newer term within Japan studies scholarship. Complicating matters further is the fact that "neoliberalism" stands at something of an awkward remove from the more familiar keywords "democracy" and "anticommunism." On the one hand, midcentury "neoliberalism" comprised a constellation of ideas that, however diffuse and complex, may be said to have advanced the "anticommunist" agenda by offering a staunch advocacy for capitalism and private enterprise. But on the other hand, few would argue that "neoliberalism" was no more than an "anticommunist" politics, as if the two were synonymous, and the most convincing recent scholarship has emphasized the advantage of reading the ambiguities of neoliberal ideas within multiple, fluctuating, and global ideological fields, rather than treating it as a monolithic position cemented within parochial Cold War binaries of opposition.[22] The relation of "neoliberalism" to "democracy" is thornier still. Most notably, the political philosopher Wendy Brown has argued in two recent book-length studies that neoliberal reason hollows out the very premises of democratic politics, ultimately "undoing the demos."[23] As an analytical frame, then, "neoliberalism" identifies a tangled web of transwar politics that crossed paths with the more familiar problems of "democracy" and "anticommunism" while also remaining irreducible to them. And for this reason, I will argue, it promises to evolve the existing conversation in new directions.

To see how, it must first be noted that the midcentury years were not a "neoliberal age," if by that is meant a time in which a fully formed neoliberalism can be counted among the hegemonic ideological dynamics.

Scholars of transatlantic politics and ideas have been more likely to describe the years during and after the Reagan and Thatcher administrations of the 1980s in those terms, whereas in the midcentury years, the neoliberal imagination was only just beginning to formulate itself in the discursive sphere of intellectual history. Its force took time to gather, and in the early days, its articulators thought of themselves as outsiders clinging to an imperiled form of imagination rather than as triumphant masters of the universe. This is why the philosopher Michel Feher has noted that "the term 'neoliberal' refers to the doctrinal revisions and strategic innovations that enabled some die-hard custodians of the classic liberal creed to chase away the feeling that history was not going their way."[24] Around the time of McClellan's 1957 *Kokoro* translation, the longer-range implications and contemporary permutations of neoliberal politics had not yet begun to appear in their more notorious forms known to us today. I take up some of the more recent articulations of the neoliberal condition in the epilogue, but the starting point for my analysis in this chapter is that the midcentury years were in fact one of the few times in which the term "neoliberalism" itself (along with its cognates) does seem to have been used by some of its own advocates to name an aspirational reconstruction of liberal sentiments.

The economic historian Philip Mirowski has observed that "the people associated with the doctrine *did* call themselves 'neo-liberals' for a brief period lasting from the 1930s to the early 1950s, but then they abruptly stopped the practice."[25] Another scholar of economic thought, Dieter Plehwe, has added that the term "neoliberalism" was already circulating in the 1920s, and took on new implications in 1938 at the Colloque Walter Lippmann, where it was offered as an appellation for a collective yearning to reconstruct—or reinvent—what was understood to have been an endangered liberal spirit of competition and enterprise. Plehwe pointed out that "neoliberalism" appeared in this context alongside other possible appellations, such as *néo-capitalisme, libéralism positif, libéralism social*, and *libéralism de gauche*.[26] I would add that in the late 1940s, at around the time Hayek organized the Mont Pèlerin Society, he spoke of what he called a "new liberal program" and a "new liberal movement."[27] Slobodian has noted that Hayek himself described the purpose of the Mont Pèlerin Society in terms of promoting "neoliberalism" and advancing a "neoliberal movement."[28] Slobodian pointed to the 1952 article "A Rebirth of Liberalism," in which Hayek wrote that "gone are the days when the few outmoded liberals walked their paths lonely, ridiculed and without response from the young. Today, on the contrary, theirs is a staggering responsibility: the new generation demands from them the answers liberalism has to offer to the great problems of our times. To erect a coherent edifice of such neo-liberal thought, and to work out its practical application to the problems of different countries, the intellectual vitality of a larger group is needed."[29] In addition, Mirowski has observed that in 1951, the Chicago economist Milton Friedman—a figure often understood to have been a popularizer of neoliberal perspectives—referred to what he called "the doctrine that, on and off, has been called neoliberalism," adding that "instead of the 19th century understanding that laissez-faire is the means to achieve this goal, neoliberalism proposes that *competition* will lead the way."[30] Daniel Stedman Jones has argued that Friedman's 1951 essay "Neo-Liberalism and Its Prospects" indicated that the economist was "one of the first American writers to claim the neoliberal moniker explicitly (though the term, as we have seen, was in fairly common usage among European neoliberals in the 1930s and 1940s)."[31]

To be sure, these citations do not imply that "neoliberalism" was the single banner under which all like-minded figures on the midcentury American right gathered. Far from it, in fact. Burgin has pointed out that "in the interwar and early postwar years 'neoliberalism' held a valence, on the rare occasions when the term was employed, that diverged significantly from that associated with it today."[32] The new liberals at midcentury were a diverse group, and their discussions naturally brought to light important differences among their number that any broad strokes nomenclature runs the risk of eliding. It is also true that whereas "neoliberalism" today is often associated with the inhumane expansions of economic rationality into formerly noneconomic realms of human life, the midcentury liberals discussed economic entrepreneurialism and rule-bound markets as the bedrock of a free society, and as the crux of civilized humanity itself. This indicates part of why Burgin has cautioned that some usages of "neoliberalism" today carry implications that would be anachronistic in the midcentury context, and that even in that earlier time, "neoliberalism" was but one term among others that circulated within a political spectrum populated by figures who often disagreed sharply with one another.

These dynamics have led scholars to warn that the invective sometimes implied by the term "neoliberal" today can obscure the sense of loss among those who once used the term during and immediately after the war years. In this vein, Burgin has pointed out that since midcentury discussions surrounding the future of liberal thought and a new philosophy of capitalism emerged in the shadows of the Great Depression and world war, their context was an "atmosphere of uncertainty," adding that these discussions should be regarded as "the product of a collapsed rather than a rigidified worldview."[33] Slobodian reminds us of this, too, when he notes that although today, "the twentieth century is commonly portrayed as the period of the triumph of neoliberalism," it should not be forgotten that in earlier times, "the dominant emotion felt by the neoliberals . . . was not hubris but anxiety."[34] The anxiety that Slobodian pointed to in the context of the midcentury neoliberals in Europe originated in their feeling that they were operating in the aftermath of the catastrophic failure of liberalism itself. This is why Hayek, writing in 1952, would begin his essay "A Rebirth of Liberalism" by noting that "when the first World War ended, the intellectual tradition of liberalism was well-nigh dead," adding that "three decades ago there hardly existed a vital world of liberal thought capable of inspiring the younger generation."[35] The death of liberal ideals to which Hayek alluded marked the loss at the origin of what Michel Feher suggested we could read as a sort of right melancholy at midcentury.[36] Feher wrote that "back in 1947, when Friedrich Hayek founded the Mont Pelerin Society, most of the economists, social scientists, and legal scholars who joined him in the Swiss Alps were perceived as outlandish figures dwelling at the right end of the political spectrum—among the participants, only the German ordoliberals were influential in their own country. Their relative marginalization lasted almost thirty years," until around the time that Hayek won the Nobel Memorial Prize in Economic Sciences in 1974.[37]

This helps us to see that reading "neoliberalism" in the history of midcentury thought requires a sensitivity to the contingency of the moment that is harder to recognize looking back. Part of the problem is that more recent theorizations of "neoliberalism" have sometimes ascribed to the term a degree of ideological certitude that runs counter to the thought of that earlier time, as Slobodian and the literary scholar Leigh Claire La Berge suggested in their critique of Brown's influential study *Undoing the*

Demos: Neoliberalism's Stealth Revolution (2015). While noting the contributions of Brown's prominent study of the rise of neoliberal politics since the fall of the Berlin Wall, Slobodian and La Berge also called it "a self-defeating handbook either to comprehend or to fight neoliberalism because it grants more autonomy to the market and closure to political struggle than neoliberals do themselves."[38] La Berge and Slobodian offered this in the context of a broader critique that held that the influential theorists of neoliberalism Harvey and Brown "have turned neoliberalism into a narrative of spiritual, political and, indeed, existential impoverishment. A viable definition for literary studies will have to ask, as [the literary scholar Rachel] Greenwald Smith does, what neoliberalism has to offer, not only what it strips away."[39] From this perspective, McClellan's 1957 *Kokoro* translation presents a compelling case study because it involves a beloved literary text that was actually conceived and received squarely within Hayek's orbit of neoliberal intellectual influence, but also carried literary implications ranging far beyond it, too—so far, in fact, that the translation's original context of reception is rarely remarked on today.

One way to recuperate the neoliberal context of this celebrated literary translation is to first reckon with something of the literary dynamic running through the neoliberal imagination itself. Moving in this direction, I recall that Slobodian has observed that although "neoliberalism" is sometimes caricatured as free-market fundamentalism, it in fact developed in the midcentury years in ways that challenged some of the more technical, data-oriented methods that were then current in the field of economics itself. While noting that "neoliberalism was born out of projects of world observation, global statistics gathering, and international investigations of the business cycle," Slobodian has also observed that "the ultimate conclusion of neoliberals about the Great Depression and its aftermath was that numbers were not enough."[40] Instead, Slobodian wrote, "neoliberals rallied around the belief that neither statistics, nor mathematically informed theory, nor the nascent science of econometrics would suffice to forecast or stave off future crises," and they even worried about a "false faith that science could make the world economy crisis-proof."[41] Hayek was one of the most intense among these skeptics. He rejected the idea that there could ever be any omniscient discipline that could explain the economy completely because he believed that knowledge in society was always dispersed rather than collected, as Slobodian has noted.[42] For this reason, the global economy presented a puzzle that mathematics, statistics, and, indeed, economics itself could not hope to solve alone.[43]

Some of the literary affordances of this perspective emerged explicitly at a 1966 meeting of the Mont Pèlerin Society in Tokyo, at which Hayek himself made revealing reference to Lao Tzu. His address revolved around defining liberalism in terms of "a self-generating or spontaneous order in social affairs," an order that he believed excessive government control and centralized economic planning threatened to obliterate. But at the conclusion of the lecture, he suggested that beneath the sorts of straightforward declaratives that made up his argument lay a more sensuous reckoning with liberty as a distinctly negative ideal whose true substance could never be fully articulated in language. Instead, Hayek implied, liberty was akin to an ineffable atmosphere that naturally precipitated in the place of its evaporated opposite, coercion. Making this point, he ended his Tokyo remarks with a literary allusion apparently intended to connect his philosophy of liberty to ideas more familiar to his interlocutors in East Asia:

> Is this all so very different
> From what Lao-Tzu says
> In his fifty seventh poem?:
> If I keep from meddling with people,
> They take care of themselves
> If I keep from commanding people,
> They behave themselves,
> If I keep from imposing on people,
> They become themselves.[44]

Another presenter at the Tokyo meeting of the Mont Pèlerin Society continued this line of inquiry, discussing how the "spontaneous orders" of liberal society and the Taoist "Way" cohered in a negative space defined by the absence of government control, human intention, and representational language. The economist Nishiyama Chiaki claimed in his lecture at the Tokyo meeting that "the Japanese" had an instinctual understanding of what Hayek described as the negative ideals of liberty because Japanese thought was founded on "the assertion of our traditional negation of reason or of intellect and of our age old perception of 'nothingness.'"[45] He argued that "for us, the Japanese, it is thus not all so difficult to tread the steps to the center of the Hayekian world. We can, in fact, even claim to Professor Hayek that it was really us, the Asians, who realized first the inescapable limitation of our intellect and that it is precisely from this realization that the sense of freedom emerges."[46] Nishiyama added that even though "the Japanese" were not yet "naturalized as respectable citizen[s] to the world of Professor Hayek," they had long intuited the negative ideals of liberalism by more poetic names, such as "the Way": "Does this mean, then, that we ['the Japanese'] have now a passport to the world of Professor Hayek or of the Mont Pelerin Society? I believe that the answer is affirmative. How much better it would be to have Rao-Tzu [Lao-Tzu] as our fellow citizen in a free society than the creep called technical economist."[47] These statements remind us that in its most romantic articulations, the neoliberal vision of market society relied on an order of imagination immeasurable by econometric analysis alone. This was so because Hayek and other leading neoliberals "concluded that the world economy was sublime, beyond representation and quantification," as Slobodian put it.[48]

Rethinking midcentury "neoliberalism" in terms of a "sublime" helps us to see that some of the most interesting questions that weigh upon a reading of the original context of McClellan's *Kokoro* translation have to do with understanding how a vision of market society premised on the all but undefinable quality of "liberty" required the powers of imagination. We begin to see the role of imagination take center stage in a lecture titled "The Prospects for Freedom" that Hayek delivered in 1946 at Stanford University. Having recently arrived in the United States from Europe, he reiterated the main claim of his 1944 bestseller *The Road to Serfdom*, which held that even the Allied nations that had been spared the scourge of wartime totalitarianism might yet succumb to it in the years after the regimes in Germany and Italy had fallen:

> What we who still regard personal liberty as the greatest good must learn again is that a stationary creed is a dying creed, that when the intellectual struggle to develop our ideas stops we have lost the battle. It is under this aspect that to the close observer of the intellectual movements of our time the prospects of freedom seem almost desperate. It cannot be denied that

> at least for a generation most of the active and productive thinkers of our time have been moving away from the philosophy of freedom, that almost every so-called progress in social thinking involved some sacrifice of individual freedom to some social good.
>
> And though most of you may feel that in these fortunate United States you are still so remote from the horrors of totalitarian government which I have painted elsewhere as not to need to worry, and though in so far as the factual developments are concerned this is still largely true, I do not feel the same assurance when I study the trend of thought in this country. When I read the more academic discussions about the desirable future order of society, when I talk to young students at the great seats of learning, I find a state of opinion which is alarmingly similar to what I knew on the European Continent twenty-five years ago and in England ten or fifteen years ago. If the state of opinion in these circles is as much an indication of future developments as it has proved elsewhere, the risk that America may go the same road is not inconsiderable.[49]

As this suggests, what worried Hayek was a climate of opinion, and a state of imagination, which he believed to have been apathetic to liberal ideals, and at times even hostile to them. In "The Prospects of Freedom," he explained that "the main reason why we are all drifting and likely to arrive at a social order which almost everybody fears is that we have no coherent social philosophy at all, that we have become afraid of general principles and have committed ourselves to a policy of experimentation without any serious effort to think out beforehand where it will lead us."[50]

This reminds us that when Hayek organized the Mont Pèlerin Society in the late 1940s, he had in mind an organization that would reconstruct the philosophy of liberty not only as an economic and political rationality rooted in the ideals of market enterprise, but as a comprehensive and expansive form of imagination. In his mind, the ravages of the Great Depression and the rise of the totalitarian menace during the global 1930s had signaled that the liberal promise of private freedom could be broken, and that the invisible hand of the market could be replaced by the authoritarian hand of a fascist or communist state. Even after the fall of the wartime regimes in Germany and Italy in 1945, Hayek sensed that the illiberal ideals that fueled their rise remained alive and well. In "The Prospects of Freedom," he observed, "We may be able to fight a defensive battle for a time and slow down the process of encroachment on liberty, but we shall not prevent the gradual advance of totalitarian control if we do not succeed in defeating the philosophy which produces it."[51] To this end, Hayek urged liberals to dream beyond the boundaries of strictly economic reason, overtly political arguments, and insiders' academic discourse. He called on them to formulate a way of looking at the world that would offer a compelling alternative to the "philosophy" that had produced "totalitarian control." It would not be easy, he warned in 1946: "This, however, is an intellectual task which we have hardly yet begun, and of the magnitude of which few people have a conception. It is not merely a task of elaborating and popularising an alternative political program. I have deliberately spoken of a philosophy, or a view of life, because it is not merely our opinions on particular issues, but the whole moral and intellectual climate which at the moment works for ever increased coercion by the state."[52]

For Hayek, in fact, the "view of life" animating the new liberalism required a form of imagination that would be as radical as any other. In "The Intellectuals and Socialism" (1949), he observed that "it may be that a free society as we have known it carries in itself the forces of its own destruction, that once freedom has been achieved it is taken for granted and ceases to be valued, and that the free growth of ideas which is the essence of a free society will bring about the destruction of the foundations on which it depends."[53] In making this claim, Hayek observed the success of socialists in capturing the popular imagination and argued that liberal intellectuals would do well to learn from their rivals: "The main lesson which the true liberal must learn from the success of the socialists is that it was their courage to be Utopian which gained them the support of the intellectuals and therefore an influence on public opinion which is daily making possible what only recently seemed utterly remote."[54] The imagination presently emerged as the key to the new liberalism. For without a radically liberal form of imagination, Hayek surmised, liberty itself might be valued only after it had been lost to "socialist totalitarianism":

> If we are to avoid such a development we must be able to offer a new liberal program which appeals to the imagination. We must make the building of a free society once more an intellectual adventure, a deed of courage. What we lack is a liberal Utopia, a program which seems neither a mere defense of things as they are nor a diluted kind of socialism, but truly

> liberal radicalism which does not spare the susceptibilities of the mighty (including the trade unions), which is not too severely practical and which does not confine itself to what appears today as politically possible.[55]

As the formulation of a "truly liberal radicalism" took as its object the nebulous matter of imagination, it called on the support of specific institutions. Understanding the formations of neoliberal thought through these institutions can help us begin to see the concrete structure of an abstract ideology in the midcentury decades. In this connection, Mirowski has argued for understanding midcentury neoliberalism as the product of a "neoliberal thought collective" that materialized in institutional and ideological orbits that cohered around one another like nesting dolls. One of the most important of these orbits in the midcentury decades was the University of Chicago: Hayek joined the faculty in 1950, and his time there overlapped with his tenure as president of the Mont Pèlerin Society, which lasted from its first meeting in 1948 until 1960. Rob Van Horn and Mirowski have argued that Hayek's activities as leader of the society and faculty member at Chicago were part of the same neoliberal program. For this reason, these scholars declared that they would clarify "neoliberalism by recounting the origins of its most famous Anglophone intellectual citadel at the University of Chicago," and argued that the Mont Pèlerin Society and the "Chicago School of Economics" "were joined at the hip from birth," noting, among other things, that "when the MPS was legally constituted, it was registered as a non profit corporation in Illinois, with offices formally listed as located in the University of Chicago Law School."[56]

At Chicago, however, Hayek was hired not into the Economics Department, but onto the Committee on Social Thought. John Nef, who was then chair of the committee, has written that "economists had opposed [Hayek's] appointment in Economics for years before largely because they regarded his *Road to Serfdom* as too popular a work for a respectable scholar to perpetrate. It was all right to have him at the University of Chicago so long as he wasn't identified with the economists."[57] The committee was (and is) a humanities consortium open to scholars of wide-ranging backgrounds and areas of expertise, rather than only to scholars of one or another discipline. Van Horn and Mirowski note that in contrast to the objections of the Economics Department, "Hayek's appointment to the Committee [on Social Thought] would require only the personal initiative of [Robert Maynard] Hutchins, since it was widely regarded as his bailiwick."[58] Remembering Hutchins's role in bringing Hayek to Chicago takes us closer to seeing the literary imperative of the liberal advocacy for the "free world" at Chicago. After all, Hutchins was not only an influential leader of the University of Chicago, but also an advocate for the "Great Books," and at Chicago, he worked with Mortimer Adler to produce *The Great Books of the Western World*, published by Encyclopædia Britannica in 1952.

The humanities scholar Mark Greif has observed that "the nobility of the Great Books was always synonymous with an idea of liberal education, advancing a simple position: men were the same in all times. Every age could produce great thinkers who examined the same human problems from their own vantage points and recorded the results."[59] In this sense, the liberal project of the Great Books implied the antihistoricist premise that the human condition is a single event unbroken by the fractures of cultural relativism. From this perspective, the best literary and philosophical writings were to be understood in relation to the common crises and catharses of humanity itself in universally legible, perennially relevant forms that anyone could—and that everyone should—read and take to heart. The scholar Tim Lacy noted in his study of Adler that broadly stated, the idea of the Great Books was part of a liberal project founded on what Lacy has called "an implicit, cosmopolitan dream of cultural democratization" by which the ideas communicated through the Great Books would "enlighten the American polis and buttress Western democratic societies against malicious political systems, such as communism and fascism."[60] Lacy also pointed out that the Cold War antifascist and anticommunist implications of the Great Books are in evidence in considering that their edifying effect, it was hoped, "would create empowered, cosmopolitan citizens comfortable with freedom in a century plagued with totalitarianism."[61]

Irony and contradiction were always part of the story, however. Lacy pointed out that to its critics, the Great Books idea thwarted social justice politics by establishing a standard of judgement that repressed people of color and women and maintained class inequality.[62] The democratic and populist premise of *The Great Books* was also complicated by its own paradoxical mix of commercialism and elitism, and in ways that recall some of the problems of "middlebrow" culture discussed in chapter 1. In fact, Dwight Macdonald's "The Book-of-the-Millennium Club" (1952) and a *Time* magazine article titled "Cashing in on Culture" (1962) implied how *The Great Books* might be read as a provocative case study in which the neoliberal concern for marketing and efficiency ironically engaged the priceless renderings of the human soul that populate the pieces of classic literature and thought included in the collection.[63] And while the capacious premise of *The Great Books* aimed to include everything that was "Great" in Western civilization, Greif has observed that "the understanding of the Great Books as it reemerged between Adler and Hutchins in Chicago became increasingly rarified and dogmatic: it held that there was a finite canon of known discoveries in all the ages of man, each revealing another aspect of a human nature that was always the same, such that readers could find the great truths only in particular books as relevant now as when they were written."[64] The conservative currents of *The Great Books* could even turn antidemocratic, ironically undoing what in some tellings was supposed to be an ennobling liberal enterprise. In this connection, Greif reminds us that Hutchins's "protoconservative return to permanent traditions analogously slipped away to the right even of Hutchins's seeming inclinations," with the result being that "the long postwar intellectual world would find the University of Chicago the single most important location in America for the revivals of antistate (or antipublic) and antidemocratic thought, which would come to be called 'neoliberalism' and 'neoconservatism.'"[65]

These were some of the contradictory currents that swirled around McClellan at Chicago as he translated *Kokoro* in the mid-1950s while still a graduate student on the Committee on Social Thought working under the tutelage of Hayek and Grene. But what was it that brought McClellan to Chicago in the first place?

McClellan in the Midcentury Midwest

Our view of the layered sentiments that collided and colluded around McClellan in the 1950s deepens in remembering that immediately before arriving at Chicago, he had earlier worked with Russell Kirk, whose best-known work, *The Conservative Mind* (1953), became a beacon of the early Cold War conservative identity, going through several editions and revisions. Aida Hirotsugu has observed that McClellan met Kirk while he was completing research for what would become *The Conservative Mind* at the University of St. Andrews, in Scotland, where McClellan was a student of Scottish Enlightenment thought.[66] In his memoir (composed in the third person), Kirk wrote that during his time at St. Andrews, "the only Oriental face was that of Edwin McClellan, half Ulsterman, half Japanese, Kirk's comrade at St. Andrews, now professor of Japanese literature at Yale. 'Pongo' McClellan maintained himself by winning prolonged games of poker from hardbitten British soldiers turned students; he seemed to do little else; yet he would become one of St. Andrews's more distinguished scholarly graduates, after some years at the University of Chicago, where he would be assistant to F. A. Hayek."[67]

Kirk would also remember McClellan in the acknowledgments to *The Conservative Mind*: "Mr. Edwin McClellan (whose company I have had in the Georgian slums round Mountjoy Square, Dublin, and in the wild country above the Falls of Ben Glas) also read my manuscript, and prepared the Index."[68] Born in Kobe to a Japanese mother and a Scottish father, McClellan left Japan during the war years, and after coming into contact with Kirk at St. Andrews, he would later move to the United States to pursue graduate study with Kirk at what is now Michigan State University. Kirk wrote that he and McClellan roomed in the same house in East Lansing, suggesting something of their closeness during these years.[69] Kirk also wrote that at Chicago, McClellan sometimes dined with Richard Weaver, the prominent conservative thinker who authored *Ideas Have Consequences* in 1948.[70] Weaver was professor of English at Chicago, and he had earlier studied at Vanderbilt with John Crowe Ransom and completed his doctorate in 1943 at Louisiana State University, where he worked with the legendary literary figures Cleanth Brooks and Robert Penn Warren.

Kirk's place in the background of McClellan's *Kokoro* translation reminds us that some of the conservative perspectives that developed during the midcentury years crossed paths with the contemporaneous development of a new liberalism. This is not to say that Kirk was intellectually or ideologically aligned with Hayek himself, nor is it to forget that Kirk's own "conservative mind" was skeptical of the sort of egotistical individualism, mechanical utilitarianism, and social disruptions that he associated with market life in general, and that are today often associated with neoliberalism in particular.[71] Yet, while noting the many conflicting threads of conservative thought and neoliberal ideas that appeared in postwar intellectual history, recent scholarship has also noted productive dialogues across their boundaries that complicate the simpler separation of conservative morality and neoliberal economics. In one study, the scholar Melinda Cooper traced aspects of a postwar conversation involving neoliberals and "new social conservatives," revealing that "brought together by their confrontation with the liberation movements of the 1960s, neoliberals and neoconservatives sought to contain the antinormative and redistributive promise of these movements by capturing them within the horizon of reinvented tradition."[72] Brown developed a resonant perspective that linked the discourses of morality and the market in opposition to the redistributive imperatives of social justice claims during this period, too. Brown argued that "neoliberal reason, especially as Friedrich Hayek formulated it, casts markets and morals as singular forms of human need provision sharing ontological principles and dynamics. Rooted in liberty and generating spontaneous order and evolution, their radical opposites are *any kind* of deliberate and state-administered social policy, planning, and justice."[73] With this, Brown expanded and revised her earlier perspective on neoliberalism in *Undoing the Demos*, which focused on the economization of everything: by introducing morality to the mix, her reading of Hayek posited neoliberal reason as a more complicated "moral-political project that aims to protect traditional hierarchies by negating the very idea of the social."[74]

Against the backdrop of this scholarly conversation about dialogues across the boundaries of neoliberal economics and conservative morality, it is worth delving into the Hayek-Kirk connection in some detail. After all, their brief moment of sympathy in the early 1950s was one condition of possibility for McClellan to move from Michigan State to Chicago. These connections are easily forgotten, though, because Kirk's relationship with Hayek quickly deteriorated. But at least in a measured sense, Hayek seems to have approved of Kirk's perspective at one point in time—and not coincidentally, precisely the point at which McClellan left Michigan State to join Hayek at Chicago. Burgin has pointed out that Hayek's impression of Kirk "shifted dramatically" over time, while also noting that "when *The Conservative Mind* was first published [1953], [Hayek] expressed admiration for the book and qualified enthusiasm for its author."[75] When Hayek was asked to review Kirk's book for the Volker Fund, which was considering making a grant for its purchase by college and university libraries, Hayek wrote in his review that he "sometimes felt quite irritated when the author claims for conservatism what really were the main contributions of classical liberalism."[76] He also wrote of the book that "I disagree with many of its values" and critiqued Kirk's text for being "much too long, and, though really excellent in some parts and throughout erudite and readable, a little uneven in the different parts."[77] But while noting that he feared *The Conservative Mind* was "much too scholarly and presumes much too much general education of its reader to receive a wide circulation," Hayek also added that "if it were at least read by all the people who can appreciate it, it should do much to shift the general discussion on the right track and generally on a higher plane."[78] With some qualification, Hayek recommended *The Conservative Mind*, writing "this is a good book which I think deserves support and will probably need it," elsewhere adding, "I can only wish that the book should be read as widely as possible."[79]

Hayek also offered an endorsement for the book when its publisher, the noted conservative Henry Regnery, asked him for one, and this seems to have meant something, considering that he declined a similar request from Regnery in the case of William Buckley's *God and Man at Yale* (1951).[80] It should be pointed out that Regnery was a major figure in his own right: the publishing house he founded in 1947, the Henry Regnery Company, would go on to become a force in the American conservative movement, and would also be the one to publish McClellan's *Kokoro* translation in 1957. Regnery himself had studied at M.I.T., then lived in Germany from 1934 to 1936, and later became a graduate student in economics at Harvard working under the tutelage of the prominent economist Joseph Schumpeter, who is remembered for developing the idea of "creative disruption," and whom Regnery described in his memoir as "a product of the Austrian school, from which have come some of the outstanding and most far-seeing economists of this century: others were Böhm-Bawerk, Menger, Mises, and Hayek."[81] Along the way, Regnery became disillusioned with the New Deal he once supported after working in its Resettlement Administration, developed an anticommunist politics, and became convinced that his purpose as a self-described "dissident publisher" was to advance the big ideas of civilization, society, and humanity in their moment of crisis, remembering, as he put it, that "it is, in the end, ideas—not newspapers, television personalities, bureaucrats, or politicians—that rule the world."[82] As this sketch indicates, Regnery's midcentury conservatism was globally oriented, and in addition to the wartime and Cold War conflicts in Europe, Asia was on his radar, too: in a chapter of his memoir titled "Communism and Foreign Policy," he recalled publishing Freda Utley's *The China Story* (1951) and John C. Caldwell's *The Korea Story* (1952), for example. The Henry Regnery Company also contracted as the publisher for the Great Books Foundation in 1949, an arrangement that would endure only until Buckley's *God and Man at Yale* angered some at the foundation, which abruptly discontinued its partnership with Regnery.[83]

As Regnery embarked on a career in publishing during the midcentury years in Chicago, he forged bonds with the Committee on Social Thought through his contacts Hutchins and Nef.[84] And it was around the time that Regnery published *The Conservative Mind* in 1953 that Hayek in fact suggested Kirk for a faculty position there. Hayek wrote in a letter to Herbert Cornuelle of the Volker Fund on May 9, 1953: "To-day Henry Regnery brought Russell Kirk out here for lunch. He seems to be a nice and very knowledgeable man who it would be nice to have around here permanently."[85] When Cornuelle asked Hayek to elaborate, Hayek replied: "As regards Russell Kirk my personal opinion is pretty clear: He ought to be at some place where his influence on the more mature students is greater than at Michigan State; the teaching of political ideas here in Chicago definitely needs some counteracting influence; and it is a subject on which the present staff of the Committee has a real gap which occasionally creates difficulties in providing for adequate supervision. In short, I for my own person should very much like to have him here."[86]

Hayek noted in his correspondence with Cornuelle that Kirk's hiring would require the approval of Nef, "whose voice is decisive."[87] In correspondence with Nef dated the same day as the correspondence with Cornuelle quoted above (May 21, 1953), Hayek sent his colleague a copy of *The Conservative Mind*, stating that he "rather liked the book for its good sense and perceptiveness and a general impression of a cultivated person it gave to me. Two or three weeks ago I met the man through

Mr. Regnery and also liked him as a person—without really getting more than a superficial pleasant impression."[88] Hayek noted that he had been in touch with Cornuelle, explaining that he had communicated to the Volker Fund that "I wished [Kirk] were here on the faculty."[89] Hayek added that while speaking only for himself, "I did say that I felt that Kirk ought to be at some better place than Michigan State College, that I did not feel that our Political Science Department was entirely satisfactory and that in the Committee we did in fact feel the lack of somebody specialising in the history of ideas and particularly American ideas."[90] Hayek concluded his letter to Nef by lauding Kirk:

> All I can say definitely about him is that he seems to me one of the rare Americans who are really at home in European traditions and that he is a thoroughly cultured and polished person, rather quiet and modest, yet quite amusing as a talker. His interests seem very wide, but how far he has an original mind I would not dare to say at this stage. He is a man of about 35, has spent two or three years at St. Andrews and appears to have surprisingly close contacts to some of the best English and Scottish circles. It is of course quite likely that we may hear nothing further about the matter; but it seems desirable that we should be prepared in case any kind of offer were made to the Committee.[91]

According to Burgin, Nef proved receptive enough to Hayek's idea of hiring Kirk to the Committee on Social Thought that he ultimately extended an offer. But Burgin noted that when the overtures from Chicago came, it seems that Kirk indicated to Nef that he was presently unavailable for faculty work.[92]

Burgin also pointed out that by the time Kirk came around to Nef's offer a few years later, Kirk "had attained a polarizing degree of notoriety through his activities as a conservative public intellectual."[93] In addition, Burgin noted, Hayek's opinion of Kirk had cooled, and skepticism came to replace what had earlier been warmer feelings of sympathy. The explosive division came at the 1957 meeting of the Mont Pèlerin Society, where Hayek (then president of the society) delivered the noted lecture "Why I Am Not A Conservative," in which he distinguished his position from Kirk's without ever mentioning Kirk by name; Kirk was present for the searing critique, and offered a response.[94] Regnery was at the meeting, too, and would write that he admired how Kirk defended his position "extemporaneously, without notes of any kind, and with great brilliance and effect," adding that "as a rather biased witness, I would not be prepared to say that the young man from Mecosta [Kirk] came out second best."[95] But Burgin has noted that Hayek's speech indicated an unbridgeable divide separating his position from Kirk's, and that this divide would lead Hayek himself to later block Kirk's petition to formally join the Mont Pèlerin Society.[96] The episode reminds us how different McClellan's two mentors could be. After all, Kirk quit the academy to live in rural Michigan, where he is said to have eschewed the convenience of many modern amenities, including the automobile, in his love for what he imagined to have been old ways; Hayek, on the other hand, was a cosmopolitan intellectual leading an international league of liberals whose activities he worked to coordinate as he traveled around the globe with seemingly indefatigable stamina and an ever-widening range of influence.[97] On the level of ideas, too, Hayek and Kirk were often far apart. Burgin has pointed out that one of the most important distinctions separating these figures was that Hayek believed that the market "was the ultimate instigator of social change, and its spontaneous dictates were a cause for celebration rather than fear," whereas Kirk "remained wary of the unpredictable and unmanageable changes that the market interactions [at the center of the modern world] necessarily produced."[98]

In some intellectual histories, these sorts of differences have become the fault lines along which the sometimes-contiguous tectonics of conservatism and neoliberalism collided and cleaved at midcentury. But their quakes do not seem to have rattled McClellan, and I would speculate that this might have been because he was never a doctrinaire ideologue who felt the need to choose sides. Whatever the differences between Kirk and Hayek may have been—and there were many, to be sure—McClellan seems to have related to both of his advisers as an engaged interlocutor rather than as a loyal partisan. He was a fellow traveler rather than an epigone or an acolyte, then, and someone who, like Hayek and Kirk, brought deep bonds to European intellectual life with him to the midcentury Midwest. Even as Kirk's relationship with Hayek deteriorated later in the 1950s, McClellan seems to have remained sympathetic to both figures. He even had a small role in their most acclaimed writings: he compiled the index for *The Conservative Mind*, for example, and was hired to enhance the prose style of Hayek's *The Constitution of Liberty* (1960). McClellan published his translation with Henry Regnery Company, whose founder, Regnery himself, was in dialogue with Hayek, would later become a member of the Mont Pèlerin Society, and had earlier published Kirk's *The Conservative Mind* and Buckley's *God and Man at Yale*. The offer Nef extended to Kirk to join the Committee on Social Thought at Chicago, although rejected, was backed by the Earhart Foundation, which was to pay the entirety of Kirk's faculty salary.[99] Earhart and its subsidiary Relm Foundation were important funding agencies for causes on the Cold War Right, and in addition to supporting the proposed hire of Kirk, they also supported the activities of Hayek and the Mont Pèlerin Society. The Earhart Foundation would also extend a graduate student fellowship to McClellan at Hayek's recommendation.

All of this suggests that McClellan's *Kokoro* translation emerged from a dense matrix of right-leaning sentiments encompassing a spectrum of persuasions among contemporaries who wrote in the shared time of the midcentury present, and whose dialogues were facilitated by some of the same institutions. In this sense, theirs was a conjuncture in which complicated and sometimes contradictory perspectives engaged one another by breathing together. Yet, it was also a conjuncture that occasioned its own disintegration, for McClellan's translation emerged from a world of what would prove to have been fragile alliances: Kirk's differences with Hayek, and McClellan's subsequent departure from the realm of liberal thought into the newly forming field of what we now know as "Japan studies," signal the position of the translation within the confluence of several cultural historical currents that came together in some moments while still retaining their own trajectories more generally. But whether in times of convergence or conflict, it was ideas that propelled these currents, at times bringing thinkers on the liberal right together, and at times driving them apart. Burgin has pointed out in this connection just how remarkable it was that in their support of Hayek and the Mont Pèlerin Society, funding agencies such as the Earhart and Relm Foundations "demonstrated an extraordinary faith in the capacity of abstract ideas to generate substantive political change."[100] And some of these ideas conspired with a distinctly literary form of imagination.

Literature and Politics

Following its *Asahi* newspaper serialization in early twentieth-century Japan, Sōseki's *Kokoro* was published in book form by a then-fledgling publishing house, Iwanami Shoten. Today, Iwanami is a giant, but the scholar Nathan Shockey has shown that in the 1910s, when it was just starting out, its founder Iwanami Shigeo attempted to gain market share by commodifying classics of literature and thought that were believed to communicate universally relevant knowledge. Shockey named this strategy "the enterprise of eternity," and Sōseki played a key role: he calligraphed the word "Iwanami" for the company logo, and his novel *Kokoro* was the publisher's breakthrough book; this is why the scholar John Nathan has written that "Iwanami was and remains the house that Sōseki built."[101] The context would be different when *Kokoro* was reborn as a novel in English translation and published by Regnery, of course. But one of the ties that bound these two otherwise vastly different idioms was an interest in the universal quality of the human condition.

In a later edition of *The Conservative Mind*, Kirk wrote that "conservatism is not an ideology, but instead a mode of looking at human nature and society."[102] The sentiments behind this statement resonate with the conclusion Watakushi comes to in *Kokoro* through his association with Sensei—namely, that excessively coherent (or "ideological") analysis (*kenkyū*) can corrupt the heart and soul of humane understanding. Early in the novel, we are told that the very bond between the student and Sensei is only possible in the absence of systematic analytical thought (*kenkyū*; research, analysis). In one scene, Sensei's mysterious behavior and terse statements confuse the student. But even so, Watakushi takes for granted that questions will never lead to answers:

> I thought his behavior very strange. But I did not visit Sensei with the purpose of studying [*kenkyū*] him. And I decided to think no more about it. My attitude towards Sensei then is one of those things that I remember with a certain amount of pride. Because of it, I believe, we were able to become so close to each other. Had I been curious in an impersonal and analytical [*kenkyūteki*] way, the bond between us would surely not have lasted. I was, of course, not aware of all this at the time. I hate to think what might have

> happened had I acted differently. Even in his relationship with me, he was in constant dread of being coldly analyzed [*kenkyū sareru*].[103]

In his prominent essay on *Kokoro*, the literary critic Komori Yōichi noted that this passage indicates a natural disposition on the part of the student to avoid turning Sensei into the object of an experiment through an empiricist gaze that engages the world and others only through cold, disinterested observation.[104] This becomes clearer in noting that what McClellan translated as "we were able to become so close to each other" appears in the Japanese original in language that might be rendered less literarily as "we were able to have a warm relationship as human beings" (*ningenrashii atatakai tsukiai*). In this context, the systematic meanings produced through intellectual analysis and purposeful explication (*kenkyū*) are taken to be the antithesis of humane (*ningenrashii*) feeling.

In this sense, Watakushi's statement might be said to offer a critique of *kenkyū* as a form of narration in general, one that is structurally limited by the same drive for explanatory conclusion that Kirk believed to be the hallmark of all ideological doctrines. Taken a step further, this helps us to see why the conservative mind at midcentury came to think that the great books of literature offered an antidote to ideological certitude: far from being doctrinaire, it held, the masterpieces of literature supply an aesthetic mode that breathes with the elusive mysteries of the human condition in an endlessly interpretable and infinitely meaningful language unattainable through more purposeful narrative schemes. The literary could leave things open-ended, then, conjuring an indeterminate space for what Hayek once called the "intellectual adventure" of liberal imagining, and this was an appealing proposition embraced by both conservative and neoliberal perspectives, which abhorred omniscient reasoning, intentional design, and centralized planning. As these premises led conservative literary culture to inoculate itself against the deconstructions of historicist investigation and the demands of social justice politics, however, the irony was that it circulated a politics all its own in the form of what were promised to have been refined cultural sensibilities and belletristic expressive styles complicit with nothing more than the timeless soul of a universal humanity. The result was a notion of the literary as something that, like Kirk's conservatism, promised to articulate not "an ideology, but instead a mode of looking at human nature and society."

This helps us to understand why Kirk believed that the potency of literary form offered welcome relief from what he viewed as the arid expositions of the "intellectual," a term that he once argued had described a figure in the nineteenth century who "neglected the imagination, the powers of insight and wonder, and the whole realm of being that is beyond private rational perception," and which in the twentieth century, he wrote, "appears to be derived from the jargon of Marxism."[105] He claimed that the "conservative mind" required the wonder of imagination and was therefore drawn to the language of the poets. As Kirk put it in a later edition of *The Conservative Mind*:

> Men conservatively inclined are not eager to be styled "intellectuals"; for that term itself is joined to the secular cult of the rationalistic Enlightenment. What occurred after 1950 was this: conservative thinkers demonstrated that "intellectuals" enjoy no monopoly of intellectual power, and that intellectualism and right reason were not synonymous terms. The principal poets of the twentieth century, indeed, never had submitted to the hegemony of liberal intellectualism; it may suffice to mention, for the moment, the names of Eliot, Yeats, and Frost.[106]

This recalls the scene in *Kokoro* in which Watakushi comes to a resonant conclusion on realizing that he wishes to see Sensei not as an intellectual, but as a humane and spiritual inspiration:

> But while my chess-loving father failed even to entertain me, Sensei, whose acquaintance I had never sought for amusement's sake, gave me far greater intellectual satisfaction as a companion. Perhaps I should not have used the word "intellectual," for it has a cold and impersonal sound. I should perhaps have said "spiritual" instead. Indeed, it would not have seemed to me then an exaggeration to say that Sensei's strength had entered my body, and that his very life was flowing in my veins.[107]

In the transatlantic world of the midcentury years, Kirk believed that the poet T. S. Eliot could inspire conservatives with a spiritual force more potent than cold intellectual argumentation. The two were actually in touch, and Eliot once wrote to Kirk stating that he was "very much impressed" with *The Conservative Mind*.[108] For his part, Kirk believed that

Eliot could guide conservatives in the twentieth century: "Not to the statistician, then, but to the poet, do many conservatives turn for insight," he wrote. "If there has been a principal conservative thinker in the twentieth century, it is T. S. Eliot, whose age this is in humane letters. Eliot's whole endeavor was to point a way out of the Waste Land toward order in the soul and in society."[109] In addition to Eliot, Kirk also seems to have found a kindred spirit in the science-fiction writer Ray Bradbury, who, Kirk once wrote, "has drawn the sword against the dreary and corrupting materialism of this century; . . . His Martians, spectres, and witches are not diverting entertainment merely: they become, in their eerie manner, the defenders of truth and beauty."[110] In this context, it comes as less of a surprise that McClellan himself would write of *Kokoro* in 1958 that it asks readers "to see the tragedy of Sensei's life as something which is not unique, but which is human."[111] He elaborated:

> Sōseki speaks often as though loneliness were peculiar to modern man. The question is whether loneliness is primarily a contemporary social phenomenon for Sōseki, or an eternal human condition. Perhaps the answer lies in the fact that a tragic writer of Sōseki's perception and sensitivity would not view man's suffering wholly as a product of some particular set of social or historical circumstances. This does not mean, of course, that Sōseki did not comment on his own times. His novels may be read profitably as social documents of late Meiji and early Taishō. But the fact remains that he wished to be read as a novelist and not as a social historian.[112]

As I turn to a reading of McClellan's *Kokoro* translation, I bear in mind that an interpretive mode premised on the inevitability of context could corrupt the complex sensibilities that animated it in the first place. It would not be convincing to insist that McClellan's interlocutors "influenced" the way he translated the novel, for example. Nor is the point that Sōseki or McClellan, Watakushi or Sensei, was a "neoliberal" himself. These deterministic lines of inquiry would threaten to reduce the pleasures of the translation to the expositions of its discursive context, and in so doing, to ironically evacuate the literary imagination from a dynamic intellectual history almost completely. With these pitfalls in mind, I proceed from the premise that because *Kokoro* does not disclose any obvious allegiance to politics, it never asks for readers' argumentative approval as any kind of political statement whatsoever. But nevertheless—and perhaps all the more—the seemingly nonideological, apparently apolitical aspects of *Kokoro* might have enchanted the romantic part of the liberal imagination that is taken with the mysterious movements of invisible hands, and the undesigned formations of spontaneous orders. In making this claim, I recall Lionel Trilling's observation in *The Liberal Imagination* (1950) that literary reading, writing, and criticism are necessary supplements to the more conventionally defined terrain of intellectual history because the literary delivers the imagination to a space of unresolved possibility that doctrinaire convictions and straightforward arguments threaten to destroy. As Trilling put it: "To the carrying out of the job of criticizing the liberal imagination, literature has a unique relevance, not merely because so much of modern literature has explicitly directed itself upon politics, but more importantly because literature is the human activity that takes the fullest and most precise account of variousness, possibility, complexity, and difficulty."[113]

To be sure, it is difficult to tell just what notion of "liberal" Trilling had in mind in writing *The Liberal Imagination*, and the scholar of the humanities Louis Menand has observed that in all likelihood, he was "treating all liberals alike."[114] But what matters in the context of the current analysis is that for Trilling at midcentury, the literary rendering of "variousness, possibility, complexity, and difficulty" was in short supply in the more "patently" political literature of the time:

> If we now turn and consider the contemporary literature of America, we see that wherever we can describe it as patently liberal and democratic, we must say that it is not of lasting interest. I do not say that the work which is written to conform to the liberal democratic tradition is of no value but only that we do not incline to return to it, we do not establish it in our minds and affections. Very likely we learn from it as citizens; and as citizen-scholars and citizen-critics we understand and explain it. But we do not live in an active reciprocal relation with it. The sense of largeness, of cogency, of the transcendence which largeness and cogency can give, the sense of being reached in our secret and primitive minds—this we virtually never get from the writers of the liberal democratic tradition at the present time.[115]

For Trilling, then, the "patently" ideological novel could have only diminished literary force because it would overwhelm the imagination with the closures of conviction, and because it would convey to readers no "sense of being reached in our secret and primitive minds." In this light, we begin to see that the liberal force of McClellan's *Kokoro* would have accumulated not in any doctrinaire appeal, but in the open-ended pleasures of the novel that conspired with the contingencies of a still-forming intellectual episteme, breathing with the efforts of Hayek and the Mont Pèlerin Society to construct a "truly radical liberalism" at midcentury, however furtively.

Kokoro *and the Market Imagination*

In reading McClellan's translation through the prism of the intellectual history introduced above, I aim for an interpretive strategy that embraces—rather than rejects or ignores—the obvious fact that at first glance, *Kokoro* would seem to be a sentimental novel about feelings that bear no trace of orientation toward the economic imperatives we often associate with a "neoliberal" imagination. I will argue that in fact, it is for this very reason that *Kokoro* offers the opportunity to rethink the shape of neoliberal thought itself in a softer aesthetic context that does not culminate in a hardline allegory of free-market fundamentalism. This is to say that treating the text as a work of literary art structured by its own formal orchestrations will challenge us to think through and beyond the discursive contexts of intellectual history outlined above, even as we explore how an economic vocabulary might allow us to sense aspects of the novel that would be harder to recognize otherwise. Balancing these commitments leads me to pursue a two-part analysis. First, I examine the submerged economic orientation of the liberal subject in *Kokoro* by close reading the nuts and bolts of its narrative language; next, I extend this economically informed reading of the liberal subject to the bifurcated form of the novel as a whole, taking into account how its two narrators speak to the reader in a novel that famously never concludes. The two-way movements of this analysis—at once moving inward toward the economics of the entrepreneurial self in particular and outward toward the form of the text in general—follow through on another two-way movement on the level of method: having first stepped outside the realm of the literary and into the domain of thought above, I now aim to show how the intellectual history of midcentury neoliberalism can enable an enhanced return to *Kokoro* by which we might be able to see something new in this long-familiar classic.

Aspects of my approach follow the lead of the literary scholar Rachel Greenwald Smith, whose study of affect and contemporary American literature showed how the novel form can articulate the workings of a deeper cultural logic in what she has called "the age of neoliberalism," particularly in narratives that conflate the realms of private feeling and private property.[116] Of special relevance to my reading of Sōseki's novel is Greenwald Smith's observation that although the uniqueness of literary characters' emotional lives might seem to form outside the rational calculations of marketplace exchange and the profit-driven motives of entrepreneurial initiative, literary subjectivities in the age of neoliberalism more often regard even their own feelings as a kind of "emotional portfolio" in need of meticulous regulation, development, and management.[117] Far from promising an escape from economic scheming, then, the interior lives of literary characters can become a marketplace all their own in which thinking and feeling individuals are transformed into entrepreneurs "exclusively responsible for themselves."[118] Making this argument, Greenwald Smith's study focused on contemporary novels that she claimed reveal how the expansions of a marketplace logic into previously noneconomic realms of human experience—such as affective life—have fueled the sorts of transformations of subjectivity that the political scientist Wendy Brown and others have identified as the crux of contemporary neoliberal politics per se.[119]

Without going so far as to posit that *Kokoro* is a "neoliberal novel," much less that Sōseki was a "neoliberal novelist" himself, we do notice that the familiar preoccupations of economic individualism conspire to conflate the realms of private feeling and private property in several moments that appear in *Kokoro*. The scholar of Japanese literature Michael Bourdaghs has examined the place of private property ownership in Sōseki's novels (including *Kokoro*) through the lens of contemporaneous trends in sociological discourse, arguing that "Sōseki's theory and practice of *bungaku* [literature] formed a critical response to modern norms of property, norms that underwrote the discipline of sociology as he knew it."[120] Building on this, we might also recall that private property has been a central concern in the canon of liberal thought, too, a canon that McClellan studied, and that informed the imagination of Sōseki's Meiji Japan. In addition to considering these ideas as an extrinsic discourse that helps us to contextualize *Kokoro*, we might also inquire after how they were metabolized into the forms of language and the structures of narrative that appear in the novel—both in the Japanese original and in McClellan's English translation. Suspended within the text itself, the liberal imagination becomes a covert literary resource easily disavowed because it is never named, but one that, once acknowledged, seems to spontaneously order the world of the novel like an invisible hand. As its influence accretes, readers begin to sense that subject formation in the novel galvanizes around marketplace competition and the incessant desire for entrepreneurial advantage, to the extent that even the most deeply held personal feelings come to be narrated within the force fields of self-interest that grip its two narrators, Watakushi and Sensei.

These dynamics are in play from the very first lines of the novel: "I always called him 'Sensei.' I shall therefore refer to him simply as 'Sensei,' and not by his real name. It is not because I consider it more discreet, but it is because I find it more natural that I do so. Whenever the memory of him comes back to me now, I find that I think of him as 'Sensei' still. And with pen in hand, I cannot bring myself to write of him in any other way."[121] *Kokoro* is a sentimental novel about feelings that would seem to exist outside the cold calculations associated with the more explicitly economic dealings of *homo economicus*. But Watakushi's insistence on the appellation "Sensei" locates his story within the transactional hierarchy of student and pupil and sets up a narrative about profitable exchange. This is a choice, for Watakushi discloses alternatives to naming the older man "Sensei": his "true [given] name" (*honmyō*) and "first initial" (*kashiramoji*) both appear as other possibilities in the first paragraph of Sōseki's Japanese-language original. But the word "Sensei" distinguishes itself from these alternatives because it necessarily implies that the younger student's relationship with the older teacher has facilitated the transfer of some kind of surplus in the form of a lesson, a feeling, and a narrative. In other words, it indicates that this is a narrative about something that has been gained. Read this way, "Sensei" is not so much a term of endearment or closeness—relational proximities that would imply something nearer to profitless equilibrium—as it is a mode of address registering the sort of difference and distance requisite to produce a surplus: the appellation "Sensei" identifies an older and wiser outsider whose narrative lesson is valuable to the extent that it would have been unattainable within Watakushi's more familiar circuits of communicative exchange.

Steering the novel in this direction, Watakushi jettisons the other possible modes of address by declaring from the start that he "will never reveal Sensei's true name" (*honmyō wa uchiakenai*), and that he "would not feel comfortable using something as cold and impersonal as a first initial" (*yosoyososhii kashiramoji nado wa totemo tsukau ki ni naranai*). With this, readers are informed that Watakushi has constructed a narrative economy of scarcity through his own strategic withholdings ("Sensei's true name"), even at the same time that he has also, as an entrepreneurial narrator himself, promised readers access to an excess (the lesson of the Sensei). By the end of the novel, readers learn that Watakushi's meticulous management of narrative scarcity and surplus is a learned strategy, a part of his inheritance from Sensei. His secretive statements at the beginning of *Kokoro* that conceal Sensei's identity link to the ending of the novel, where Sensei closes his letter with this statement: "I want both the good and bad things in my past to serve as an example to others. But my wife is the one exception—I do not want her to know about any of this. My first wish is that her memory of me should be kept as unsullied as possible. So long as my wife is alive, I want you to keep everything I have told you a secret—even after I myself am dead."[122] The beginning and ending of *Kokoro* bond the two narrators through a language of secrets. And as a secret confided through narrative, Sensei's life story becomes proprietary knowledge requiring Watakushi's careful management. This explains why Watakushi contracts himself in the first lines of the novel as a limited liability intermediary who will broker readers' investments in a narrative and sentimental economy centered on Sensei, but only within the parameters put forth by the negotiations that open the novel, the most prominent of which is the provision that the older man be known to the reader only as "Sensei." Perhaps it was in the spirit of secrecy, too, that in McClellan's translation, Sensei's and Watakushi's strategic withholdings were compounded by the fact that one of the alternative appellations for "Sensei" that was listed in the first lines of Sōseki's original—"a cold and impersonal first initial"—mysteriously disappeared altogether. Unlike Watakushi, however, McClellan never disclosed his own narrative withholding to the reader as he laundered it through the "derivatives market" of translation, so to speak.

More generally, my reading of the first lines of the novel elaborates a thread that has developed in scholarship on *Kokoro* according to which the opening paragraph reveals a crucial dynamic in the younger student's relationship with the older man Sensei. This thread holds that while it might seem that the student is loyal to Sensei, the language of the younger narrator's prose actually reveals that he does not faithfully transmit the story of the older man transparently, but rather responds to Sensei in his own terms, at times even undermining the older man in subtle but unmistakable ways. The scholar of Japanese literature Atsuko Sakaki has explained that it was Komori's influential 1985 reading of the novel that most prominently revealed how small details like the impersonal initial referenced by the student indicated that "the narrator [Watakushi] has come to differentiate his relationship with Sensei, which was human and warmhearted, from Sensei's relationship with K, which was distant and cold."[123] While this may sound like a simple matter of plot development, Sakaki explained that it was, for Komori, a key to the larger argument that beyond the frame of the narrative, the student went on to have a sexual relationship with Sensei's widow after the older man's death, and that as a result, the student had in fact fathered a child by her (in contrast to Sensei, who had no children with his wife).[124] Although controversial, to be sure, Komori's reading is now regarded as fundamental to the contemporary interpretation of *Kokoro*: it launched the so-called *Kokoro* debates (*Kokoro ronsō*), and the scholar of Japanese literature John Nathan noted in his biography of Sōseki that "of the five hundred articles on the book [*Kokoro*] written since its publication in 1914, more than two hundred appeared in the first ten years after Komori's [1985] essay."[125]

Moving closer to the matter at hand in this chapter, the scholar of Japanese literature Keith Vincent has argued that some of the subtle textual evidence on which Komori's thesis rose is downplayed or obscured in McClellan's translation.[126] By re-reading McClellan's translation through the insights generated by the *Kokoro* debates, Vincent showed how the skeptical attitude that drove Komori's critique of canonical conservatism in Japan could deconstruct paternalistic sensibilities on both sides of the Pacific that had ascribed to novels like *Kokoro* an ethical clarity to be believed at face value. This helps us to see why Bourdaghs has summed up the implications of the *Kokoro* debates in the economic terms of possession, arguing that "the crucial issues under dispute in the *Kokoro* ronsō, in fact, revolved largely around the ideological issues of ownership. Who did the novel belong to, the author, its original readers in early Taishō, or the contemporary critic? . . . Ultimately, the *Kokoro* ronsō represented a struggle over ownership of Sōseki and his works: which school of interpretation was going to win the right to legitimacy for its readings of the novel?"[127]

Within this wider dialogue, my heavy-handed analysis above represents an intentional barbarization of a moving novel, one that breaks apart the subtlety of Watakushi's language in order to expose the contractual implication made manifest by its very forms. Although inelegant, this approach at least establishes a starting point that prepares us to extend other readings of the young student's relationship with Sensei in the direction of an economic imagination, and to see in *Kokoro* what literary critics studying the connections between (neo)liberal economic thought and the novel form have argued in other contexts—namely, that the marketplace rationality premised on exchange is not contained by the marketplace itself, but rather insinuates itself into ever greater territories of social and private life, such that the market mechanism becomes the heartbeat of many (or even all) aspects of human life. One of the implications that follows from this premise is that the strategic calculations of market enterprise leave their residues on the very forms of language and narrative that are available to articulate even thoughts and feelings that seem to bear no trace of economic imperative. In this connection, Greenwald Smith has noted in her study of contemporary American fiction that the building blocks of neoliberal subject formation accrete in the tendency to narrate human feelings in the language of entrepreneurial enterprise. As she put it: "In the neoliberal context, recognizing the presence of emotions, in art, in other people, and in the self, does not challenge market-oriented thinking. Instead, feelings frequently become yet another material foundation for market-oriented behavior: emotions are acquired, invested, traded, and speculated upon."[128]

In a related vein, the literary critic Ian Watt described contractual associations and economic individualism in *The Rise of the Novel*, an iconic study that appeared in 1957, the same year as did McClellan's translation of *Kokoro*. Watt argued that the "rise of the novel" took as its condition of possibility "a society characterised by that vast complex of interdependent factors denoted by the term 'individualism,'" adding that these "factors" were largely animated by capitalism, which, Watt noted, "brought a great increase of economic specialisation" and a "new economic order" centered on the "individual: he alone was primarily responsible for determining his own economic, social, political and religious roles."[129] In his reading of *homo economicus* in *Robinson Crusoe* (1719), Watt observed that contracts and bookkeeping textually formalize exchange relationships in ways that replace "the unwritten, traditional and collective relationships of previous societies," and that indicate the "theoretical development of political individualism."[130] By extension, Watt's observations suggest that the contractual language in Watakushi's first utterances in *Kokoro* evidence the workings of an exclusive liberal worldview, one that obliterates other sensibilities. As Watt put it: "The hypostasis of the economic motive logically entails a devaluation of other modes of thought, feeling and action: the various forms of traditional group relationship, the family, the guild, the village, the sense of nationality—all are weakened, and so too are the competing claims of non-economic individual achievement and enjoyment, ranging from spiritual salvation to the pleasures of recreation."[131] These sorts of erasures figure centrally in *Kokoro*: most notably, the rich spiritual life of "K" is overcome by Sensei's strategic contracting of Okusan in his bid to marry Ojosan, and Sensei's inheritance, once usurped, takes with it his bonds to blood kin.

The fate of K is particularly noteworthy in this connection because his demise coincides with the collapse of a spiritual space in *Kokoro* untrammeled by economic scheming. K abandons the credentialing institution of academe, and in his solitary studies of religious texts such as the Bible and Buddhist sutras, he strives to develop a strength of spirit immeasurable by the metrics of entrepreneurial self-advancement and material accumulation. But when Sensei destroys his friend, body and soul, the novel dramatizes what Watt called the "hypostasis of the economic motive," which obliterates the sort of space of spirit that had until then been held out by K. In the beginning, Sensei's plan in inviting K to live with Ojosan and Okusan was to "humanize" (*ningenrashiku suru*) his holier friend; put more bluntly, he wanted the chaste K to know carnal temptation. Okusan correctly foresaw that Sensei's inviting K into their home would upset its Edenic equilibrium by initiating a competition for Ojosan's favor between the two young men. She advised Sensei against the plan, even though it would have been more lucrative for her take on another boarder:

> As I said, Okusan was against this arrangement from the first. In a boarding house, she said, two lodgers would be more convenient than one, and three would be more profitable than two. But, she pointed out, she was not running a boarding house, and she had no wish to take in another lodger. I said that my friend would give her no trouble. Trouble or no trouble, she answered, she disliked having a stranger in the house. But I was a stranger too, I said. Her answer was that she had from the first known that she could trust me. I smiled. She then changed her tactics. She said that I would later regret having brought such a person into the house. I asked her why she thought so. It was her turn to smile.[132]

Sensei wins the argument with Okusan, but at his own expense. As it later becomes clear that K, too, has fallen in love with Ojosan, Sensei begins to scheme against his friend: "I watched him carefully, as though he were my fencing opponent. There was not one part of me that was not on guard. I did not relax for one single moment my eyes, or my heart, or my body. To say that K did not guard himself well would be an understatement. In his innocence, he put himself completely at my mercy. I was allowed to observe him in leisure, and to note carefully his most vulnerable points."[133] In what turns out to be a battle to the death, K's moral superiority becomes a competitive disadvantage. As a good man, K is a bad entrepreneur, and this enchants Sensei: "[K] was too honest, too simple, and altogether too righteous to see through me. I was in no mood to admire his virtues, however. Instead, I saw them only as weaknesses."[134]

Gripped with fear that K will abandon the celibacy required of his spiritual devotions and seduce Ojosan, Sensei destroys him by cynically ventriloquizing K's own moral language. The piety of K's words, once turned against him, takes on the sinister form of a black magic incantation:

> I said cruelly, "Anyone who has no spiritual aspirations is an idiot." This was what K had said to me when we were traveling in Boshu. I threw back at him the very words that he once used to humiliate me. Even my tone of

> voice was the same as his had been when he made the remark. But I insist that I was not being vindictive. I confess to you that what I was trying to do was far more cruel than mere revenge. I wanted to destroy whatever hope there might have been in his love for Ojosan.[135]

Sensei later repeats the damning curse: "What I feared was the harm he might cause me if he decided to change his ways. It was simply self-interest that prompted my remark. I said again: 'Anyone who has no spiritual aspirations is an idiot.' I watched K closely. I wanted to see how my words were affecting him."[136]

This exchange reveals that for Sensei, language is a simple tool to be manipulated for his own advantage. Whereas K communed with a spiritual poetics that connected him to the souls of the prophets, Sensei hides his true intentions behind pieces of jargon that he maneuvers like so many chess pieces: "I remember that I used constantly the word 'human' in defending my position and in attacking his. K insisted that I was trying to hide all my weaknesses behind this word. Now, I see that he was right. But in trying to point out his limitations I had become aggressive, and I was in no mood to be objective about myself. I became more dogmatic than ever."[137] And crueler, too, for Sensei comes to compare himself to a "wolf jump[ing] at the lamb's throat."[138] As the spiritual realm held out by K collapses, the intuitive poetry of the prophets that K felt deeply is overwritten by the learned logic of men like Sensei. The jargon of self-interested argument that allowed Sensei to prevail upon Okusan and K presently becomes the vernacular in a society of ceaseless competition whose ever-expansive influence spares no one and nothing, as Sensei ultimately comes to understand:

> When I was cheated by my uncle, I felt very strongly the unreliableness of men. I learned to judge others harshly, but not myself. I thought that, in the midst of a corrupt world, I had managed to remain virtuous. Because of K, however, my self-confidence was shattered. With a shock, I realized that I was no better than my uncle. I became as disgusted with myself as I had been with the rest of the world. Action of any kind became impossible for me.[139]

And so we see that one of the central problems of *Kokoro* is the age-old question that haunts market society in general: How can the self-interest that drives economic activity and spills over into even noneconomic situations ever square with a sentimental desire to lead a moral life?

The Thought of Kokoro

The scholar Duncan Foley explored this question in his survey of foundational texts in the history of economic thought. He began by describing this corpus in terms of an "economic theology" because, he explained, "at its most abstract and interesting level, economics is a speculative philosophical discourse, not a deductive or inductive science."[140] His narrative began with Adam Smith, who, Foley observed, "addresses more directly than anyone else the central anxiety that besets capitalism—the question of how to be a good person and live a good and moral life within the antagonistic, impersonal, and self-regarding social relations that capitalism imposes."[141] This is the sort of question that I understand Sōseki to be raising in my reading of *Kokoro* above, and in the realm of economic thought, it led Foley to argue that the "most important feature of Adam Smith's work is not what it tells us concretely about how the economy works (although it tells us a great deal about that), but its discussion of how we should feel about capitalist economic life and what attitude it might be reasonable for us to take toward the complicated and contradictory experience it affords us. These are discussions above all of faith and belief, not of fact, and hence theological."[142] To some extent, we could just as easily say "and hence literary." And in this light, Foley's reflection on "economic theology" helps us to see why the axioms of economic individualism examined above come alive in *Kokoro* as they breathe with layers of more abstract thinking about self and society that have appeared in the lengthier history of economic thought, too, rather than only through narrations of explicitly market-oriented behavior or simple parables of free-market fundamentalism.

Exploring these layers of complexity transitions my reading of the novel away from the self-interested figure of *homo economicus* analyzed above, and toward the insight of the scholar of art and philosophy Pedro Erber, who in another context has observed that even if it is true that *homo economicus* has left his perch in the market and insinuated himself into other areas of human experience, as neoliberal theory holds, "this does not amount to a simple elimination of every other aspect of human psychology and a purification of the utility-maximizing, interest-seeking instinct"; instead, it indicates a blurring of boundaries that puts economics into a two-way dialogue with aesthetics—a dialogue in which the "transit" between economic ideas and aesthetic life "is open in both directions," as Erber put it.[143] What makes these connections more difficult to see in the case of *Kokoro*, however, is the fact that its subtle literary form resists any hard-driving argument about its ultimate politics or definite links to intellectual history. Rather than adding up to an argument, in fact, we notice that many of the questions raised by the novel go unanswered. In this regard, Alan Tansman has observed that whatever the promise of a concrete lesson from the "Sensei" might be in Sōseki's novel, readers "finally come to sense that the only thing there is to learn is that there is nothing to learn that will change anything at all. This is the lesson of Japan's most ardent and regarded public teacher of the modern condition."[144] Tansman wrote that "if there is hope, or a positive pedagogical project, in the novel, it is not about being a person in the world," adding that in the final section of the novel, "there is a merging of consciousnesses through reading and the possibility of direct communication. But society, the sphere of public action, has disappeared."[145]

The absence of any obviously interventionist impulse or definite social politics in *Kokoro* is part of what creates the impression that this is a "Great Book" of the human condition that is awesome in its insight, but purposeless in its politics. In another sense, though, the seemingly apolitical turn away from social action in *Kokoro* actually resonates with perspectives that developed in the right-liberal imagination at midcentury. If "society" as a realm of transformative "public action" does not exist, for example, then there can be no conceptual basis for any notion of "social justice"—a perspective promoted by the neoliberal mind in particular, and elaborated by Hayek in *Law, Legislation and Liberty*, vol. 2, *The Mirage of Social Justice* (1976). This would suggest that when a liberal agnosticism holds that there is no lesson to be learned about "being a person in the world," all individuals remain exclusively responsible for their own contingent circumstances in a marketplace organized more by spontaneous orders and invisible hands than any legible logic that might be evaluated, and transformed, according to a normative political and ethical horizon. These were some of the trends in thought that in another context led the political philosopher Wendy Brown to argue that as the ever-expansive realm of individualist economic competition erodes the possibility of transformative and collective political action in society, neoliberalism articulates itself in the "vanquishing of *homo politicus*."[146]

Some of the deeper intellectual architecture of these perspectives originated in part with a skepticism toward the powers of the rational mind to plan, design, and foresee. And this has implications for a reading of *Kokoro* because it was tied to what Hayek called "individualism," the same topic as Sōseki's most famous essay, "Watakushi no kojinshugi" (My Individualism), and one of the most familiar themes in the novel. In a December 1945 lecture titled "Individualism: True and False," Hayek traced what he called the "true individualism" to the thought of John Locke, Adam Smith, and Edmund Burke, among others. This Anglo-liberal tradition of individualists stood against the socialists, of course—Hayek even wrote of "individualism" that "the term has the distinction that the word 'socialism' was deliberately coined to express its opposition to individualism."[147] But Hayek's more nuanced critique took aim at what he called the "false" individualists of the French tradition (including Descartes and Rousseau in particular), whom he blamed for an excessive faith in the intentional designs of the rational mind. Hayek specified that in contrast, the "true individualism" of the Anglo-liberal tradition emphasized the inarguable limitations and imperfection of human knowledge. He suggested that the "true individualism" respects authorless traditions and conventions, viewing them as the social grammar that protects liberty in an undesigned world beyond any individual's conscious planning.

This led Hayek to revise what he viewed as the major misconceptions about "individualism." Among other things, Hayek's rumination on what he called the "true individualism" criticized the crude model of "economic man" (*homo economicus*) that he argued had been erroneously attributed to Adam Smith. He countered that Smith's great insight was not that people are rational, calculating, and savvy by nature, but that "man was by nature lazy and indolent, improvident and wasteful, and that it was only by the force of circumstances that he could be made to behave economically or carefully to adjust his means to his ends."[148] And whereas "individualism" might seem to indicate an unrestrained free will enabled by an attitude of laissez-faire, Hayek in fact emphasized that the true individualism is actually structured by universally applied rules, writing that "the most general principle on which an individualist system is based is that it uses the universal acceptance of general principles as the means to create order in social affairs."[149] Elsewhere, he responded to those who condemn "individualism" for encouraging selfishness and greed by arguing that the "true individualism" is a broader philosophy that proceeds from "the constitutional limitation of man's knowledge and interests, the fact that he *cannot* know more than a tiny part of the whole of society."[150] Perhaps most surprisingly, Hayek argued that the "true individualism" obeys the accumulated authority of tradition even when its conventions do not seem to make sense, writing that the individual must "submit to conventions which are not the result of intelligent design, whose justification in the particular instance may not be recognizable, and which to him will often appear unintelligible and irrational."[151]

Brown helps us to see that these remarks on "convention" in "Individualism: True and False" are broadly consistent with Hayek's wider perspective on how the authorless agency of tradition sanctioned markets and morals, both of which Hayek believed had the virtue of creating consensus without coercion.[152] Hayek's fear was that in contrast, the rational mind could turn authoritarian, imposing its own coercive designs over those evolved by tradition and codified by rules. This is why he wrote in *The Fatal Conceit: The Errors of Socialism* (1988) that "the curious task of economics is to demonstrate to men how little they really know about what they imagine they can design."[153] He had already made this point decades earlier at the end of "Individualism: True and False," where he drew on the conservative thinker Edmund Burke as he argued that engaging a world beyond our minds and forms of society beyond our selves requires a sensitivity to all that we cannot plan, and all that we cannot change. And this sensitivity, Hayek argued, was the crux of the true individualism:

> What individualism teaches us is that society is greater than the individual only in so far as it is free. In so far as it is controlled or directed, it is limited to the powers of the individual minds which control or direct it. If the presumption of the modern mind, which will not respect anything that is not consciously controlled by individual reason, does not learn in time where to stop, we may, as Edmund Burke warned us, "be well assured that

> everything about us will dwindle by degrees, until at length our concerns are shrunk to the dimensions of our minds."[154]

Although rarely read as a resource for literary criticism, Hayek's perspective on the spontaneous order that materializes beyond the rational powers of the human mind supplies an unlikely but revealing vantage point from which to rethink aspects of *Kokoro*. Most obviously, the novel is associated with the problems and paradoxes of "individualism," and so Hayek's essay on the subject provides insight into a foundational concept that Sōseki rendered in fiction. With that said, though, simply overlaying a subtle novel with the grid of Hayek's thought would not only be an unconvincing way to read *Kokoro*, but would also ironically replicate the tendency to impose systematic ideas and the foregone conclusions of complete designs that Hayek himself warned against. A better way to work from ideas to literature and back again might be to ask how *Kokoro* can enrich a reading of Hayek by drawing out some of the submerged implications for aesthetics and interpretation that emanate from his skepticism toward the powers of the rational mind. To make this connection, it serves to recall that at around the same time that Hayek conceptualized the limits of human rationality with reference to market life, a resonant idea took shape in the realm of midcentury literary criticism, later becoming a commonplace of the field that endures to this day. This idea is known to literature scholars as the "intentional fallacy," and it holds that the purposeful designs of an author do not determine the ultimate meaning of a literary text. The scholar Michael Szalay has pointed to these connections in his study of literature and economics in another context, and drawing on his perspective, it might be said that reading *Kokoro* with Hayek in mind would suggest that it is no easier for an author's intentions to strategically plan the meaning of a literary work of art than it is for a government bureaucrat or economist to effectively plan economic activity.[155]

By the same measure, though, it must not be forgotten that placing limits on the scope of intentional design is supposed to be liberating in the Hayekian view inasmuch as it enables a world of unscripted possibilities to materialize beyond the strict confines of specific plans and known-in-advance endings—that is, beyond the limitations of human reason itself. That is why he argued that "if left free, men will often achieve more than individual human reason could design or foresee."[156] Likewise, the skepticism toward authorial intention in literary criticism is supposed to release the aesthetic power of literary language from the limitations imposed by the specificity of an author's personal life, historical circumstances, and creative intentions, and to allow the text itself, as an autonomous work of art and an independent structure of meaning, to say more than the author alone could have ever knowingly designed in advance. That is why the midcentury critics W. K. Wimsatt Jr. and M. C. Beardsley, writing at nearly the same time as Hayek in "Individualism: True and False," would argue in their essay "The Intentional Fallacy" (1946) that literary works of art do not merely signify in relation to the parochial circumstances of their creators; rather, "the work is measured against something outside the author."[157] Roland Barthes would corroborate this perspective in his iconic essay "The Death of the Author" (1968), writing that "to give a text an Author is to impose a limit on that text, to furnish it with a final signified, to close the writing."[158] He argued that in contrast, the liberated text that emerges after the metaphorical "death of the author" can signify freely, unlimited by any ultimate horizon of implication or specific source of original meaning.

These liberations are never of a formless and unpoliced kind, however. To the contrary, and however paradoxically, they unfold within the confines of laws and orders that take shape in either a political economic framework (as in the case of the market) or a specific genre, grammar, and narrative structure (as in the case of literature). Michel Foucault alerted us to this when he emphasized the role of form in Hayek's advocacy for law-bound markets that are governed by universally applied rules and regulations, rather than by the content of purposeful economic plans with definite intentions. He wrote that for Hayek and other neoliberals, laws are like the rules of a game that is played with an unplanned outcome, adding that for this reason, the neoliberal mind believed that laws are the opposite of a preconceived design concocted with the specific aim of arriving at a known-in-advance ending.[159] In the literary realm, too, we notice that the "death of the author" and the "intentional fallacy" do not mean that reading becomes an amorphous or purely subjective experience in which anything goes; rather, it indicates that all readers of a given text submit to the specific narrative laws and genre-bound orders that the text establishes, finding in them a form of structured-yet-spontaneous meaning in an aesthetic realm that never culminates in any narrowly defined point, planned-in-advance argument, or avowedly ideological purpose. Like rule-bound markets in the Hayekian view, then, literary works of art are endowed with a sublime implication to the extent that they are allowed to function as self-legislating structures of meaning—the extent, that is, to which they are "left free." Among other things, this is why the "Great Books" are believed by their advocates to be inexhaustible—because they never reduce to a single line of thinking, or historicist grid of contextual coordinates, but rather supply a formal structure that opens up infinitely and spontaneously in reading after reading. Rewriting Hayek's quotation above, it might be said that what the "true individualism" teaches the liberal imagination is that the realm of literature and art (like society) is greater than the individual only insofar as it is free.

This makes clear that as a structure of thought, Hayek's notion of "true individualism" raised questions of form that were not purely intellectual, nor merely economic. In addition, these questions had to do with narrating the shape of society and the mind of the self in a world that cannot be completely known to any individual imagination. Needless to say, these are matters that have been given aesthetic representation, and subjected to literary interpretation, too. This comes through in the case of *Kokoro* in particular as we witness the limits of language and the imperfection of intentional human designs unfold within a narrative structure that frames the self-limiting perspective of each of its two narrators against the judgmental gaze of the other. In so doing, *Kokoro* balances the self-interested motivations of Sensei and Watakushi against the disinterested judgement of the reader, who engages the novel from outside its frame as a pensive spectator contemplating a work of literary art.[160] As we read the selfish drive of the characters suspended within the purposeless drive of the novel itself, we come to realize that as surprising as it may sound, part of what makes *Kokoro* a novel about the "true individualism" has little to do with its content—the story that it tells, the events that it describes, and the historical context in which it was written and set. In addition, and more compellingly, it is the form of the novel—split between two narrators and ultimately inconclusive—which polices the laws and order of a text inviting continual contemplation from each and every individual reader at the same time that it will always refuse to be summed up, completely known, ultimately judged, or contextualized once and for all—refuse, that is, to ever be "shrunk to the dimensions of our minds."

Living with Strangers

It all starts with a spontaneous encounter that is nevertheless structured. At the beginning of the novel, Watakushi's friend invites him to Kamakura, only to abandon him there. Left alone, Watakushi spies Sensei on the beach in a moment of chance encounter, and notices that the older man is accompanied by a mysterious foreigner. The next day, Watakushi returns to the same place he had first laid eyes on Sensei, carefully timing his surveillance to precisely twenty-four hours after the original encounter. His effort to contrive another "chance" meeting pays off, and leads to his first conversation with Sensei in the changing room near the beach:

> It was, I think, on the afternoon of the third day following our swim together that Sensei, when we met at the tea house, suddenly asked me, "Do you intend to stay in Kamakura long?" I had really no idea how much longer I would be in Kamakura, so I said, "I don't know." I then saw that Sensei was grinning, and I suddenly became embarrassed. I could not help blurting out, "And you, Sensei?" It was then that I began to call him "Sensei."[161]

The language of this encounter emphasizes its spontaneity, as a less literary translation might make clearer. Sensei poses a question "out of the blue" (*totsuzen*) to Watakushi, who is "caught thoughtlessly off guard" (*kangae no nai watakushi*) and responds that he "has no idea" what he will do (*dō da ka wakarimasen*). The emptiness of thought and the absence of design mysteriously call forth the appellation "Sensei," which Watakushi paradoxically "cannot help but respond with" (*kikikaesazu ni wa irarenakatta*) even though "this was the first time that the word 'Sensei' had ever crossed [his] lips" (*kore ga watakushi no kuchi o deta sensei to iu kotoba no hajimari de aru*).

A readerly mind attuned to the moral side of market thinking would be prepared to see the encounter at Kamakura cast the older man in a role akin to what Adam Smith called the "impartial spectator": rather than being a "Sensei" in the sense of a teacher who gives a lesson in a school, he could be read as a stranger in society who regards Watakushi disinterestedly, first as an actual interlocutor and later as an internalized form of conscience speaking from within. Smith described the workings of the invisible hand of the marketplace in *The Wealth of Nations* (1776) and considered the sentimental life of the entrepreneurial subject whose world is ordered by it in *The Theory of Moral Sentiments* (1759). In the mid-century years, Smith's perspective seems to have been one of Hayek's own inspirations: in "Individualism: True and False," Hayek described Smith as one "to whom nobody will deny the title of individualist," and ventured "the opinion that for all practical purposes we can still learn more about the behavior of men from the *Wealth of Nations* than from most of the more pretentious modern treatises on 'social psychology.'"[162] But it was in *The Theory of Moral Sentiments* that Smith analyzed the moral economy of interpersonal judgment in ways that best illuminate the spontaneous order of *Kokoro*. In that text, Smith sketched the social imagination of a modern self that relies on the power of imagination to make sense of a world that can never be fully known to any individual mind, and to judge ambiguous moral matters in social interactions that exceed one's own self-centered perspective. This led Smith to take up the question of how the power of imagination allows the individual in market society to envision his or her own actions in terms of being praiseworthy or blameworthy in the eyes of others, given that the force field of one's own self-interest must necessarily compromise any pretense to objective self-judgment. He observed: "When I endeavour to examine my own conduct, when I endeavour to pass sentence upon it, and either to approve or condemn it, it is evident that, in all such cases, I divide myself, as it were, into two persons; and that I, the examiner and judge, represent a different character from that other I, the person whose conduct is examined into and judged of."[163] This statement reverberates with the bifurcated form of *Kokoro* itself, a sentimental meditation with two narrators (Sensei and Watakushi) who alternately play the role of "I, the examiner and judge" of his interlocutor, and "I, the person whose conduct is examined into and judged of" by the other (and implicitly by the reader of *Kokoro*, too). In this sense, the two first-person narratives in *Kokoro* would seem to reflect something of the doubled-nature of the self that Smith described, a self that divides into reciprocal halves that alternately judge and are "judged of."

In making this point, Smith revealed that subjective judgement in market society relies on a power of imagination that envisions the world and the self through the eyes of strangers. He believed that the self-interested individual locked in isolation could never be a perfect judge of himself because, left alone, his own self-love would bond him to a hermetic world in which truly disinterested judgment would always be impossible. Smith argued that even the company of friends, family, and other sympathetic confidants would be insufficient to ventilate the mind of any individual; instead, it was conversation with the "impartial spectator," a kind of stranger, which could best regulate the distorted self-image of the self-interested and self-loving subject:

> In solitude, we are apt to feel too strongly whatever relates to ourselves: we are apt to over-rate the good offices we may have done, and the injuries we may have suffered: we are apt to be too much elated by our own good, and too much dejected by our own bad fortune. The conversation of a friend brings us to a better, that of a stranger to a still better temper. The man within the breast, the abstract and ideal spectator of our sentiments and conduct, requires often to be awakened and put in mind of his duty, by the presence of the real spectator: and it is always from that spectator, from whom we can expect the least sympathy and indulgence, that we are likely to learn the most complete lesson of self-command.[164]

Smith almost suggests that the lonely liberal cannot abandon his moral and sentimental life to a simple philosophy of laissez-faire. Instead, thoughts and feelings require strategic regulation, both through actual contact with "real" spectators in our midst, and through introspective dialogue with the "ideal" spectator that lives within our hearts as a kind of conscience. The real and ideal spectators moderate and clarify our sentiments by offering the counsel of the stranger, as Smith argued in *The Theory of Moral Sentiments*: "Are you in adversity? Do not mourn in the darkness of solitude, do not regulate your sorrow according to the indulgent sympathy of your intimate friends; return, as soon as possible, to the day-light of the world and of society. Live with strangers, with those who know nothing, or care nothing about your misfortune."[165]

This statement resonates with the themes of *Kokoro* inasmuch as the novel addresses the relationship of two strangers, Watakushi and Sensei, who regard one another in their respective narratives. But on a deeper level, it also tells us something about the readerly imagination that engages a literary text more generally. After all, reading a novel is itself an opportunity to "live with strangers," so to speak, at least inasmuch as the act of reading fiction both requires and develops a force of imagination that allows one to momentarily inhabit the perspectives of others. And this force of imagination occasions a contemplative cast of mind capable of rendering judgement. In this vein, Erber has observed that inasmuch as *The Wealth of Nations* and *The Theory of Moral Sentiments* present Smith's insights into structures of interest and disinterestedness in market society, they are part of a larger philosophical conversation that has revealed how the questions of moral and economic judgement have appeared in proximity to the adjacent realm of aesthetic judgment.[166] Taken a step further, we begin to see why literature has been said to give aesthetic form to the ideal structures of spectatorship and judgement that Smith conceptualized in his moral and economic philosophy, as the scholar Martha Nussbaum has observed.[167]

Part of how these dynamics come through in *Kokoro* revolves around the appearance of Sensei as a kind of spectator who is both real and ideal. At the beginning of their relationship, Sensei encounters Watakushi as one of the many beachgoers gathered in Kamakura, and in this context, Sensei regards Watakushi as a kind of indifferent other who says that he cares little for the younger student. In fact, when Sensei noted in his testament that he had recently received correspondence from Watakushi asking if he could help the student find a job, he wrote: "Unfortunately, it would not be an exaggeration to say that at the time I was hardly aware of your existence. To go further, such a matter as your future livelihood was to me almost totally without significance. I did not care what you did. It was not, to my way of thinking, worth all the fuss."[168] Sensei also wrote that when Watakushi would argue about "contemporary ideas,"

> you will remember too what my attitude was. Though I did not exactly disdain your opinions, I must admit I could not bring myself to respect them either. Your thoughts were without solid foundation, and you were too young to have had much experience. Sometimes, I laughed. Sometimes, you used to look at me discontentedly. In the end, you asked me to spread out my picture scroll before your eyes. Then, for the first time, I respected you. I was moved by your decision, albeit discourteous in expression, to grasp something that was alive within my soul.[169]

Sensei's impartiality toward Watakushi endows his judgements with an intense power. It is the sort of power which, for Smith, would form the very conscience by which "the man of real constancy and firmness, the wise and just man who has been thoroughly bred in the great school of self-command" lives his life. Smith explained that the praiseworthy man lives with the eye of the impartial spectator upon him, and within him:

> He has never dared to forget for one moment the judgment which the impartial spectator would pass upon his sentiments and conduct. He has never dared to suffer the man within the breast to be absent one moment from his attention. With eyes of this great inmate he has always been accustomed to regard whatever relates to himself. This habit has become perfectly familiar to him. He has been in the constant practice, and, indeed, under the constant necessity, of modelling, or of endeavouring to model, not only his outward conduct and behaviour, but, as much as he can, even his inward sentiments and feelings, according to those of this awful and respectable judge. He does not merely affect the sentiments of the impartial spectator. He really adopts them. He almost identifies himself with, he almost becomes himself that impartial spectator, and scarce even feels but as that great arbiter of his conduct directs him to feel.[170]

In *Kokoro*, too, Sensei is not only an external interlocutor with whom Watakushi has dialogue; he also desires to become what Smith would have called "the man within the breast," that idealized and internalized form of the "impartial spectator." In his letter to Watakushi, in fact, Sensei describes his own transition from real to ideal spectator: "You wished to cut open my heart and see the blood flow. I was then still alive. I did not want to die. That is why I refused you and postponed the granting of your wish to another day. Now, I myself am about to cut open my own heart, and drench your face with my blood. And I shall be satisfied if, when my heart stops beating, a new life lodges itself in your breast."[171]

Taken in isolation, the gravity of Sensei's testament articulates in literary terms something of what Smith came to believe as a moral philosopher—namely, that the judgment of the impartial spectator is awesome in the classic sense of terrifying. Smith wrote in *The Theory of Moral Sentiments* that "it is so disagreeable to think ill of ourselves, that we often purposely turn away our view from those circumstances which might render that judgment unfavourable. He is a bold surgeon, they say, whose hand does not tremble when he performs an operation upon his own person; and he is often equally bold who does not hesitate to pull off the mysterious veil of self-delusion, which covers from his view the deformities of his own conduct."[172] The bold man who pulls back the "veil of self-delusion" must be prepared for the horror of seeing himself as others do: "This self-deceit, this fatal weakness of mankind," Smith wrote, "is the source of half the disorders of human life. If we saw ourselves in the light in which others see us, or in which they would see us if they knew all, a reformation would generally be unavoidable. We could not otherwise endure the sight."[173] This conjures images redolent of Sensei in *Kokoro*, a man who cut out his own heart and drenched Watakushi's face with its blood, performing "an operation upon his own person" with a hand as steady as the judgement he renders as an impartial spectator. For Sensei, though, there is no "reformation" possible at the end of his self-judgment in the letter he sends to Watakushi. He cannot survive his own self-regarding narrative, for the incontrovertible truth of his own actions, once reckoned with in language set down in ink, condemns him to death. In Sensei's case, the self that judges kills the self that "is judged of." As the ink running from his brush becomes the blood running from his body, the ultimate referent of his words becomes a dying wish to live on as "the man within the breast" of Watakushi.

To what extent this transmission actually happens remains the matter of interpretive debate. On the one hand, as mentioned already, the student describes Sensei at one point as more of a spiritual than an intellectual inspiration, and even writes that "indeed, it would not have seemed to me then an exaggeration to say that Sensei's strength had entered my body, and that his very life was flowing in my veins."[174] But although this would suggest that the student had indeed internalized Sensei's presence, it is also true that the student's own language in the first portion of the narrative is clearly strategic and manipulative, as examined above, too, and he seems to draw clear distinctions between himself and Sensei, as the *Kokoro* debates and their interpreters have revealed. This makes it harder to imagine a purely faithful reception of Sensei's intentions. Furthermore, Vincent reminds us that the very premise of a transparent transmission from Sensei to the student is tied up with an interpretive conservatism. He noted that for paternalistic readers "who tend to identify with Sensei's values and who see his dilemma as a tragic one, the idea that *watakushi* has faithfully transmitted Sensei's story to them will be extremely important, just as it was important for Sensei that *watakushi* be the right narrator for his testament."[175] Vincent added that it was this fantasy of "belated but sincere communication between men that informed the vast majority of male-authored critical readings of *Kokoro* throughout most of the postwar period, when *Kokoro* first achieved its canonical status."[176] Vincent showed that McClellan's was one of these readings, and by deconstructing its implicit assumptions, he revealed that the dialogue between Sensei and the student is so complex that nothing in it can be taken at face value.

In the end, these are the sorts of literary ambivalences that enliven (rather than dampen) the affordance of *Kokoro* as a literary text first and foremost. They reveal that McClellan's translation does more than simply reflect the intellectual history that preceded it, and that surrounded it; more precisely, the translation converses, and conspires, with that history, at times through confluence, at times through conflict. Reading within these tensions suggests how the translation could be read as one compelling vector within what the humanities scholar Mark Greif has called "the age of the crisis of man," a midcentury moment in which the novel became a kind of philosophy by other means for writers and intellectuals reflecting on the human condition itself. Greif argued that what began as a group of philosophical questions about "the human condition" in these years later migrated into "other spheres of representation—including the demand that artists answer the problems of the age. One such mode of representation would be, specifically, *the novel.* What a generation of American thinkers could not do only with philosophy or international organization, the critics among them sought to do with the aesthetics of their dominant literary form, fiction."[177] This led Greif to arrive at a deeper observation—namely, that the literary is a crucial consideration for intellectual historians because "the challenge for all histories of high 'ideas' is to find their entryways into vernacular thinking and practice. How does high discourse weigh upon other levels, if it does? How does one know, or prove that it does? Many inquirers choose not to find out. Here, fiction becomes key."[178] By reading *Kokoro* as a key to understanding the formation of neoliberal thought in midcentury America, this chapter has explored how the novel breathed with trends in intellectual history from long before and well after its original publication in the *Asahi* newspaper, while also remaining a literary aesthetic representation that has never simply said the same thing as its expository others.

Styling Neoliberal Thought

In the years following the publication of McClellan's *Kokoro* translation in 1957, Hayek visited Japan several times, and he counted among his contacts there heads of industry and banking, elected officials and academics. The economist Nishiyama Chiaki, who had been a student of Hayek's at Chicago at the same time that McClellan was, too, proved to be a strategic ally to his mentor in Japan: he translated Hayek's *The Road to Serfdom* (1944) and Milton Friedman's *Free to Choose* (1980) into Japanese, and he even served as president of the Mont Pèlerin Society from 1980 to 1982. Beyond the academic world, Hayek also reached out to captains of industry. In 1965, for example, he encouraged Matsushita Kōnosuke, founder of Panasonic, to join the society. In addition to extending the official invitation, Hayek wrote to personally assure Matsushita that the activities of the society would not complicate his leadership of the electronics firm, and that Hayek himself "should be pleased personally if you were to honour the Society by accepting the invitation to become a member."[179] In the realm of politics, Hayek's visits to Japan in the 1960s coincided with the consolidation of the Liberal Democratic Party (LDP), a conservative force that in 1955 began its rise to what would be a decades-long run in power. In 1965, Hayek met Fukuda Takeo, who would later become minister of finance and prime minister, and in a 1967 letter to Tanaka Seigen, Hayek discussed at length several ideas that he would have liked to propose to "such an experienced and responsible politician as Mr. Fukuda" during a recent visit to Japan.[180]

Without having set this chain of events into motion, to be sure, Hayek's reading of *Kokoro* does stand near the chronological beginning of his years-long interest in Japan. Looking back on that formative time, McClellan once recalled that Hayek had intuitively grasped the gravity of *Kokoro* when he first read it in the 1950s. In fact, he said that Hayek had felt the novel with greater clarity and depth than could most of his colleagues in the field of Japan studies. As McClellan recounted in a 1998 lecture:

> The incredible thing is that both Hayek, this economist, and David Grene, who was, of course, a classical Greek scholar, were both terribly moved by the novel. And I think here, for example, you see their capacity to understand—I'm just giving one example—what it was like for Sensei, or the old man, to see their era end.
>
> It has nothing to do whether Sensei was happy in it [the Meiji period] or not. He wasn't. I don't think he liked Meiji Japan very much, but when the Emperor dies, a part of him goes with him.
>
> I think that Hayek understood, and I'm not so sure that there were that many Japanese or Japanologists, say, who would have understood it the way Hayek understood it, or the way David Grene understood it.[181]

Soon after the *Kokoro* translation appeared in 1957, Hayek hired McClellan to style the prose of his own manuscript of *The Constitution of Liberty* (1960). The reason for the hire seems to have been that Hayek's own rhetoric had become an impediment to his goal of reaching the widest audience possible. In this connection, Burgin has observed that Hayek's early writings were characterized by a forbidding style, noting that in the early 1930s, Hayek "was reluctant to connect economic analysis to any social or political ideology," and that "his writing was still thematically abstruse, stylistically Germanic, and preoccupied with problems in capital theory that even many economists found difficult to comprehend."[182]

As late as the 1950s, Hayek found some of his writings rejected even by sympathetic fellow travelers. When he sent his manuscript of *The Sensory Order* to Henry Regnery for consideration, for example, the publisher declined to pursue the project further in a 1952 letter he sent to Hayek with a reader's report enclosed. Part of the problem was that the manuscript had to do with matters of psychology and mind, and that Regnery felt that this was a field remote from his usual areas of publishing. But another part of the problem was Hayek's style, which the reader's report critiqued for its opacity.[183] As Hayek's ambition to influence the imagination of a broader audience developed in the midcentury years, style and readability became more pressing concerns. He wrote to the

Earhart Foundation in 1958 complaining about the delays encountered in polishing the prose style of the manuscript that would become *The Constitution of Liberty* (1960):

> Quite apart from the ordinary technical difficulties as checking references etc., the chief thing, revising the English style, is a matter which would take me years if I had to do it myself. I feel I could for the next twelve months really profitably employ a half time research assistant to help me in this matter. I should mainly want somebody who himself writes very good English and is sufficiently familiar with my ideas.
>
> As I mentioned in my earlier letter, your former fellow McClellan would seem the most suitable person available and when I talked to him before the summer, seemed willing to undertake the task.[184]

One is tempted to speculate that it must have been McClellan's translation of *Kokoro* that persuaded Hayek that McClellan was best positioned to endow his texts with a literary touch, considering that the translation had been published the year before Hayek's 1958 letter to Earhart. When Hayek petitioned the Relm Foundation several years later, in 1966, for funding to hire McClellan to edit another manuscript—*Law, Legislation and Liberty*—he wrote: "I believe that it is important that when the book comes out it should be fairly polished in exposition. If *The Constitution of Liberty* has been fairly successful, this is in a large measure due to what Edwin MacClellan [*sic*] did to my original draft."[185] Hayek would later rejoice at McClellan's willingness to collaborate on the manuscript of *Law, Legislation and Liberty*, exclaiming: "To my equal surprise and gratification Edwin McClellan declared himself willing to do for my forthcoming book what he did for the *Constitution of Liberty.* Since he writes the kind of English I would like to write and is, of course, now thoroughly familiar with my ideas, this seems to me greatly preferable to any other solution."[186] The fact that McClellan was twice hired to edit Hayek's own manuscripts reminds us that the voices of Sōseki and Hayek sometimes come to Anglophone readers in something of the same language—McClellan's. In this sense, their texts share a genetic reference to one another, however recessive, and this is part of why it might be said that we breathe with McClellan when we read some of Hayek's texts, following the ripples created by their language out toward a vanishing horizon of liberal *kokoro.*

The connections between literature and thought examined in this chapter would not be clear from reading McClellan's translation of *Kokoro* alone, however. They only come to light in analyzing the confluence by which one of modern Japan's best-known novels breathed with ideas. What made McClellan's dialogue with Hayek so extraordinary was that it created the conditions of possibility in which literary form and right-leaning liberal politics could mix within the magic of their own "spontaneous order," so to speak, guided by the invisible hand of coincidence. After all, *Kokoro* did not become a piece of neoliberal propaganda in McClellan's hands, and neither did Hayek exert any palpable "influence" that dictated how McClellan rendered Sōseki's prose in English. Instead, their connection materialized in the more nebulous and organic realm of sensibility and sympathy. The translation has proven to be so satisfying in literary terms alone that its connections to the politics of the Right within which it was originally conceived and received have rarely been noticed, even though it has long been one of the most widely read Japanese novels available in English translation. This is so because the compelling aesthetics of language rendered in McClellan's moving prose style commune with the original Japanese in an almost musical rhythm, as if the languages of each were born together as blood kin who come from the same place. Their consanguinity sings a song of style that allows English-language readers to feel that they, too, are moving in tune to a classic of the human condition unmediated by the distortions of any interventionist design. But as McClellan's rendering of Sōseki's prose evaporates readerly feeling into the air of literary enchantment, it also precipitates a self-effacing liberal politics whose telltale sign has often been its own disavowal.

EPILOGUE

Tracing the Neoliberal Aesthetic in 1980s Japan

Chapter 4 examined how the sentiments of a right-leaning liberalism in midcentury America informed the context in which McClellan implicitly wrote *Kokoro* into the pantheon of "Great Books." In making this claim, I tried to show how McClellan's translation emerged from a wider intellectual historical conjuncture in which dialogues about liberal subjectivity that originated during the war years continued into the midcentury years, too. This epilogue offers a coda to that analysis by tracing the neoliberal aesthetic to the 1980s—a decade that has often been associated with the rise of neoliberal politics in the transatlantic world, and during which the momentum created by Japan's celebrated "economic miracle" culminated in the transpacific realm. Drawing these threads together, my analysis here considers the articulation of more recent neoliberal politics as a matter of cultural common sense rather than of ideas that have to be argued. This prompts me to turn my attention from the "Great Books" at Chicago to the realm of pop culture, and to take up aspects of the early fiction of Murakami Haruki (1949–) in particular, whose novels have long been promoted in the global literary marketplace, becoming international bestsellers time and again. I conclude the study as a whole with a sketch of how his 1980s fiction opens up a space in which to think about, and feel, the deeper historical complexions that have become suspended within the neoliberal condition in more recent times.

This analysis begins with the observation that Murakami rose to prominence in Japan's flush 1980s as a nuanced chronicler of the materially privileged but existentially precarious life of young adults in Tokyo.[1] By this time, the transpacific dynamic that had earlier cast Japan as a defeated imperialist belligerent in need of rehabilitation had evolved, with the image of a seemingly indomitable Japanese economic prowess in the global marketplace creating anxieties in America. At around the same time that Murakami's first novels appeared, Ezra Vogel's *Japan as Number One: Lessons for America* (1979) praised the rapidity of Japan's postwar rebirth as an economic (rather than imperial) agent, and wondered aloud what the former foe who had surrendered to Allied forces in 1945 might be able to teach Cold War America, whose confidence once brimmed in an earlier era of Pax Americana but had more recently been rocked by scandals surrounding the Vietnam War and Richard Nixon's presidency.[2] The American fascination with Japanese business practices also took center stage in a 1981 made-for-television piece called *The Colonel Comes to Japan*, which narrated the quest of Kentucky Fried Chicken to penetrate the Japanese marketplace by mimicking what were thought to be native customs. In 1986, the *Nihon Keizai Shinbun* published a bestselling manga drawn by the celebrated artist Ishinomori Shotaro that was titled *Manga Nihon Keizai nyūmon* (A Manga Introduction to Japanese Economics), which linked fundamental principles of political economy to Japan's place in the globalized marketplace of the 1980s. The manga referred to the legendary Chrysler executive Lee Iacocca, whose autobiographical meditation on business and management, *Iacocca* (1984), had become an explosive bestseller in America and Japan. It went through thirty-six printings totaling two million copies in its first nine months in America, with an additional half million sold in Japan. It is said to have generated five hundred fan letters per day addressed to Iacocca, and one thousand speaking invitations per month.[3] And Japan was part of the story: one of the last chapters of *Iacocca* was titled "The Japanese Challenge," the same title, in fact, as part 1 of Vogel's *Japan as Number One.*

At around the time that rivalries in the automotive industry informed Ishinomori's and Iacocca's narratives, the cofounder and CEO of Sony, Morita Akio, wrote in his autobiography, *Made in Japan* (1986), about Japanese management practices and corporate culture in ways that celebrated what he suggested was a Japanese style mixing equal parts native intuition and global competitiveness, as if the universal model of *homo economicus* had taken on culturally specific forms to be narrated in the genre of *Nihonjinron* (so-called theories of the Japanese people). It would later be revealed that while courting American consumers, Morita was also giving speeches in Japan alongside the far-right-wing novelist-turned-politician Ishihara Shintarō, whose nationalist vision of Japan overcoming both the United States and the Soviet Union to lead the post–Cold War world emerged in *"NO" to ieru Nihon* (The Japan That Can Say "No," 1989). In his study of the perceived prowess of Japanese corporations, entrepreneurs, and management techniques in the 1980s, the cultural historian Andrew McKevitt wrote that "the globalized future looked much more Japanese in the 1980s than we acknowledge three decades later."[4] *Iacocca* reminds us of this, too: in its last chapter, "Making America Great Again," the executive wrote that "by combining the skills and efficiencies of their culture with a whole host of unfair economic advantages, Japan appears capable of looting our markets with impunity. In Washington this is known as laissez-faire economics, and they love it. In Tokyo they call it *Veni, Vidi, Vici* economics, and believe me, they love it even more. The Japanese have come, they've seen, and they are conquering. And our dependence on Japan will continue to grow until we establish some practical limits to their enjoyment of our markets."[5]

Across these narratives of economic life in the transpacific 1980s, the shrewd executive, the savvy manager, and the loyal salaryman populated stories about how Japan played the game of capitalism in the same decade that witnessed the ascending transatlantic influence of Ronald Reagan and Margaret Thatcher. Told from the perspective of the corporate elite, these narratives predictably revolved around robust production, careful management, and progress leading to an ever-brighter future. In this sense, they reflected a faith in the global economy as a structure of meaning, an *oikos* in which hope could shelter. Murakami would tell a different kind of story, to be sure, one that focused more on the melancholy and angst of the age for young adults than on the inexorable progress of the Japanese economy and corporate institutions. But his rise as an international literary icon was buoyed by the ballyhooed economy of the age. And since then, his popularity has been understood to be a recession-proof emblem of "Japan's Gross National Cool," a form of cultural capital accumulating value as it has circulated through the conduits created by the globalized marketplace with relevance undiminished—and perhaps even augmented—by the bursting of the economic bubble in Japan at the end of the 1980s.[6]

The scholar of Japanese literature John Treat has remarked on the enterprising nature of Murakami himself, noting that "when neoliberalism became fashionable in the UK and the US, Murakami Haruki did in Japan. In one sense he has been the perfect neoliberalist writer. Breaking all the guild rules imposed by the Japanese publishing industry, Murakami has been the entrepreneur extraordinaire."[7] But Treat was quick to contrast the author himself with his fictional characters, pointing out that "the content of Murakami's novels themselves do not so obviously look neoliberal to us. His characters are nothing as entrepreneurial as their author. They are lazy, in fact."[8] This, however, does not convince Treat that the novels themselves are unrelated to the neoliberal world. "But glance elsewhere," he invites us. "Murakami's characters, with their psychic maladies such as depression and dissociation, express a profound crisis of freedom."[9] The scholar Matthew Strecher has put the matter in starker terms still, writing that "Murakami Haruki's *raison d'être* as a writer lies in certain key questions he raises about the nature (and ultimate fate) of individual identity in contemporary Japan," adding that the problem Murakami's fiction takes up is that "as a result of hyper-commodification of late-model capitalism, the total focus on economic prosperity, and the need in such an economy to control the desire of the consumer, individual identity has been gradually lost, replaced by what might be termed a 'manufactured' subjectivity, a 'ready-made' identity."[10] In making these observations, Treat and Strecher raised the question of how an internationally popular novelist might have engaged the beginning of what is widely regarded to be the neoliberal age through a literary idiom that never feels doctrinaire, insistent, or even all that political. For as Strecher has observed, it has been said that Murakami is "a 'totally *un*-political' writer whose works nevertheless always made us think of politics. This is one way to phrase the matter. Another would be to say that Murakami is a totally political writer who always pretends he is not."[11]

With these paradoxes in mind, I aim to show how Murakami's early novel *Hitsuji o meguru bōken* (A Wild Sheep Chase, 1982) rendered elements of the neoliberal condition, however unintentionally. The point is not that Murakami and his literary characters are neoliberals themselves, nor that the author knowingly composed literary writings in order to advance an ideological agenda, as if he were Ayn Rand. In the case of Rand, the scholar Lisa Duggan has shown how her sexually charged hommages to what Rand viewed as the libidinous force of capitalism itself have become touchstones of the neoliberal world today—and not because they formulated sophisticated neoliberal ideas, but because they represent, in Duggan's words, "conversion machines that run on lust," and because "they provide a structure of feeling—optimistic cruelty—that morphs throughout the twentieth century and underwrites the form of capitalism on steroids that dominates the present."[12] This helps us to see that the literary history of neoliberal politics need not resolve to the original articulation of neoliberal ideas per se. It also helps us to see that the challenge posed by Murakami's early fiction is that unlike Rand's "optimistic cruelty" (Duggan's inversion of Lauren Berlant's iconic formulation of "cruel optimism"), he offers a softer, less doctrinaire narrative structure in which to sense the market-ordered world. And in the context of this study, this narrative structure opens up a vantage point from which to consider the longer duration and wider distributions of neoliberal sentiment extending from the interwar years onward to our own historical present. Without positing an unbroken history or any direct line of transmission from that earlier time to today, this epilogue explores how Murakami's fiction allows readers to reflect on how the neoliberal condition in recent times continues to breathe with its own past.

Attuning to an Apolitical World

My reading of Murakami joins other recent studies that have interpreted aspects of Japanese cultural history from the postwar period of "high economic growth" to the recessionary millennial years through the economic logic and cultural complexions of neoliberalism.[13] The most important of these is *Ambient Media: Japanese Atmospheres of Self* (2016), in which the media studies scholar Paul Roquet argued that the ambient aesthetics and healing promise of various media ecologies that developed in Japan (and elsewhere) from the 1970s onward inflected a neoliberal logic of self-care. By this logic, the burden of mood regulation and spiritual homeostasis is distributed in the direction of the increasingly isolated individual subject, who alone is left responsible for him- or herself.[14] In a section of the study titled "Techniques of the Neoliberal Self," Roquet observed that "the proliferation of new techniques of ambient subjectivation in the 1970s reflected a shifting understanding of the person: away from forms of collective self-understanding and toward a model rooted in a liberal ideal of autonomy and self-determination."[15] Roquet elaborated on the implications of this "neoliberal self" in relation to media arts in both industrial and avant-garde contexts. What he discovered was a paradoxical mix of liberation through self-care and casual coercion through meticulously managed mass mediations:

> Personal media use holds out the promise of self-determination, but the technologies also serve as ways for governments and other social institutions to offload more and more of the labor of subjective maintenance onto an increasingly isolated subject. In Japan, as elsewhere, demands placed on the individual to preserve and develop their own health and social utility rose in direct proportion to the dismantling of social services and welfare programs. People were "free" to adjust to these new forms of insecurity, and the new technologies of self served as crucial tools for doing so.[16]

In Roquet's account, then, the "techniques of the neoliberal self" were techniques of aesthetic attunement by which increasingly isolated and self-reliant subjects maintained the premise of control over what were, in fact, ever more precarious circumstances in which their political agency had become only more tightly circumscribed.

Roquet found one particularly rich rendering of these techniques in Ichikawa Jun's 2004 film *Tony Takitani*, a piece of ambient cinema inspired by the Murakami short story of the same name. He noted in particular how the ambient aesthetics of the film emerge in the course of a narrative progression that strips away, discards, and dissolves. *Tony Takitani* tells the story of its eponymous protagonist who, already an introvert by nature, comes to lose the two most meaningful relationships he does form in life, one with his father, a jazz musician who dies of cancer, and the other with a lover who becomes his wife, only to be killed in a car accident. Roquet's analysis considered how the "solitary style" portrayed in the melancholic film intersects with a broader design trend in contemporary Japanese consumer culture geared toward a "low-affect lifestyle," which has been epitomized by the retail chain Muji, a purveyor of simply designed consumer goods. He suggested that these consumer trends reverberate with Ichikawa's cinematic adaptation of Murakami's literary rendering of isolation and desolation in 1980s Japan insofar as they all articulate aspects of one of the techniques of the neoliberal subject that Roquet named "subtractivism." By this he meant a lifestyle management strategy defined by stripping away distraction and eliminating lingering attachments in an effort to construct an autonomous and anonymous lifestyle without style. Roquet's notion of "subtractivism" drew on the ambient video producer Aria Man's description of the era starting in the late 1970s as "the Age of Subtraction" (*hikizan no jidai*), an appellation that, according to Roquet, articulated "a general fatigue in Japan from too much stuff and too many people, leading to a desire for emptied-out environments with no one around."[17] Taking cues from both commercial agents (such as the retailer Muji) and trends in aesthetic life (epitomized by Ichikawa's film), "subtractivist" practices constitute an attempt to exercise agency over a volatile everyday life by corralling the more intense waves of nonambient feelings—such as frustration, anxiety, and anger—into a more moderated midrange within the sinusoidal rhythms of affective amplitude.

In this sense, subtractivism might be counted among the "techniques of the neoliberal self" insofar as it dissolves the more strongly felt sense of private crisis in the neoliberal age into a more palatable—or at least ignorable—kind of background atmospheric. But these techniques of self-care have their compromises, as Roquet points out frequently. We begin to see these compromises more clearly still if we layer Roquet's analysis of ambient aesthetics with the political philosopher Wendy Brown's perspective on the crises of contemporary neoliberalism. Working in different fields, both analysts drew in part on Michel Foucault's earlier critique of neoliberalism and self-care, and so it makes sense that aspects of their studies would reverberate with one another. In his analysis of *Tony Takitani*, Roquet concluded that "in this world, personal autonomy is everything and can be found only through letting go. But as the ambient design of Ichikawa's film insistently reminds us, this world of soft surfaces and low-affect living will always arrive tinted by the sadness of all that was left behind."[18] As a "technique of the neoliberal self," then, it might be said that subtractivism implicitly negotiates the paradoxical subjective condition of the neoliberal age that Brown has identified, a condition in which the properly interpolated individual is prepared to sacrifice everything for a group or cause—be it a nation, a job, or even the abstract ideal of "freedom" itself—which offers almost nothing in return: no epistemological certitude, no hope for the future, no increased life prospects. By strategically accommodating to a capricious present through ever more advanced forms of technologically mediated self-care, the neoliberal subject winds up setting aside the ideals of political identity that had formerly been the origin of hope for progress and justice in the future. Brown has noted that in this balance of self-care and self-sacrifice, we find a startling historical echo: insofar as the contemporary neoliberal subject is prepared to give all for a collective ideal from which it asks for no form of compensation whatsoever, it ironically recapitulates some of the ideals of self-sacrifice to the imagined whole that had earlier informed the fascist imagination of the war years—an imagination that midcentury neoliberalism had promised to overcome by positing the origin of freedom in the entrepreneurial marketplace rather than in the collectivist state.[19]

Bringing these threads together, we begin to see that the subtractivist subject deletes the noise of emotional life at the same time that he or she also jettisons a hopeful narrative for an improved self and society in the future. In the case of *Tony Takitani*, these deletions come through most clearly in a cinematically rendered "world of soft surfaces and low-affect living," as Roquet put it. But beyond the delicately wrought aesthetics of professional filmmaking, not all neoliberal surfaces are so soft, and sometimes, "low-affect living" is simply another name for spiritual vacancy in a futureless world without hope. This conclusion is suggested by the perspectives of anthropologists Hirokazu Miyazaki and Anne Allison, who in different ways have examined the deteriorating conditions of hope itself in neoliberal Japan today.[20] Their studies would suggest that as affective life comes to be meticulously managed like the investment portfolio of an entrepreneurial strategist, the premise of politics itself unwinds to the point that the possibility of a better world comes to be nearly unimaginable. In the vacated place of an evaporated future that was exclusively possible through political intervention, the *oikos* of the economic precipitates the only "household" of meaning. In this sense, reading Roquet and Brown together reminds us that if neoliberalism is to be understood in terms of *homo economicus* vanquishing *homo politicus*, then it should come as no surprise that one of the things deleted by the subtractivist "techniques of the neoliberal self" is the promise of politics per se.

A Wild Sheep Chase

It all begins in *A Wild Sheep Chase* with the subtraction of politics from the memory of the 1960s, a decade that has, of course, been remembered in Japan (as elsewhere) for its protests, student activism, and antiestablishment counterculture—in other words, for its promise of political possibility. But in Murakami's telling from the vantage point of the flush 1980s, the 1960s was an interesting period for pop culture but an impotent time for politics. A lot may have happened, Murakami seems to tell us, but nothing changed. It is almost as if some of Murakami's protagonists were born knowing the lesson Watakushi learned in *Kokoro*—that there is nothing to learn about the world that will ever change anything at all, as Tansman summed up in his reading of Sōseki's classic. Murakami came close to saying something like this in the 1989 short story "Warera no jidai no fōkuroa: Kōdo shihonshugi zenshi" (The Folklore of My Generation: A Prehistory of Late Capitalism), in which he reflected on coming of age in the 1960s with a mix of nostalgia and resignation, writing: "But as to whether the era brought us—my generation, that is—any special radiance, well, I'm not so sure. In the final analysis, perhaps we simply passed through it as if we were watching an exciting movie: we experienced it as real—our hearts pounded, our palms sweated—but when the lights came on we just walked out of the cinema and picked up where we'd left off. For whatever reason, we neglected to learn any truly valuable lesson from it all. Don't ask me why."[21] This description of the 1960s prepares us to see what others have viewed as a global moment of intense struggle in the opposite terms: as a "prehistory of late capitalism" (*kōdo shihonshugi zenshi*) that cleared the path for the rise of a conservative corporate class and what Brown has described as the neoliberal turn away from politics. In this connection, Strecher would remind us that the trope of *kōdo shihonshugi* in Murakami's fiction—a trope that I have rendered as "late capitalism," and that he has translated as "rapid capitalism"—evokes the specter of the economic overwhelming other aspects of human life generally, for it indicates the "intrusive commodification of areas of human relationships that had previously remained aloof from the consumerist ethic—friendship, love, even family roles."[22] In the quotation above, we see how this perspective could undergird a version of events in which the perceived political promise of the 1960s was as chimeric as the cinematic shadows that dance on the movie screen.

A Wild Sheep Chase had already rehearsed this subtraction of politics from the memory of the 1960s. Published in 1982 and set in the 1970s, the novel opens as the unnamed first-person protagonist known as "Boku" learns that a lover he knew years ago while still in college has died in a traffic accident.[23] It had been years since the two last saw each other, and even her name has been forgotten; we are told that she is remembered simply as the "girl who'd sleep with anyone." We are also told that their liaison unfolded as "the curtain was creaking down on the shambles of the Sixties," indicating that it coincided with the subtraction of the 1960s itself from Boku's life. As if to make the point unmistakable, the beginning of the novel is precisely dated November 25, 1970, the very day that the writer and right-wing nationalist Mishima Yukio occupied the Japanese Self-Defense Force headquarters, issued a call to arms, and then committed ritual suicide (*seppuku*). It was one of the most explosive flash points in postwar Japanese cultural history, and it could be interpreted as a kind of culmination—or end—of the 1960s in a spectacle of public violence. But in Murakami's telling, Mishima's suicide becomes an ignorable image fading into the background without any lasting substance:

> We walked through the woods to the ICU campus, sat down in the student lounge, and munched on hot dogs. It was two in the afternoon, and Yukio Mishima's picture kept flashing on the lounge TV. The volume control was broken so we could hardly make out what was being said, but it didn't matter to us one way or the other. A student got up on a chair and tried fooling with the volume, but eventually gave up and wandered off.
>
> "I want you," I said.
>
> "Okay," she said.
>
> So we thrust our hands back into our coat pockets and slowly walked back to the apartment.[24]

A world without politics begins to materialize as the novel polices a controlled narrative force field in which the harsher realties symbolized by Mishima, the 1960s, violence, and ideology "didn't matter to us one way or the other" (*dochira ni shitemo sore wa wareware ni totte wa dō demo ii koto datta*).[25]

The deletions in Boku's life continue to accrete as the mainline narrative takes shape. After the faint memory of an almost-forgotten lover lost in a senseless accident passes, the novel moves ahead several years, and turns to another loss, Boku's divorce, which empties out time itself of structuring content and initiates one of the first feelings of drift that will return throughout the novel. "A month had passed since I agreed to the divorce and she moved out," Boku tells the reader. "A non-month. Unfocused and unfelt, a lukewarm protoplasm of a month. . . . I passed through the month the way people X out days on a calendar, one after the other."[26] As the numbing effect of the divorce filters through the subtractivist imagination, it is strategically metabolized as just one more deletion to be let go in the name of perceived control: "I would be thirty in a few months; she would be twenty-six. And if you considered the vastness of the rest of our lives, the foundations we'd laid barely scraped zero. All we'd done our four years together was to eat through our savings."[27] As the narrative progresses from here, readers learn that even beyond his failed marriage, Boku self-identifies as an intensely bored and mediocre person leading a life so ordinary as to leave no legible trace behind: "I grew up in an ordinary [*heibon*] little town, went to an ordinary [*heibon*] school," he explains early in the novel. "I was a quiet child, but grew into a bored [*taikutsu*] kid. I met this ordinary [*heibon*] girl, had an ordinary [*heibon*] first romance. . . ."[28] And on and on from there until Boku realizes, "Maybe my life isn't boring [*taikutsu*], maybe I don't really seek a boring [*taikutsu*] life. But effectively it's the same thing. Either way I've already got what's coming. Most people, they're trying to escape from boredom [*taikutsu*], but I'm trying to get into the thick of boredom [*taikutsu*]. That's why I'm not complaining when I say my life is boring [*taikutsu*]."[29]

Boredom (*taikutsu*) becomes the desired attunement of the resigned subtractivist who has dissolved extraneous stimuli and painful memories into a comfortingly ordinary (*heibon*) atmospheric. This tranquilizes any interventionist impulse with the bored realization that no matter what might be done, "I've already got what's coming" (*dochira ni shitemo boku wa sude ni sore o te ni ireteirunda*). But Boku's ambient attunement to the boredom of his own life is threatened when he is visited one day by mysterious men demanding that he locate a sheep with a black mark on its back. They explain that the sheep had come to their attention after Boku featured a photograph of it in the promotional materials that his firm produces for clients. Boku had chosen the photograph thoughtlessly, but the men will accept nothing less than its capture as they reveal that they work on behalf of an enigmatic "Boss" (*Sensei*) who means business. From this point on, the readerly temptation is to figure out what it all means under the assumption that all of the pieces of the puzzle somehow fit together to reveal a larger whole. But I would argue that trying to explain the surrealist narrative—Who are these men? What is the meaning of the sheep? Why Boku? What is the point?—can distract us from how the deeper narrative preoccupations of the novel engage an undesigned world organized only by spontaneous arisings and happenstance encounters with no internal logic, and no necessary outcomes. They cannot be changed because they have no reason for being in the first place. In this sense, the novel meditates on a world in which there is "neither coincidence nor possibility," as Boku put it right around the time the mysterious men appear:

> We can, if we so choose, wander aimlessly over the continent of the arbitrary. Rootless as some winged seed blown about on a serendipitous spring breeze.
>
> Nonetheless, we can in the same breath deny that there is any such thing as coincidence. What's done is done, what's yet to be is clearly yet to be, and so on. In other words, sandwiched as we are between the "everything" that is behind us and the "zero" beyond us, ours is an ephemeral existence in which there is neither coincidence nor possibility.
>
> In actual practice, however, distinctions between the two interpretations amount to precious little. A state of affairs (as with most face-offs between interpretations) not unlike calling the same food by two different names.[30]

This might be taken for a kind of self-interpreting moment in the novel that warns readers away from approaching its narrative through cause-and-effect logic. Drawing on the analysis of *Kokoro* in chapter 4, it might be said that this passage suggests that any straightforward analysis (*kenkyū*) of *A Wild Sheep Chase* can become a "wild goose chase" of its own tasked with corralling the anarchic dispersion of knowable information into a contrived narrative scheme. Murakami's novel subtracts this inclination with a title drawn from the English language idiom that asks, why bother?

Things move forward after the mysterious men tell Boku to find the sheep, or else. The "wild sheep chase" that follows takes him to the remote reaches of Hokkaido, deep in the north. This becomes a welcome excursion that affords Boku the chance to finally subtract some of the last lingering residues of everyday middle-class life that have stubbornly clung to him. As the frontier sheep chase replaces the Tokyo rat race, deeper shades of nothingness submerge Boku in new waves of blasé boredom:

> Boarding a long-distance train without any luggage gave me a feeling of exhilaration [*sutekina kibun*]. It was as if while out taking a leisurely stroll, I was suddenly like a dive-bomber caught in a space-time warp. In which there is nothing [*soko ni wa marude nanimo nai*]: no dentist's appointments, no pending issues in desk drawers, no inextricably complicated human involvement, no favors demanded. I'd left that behind, temporarily. All I had with me were my tennis shoes with their misshapen rubber soles. They held fast to my feet like vague memories of another space-time. But that hardly mattered. Nothing that some canned beer and dried-out ham sandwiches couldn't put out of mind.[31]

With this, Boku begins to sense that he has been drifting away from the contextual coordinates that had earlier tethered him to a wider social world. He reflects on the trip home four years earlier to complete paperwork related to his divorce, realizing: "From that point on there was no hometown for me. Nowhere to return to. What a relief! No one to want me, no one to want anything from me."[32] As Boku subtracts individuals from his life, he also arrives at the more metaphysical conclusion that the world itself does not need him, and that he may not need it. "The world goes on without me," he realizes. "People cross streets through no intervention on my part, sharpen pencils, move fifty yards a minute west to east, fill coffee lounges with music that's refined into nothingness. The 'world'—the word always makes me think of a tortoise and elephants tirelessly supporting a gigantic disc. The elephants have no knowledge of the tortoise's role, the tortoise unable to see what the elephants are doing. And neither is the least aware of the world on their backs."[33]

This is redolent of the world that Watakushi learned of in *Kokoro*, too, a world of undesigned features and lives that unfold in the confluences of unknowable forces. As the unnamed first-person protagonists Watakushi and Boku—each haunted by an enigmatic "Sensei"—ultimately come to understand that they move through the world without any hope of understanding it, much less of transforming it, they stand ready to sacrifice themselves in circular narratives that move from the city to the provinces and at least implicitly loop back to the city, completing a circle centered on the self. Lonely and liberated, Watakushi and Boku find themselves on quests that never come to any articulable fruition: in *Kokoro*, Watakushi comes from a middle-class family who sends him to Tokyo for an elite education and a promising career beyond, but he ultimately decides that universities and careers are meaningless and abandons the provincial family that set him on track in the first place; in *A Wild Sheep Chase*, similarly, Boku is an affluent white-collar worker who comes to be convinced that his life has become a collection of meaningless relationships and objects that could just as easily be abandoned.

That is why Boku goes on the "sheep chase" in the first place—because he has nothing to lose. "Simply put," he explains in a conversation, "from tomorrow I'm thinking of going off in search of that sheep. I thought it over a lot, but in the end that's what I decided." He continues:

> What have I got to feel threatened about? Next to nothing. I broke up with my wife, I plan to quit my job today, my apartment is rented, and I have no furnishings worth worrying about. By way of holdings, I've got maybe two million yen in savings, a used car, and a cat who's getting on in years. My clothes are all out of fashion, and my records are ancient. I've made no name for myself, have no social credibility, no sex appeal, no talent. I'm not so young anymore, and I'm always saying dumb things that I later regret. In a word, to borrow your turn of phrase, I am an utterly mediocre person. What have I got to lose?[34]

The subtractivist sensation of soothing simplicity follows: "With the job out of the picture, I felt a surge of relief. Slowly but surely I was making things simpler. I'd lost my hometown, lost my teens, lost my wife, in another three months I'd lose my twenties. What'd be left of me when I got to be sixty, I couldn't imagine. There's no thinking about these things. There's no telling even what's going to happen a month from now."[35] For Boku, there is only a shallow past to recall and not much of a future to anticipate. His life does not play out on a linear trajectory bending toward ever-greater success that can be measured by promotions at work and progeny at home. In an age of accumulation, he dreams of subtraction. Family does not figure, and the future is almost unimaginable. At one point, he sees children playing in a train station plaza, and reflects on his solitude: "Casually taking it all in, I thought of my ex-wife's parting remark that maybe we ought to have had children. To be sure, at my age it wouldn't have been unreasonable to have kids, but me a father? Good grief. What kid would want to have anyone like me for a father?"[36]

Yet, just because the force of the economic miracle does not feel very miraculous to Boku does not mean that he is a critic of it, as if he somehow resists the temper of his times. I would argue that he is more akin to a fish that does not know that water is wet. Drawing on Georg Simmel's classic essay "The Metropolis and Mental Life," it might be said that Boku's self-identity materializes the blasé metropolitan attitude of an affluent middle class that takes prosperity and choice for granted, and that accommodates itself to superficial social patterns based mostly on scripted economic transactions, rather than on trusting relationships premised on genuine and humane sympathy. As Treat put it, this is a world in which the liberal dictate to laissez-faire turns into the bored bourgeois privilege to *laissez-faire rien*.[37]

By the same token, though, doing nothing and being bored have their appeal. For one thing, they save Boku from the sorts of extreme positions symbolized by Mishima. And for another, they become the conditions of possibility for his most capacious aesthetic experiences, suggesting that a world without politics allows a peculiar kind of beauty to emerge in Boku's perceptual field. It may not feel very miraculous, to be sure, but his strategic deletions set him on course for intense engagements with atmospheric moments that exceed the narrative order of things involving the Sheep, the Rat, and the Boss. Unburdened and alone, Boku's sensibilities open up to moments of drifting, dissolving, and melting in particular. The following excerpt offers one example:

> The drizzle still hadn't let up by five o'clock the next evening. The rain had been preceded by four or five days of crisp, clear early summer skies, fooling people into thinking the rainy season was over. From the eighth-floor window, every square inch of ground looked dark and damp, and a traffic jam stretched for several miles on the eastbound lanes of the elevated expressway.
>
> As I stared out long and hard, things began to melt in the rain. In fact, everything in town was melting. The breakwater, the cranes, the rows of buildings, the figures beneath their black umbrellas, everything. Even the greenery was flowing down from the hills. Yet when I shut my eyes for a few seconds and opened them again, the town was back the way it had been. Six cranes loomed in the dark haze, trains headed east as if their engines had just restarted, flocks of umbrellas dodged back and forth across the streets of shops, the green hills soaked up their fill of June rain.[38]

This passage conveys a cool mood of melancholic blue uncomplicated by the narrative momentum that accelerates in the "sheep chase" plotline. The novel elsewhere amplifies this mood, delivering Boku and the reader to a more intensely articulated encounter with the sadness of solitude.

In one case, Boku reflects on his ex-wife, recalling that she kept "precise records about sex." "That she kept records about sex is the full extent of my knowledge," Boku confides. "What and how much she wrote, I have no idea. And now that we're no longer together, I'll probably never know."[39] With this, the amplitudes of melancholic blue begin to roll in more powerful waves:

> "If I die," she told me, "burn these notebooks. Douse them in kerosene and let them burn till ash, then bury them. I'd never forgive you if one word remained."
>
> "But I'm the one who's been sleeping with you. I pretty much know every inch of your body. What's there to be ashamed of at this late date?"
>
> "Body cells replace themselves every month. Even at this very moment," she said, thrusting a skinny back of her hand before my eyes. "Most everything you think you know about me is nothing more than memories."
>
> The woman—save for the month or so prior to our divorce—was singularly methodical in her thinking. She had an absolutely realistic grasp on her life. Which is to say that no door once closed ever opened again, nor as a rule was any door left wide open.

> Now all I know about her is my memories of her. And these memories fade further and further into the distance like displaced cells. Now I have no way of knowing precisely how many times she and I had sex.[40]

Eros subtracted from sex leaves only cells. In one sense, Boku's marriage itself has become a group of self-contained memories organized cellularly like bricks in a wall, each one alone, and all of them together. In one such cellular memory, described in the scene above, Boku realizes that as the cells of the body regenerate, they metabolize an older self and create a newer one in a self-consuming circuit that devours the body's tactile connection to its own past. Even the most intimate physical encounters dissolve as the most seemingly stable measure of self-identity—the body—replaces itself. Everything becomes a memory, every body disappears, and the most meticulous written record of it all is destined only for ashes. Nothing adds up to anything because everything is eventually subtracted. Boku makes this point explicitly later in the novel: "I thought about cells. Like my ex-wife had said, ultimately every last cell of you is lost. Lost even to yourself. I pressed the palm of my hand against my cheek. The face my hand felt in the dark wasn't my own, I didn't think. It was the face of another that had taken the shape of my face. But I couldn't remember the details. Everything—names, sensations, places—dissolved and was swallowed into the darkness."[41]

Scenes like this alert readers to the dangerous undertow that lurks beneath the mainline narrative about the Sheep, the Boss, and the Rat. In its strongest articulations, this undertow takes on an almost apocalyptic implication in which the beauty of an impersonal universe overwhelms Boku. Below is one example from near the end of *A Wild Sheep Chase*:

> We were totally alone. As if we'd been dropped off at the edge of the world.
>
> We set our backpacks on the ground and stood there saying nothing, trying to get our bearings. Below us a slender ribbon of silver river wound its way through the valley, both banks covered in dense green forest. Across the valley broke waves of low, autumn-tinged hills and beyond that a hazy view of the flatlands. Thin columns of smoke rose from the fields where rice straw was being burned after the harvest. A breathtaking panorama, but it made me feel no better. Everything seemed so remote, so . . . alien.

> The sky was weighed down with a moist, uniform gray—clouds that seemed, as one, to blanket all light. Below, lumps of dense black cloud matter blew by, almost within touching distance. The clouds raced eastward from the direction of the Asian continent, cutting across the Japan Sea to Hokkaido on their way to the Sea of Okhotsk with remarkable speed. It all contributed to making us aware of the utter precariousness of where we stood. One passing gust and this whole crumbling curve plastered against the cliff could easily drag us to the bottom of the abyss.[42]

At the end of *Kokoro*, Watakushi melts into his own narrative as he boards a train after receiving Sensei's letter at the moment that his father lay dying, and at the end of *A Wild Sheep Chase*, we find an inadvertent echo of *Kokoro* in which transiting by train again comes to resonate with the circuits of storytelling itself: "There was a train leaving at twelve o'clock sharp. Not a soul on the platform. On board only four passengers, including myself. Even so, it was a relief to see people after so long. One way or another, I'd made it back to the land of the living. No matter how boring [*taikutsu*] or mediocre it might be, this was my world."[43] On the one hand, this might seem to imply a return to the realm of the social, a rejection of the subtractivist drift that appears throughout *A Wild Sheep Chase*, and an anticipation of Murakami's writings in the 1990s that engaged social problems more directly.[44] But even if that is the case, it is also true that in *Dansu Dansu Dansu* (Dance Dance Dance, 1988), the sequel to *A Wild Sheep Chase*, the economic imperatives of the neoliberal world implicit in the earlier novel became only all the more explicit. These dynamics are at times unmistakable, as in passages such as the following, in which the novel tells the reader what it is about:

> That's how the system works. That's capital investment. Granted, this sort of thing isn't new to the modern age. But everything before is nothing compared to the exacting detail and sheer power of invulnerability of today's web of capitalism. And it's megacomputers that have made it all possible, with their inhuman capacity to pull every last factor and condition on the face of the earth into their net calculations. Advanced capitalism has transcended itself. Not to overstate things, financial dealings have practically become a religious activity. The new mysticism. People worship capital, adore its aura, genuflect before Porsches and Tokyo land values. Worshiping everything their shiny Porsches symbolize. It's the only stuff of myth

> that's left in the world. Latter-day capitalism [*kōdo shihonshugi shakai*]. Like it or not, it's the society we live in. . . . It's the way of the world—philosophy starting to look more and more like business administration.[45]

In the trajectory of Murakami's literary imagination in the 1980s, then, the path traced by *A Wild Sheep Chase* accelerated toward the sort of overflow of market-based thinking into previously noneconomic aspects of human life that analysts have more recently understood in terms of the neoliberal condition today.

Merely Academic

As a method of conclusion, reflecting on Murakami's early fiction opens up to broader and ongoing conversations about the intellectual genealogies of our own historical present.[46] I have already mentioned that in one case, the political philosopher Wendy Brown suggested in *Undoing the Demos* that neoliberal precarity today inculcates in citizens a readiness to be sacrificed, which she argued ironically resonates with aspects of the fascist politics that the midcentury neoliberals themselves had endeavored to overcome.[47] But the layers of irony only accumulated further in Brown's 2019 study, *In the Ruins of Neoliberalism: The Rise of Antidemocratic Politics in the West*, in which she wrote that however influential the midcentury neoliberal intellectuals like Hayek and Milton Friedman might have been, this does not mean that they "aimed at the political and economic present" we are living in today, as if their ideas had been perfectly translated into our world.[48] Instead, she emphasized, many aspects of contemporary neoliberal politics in fact contradict the writings of the earlier neoliberal intellectuals themselves. The irony for Brown was that although the range of ideas and practices "that may be gathered under the sign of neoliberalism has importantly constituted the catastrophic present, this was not neoliberalism's intended spawn, but its Frankensteinian creation."[49] This led Brown to complicate the linkages between the politics of today and those of the past, even while acknowledging deeper historical reverberations. She wrote that although her 2019 study "does not argue that neoliberalism *aimed* at the current conjuncture of principles, policies, practices, and forms of rationality, neither does it argue that the fascisms of the 1930s are 'returning'"; instead, it sees "the current formation as relatively novel" and therefore different from the politics of earlier times.[50]

Brown's studies of neoliberal politics over the long duration raise the unresolved question of how this ideological formation that emerged from the crises of the interwar years relates to its own past. Closer to the literary realm, Joseph North's *Literary Criticism: A Concise Political History* (2017) set out to show that this interpretive work of excavating our own intellectual inheritances—ironies and all—carries distinctive implications for the practice of literary criticism in particular. He made this point by engaging the fate of academic reading from the "conservative" midcentury years to the neoliberal present. Examining this chronology, North argued the provocative perspective that although the conservative, right-leaning formalisms of the midcentury New Critics have largely been eclipsed by competing historicist alternatives carried forward by scholarly approaches with more avowedly left-leaning political implications, it has not necessarily been true that the political purchase of contemporary literary criticism has been saved the fate of *homo politicus* in the ascendant age of *homo economicus*. He offered that while "the turn to the historicist/contextualist paradigm has generally been understood as a local victory for the left over the elitisms of midcentury criticism, this has been largely an error. In fact, it is better to say the opposite is true: in its most salient aspects, the turn to the current paradigm in the late 1970s and early 1980s was symptomatic of the wider retreat of the left in the neoliberal period and was thus a small part of the more general victory of the right."[51] North explained that the gains secured by scholarly historicism, however politically insistent, have come at the considerable expense of forfeiting the impulse to influence society beyond the academy through the cultivation of aesthetic judgement—the sort of impulse that he argued had been the hallmark of an earlier model of conservative midcentury literary criticism. One of the surest marks of this interventionist inclination was the premise that at least on an aspirational level, the audience for literary criticism would extend to a public beyond the academy.[52] North concluded that the erosion of this sort of outward-facing perspective leaves us to confront the uncomfortable conclusion that the circle of influence that the world of scholarly discourse can claim for itself in literary studies has, in fact, deteriorated in proportion to the more general demise of *homo politicus* in the age of neoliberalization.[53]

To be sure, I engage North's controversial perspective as an object of study (rather than as an objective statement), one which, in the limited context of my own narrative, reminds me that the arguments I have made in this study of literature and thought may have been ironically compromised by the academic form in which I myself have made them. This puts me in mind of the deeper pitfalls of "critique" that the literary scholar Rita Felski has notably examined, for needless to say, the spirit of critique is implicit in the notion of "conspiring" at the heart of this study. In *The Limits of Critique* (2015), Felski described "critique" as a style of thought common in literary studies that is premised on scholarly skepticism, interrogation, and even disenchantment. The object of Felski's own suspicion was a mood and a method according to which scholars of literature work "against the grain and between the lines; their self-appointed task is to draw out what a text fails—or willfully refuses—to see."[54] Felski argued that the result of this suspicious practice can be "dramatic or melodramatic narratives in which everything is connected. The scholar-turned-sleuth broods over matters of fault and complicity, she pieces together a causal sequence that allows her to identify a crime, impute a motive, interrupt clues, and track down a guilty party."[55] But this is strange, Felski argued: "There is, after all, something perplexing about the ease with which a certain style of reading has settled into the default option. Why is it that critics are so quick off the mark to interrogate, unmask, expose, subvert, unravel, demystify, destabilize, take issue, and take umbrage?"[56] She even questioned the same statement by Althusser that I chose for the introduction's epigraph—a statement about the inevitable guilt of reading and interpretation—noting with wry irony that it "suggests a secular spin on Christian doctrine: we are all stained by the original sin of interpretation," then qualifying this remark with the observation that within our own self-suspecting hermeneutics, "in contrast to Christian theology, there is no hope of final salvation!"[57] If we persist, Felski suggested, the damage is done as the magnetic appeal of suspicious "critique" rules out "a wider range of affective styles and modes of argument" in literary scholarship.[58]

Taken together, Felski's and North's perspectives offer themselves as sobering reminders of how academic supplements to literary writing—

however "critical"—can ironically conjure the specter of those other meanings of the word "academic" itself: "not leading to a decision," "unpractical" "strictly theoretical or formal," and more damningly, "of no consequence, irrelevant," as the dictionary tells us.[59] The art critic Dave Hickey has put the matter frankly, too, saying that "criticism is the weakest thing you can do in writing. It is the written equivalent of air guitar—flurries of silent, sympathetic gestures with nothing at their heart but the memory of the music. . . . It's a loser's game, and everybody knows it."[60] But in reckoning with the limits of my own analysis, I would also remember in closing that however paradoxically, reflecting on the quandaries of literary criticism can elucidate aspects of the normative force of literature that I have been examining throughout this study, even (or especially) if it does so through chastening reminders of the broken tools with which I have worked. On the one hand, the allure of the literary examined in the chapters of this study was always bound to outpace my scholarly "investigations" and "critiques" that materialized in failed pursuit. But then again, this could be taken for a confirmation of the force of the literary examined in this study, a force which engages with argumentative expositions and nonliterary narrative neighbors even as it evades their grasp—and my own—by slipping into the suspensions occasioned by its own aesthetic forms. From this perspective, it might be said that the limitations of literary criticism pay a kind of tribute to the literary thing that criticism itself can never fully explain.

This is another way of phrasing the problem that Sōseki faced when he lamented the peril of "washing blood with blood" that awaits the literary critic who uses language to talk about language. And as I argued at the beginning of this study, the blood of language connects literature to thought. Exploring these connections led my reading of *A Wild Sheep Chase* to suggest how the longer history of neoliberal ideas that first gathered in the global 1930s and once coursed through *Kokoro* still pulsates in the alchemy of readerly moments that convert the harshness of politics into the more soothing atmospheres of aesthetic form. That this could happen in contemporary pop fiction is perhaps unsurprising: it is an old ruse, after all, as studies of culture and politics during the war years remind us. But insofar as it is a ruse that continues to articulate itself no matter how often its sleight of hand is exposed, it would seem to attest to the power of literature and thought, culture and politics, in conspiratorial relation. And suspended within the prism of time, from the crisis of the global 1930s to our own age of neoliberal globalization, it is a ruse that invites our readerly experience today to breathe with parts of a past that are not yet over, and to reflect on aspects of a history that yet remain contemporary.

Notes

Introduction

1. Louis Althusser, "Part One: From *Capital* to Marx's Philosophy," in *Reading Capital: The Complete Edition*, trans. Ben Brewster and David Fernbach (London: Verso, 2015), 12.

2. Natsume Sōseki, *Natsume Sōseki zenshū* (Tokyo: Iwanami Shoten, 1995), 14:9.

3. This is the observation of D. Cuong O'Neill, who has written that Sōseki sensed that the "mastery of literature is to be had, we are told in the preface [to *Bungakuron*], by stepping outside of literature into the domain of criticism." O'Neill described this as a "decision to leave literature in order to return to it." D. Cuong O'Neill, "Tragedy, Masochism, and Other Worldly Pleasures: Reading Natsume Sōseki's *Bungakuron*," *Discourse* 28, no.2/3 (Spring / Fall 2006): 81–82.

4. Tosaka Jun, *Tosaka Jun zenshū* (Tokyo: Keisō Shobō, 1966), 4:3.

5. In a study of cinema and philosophy, the scholar Philip Kaffen has written that the writings of the philosopher Nakai Masakazu help us to see that "in the simplest terms, cinema constitutes not merely an object of thought but a kind of ground for thinking." Kaffen, "Nakai Masakazu and the Cinematic Imperative," *positions: asia critique* 26, no. 3 (August 2018): 484. In another context, the scholar of Japanese literature Inden Masashi has recently analyzed the literary modernism of the novelist Yokomitsu Riichi through a philosophical prism with particular reference to the concept of "ground" (*konkyo*). See Inden Masashi, *Kankaku to sonzai: Yokomitsu Riichi o meguru konkyo eno toi* (Tokyo: Meiji Shoin, 2014).

6. The etymology of the keyword "conspire" appears in the Oxford English Dictionary as follows: "< French *conspire-r* (15th cent. in Littré) (= Provençal *cospirar*, Spanish *conspirar*, Italian *conspirare*), < Latin *conspīrāre* lit. 'to breathe together', whence, 'to accord, harmonize, agree, combine or unite in a purpose, plot mischief together secretly." *OED Online*, s.v. "conspire, v.," accessed January 19, 2021, www.oed.com/view/Entry/39777.

7. Lionel Trilling, *The Liberal Imagination* (New York: New York Review of Books, 2008), 286, 293–94.

8. As Benjamin put it in his noted essay "The Storyteller," "'A man who dies at the age of thirty-five,' said Moritz Heimann once, 'is at every point of his life a man who dies at the age of thirty-five.' Nothing is more dubious than this sentence—but for the sole reason that the tense is wrong. A man—so says the truth that was meant here—who died at thirty-five will appear to *remembrance* at every point in his life as a man who dies at the age of thirty-five. In other words, the statement that makes no sense for real life becomes indisputable for remembered life." Walter Benjamin, "The Storyteller: Reflections on the Works of Nikolai Leskov," in *Illuminations: Essays and Reflections*, trans. Harry Zohn (Boston: Mariner Books, 2019), 46.

9. This point is informed by Pheng Cheah's discussion of Hannah Arendt's description of an "interest" as something that is between (*inter-est*) in the sense that it "lies between people and therefore can relate and bind them together," as Arendt put it. See Cheah, *What Is a World? On Postcolonial Literature as World Literature* (Durham, NC: Duke University Press, 2016), 149.

10. Sianne Ngai, *Theory of the Gimmick: Aesthetic Judgment and Capitalist Form* (Cambridge, MA: Belknap Press of Harvard University Press, 2020), 105.

11. Mary McCarthy, *Ideas and the Novel* (New York: Harcourt Brace Jovanovich, 1980), 3.

12. McCarthy, *Ideas and the Novel*, 3.

13. Jonathan Abel, *Redacted: The Archives of Censorship in Transwar Japan* (Berkeley: University of California Press, 2012), 17–18.

14. Alan Tansman, "Introduction: The Culture of Japanese Fascism," in *The Culture of Japanese Fascism*, ed. Alan Tansman (Durham, NC: Duke University Press, 2009), 9.

15. Marshall Berman, *All That Is Solid Melts into Air: The Experience of Modernity* (New York: Penguin Books, 1988), 15.

16. Harry Harootunian has described the experience and fantasy of "modern life" in terms of fracture and discontinuity: "In Japan and elsewhere, modernity was seen as a spectacle of ceaseless change (the narrative of historical progress and law of capitalist expansion) and the specter of unrelieved uncertainty introduced by a dominant historical culture no longer anchored in fixed values but in fantasy and desire." Harootunian, *Overcome by Modernity: History, Culture, and Community in Interwar Japan* (Princeton, NJ: Princeton University Press, 2000), xix. Also see Harootunian, *Overcome by Modernity*, 3–33.

17. Harootunian, *Overcome by Modernity*, xxv.

18. For example, see Peter Duus and Daniel I. Okimoto, "Fascism and the History of Pre-war Japan: The Failure of a Concept," *Journal of Asian Studies* 39, no. 1 (November 1979): 65–76, and Gilbert Allardyce, "What Fascism Is Not: Thoughts on the Deflation of a Concept," *American Historical Review* 84, no. 2 (April 1979): 367–88. For a more recent argument against studying Japanese history through the lens of "fascism," see Sheldon Garon, "Transnational History and Japan's 'Comparative Advantage,'" *Journal of Japanese Studies* 43, no. 1 (Winter 2017): 90–91. The historian Federico Marcon has also critiqued the discussion of fascism in wartime Japan, arguing that

> Japan in the 1930s, to which the term "fascist" is often attributed, can be in fact better explained as a case of pseudo-democratic institutions becoming qualitatively more authoritarian with the intensification of its military efforts in China without any revolutionary transformation, coups d'état, or marches on Tokyo: the limited democratic scope of the institutions established by the 1889 Constitution, the structural knots of private interests binding together armed forces, state bureaucracy, political parties, and industrial conglomerates, and a long and brutal war with China explain the imperialist and ultranationalist militarism of the late 1930s better than the appeal to "global fascism."

Marcon, "Historical Knowledge, Historians' Categories, and the Question of 'Fascism,'" *positions*, February 19, 2020, http://positionswebsite.org/federico-marcon-historical-knowledge-historians-categories-and-the-question-of-fascism/.

But while some have argued that there is no suitable definition of fascism, others have suggested that there are in fact many, and that the true challenge of studying "fascism" in global context lies in interpreting the competing perspectives on all that it can mean. In this regard, the historian Leslie Pincus has surveyed the productive controversy generated by the question of how to understand "fascism" as a global concept with relevance to the specific context of interwar Japan. She has observed that

> a basic definition of fascism continues to be the subject of heated controversy. While Marxist historians have routinely defined fascism as a profound structural crisis of late capitalism, others of a more psychoanalytic bent have focused on monolithic leadership cults and authoritarian personalities. Western scholars committed to liberal political philosophy are more likely to view fascism as an aberrant and localized solution to a unique set of sociopolitical problems, if they consent to use the term at all. In contrast, "fascism" is a term accepted by many postwar Japanese historians, Marxists as well as progressive historians like Maruyama Masao, though not without provisos meant to distinguish the Japanese version from its European model.

Pincus, *Authenticating Culture in Imperial Japan: Kuki Shūzō and the Rise of National Aesthetics* (Berkeley: University of California Press, 1996), 214–15.

19. Andrew Gordon, *Labor and Imperial Democracy in Prewar Japan* (Berkeley: University of California Press, 1991), 334, 335. Emphasis in original.

20. For example, the historian Leslie Pincus has argued for reading fascism in terms of ideology, noting that she understood "the term 'ideology' as [Louis] Althusser defined it—the 'representation of the imaginary relationship of individuals to their real conditions of existence.' It is in this ideological elaboration of fascism that students of Japan's interwar years will discover common ground with European fascism." Pincus, *Authenticating Culture*, 216. In another study, Harootunian wrote that "one of the problems that has inhibited historians is the failure to draw a distinction between fascist movements and regimes, on the one hand, and ideology, on the other, between cultural and political impulses and institutions and performatives. The cultural analyses that configure conceptions of political order are not always the same as the forces that mobilize movements and establish regimes, even though they might share a fund of common

ideologemes." Harootunian, *Overcome by Modernity*, xxix. In a more recent analysis, the historian Max Ward has similarly specified his usage of the term "fascism" to indicate an ideological orientation rather than "the doctrine of a specific fascist party" or "an identifiable fascist state regime," noting that "fascism in all its national inflections during the interwar period was first and foremost an ideological phenomenon." Max Ward, "Crisis Ideology and the Articulation of Fascism in Interwar Japan: The 1938 Thought-War Symposium," *Japan Forum* 26, no. 4 (2014): 478–79. My use of the term "reactionary modernism" is informed by Jeffrey Herf's *Reactionary Modernism: Technology, Culture, and Politics in Weimar and the Third Reich* (Cambridge: Cambridge University Press, 1984).

21. As Zeev Sternhell has written: "Fascism wished to rectify the most disastrous consequences of the modernization of the European continent and to provide a solution to the atomization of society, its fragmentation into antagonistic groups, and the alienation of the individual in a free market economy. Fascism rebelled against the dehumanization that modernization had introduced into human relationships, but it was also very eager to retain the benefits of progress and never advocated a return to a hypothetical golden age." Sternhell, with Mario Sznajder and Maia Asheri, *The Birth of Fascist Ideology: From Cultural Rebellion to Political Revolution*, trans. David Maisel (Princeton, NJ: Princeton University Press, 1994), 6–7.

22. Hofmann began his study of fascism in Japan and Italy with the paradox of "restoration-revolution" (*ishin-kakumei*), explaining that this dynamic suggested "the mechanism of fascism, its role in revolutionizing the old and restoring the new in order to reconcile the tension between capital and the nation." Hofmann, *The Fascist Effect: Japan and Italy: 1915–1952* (Ithaca, NY: Cornell University Press, 2015), 1. He also elucidated a "fundamental contradiction at the heart of this ideology. On the one hand, fascism stood for particularism. It claimed to represent the deep spiritual essence of the nation," but on the other hand, "fascism's declared aim to counteract the negative effects of capitalist modernity (though not capitalism itself) implied a universal valence" (2).

23. As Federico Finchelstein put it, "Fascism was essentially revolutionary in that it created a new political order, but it was less revolutionary in its relationship to capitalism. In fact, it never threatened it." Finchelstein, *From Fascism to Populism in History* (Oakland: University of California Press, 2017), 43. In a study focused on interwar Japan in global context, Harootunian observed that "fascism in Japan, and elsewhere, appeared under the guise of what might be called gemeinschaft capitalism and the claims of a social order free from the uncertainties and indeterminacies of an alienated civil society, where an eternalized and unchanging cultural or communal order was put into the service of the capitalist mode of production to establish a 'capitalism without capitalism.'" Harootunian, *Overcome by Modernity*, xxx.

24. Alan Tansman, *The Aesthetics of Japanese Fascism* (Berkeley: University of California Press, 2009).

25. Trilling, *Liberal Imagination*, 292–93.

26. Trilling, *Liberal Imagination*, 296.

27. Trilling, *Liberal Imagination*, 296–97.

28. Trilling, *Liberal Imagination*, 297.

29. Trilling, *Liberal Imagination*, 295.

30. This description of neoliberalism is informed by Angus Burgin, *The Great Persuasion: Reinventing Free Markets since the Depression* (Cambridge, MA: Harvard University Press, 2012), and Quinn Slobodian, *Globalists: The End of Empire and the Birth of Neoliberalism* (Cambridge, MA: Harvard University Press, 2018).

31. The historian Quinn Slobodian observed that the confrontation with democracy was "at the heart of the [twentieth] century for neoliberals," explaining that although neoliberals "embraced democracy for providing a means of peaceful change" and were therefore not "opposed to democracy as such," they also believed that "democracy bore the seed of destruction for the totality" because it empowered the masses to an excessive degree, at times with the disastrous consequences of upending order and throwing the market into disarray. Slobodian, *Globalists*, 14. For a critique of "social justice" from a prominent neoliberal thinker, see Friedrich Hayek, *Law, Legislation and Liberty*, vol. 2, *The Mirage of Social Justice* (Chicago: University of Chicago Press, 1976). For a critical scholarly interpretation of neoliberal thought vis-à-vis the social, the political, and democracy, see Wendy Brown, *In the Ruins of Neoliberalism: The Rise of Antidemocratic Politics in the West* (New York: Columbia University Press, 2019).

32. See David Harvey, *A Brief History of Neoliberalism* (Oxford: Oxford University Press, 2005), and Wendy Brown, *Undoing the Demos: Neoliberalism's Stealth Revolution* (New York: Zone Books, 2015).

33. Foucault observed that for those "who inspired the programming of neo-liberal politics in Germany . . . the experience of Nazism was at the heart of their reflections," for "Nazism enabled them to define what I would call the field of adversity that they had to define and cross in order to reach their objective." Michel Foucault, *The Birth of Biopolitics: Lectures at the College de France, 1978–1979*, ed. Michel Senellart, trans. Graham Burchell (New York: Picador, 2008), 106.

34. Michel Feher, *Rated Agency: Investee Politics in a Speculative Age* (New York: Zone Books, 2018), 7.

35. Harvey, *Brief History of Neoliberalism*, 5.

36. Harvey, *Brief History of Neoliberalism*, 39.

37. Pincus, *Authenticating Culture*, 8.

38. Fukuyama noted that "the first Asian alternative to liberalism to be decisively defeated was the fascist one represented by Imperial Japan," adding that in the postwar years thereafter, "the very fact that the essential elements of economic and political liberalism have been so successfully grafted onto uniquely Japanese traditions and institutions guarantees their survival in the long run." Francis Fukuyama, "The End of History?," *The National Interest* 16 (Summer 1989): 10.

39. See Karatani Kōjin, "The End of the Modern Novel," trans. Michael K. Bourdaghs, in Karatani, *History and Repetition*, ed. Seiji M. Lippit (New York: Columbia University Press, 2012), 150–71. Karatani mentions Fukuyama's thesis at the beginning of *History and Repetition*. See "Introduction: On *The Eighteenth Brumaire of Louis Bonaparte*," in Karatani, *History and Repetition*, 1. Baryon Tensor Posadas has also examined Karatani's notion of historical repetition, paying particular attention to what it would mean to understand repetitions of the 1930s in more contemporary times as an expression of a past that is not completed nor closed off. See Posadas, *Double Visions*,

Double Fictions: The Doppelgänger in Japanese Film and Literature (Minneapolis: University of Minnesota Press, 2018), 154–60.

40. Karatani Kōjin, "Author's Preface to the English Edition," in *History and Repetition*, vii–viii.

41. Maruyama Masao, *Nihon no shisō* (Tokyo: Iwanami Shoten, 1961), 5. As the intellectual historian Andrew Barshay has remarked in this connection, "For Maruyama, the essence of Japanese thought is to have no essence. Japanese tradition has no 'axis' analogous to Christianity in the West or Confucianism in China. It is a 'tradition without structure.'" Barshay, *The Social Sciences in Modern Japan: The Marxian and Modernist Traditions* (Berkeley: University of California Press, 2004), 224.

42. As Sartre put it:

> We were not unaware of the fact that a time would come when historians would be able to survey from all angles this stretch of time which we lived feverishly minute by minute, when they would illuminate our past by our future and would decide upon the value of our undertakings by their outcome and upon the sincerity of our intentions by their success.
>
> But the irreversibility of our age belonged only to us. We had to save or lose ourselves gropingly in this irreversible time. These events pounced upon us like thieves and we had to do our job in the face of the incomprehensible and the untenable, to bet, to conjecture without evidence, to undertake in uncertainty and persevere without hope. Our age would be explained, but no one could keep it from having been inexplicable to us.

Jean-Paul Sartre, "Situation of the Writer in 1947," in *"What Is Literature?" and Other Essays* (Cambridge, MA: Harvard University Press, 1988), 184–85. The paragraph break in this quotation has been added here for clarity.

43. Jacques Rancière, "The Pensive Image," in *The Emancipated Spectator*, trans. Gregory Elliott (London: Verso, 2009), 107.

44. Rancière, "Pensive Image," 107.

45. In their readings of texts as widely various as the novels of Fyodor Dostoyevsky and the historical fiction of the Shoah, Morson and Bernstein explained sideshadowing as a critical sensibility that works against the fallacies of teleological thinking by remaining attuned to the conflicting possibilities and indeterminate temporality of moments that seem in retrospect to be bounded by indisputable endings. They argued that whereas the logic of *fore*shadowing fixes meaning to a stable narrative endpoint, consolidating explanatory power in moments of climax and conclusion, sideshadowing understands the past to be an open-ended kind of present whose future remains deferred, and whose life course unfolds without any determinate trajectory. Bernstein has observed in this regard that sideshadowing does not propose to treat any historical period as "a monad, unconnected to what preceded or followed," and neither does it "argue against relationships and consequences evolving over time; it only says that few of these consequences are either necessary or consistently predictable, and it urges that the multiple choices of action available at a given moment, and the realization that the present contains the seeds of diverse and mutually exclusive possible futures, be included in one's understanding of what any single moment entails." Michael André Bernstein, *Foregone Conclusions:*

Against Apocalyptic History (Berkeley: University of California Press, 1994), 31–32. In a complementary observation, Morson has noted that "sideshadowing suggests that to understand any moment is to grasp its field of possibilities." Gary Saul Morson, *Narrative and Freedom: The Shadows of Time* (New Haven, CT: Yale University Press, 1994), 120.

46. See Harry Harootunian, "The Postwar Genealogy of Fascism and Tosaka Jun's Prewar Critique of Liberalism," *Journal of Pacific Asia* 2 (1995): 104.

1. Middlebrow as Method

1. Virginia Woolf, "Middlebrow," in *The Death of the Moth and Other Essays* (New York: Harcourt Brace Jovanovich, 1942), 186.

2. Dwight Macdonald, "Updating the Bible," in *Masscult and Midcult: Essays against the American Grain*, ed. John Summers (New York: New York Review of Books, 2011), 153. Macdonald cited the opinion of John Livingston Lowes in support, quoting him as having said of the King James Version, "Its phraseology has become part and parcel of our common tongue. . . . Its rhythms and cadences, its turns of speech, its familiar imagery, its very words are woven into the texture of our literature. . . . The English of the Bible . . . is characterized not merely by a homely vigor and pithiness of phrase but also a singular nobility of diction and by a rhymic quality which is, I think, unrivaled in its beauty" (153).

3. Macdonald, "Updating the Bible," 153.

4. Macdonald, "Updating the Bible," 161. Emphasis in original.

5. Michael Emmerich, "The Tale of Genji": *Translation, Canonization, and World Literature* (New York: Columbia University Press, 2013), 11.

6. Yamada was named in Odagiri Hideo's well-known essay on literature and war responsibility. See Odagiri Hideo, "Bungaku ni okeru sensō sekinin no tsuikyū," *Shin Nihon Bungaku* 1, no. 3 (May / June 1946): 65.

7. One of the stronger critiques appeared in Peter Dale's *The Myth of Japanese Uniqueness* (1986), in which Dale paraphrased Tanizaki's argument in *Bunshō tokuhon* (A Manual on Style, 1934) and concluded:

> At first reading, there is something engaging in this critique of the influx of jargon into the modern world, in this advocacy of a lean and nuanced idiom. But read in the sociopolitical context of the times, Tanizaki's thesis takes on rather ominous echoes. At a time of militant aggression in China, antagonisms abroad and vigorous repression on the home front, Tanizaki's extolling of the virtues of circumspection, deference to authority, reverence for the past and accommodation to the established order, conjoined to this fastidious rejection of foreign words, and an attribution of diplomatic failure to the native virtue of diffident reticence, lend sympathy at the level of primarily aesthetic discourse to the dominant rhetoric and values stressed in Japan's emerging fascist order.

Peter N. Dale, *The Myth of Japanese Uniqueness* (London: Croom Helm, 1986), 81.

Masao Miyoshi called Dale's reading wrongheaded, but also pointed out that Tanizaki celebrated the fall of Singapore in a 1942 radio broadcast speech that was full of "imperial clichés." Masao Miyoshi, *Off Center: Power and Culture Relations between*

Japan and the United States (Cambridge, MA: Harvard University Press, 1991), 138; see also 265n30. Miyoshi wrote of Tanizaki's speech: "There is neither irony nor reservation: Tanizaki's pride in his country's victory is total" (138). But while noting that "Tanizaki was indeed carried away by the triumphant turn of events at the very beginning of the Pacific War," Miyoshi also wrote that Tanizaki offered few such statements in the time of crisis, and that for this reason, "it might be necessary finally to be satisfied with Tanizaki's having written so few pieces in any way supportive of the war, rather than to be repelled by these few words of collaborative evidence" (138–39). Miyoshi concluded his reading of Tanizaki's wartime fiction by stating, "In his so-called return to Japan *monogatari*, there is not one item that is nationalistic or chauvinistic. The tales are as preoccupied with aesthetic/epistemological queries as his works in the first period, though the subjects and settings in time and space are restricted to Japan" (144). Miyoshi wrote of Tanizaki's famous essay *In'ei raisan* (In Praise of Shadows, 1933–34) that "an element of racism—though against his own race in this case—is undeniable, and to ignore it would be a mistake. One does need to recall, however, that this was written in the middle of gradually heightening nationalism and chauvinism. A few years later, *In Praise of Shadows* would have been at least frowned upon, if not outright censored. In that sense, perverse as it is, Tanizaki's aesthetic manifesto could be appreciated for refusing to surrender to the growing fanatic self-congratulation and for inserting a moment of self-mockery" (142). Citing these arguments, Eric Cazdyn has written that "Masao Miyoshi argues that, although Tanizaki's work during this period might seem escapist and collaborationist, his stories and relative reticence at times of such nationalist fervor are indeed a remarkably bold attempt at resistance." Eric Cazdyn, *The Flash of Capital: Film and Geopolitics in Japan* (Durham, NC: Duke University Press, 2002), 97.

8. Thomas LaMarre, *Shadows on the Screen: Tanizaki Jun'ichirō on Cinema and "Oriental" Aesthetics* (Ann Arbor: Center for Japanese Studies, University of Michigan, 2005), 12–13.

9. LaMarre, *Shadows on the Screen*, 19.

10. Nishino Atsushi, "Hai o yoseatsumeru: Yamada Yoshio to Tanizaki Jun'ichirō yaku *Genji monogatari*," in *Kindai bungaku ni okeru* "Genji monogatari," ed. Chiba Shunji (Tokyo: Ōfū, 2007), 120–25.

11. Ward's history of the Peace Preservation Law considered the discourse through which "state officials in Tokyo attempted to craft an antiradical law in order to safeguard the empire against imported ideologies such as communism. In order to criminally identify this foreign threat, officials were required to define what exactly was being threatened. They chose the term 'kokutai' for its apparent concreteness and consistently defined it as signifying the location of sovereignty in the 'line of Emperors unbroken for ages eternal' (*bansei ikkei no tennō*) as defined in Articles 1 and 4 of the Meiji Constitution." Max Ward, *Thought Crime: Ideology and State Power in Interwar Japan* (Durham, NC: Duke University Press, 2019), 47.

12. As Ward put it: "Certainly, the imperial state legitimated the suppression of political activists as protecting Japan's timeless cultural traditions or, later, celebrated its rehabilitation policies as expressions of Japan's unique imperial benevolence toward wayward subjects. However, we should not confuse the rhetoric of these cultural claims with the ideological forms through which the imperial state exercised its power, for when

we do, our analytical explanations replicate the very claims that officials used to legitimize these policies. As I argue in *Thought Crime*, in essence, the Japanese campaigns to suppress and rehabilitate political criminals were based on modes of power that various modern states utilize in periods of political crisis, including attempts to guide social morality and behavior." Ward, *Thought Crime*, 5.

13. Woolf, "Middlebrow," 177, 178. Joan Shelley Rubin also discusses the discourse on "middlebrow" with reference to Woolf, Greenberg, and Macdonald, among others. See Rubin, *The Making of Middlebrow Culture* (Chapel Hill: University of North Carolina Press, 1992), xi–xx.

14. Woolf, "Middlebrow," 178.

15. Woolf, "Middlebrow," 179.

16. Woolf, "Middlebrow," 180.

17. Woolf, "Middlebrow," 183.

18. Woolf, "Middlebrow," 184.

19. Woolf, "Middlebrow," 186.

20. My understanding of the pedagogical element of middlebrow culture is informed by the perspectives of several scholars. In *The Making of Middlebrow Culture*, Rubin pointed to the pedagogical orientation of John Erskine's and Mortimer Adler's "Great Books" curriculum, and elsewhere examined how the "Book-of-the-Month Club" taught a kind of literary taste to millions of what its organizers called "average intelligent readers" (xix). In *Cold War Orientalism: Asia in the Middlebrow Imagination, 1945–1961*, the scholar Christina Klein also examined the pedagogical impulse behind middlebrow culture by exploring "how middlebrow intellectuals, texts, and institutions tried to educate Americans about their evolving relationships with Asia, and how they created opportunities—real and symbolic—for their audiences to participate in the forging of these relationships." Klein, *Cold War Orientalism: Asia in the Middlebrow Imagination, 1945–1961* (Berkeley: University of California Press, 2003), 7. In another context, Alan Tansman has discussed pedagogy and literary culture in modern Japan. See Tansman, "The Pedagogy of the Japanese Novel," *Novel: A Forum on Fiction* 47, no. 1 (2014): 57–66.

21. Macdonald, "Masscult and Midcult," in *Masscult and Midcult*, 35.

22. Christopher Chowrimootoo, *Middlebrow Modernism: Britten's Operas and the Great Divide* (Oakland: University of California Press, 2018), 16.

23. Chowrimootoo, *Middlebrow Modernism*, 15. For a discussion of middlebrow culture in postwar Japan, see Hidetoshi Katō, "Middle-Brow Culture," *Journal of Social and Political Ideas in Japan* 2, no. 1 (April 1964): 70–74, and Adam Bronson, *One Hundred Million Philosophers: Science of Thought and the Culture of Democracy in Postwar Japan* (Honolulu: University of Hawai'i Press, 2016), 176–79.

24. Edward Mack, *Manufacturing Modern Japanese Literature: Publishing, Prizes, and the Ascription of Literary Value* (Durham, NC: Duke University Press, 2010), 140.

25. Nathan Shockey, *The Typographic Imagination: Reading and Writing in Japan's Age of Modern Print Media* (New York: Columbia University Press, 2020), 52.

26. Shockey noted in the context of *Kingu* that "this mass-media complex was actively complicit in Japan's road to fascist empire and total war. . . . If the circulation of multimedia print publications like Kōdansha's helped readers imagine a shared national

culture, then magazines were primed to play a key role in bolstering fascist attitudes among the populace." Shockey, *Typographic Imagination*, 57. Satō's study of *Kingu* and fascism appears in Satō Takumi, "Kingu" *no jidai: Kokumin taishū zasshi no kōkyōsei* (Tokyo: Iwanami Shoten, 2002), 323–87.

27. Clement Greenberg, "Avant-Garde and Kitsch," in *Art and Culture: Critical Essays* (Boston: Beacon Press, 1961), 19. Greenberg had earlier explained that the rise of the modernist avant-garde in the early twentieth century had occasioned the rise of its opposite, too, noting that "a second new cultural phenomenon appeared in the industrial West: that thing to which the Germans give the wonderful name of *Kitsch:* popular, commercial art and literature with their chromeotypes, magazine covers, illustrations, ads, slick and pulp fiction, comics, Tin Pan Alley music, tap dancing, Hollywood movies, etc., etc." Greenberg, "Avant-Garde and Kitsch," 9.

28. These etymological details appear in Robert Hendrickson, *The Facts on File Encyclopedia of Word and Phrase Origins*, 4th ed. (New York: Facts on File, 2008), 402, 274.

29. Masao Miyoshi has credited Tanizaki's experience writing film scenarios with allowing him to gain "a better understanding than any other recent writer of his country about the relationship between popular and high culture," later adding that "in Tanizaki's work the high and low, the foreign and native mix, as the traditional and emergent clash in ever more intriguing interplay." Miyoshi, *Off Center*, 126, 128–29.

30. Emmerich, *Translation, Canonization*, 315. Emmerich has examined in detail the rise of *Genji* as a classic of world literature, noting, "This elevation of the tale to the status of world literature, both within and without Japan, was also what made it possible to frame it as the wellspring, or at least one among a number of competing candidates for the wellspring, of Japanese literature, of 'the traditional aesthetics of the Japanese people,' of the Japanese national essence itself, as it was defined and redefined at various points in Japan's modern history." Emmerich, *Translation, Canonization*, 236. For other studies of Tanizaki and Yamada's *Genji* translation, see Nishino, "Hai o yoseatsumeru," 113–61, and Ibuki Kazuko and G. G. Rowley, "The 'Tanizaki Genji': Inception, Process, and Afterthoughts; with Translations by Thomas Harper of Tanizaki Jun'ichirō's 'On Translating *The Tale of Genji* into Modern Japanese' (1938) and 'Some Malicious Remarks' (1965)," in *The Grand Old Man and the Great Tradition: Essays on Tanizaki Jun'ichirō in Honor of Adriana Boscaro*, ed. Luisa Bienati and Bonaventura Ruperti (Ann Arbor: Center for Japanese Studies, University of Michigan, 2009), 25–52.

31. The historian Jordan Sand has interpreted the emergence of a bourgeois "middle-class" culture in late nineteenth- and early twentieth-century Japan with emphasis on housing and domestic lifestyle. He observed that while the problem of definition persists,

> the rhetoric of class and the normative value of middle-classness nevertheless deserve historians' attention because they are themselves fundamental to capitalist society. The modalities of class rhetoric also extend far beyond explicit verbal declarations, encompassing nuances of expression, physical comportment, dress, personal belongings, and every expression of taste. Even if class categories evade a single social scientific formulation, there can be no question that the language of class emerged from a systematic transformation of tremendous weight, that is, the

abandonment of a social structure in which status was largely hereditary, unambiguous, and unquestioned.

Sand, *House and Home in Modern Japan: Architecture, Domestic Space and Bourgeois Culture, 1880–1930* (Cambridge, MA: Harvard University Asia Center, 2003), 10.

32. See Gregory L. Golley, "Tanizaki Junichiro: The Art of Subversion and the Subversion of Art," in *Journal of Japanese Studies* 21, no. 2 (Summer 1995): 365–404.

33. Emmerich, *Translation, Canonization*, 343.

34. Quoted in Emmerich, *Translation, Canonization*, 354.

35. Quoted in Emmerich, *Translation, Canonization*, 354.

36. See Yamada Yoshio, *Renga gaisetsu* (Tokyo: Iwanami Shoten, 1937), 181, and Takiura Masato, *Yamada Yoshio: Kyōdōtai no kokugaku no yume* (Tokyo: Kōdansha, 2009), 142–43.

37. For a study of Yamada's place in language debates, see Shockey, *Typographic Imagination*, 165–69.

38. Walter A. Skya, *Japan's Holy War: The Ideology of Radical Shintō Ultranationalism* (Durham, NC: Duke University Press, 2009), 302, 308.

39. This biographical sketch is informed by the following sources: Skya, *Japan's Holy War*, 289–95, 301–10; Takiura, *Yamada Yoshio*; Satō Kiyoji, "Yamada Yoshio," in *Nihongo gakusha retsuden* (Tokyo: Meiji Shoin, 1997), 94–119; Nishino, "Hai o yoseatsumeru," 113–14; Ōiwa Masanaka, "Yamada Yoshio den: Sono ichi," *Bunpō*, November 1968, 136–39; Ōiwa Masanaka, "Yamada Yoshio den: Sono ni," *Bunpō*, December 1968, 140–43; Ōiwa Masanaka, "Yamada Yoshio den: Sono san," *Bunpō*, January 1969, 132–35; Ōiwa Masanaka, "Yamada Yoshio den: Sono yon," *Bunpō*, February 1969, 128–31; and Ōiwa Masanaka, "Yamada Yoshio den: Sono go: kan," *Bunpō*, March 1969, 126–29.

40. Alan Tansman, *The Aesthetics of Japanese Fascism* (Berkeley: University of California Press, 2009), 150.

41. Tansman has noted in this connection: "As is indicated by the publication and distribution of dozens of interpretive books on *The Essence of the National Polity*, it was probably not easily understood by most of its readers—a readership composed of the general population, including every schoolchild. Its prestige would seem to have grown out of its very abstruseness, its ability to persuade readers that they could 'get' the essence of its 'venerable' words and phrases without discerning their precise meanings. It was, in essence, a performative document." Tansman, *Aesthetics of Japanese Fascism*, 152.

42. John Brownlee lists the following professors as members of the committee that wrote *Kokutai no hongi*: Fujikake Shizuya (Tokyo Imperial University; art); Hisamatsu Sen'ichi (Tokyo Imperial University; Japanese literature); Kuroita Katsumi (Tokyo Imperial University; Japanese history); Ui Hakuji (Tokyo Imperial University; Indian philosophy and Buddhism); Watsuji Tetsurō (Tokyo Imperial University; philosophy); Sakuta Shōichi (Kyoto Imperial University; economics); Yamada Yoshio (Tohoku Imperial University; Japanese literature); Iijima Tadao (The Peers School; history); Kōno Seizō (Kokugakuin University, president). John S. Brownlee, *Japanese Historians and the National Myths, 1600–1945: The Age of the Gods and Emperor Jinmu* (Vancouver: UBC Press, 1997), 152–53.

43. Tansman, *Aesthetics of Japanese Fascism*, 150–51.

44. Tomiko Yoda, *Gender and National Literature: Heian Texts in the Constructions of Japanese Modernity* (Durham, NC: Duke University Press, 2004), 60.

45. Kobayashi Masaaki, "Wartime Japan, the Imperial Line, and *The Tale of Genji*," trans. Michael Emmerich, in *Envisioning* "The Tale of Genji": *Media, Gender, and Cultural Production*, ed. Haruo Shirane (New York: Columbia University Press, 2008), 288.

46. Kobayashi, "Wartime Japan," 289.

47. In this connection, Emmerich has written that "it is impossible to discuss this translation, however, without at least touching on its infamy as an example of wartime censorship, or perhaps self-censorship," adding that Tanizaki and Yamada

> scrupulously expunged every reference to Genji's sexual liaisons with women who were, or would be, intimately involved with an emperor. This includes not only Genji's secret affair with his stepmother, Fujitsubo, which leads to the birth of the future emperor Reizei, but also his relationship with Oborozukiyo, the daughter of the powerful Minister of the Right, who had a good chance of becoming the next empress. Needless to say, the excision of Genji's affair with Fujitsubo obscures the fact that Emperor Reizei is his son, and thus a commoner by birth. Tanizaki also suppressed Genji's attainment of the rank of honorary retired Emperor.

Emmerich, *Translation, Canonization*, 334–44.

48. Yamada Yoshio, "Tanizaki shi to *Genji monogatari*: Kōetsusha no kotoba," *Chūō Kōron*, January 1939, 335.

49. Yamada, "Tanizaki shi to *Genji monogatari*," 335–38. Yamada mentions *kokutai* on pages 335 and 336.

50. Yamada Yoshio, "Genji monogatari" *no ongaku* (Tokyo: Hōbunkan, 1934), 1.

51. Tanizaki Jun'ichirō, *Tanizaki Jun'ichirō zenshū* (Tokyo: Chūō Kōronsha, 1966–70), 21:518. Tanizaki uses the term "feminist" to mean something like "woman worshipper," or a man devoted to a single woman. Genji's philandering made him the opposite of a Tanizakian feminist (one who worships a single woman with absolute devotion) because Genji made overtures to several women at once and, in Tanizaki's opinion, treated them as mere playthings.

52. Tansman, *Aesthetics of Japanese Fascism*, 153.

53. Tansman, *Aesthetics of Japanese Fascism*, 160.

54. Kobayashi, "Wartime Japan," 291.

55. Kobayashi, "Wartime Japan," 291.

56. Nishino, "Hai o yoseatsumeru" 125.

57. Steven Botterill, ed. and trans., *Dante: De vulgari eloquentia* (Cambridge: Cambridge University Press, 1996), 3, 5.

58. Haruo Shirane explains the place of *monogatari* in the larger hierarchies of writing in the introduction to his study of *Genji*. See Haruo Shirane, *The Bridge of Dreams: A Poetics of* "The Tale of Genji" (Stanford, CA: Stanford University Press, 1987), xv–xxiii. Shirane notes in particular that "the literature most highly esteemed by the Heian aristocracy was not vernacular prose, but poetry and prose in classical Chinese, a written language employed exclusively by men, and *waka*, the thirty-one syllable native poetry composed by both sexes" (xv).

59. Minamoto no Tamenori, "Illustration of the Three Jewels," trans. Edward Kamens, in *Traditional Japanese Literature: An Anthology, Beginnings to 1600*, ed. Haruo Shirane (New York: Columbia University Press, 2007), 216, 217.

60. The scholar of Japanese literature Tomiko Yoda has observed that Norinaga's method of textual analysis combined philological rigor with literary imagination, and in so doing, linked ancient Japanese texts to what we now think of as a modern aesthetics. As she put it, "The influence that Norinaga's thesis had on subsequent Japanese intellectual history may be understood, in part, by the prescience with which his poetics anticipated the conceptualization of literature in a modern sense: the 'concrete universal' that brings together individuality and collectivity, particularity and generality, or unity and difference." Yoda, *Gender and National Literature*, 39.

61. Motoori Norinaga, "*The Tale of Genji*: A Little Jeweled Comb," trans. Thomas Harper, in *Reading* "The Tale of Genji": *Sources from the First Millennium*, ed. Thomas J. Harper and Haruo Shirane (New York: Columbia University Press, 2015), 420–21. The corresponding Japanese-language source text is Motoori Norinaga, "*Genji monogatari* Tama no ogushi," in *Motoori Norinaga zenshū* (Tokyo: Chikuma Shobō), 4:174.

62. Pheng Cheah, *What Is a World? On Postcolonial Literature as World Literature* (Durham, NC: Duke University Press, 2016).

63. In this vein, Harootunian has observed that Norinaga's writings on *Genji* revealed that "what people did in their everyday life, Motoori [Norinaga] seemed to propose, was far more important as an example of honest emotion than any instruction on proper or improper conduct," later adding that for Norinaga, "nothing human could be outside the penumbra of *mono no aware*, and nothing should be beyond the natural human propensity to know, feel, and understand." Harootunian, *Things Seen and Unseen: Discourse and Ideology in Tokugawa Nativism* (Chicago: University of Chicago Press, 1988), 110.

64. Norinaga, "Little Jeweled Comb," 470; Norinaga, "*Genji monogatari* Tama no ogushi," 214.

65. Norinaga, "Little Jeweled Comb," 470; Norinaga, "*Genji monogatari* Tama no ogushi," 214.

66. Norinaga, "Little Jeweled Comb," 471; Norinaga, "*Genji monogatari* Tama no ogushi," 215.

67. Yamada Yoshio, *Kokugaku no hongi* (Tokyo: Unebi Shobō, 1942), 58.

68. Yamada, *Kokugaku no hongi*, 47.

69. Yamada, *Kokugaku no hongi*, 51.

70. Yamada, *Kokugaku no hongi*, 43–44.

71. Yamada, *Renga gaisetsu*, 173.

72. Yamada, *Renga gaisetsu*, 173.

73. Yamada, *Renga gaisetsu*, 185.

74. Tanizaki, *Tanizaki Jun'ichirō zenshū*, 14:493.

75. LaMarre, *Shadows on the Screen*, 14.

76. LaMarre has argued in this regard that in Tanizaki's case, "cultural nationalism involves not only the territorial nation but also the nation in expansion, the national empire." LaMarre, *Shadows on the Screen*, 14.

77. Tomi Suzuki, "*The Tale of Genji*, National Literature, Language, and Modernism," in Shirane, *Envisioning* "The Tale of Genji," 272.

78. Tanizaki, *Tanizaki Jun'ichirō zenshū*, 21:102.
79. Tanizaki, *Tanizaki Jun'ichirō zenshū*, 20:183.
80. Tanizaki, *Tanizaki Jun'ichirō zenshū*, 21:126–27.
81. Tanizaki, *Tanizaki Jun'ichirō zenshū*, 20:199.
82. Tanizaki, *Tanizaki Jun'ichirō zenshū*, 20:199.
83. Tanizaki, *Tanizaki Jun'ichirō zenshū*, 21:118.
84. Margherita Long has also analyzed race in *In Praise of Shadows*. See Long, *This Perversion Called Love: Reading Tanizaki, Feminist Theory, and Freud* (Stanford, CA: Stanford University Press, 2009), 18–22.
85. Tanizaki, *Tanizaki Jun'ichirō zenshū*, 20:547, 548.
86. Tanizaki, *Tanizaki Jun'ichirō zenshū*, 20:548.
87. Tanizaki, *Tanizaki Jun'ichirō zenshū*, 20:547.
88. Tanizaki, *Tanizaki Jun'ichirō zenshū*, 20:557.
89. Harootunian, *Things Seen and Unseen*, 108.
90. Harootunian, *Things Seen and Unseen*, 108.
91. Emmerich, *Translation, Canonization*, 316. Chiba Shunji has also discussed the Waley translation and Hakuchō's essays vis-à-vis *Genji* in modern times. See Chiba, "Kindai bungaku no naka no *Genji monogatari*," in Chiba, *Kindai bungaku ni okeru*, 9–28.
92. Hakuchō quoted in translation by Emmerich, *Translation, Canonization*, 324.
93. Hakuchō quoted in translation by Emmerich, *Translation, Canonization*, 328.
94. Emmerich, *Translation, Canonization*, 342.
95. Shimanaka Yūsaku, "*Genji monogatari* no kankō ni atatte," *Chūo Kōron*, January 1939, 328. For a detailed commentary on the genesis of the 1939 Tanizaki-Yamada *Genji*, including analysis of its relationship to Waley's translation, see Mizukami Tsutomu and Chiba Shunji, eds., *Tanizaki Sensei no shokan: Aru shuppansha shachō e no tegami o yomu* (Tokyo: Chūō Kōron Shinsha, 2008), 346–51, and Ibuki and Rowley, "Tanizaki Genji," 25–36.
96. Shimanaka, "*Genji monogatari* no kankō ni atatte," 329.
97. Arthur Waley correspondence to Tanizaki Jun'ichirō, in *Ashiya-shi Tanizaki Jun'ichirō kinenkan shiryōshū (4): kizō kitaku shokan: Heisei jūhachi-nen-nijūni-nen* (Ashiya-shi Tanizaki Jun'ichirō kinenkan, 2011), 53. The date of this correspondence is not certain, but editors speculate it may have been written in 1955.
98. Arthur Waley correspondence to Tanizaki Jun'ichirō in *Ashiya-shi Tanizaki Jun'ichirō kinenkan shiryōshū (4)*, 51. In addition, Donald Keene has written about

> a gift I received in 1951 from the great translator Arthur Waley, whose work had been an inspiration ever since I began the study of Chinese and Japanese. I got to know Waley while I was living in England, and on some occasion he gave me the three volumes of *The Makioka Sisters* (*Sasameyuki*) that Tanizaki had sent him. The volumes, printed on conspicuously better paper than other novels of that time, were inscribed by Tanizaki to Arthur Waley. I guessed that Tanizaki had sent Waley the books hoping that the celebrated translator of *The Tale of Genji* would translate his own novel, often compared with *Genji*. Waley had no intention of making a translation—it had been years since he had translated anything from Japanese—

and gave the books to me after reading them. It was difficult to obtain books from Japan at the time because of British currency restrictions, and I was delighted with the gift.

Keene, *Five Modern Japanese Novelists* (New York: Columbia University Press, 2003), 2.

99. Tanizaki, *Tanizaki Jun'ichirō zenshū*. 21:126.

100. Tanizaki, *Tanizaki Jun'ichirō zenshū*, 21:126.

101. Masao Miyoshi, "Translation as Interpretation," *Journal of Asian Studies* 38, no. 2 (February 1979): 301.

102. Miyoshi, "Translation as Interpretation," 300.

103. Miyoshi, "Translation as Interpretation," 301.

104. Tanizaki, *Tanizaki Jun'ichirō zenshū*, 21:126.

105. Anne Carson, *Economy of the Unlost (Reading Simonides of Keos with Paul Celan)* (Princeton, NJ: Princeton University Press, 1999), 84.

106. Yamada, "Tanizaki shi to *Genji monogatari*," 336.

107. Yamada, "Tanizaki shi to *Genji monogatari*," 338.

108. Tanizaki Jun'ichirō, trans., Yamada Yoshio, ed., *Genji monogatari* (Tokyo: Chūō Kōron, 1939–41), 5:1–2. Although there are many variant editions of *Genji*, I refer to the text found in Kaneko Motoomi, ed., *Teihon* "Genji monogatari" *shinkai: Jō* (Tokyo: Meiji Shoin, 1925) as the source text "original" (*genbun*) in order to indicate the version of *Genji* that Tanizaki and Yamada likely referred to as they completed their 1939 translation. Although I have not been able to conclude with certainty that this was the version that they both used, Nishino Atsushi has shown that there is a strong correlation between Yamada's notations in his personal copy of this edition of *Genji* (housed in the Yamada Yoshio Bunko at the Toyama City Library) and the expurgations of the 1939 translation, suggesting that this may well have been the text on which he and Tanizaki based their 1939 translation. Nishino, "Hai o yoseatsumeru," 143–44.

I have considered verb endings that Tanizaki and Yamada modernized to have been insignificant departures from the source text because such alterations were inevitable in a modern translation. For example, whereas the original text of the first line of this excerpt reads "hito no sumika nado mo arikere" and Tanizaki and Yamada changed the verb *arikere* to *atta*, I do not consider this to have been a meaningful departure from the original since Tanizaki and Yamada's only intervention was to modernize the verb conjugation. In other cases, however, they added circumlocutions, changed the vocabulary, or otherwise significantly altered the source text. I count these sorts of alterations as more significant and discretionary departures from the source text.

109. Lady Murasaki, *The Tale of Genji: A Novel in Six Parts*, trans. Arthur Waley (New York: Modern Library, 1960), 229.

110. I am grateful to Anthony Chambers for pointing out to me that Tanizaki and Yamada's translation contained far more syllables than both the original and Waley's English translation.

111. Quoted and translated in Emmerich, *Translation, Canonization*, 349.

112. Quoted and translated in Emmerich, *Translation, Canonization*, 349–50.

113. Tanizaki, *Tanizaki Jun'ichirō zenshū*, 23:169.

114. Bernard Groethuysen, *The Bourgeois: Catholicism vs. Capitalism in Eighteenth-Century France*, trans. Mary Ilford (New York: Holt, Rinehart and Winston, 1968), 38.

115. Groethuysen, *Bourgeois*, 38.

116. Franco Moretti, *The Bourgeois: Between History and Literature* (London: Verso, 2013), 15, 19.

117. Tanizaki, *Tanizaki Jun'ichirō zenshū*, 22:348–49. For other citations of Tanizaki's support of the war, see Hosoe Hikaru, *Tanizaki Jun'ichirō shinsō retorikku* (Osaka: Izumi Shoin, 2004), 487–525.

118. Cited by Hosoe, *Tanizaki Jun'ichirō shinsō retorikku*, 495.

119. Tanizaki, *Tanizaki Jun'ichirō zenshū*, 23:253.

120. Emmerich, *Translation, Canonization*, 315.

121. Cheah, *What Is a World?*, 3.

122. Cheah, *What Is a World?*, 3.

123. Virginia Woolf, "*The Tale of Genji*: The First Volume of Mr. Arthur Waley's Translation of a Great Japanese Novel by the Lady Murasaki," in Harper and Shirane, *Reading* "The Tale of Genji," 566–67.

2. A Worldly World in Fiction and Philosophy

1. Aldous Huxley, *Point Counter Point* (New York: Doubleday, Doran, 2009), 294–95.

2. Yokomitsu Riichi quoted in roundtable discussion titled "'Junsui shōsetsu' o kataru," in *Teihon Yokomitsu Riichi zenshū*, ed. Hoshō Masao, Inoue Ken, and Kuritsubo Yoshiki (Tokyo: Kawade Shobō Shinsha, 1983), 15:198.

3. See Seiji Lippit, *Topographies of Japanese Modernism* (New York: Columbia University Press, 2002), 205.

4. See Inden Masashi, *"Kankaku" to "sonzai": Yokomitsu Riichi o meguru konkyo e no toi* (Tokyo: Meiji Shoin, 2014).

5. Inden, *"Kankaku" to "sonzai,"* 155–76.

6. As the scholar Travis Workman has noted in his exploration of philosophy and the question of world history in the context of the Japanese empire, "most importantly for colonial subjects and colonial intellectuals, this discourse stated that overcoming Western modernity was a universal matter for humanity at large. The Japanese nation-state, with its particular culture, space, and history, not only represented the other nations of East Asia, but was also responsible for solving the problems of Western metaphysics for the world at large." Workman, *Imperial Genus: The Formation and Limits of the Human in Modern Korea and Japan* (Oakland: University of California Press, 2016), 174.

7. As Cheah put it: "The world's reality is neither objective nor subjective because it is a process grounded in the force of temporalization. Literature has a similarly curious ontological status: it is not something objective and so cannot be reduced to the subject's rational powers of determination and calculation." Cheah, *What Is a World? On Postcolonial Literature as World Literature* (Durham, NC: Duke University Press, 2016), 10.

8. Lippit, *Topographies of Japanese Modernism*, 216. For Lippit's reading of the novel, see *Topographies of Japanese Modernism*, 197–228.

9. For an overview of the "novel of ideas," see Michael Lemahieu, "The Novel of Ideas," in *The Cambridge Companion to British Fiction since 1945*, ed. David James (Cambridge: Cambridge University Press, 2015), 177–91.

10. Sianne Ngai, *Theory of the Gimmick: Aesthetic Judgment and Capitalist Form* (Cambridge, MA: Belknap Press of Harvard University Press, 2020), 105–44.

11. Huxley, *Point Counter Point*, 295.

12. Biographical information on Yura Tetsuji appears in Yomota Inuhiko, *Sensei to watashi* (Tokyo: Shinchōsha, 2007), 101–21, Inoue Ken, Kamiya Tadataka, and Hatori Tetsuya, eds., *Yokomitsu Riichi jiten* (Tokyo: Ōfū, 2002), 456–57, and in the chronology of Yura's life appended to Yura Tetsuji, *Yokomitsu Riichi no geijutsu shisō* (Tokyo: Nihon Tosho Sentā, 1984), 129–30.

13. For a study of this debate, see Peter E. Gordon, *Continental Divide: Heidegger, Cassirer, Davos* (Cambridge, MA: Harvard University Press, 2010).

14. Yura's connection to Yamada and the Jingū kōgakkan is described in Yomota, *Sensei to watashi*, 114.

15. Inaga has written that "it is well known that Yokomitsu Riichi (1898–1947), who went to Europe in 1936, chose Yura Tetsuji as his model for Yashiro, the ultranationalist protagonist in his final and unfinished long novel, *Ryoshū* (1948) [*The Melancholy of Travel*]." Inaga Shigemi, "Japanese Philosophers Go West: The Effect of Maritime Trips on Philosophy in Japan with Special Reference to the Case of Watsuji Tetsurō (1889–1960)," *Japan Review* 25 (2013): 129. Inden has remarked on the connections linking Yura and Yokomitsu, noting print sources that suggest that Yura himself was a model for Yashiro in *The Melancholy of Travel*. See Inden, *"Kankaku" to "sonzai,"* 39, 57n1.

16. Yomota, *Sensei to watashi*, 133, and Inoue Ken, "Kaisetsu," in Yura, *Yokomitsu Riichi no geijutsu shisō*, 6.

17. Yura Tetsuji, "Yokomitsu Riichi to Kawabata Yasunari," in *Yokomitsu Riichi no bungaku to shōgai: Botsugo sanjūnen kinenshū*, ed. Yura Tetsuji (Tokyo: Ōfūsha, 1977), 263.

18. Yura, "Yokomitsu Riichi to Kawabata Yasunari," 261. Yura wrote that several lines of Yashiro's dialogue in a scene late in the novel "were nearly all very close to my own notes" (*kono sanjū sūkō wa, hotondo watashi no nōto ni chikai*) (261).

19. The literary scholar Kim Te-Gyun has written that *The Melancholy of Travel* is widely read as a "love story novel of ideas" (*ren'ai shisō shōsetsu*) because it mixes intellectual questions with a romantic plotline. Kim Te-Gyun, *Yokomitsu Riichi to "kindai no chōkoku": "Ryoshū" ni okeru kenchiku, kagaku, shokuminchi* (Tokyo: Kanrin Shobō, 2014), 151. The mix of romance and ideas would seem to be consistent with Yura's claim that his own "marriage problem" was the basis of Yokomitsu's comparative exploration of global intellectual histories.

20. Yura, "Yokomitsu Riichi to Kawabata Yasunari," 257–58.

21. Yura, "Yokomitsu Riichi to Kawabata Yasunari," 258.

22. Tosaka Jun, *Tosaka Jun zenshū* (Tokyo: Keisō Shobō, 1966–79), 4:114. See also 3:171–76.

23. Dennis Washburn, *Translating Mount Fuji: Modern Japanese Fiction and the Ethics of Identity* (New York: Columbia University Press, 2007), 147.

24. Irena Hayter, "Figures of the Visual: Japanese Modernism, Technology, Vitalism," *positions: asia critique* 25, no. 2 (2017): 294.

25. Hayter, "Figures of the Visual," 300.

26. My use of the term "deep communication" is informed by Cheah's reading of Amitav Ghosh's *The Hungry Tide* (2004). See the section titled "Deep Time and World Literature as Deep Communication," in Cheah, *What Is a World?*, 267–70.

27. Harry Harootunian, "Philosophy and Answerability: The Kyoto School and the Epiphanic Moment of World History," in *Confronting Capital and Empire: Rethinking Kyoto School Philosophy*, ed. Viren Murthy, Fabian Schäfer, and Max Ward (Leiden: Brill, 2017), 30. In a resonant observation, the intellectual historian Takeshi Kimoto has concluded that the discussions collected in "The World Historical Perspective and Japan" reveal that in the Kyoto School imagination, warfare in the present "involved at its core Japan's world-historical destiny to transform the world order created by Western modernity and subsequently imposed on the rest of the world so as to establish a new world order." Kimoto, "Antinomies of Total War," *positions: east asia cultures critique* 17, no. 1 (Spring 2009): 110.

28. Christopher Goto-Jones has pointed out that in the essay "Sekai shinchitsujo no genri" (Principles for a New World Order), Nishida argued that the mid-twentieth century was a "period of worldly self-consciousness" (*sekaiteki jikaku*) that necessitated a global awareness of what Nishida called a "world-historical world" (*sekaishiteki sekai*). Goto-Jones has also examined how Tanabe Hajime, another Kyoto School thinker, did not merely observe "the nature and meaning of history" but rather found "within it an ethical imperative (*tōi*) to transform the discipline of history, including centrally the history of philosophy and political thought. Indeed, he talks of an obligation and mission in the present to achieve this world-historical standpoint (*sekaishi-teki tachiba*)." Goto-Jones, "The Kyoto School, the Cambridge School, and the History of Political Philosophy in Wartime Japan," *positions: east asia cultures critique* 17, no. 1 (Spring 2009): 22, 25. Elsewhere, Richard Calichman has translated Nishitani Keiji's "My Views on 'Overcoming Modernity,'" an essay presented at the "Overcoming Modernity" conference in which Nishitani argued that the "state life" of Japan had "flowed into world history and become its bloodline, so to speak, and together with this the fountainhead of state life and the ideals that run throughout its history have become the guiding ideals within world-historical reality." Nishitani, "My Views on 'Overcoming Modernity,'" in *Overcoming Modernity: Cultural Identity in Wartime Japan*, ed. and trans. Richard Calichman (New York: Columbia University Press, 2008), 62. For analysis of Miki Kiyoshi's involvement in the discourse of "world history," see Lewis E. Harrington, "Miki Kiyoshi and the Shōwa Kenkyūkai: The Failure of World History," *positions: east asia cultures critique* 17, no. 1 (2009): 43–72. For analysis of Tanabe Hajime's vision of empire, see Naoki Sakai, "Subject and Substratum: On Japanese Imperial Nationalism," *Cultural Studies* 14, no. 3–4 (2000): 462–530.

29. The term *sekaisei* (worldliness) also appears in the noted Kyoto School roundtable on world history and Japan. See Kōsaka Masaaki, Nishitani Keiji, Kōyama Iwao, and Suzuki Shigetaka, *Sekaishiteki tachiba to Nihon*, ed. Fujita Chikamasa (Tokyo: Chūō Kōronsha, 1943), 82, 90.

30. Yura Tetsuji, *Minzoku kokka to sekaikan* (Tokyo: Minzoku Kagakusha, 1943), 138.

31. Yura, *Minzoku kokka to sekaikan*, 139. Emphasis in original on "makes" (*tsukuru*).

32. Cheah, *What Is a World?*, 211.

33. Cheah, *What Is a World?*, 42.

34. Cheah, *What Is a World?*, 19.

35. Harry Harootunian, *Marx after Marx: History and Time in the Expansion of Capitalism* (New York: Columbia University Press, 2015), 238–39.

36. Yura Tetsuji, *Hittorā to Doitsu minzoku kokka* (Tokyo: Kokumin Kyōiku Fukyūkai, 1944), 1.

37. Tetsuo Najita and H. D. Harootunian, "Japanese Revolt against the West: Political and Cultural Criticism in the Twentieth Century," *The Cambridge History of Japan*, vol. 6, *The Twentieth Century*, ed. Peter Duus (Cambridge: Cambridge University Press, 1988), 741.

38. *Shin Nihon no shisō genri*, in Miki Kiyoshi, *Miki Kiyoshi: Tōa Kyōdōtai ronshū*, ed. Uchida Hiroshi (Tokyo: Kobushi Shobō, 2007), 176.

39. *Shin Nihon no shisō genri*, 177.

40. Hannah Arendt, *The Human Condition*, 2nd ed. (Chicago: University of Chicago Press, 1998), 167–68. The literary scholar Shu-Mei Shih has observed the implications of Arendt's notion of the useless art object for our understanding of worldliness and literature. See Shih, "World Studies and Relational Comparison," *PMLA* 130, no. 2 (2015): 437. Cheah has also considered the implications of Arendt's thought for our reckoning with the nexus of world and text. See Cheah, *What Is a World?*, 131–60.

41. Cheah, *What Is a World?*, 126.

42. Cheah, *What Is a World?*, 126.

43. Cheah, *What Is a World?*, 127. Language thus has the world-making force of meaning because, as Cheah put it, "the logos is a whole of connections that gathers and holds every being together such that the parts belong to each other. This holding-together is the condition of possibility of meaning." Cheah, *What Is a World?*, 127–28.

44. Cheah, *What Is a World?*, 10–11.

45. Cheah, *What Is a World?*, 180.

46. Cheah, *What Is a World?*, 180.

47. Cheah, *What Is a World?*, 129.

48. Cheah, *What Is a World?*, 210.

49. Jean-Paul Sartre, "Situation of the Writer in 1947," in *"What Is Literature?" and Other Essays* (Cambridge, MA: Harvard University Press, 1988), 182–83.

50. Sartre, "Situation of the Writer," 175. Emphasis in original.

51. This is not to deny that even a geographical designation such as "the West" can be understood in more than physical terms in *The Melancholy of Travel.* As Lippit has pointed out, "The novel poses the question of where, for the Japanese intellectual, 'the West' is located. It is not merely an external, material *place*, as Yashiro discovers through his journey to Europe. It is also located in consciousness—as image and concept—and Yashiro's struggle is thus an internal struggle. The West exists as a phantasm and a specter for Yashiro, just as it did for generations of Japanese writers, and the crisis presented in Yokomitsu's novel results in part from the realization of the difference between the internal and external manifestations of the West." Lippit, *Topographies of Japanese Modernism*, 219. Emphasis in original.

52. Cheah, *What Is a World?*, 192.

53. Inoue Ken has noted Yokomitsu's inclinations to abort (*chūzetsu*) the novel during the course of its serialization. See Inoue Ken, *Hyōden Yokomitsu Riichi* (Toyo: Ōfūsha, 1975), 360–61. On Yokomitsu's unrealized plan to continue the narrative, see Mogi Masao, *Yokomitsu Riichi no hyōgen sekai: Nihon no shōsetsu* (Tokyo: Benseisha, 1995), 69–70, and Yura Tetsuji, "Yokomitsu Riichi to *Ryoshū* no kōsō," *Yomiuri Shinbun*, March 22, 1973 (evening ed.), 5.

54. Toeda Hirokazu, "*Ryoshū*—samayoeru honbun," in *Yokomitsu Riichi no bungaku sekai*, ed. Ishida Hitoshi, Shibuya Kaori, and Nakamura Miharu (Tokyo: Kanrin Shobō, 2006), 136. Toeda discusses the postwar censorship of the novel in depth in this essay (130–41). Kim Te-Gyun also analyzes the wartime and postwar editions of the novel. See Kim, *Yokomitsu Riichi to "kindai no chōkoku,"* 137–63.

55. Publishing information in this paragraph appears in Inoue et al., *Yokomitsu Riichi jiten*, 217–18, and Kuritsubo Yoshiki, "Kaidai," in Yokomitsu, *Teihon Yokomitsu Riichi zenshū*, 9:301–3.

56. The chronology and historical context of the novel is discussed in Hamakawa Katsuhiko, *Ronkō Yokomitsu Riichi* (Osaka: Izumi Shoin, 2001), 217, and in Inoue et al., *Yokomitsu Riichi jiten*, 218–20.

57. Judt wrote that "Léon Blum today is a half-forgotten man," while adding that

> in his day Blum was a strikingly controversial figure: the leader and exemplar of French Socialism in all its doctrinal fidelity and contradictions; the head of the Popular Front government of 1936, from which so much was expected and feared; France's first socialist prime minister and its first Jewish one at a time of widespread anti-Semitism; the chief target of Pétainist revenge following the installation in 1940 of the Vichy regime, as well as "enemy number one," as Blum himself put it, of the French Communist Party. That such a man, around whom swirled and stormed for three decades the anger, the hatreds, and the political divisions of his country, should now be the object of benign neglect is an index of the changes that have taken place in France since the 1950s.

Tony Judt, *The Burden of Responsibility: Blum, Camus, Aron, and the French Twentieth Century* (Chicago: University of Chicago Press, 1998), 29.

58. Thomas Mann, *The Magic Mountain*, trans. John E. Woods (New York: Vintage Books, 1995), xi–xii. Emphasis in original.

59. Lauren Berlant, *Cruel Optimism* (Durham, NC: Duke University Press, 2011), 4.

60. Berlant, *Cruel Optimism*, 5. Emphasis in original.

61. Yokomitsu, *Teihon Yokomitsu Riichi zenshū*, 8:198–99.

62. Mary A. Favret, *War at a Distance: Romanticism and the Making of Modern Wartime* (Princeton, NJ: Princeton University Press, 2010), 11.

63. Favret, *War at a Distance*, 21–22.

64. Favret, *War at a Distance*, 18.

65. This scene appears in Yokomitsu, *Teihon Yokomitsu Riichi zenshū*, 8:25–26.

66. In another reading of the novel, Lippit has written that "symbolically, [the cathedral sculpture] functions as the material remains of a former ideal, which now call

forth only sensations of revulsion and horror." Lippit, *Topographies of Japanese Modernism*, 220.

67. Ngai, *Theory of the Gimmick*, 127–30.

68. Yokomitsu, *Teihon Yokomitsu Riichi zenshū*, 8: 123.

69. Gordon, *Continental Divide*, 88.

70. Mann, *Magic Mountain*, 4.

71. Yokomitsu, *Teihon Yokomitsu Riichi zenshū*, 8:146–47.

72. Yokomitsu, *Teihon Yokomitsu Riichi zenshū*, 8:148.

73. See Alan Tansman, *The Aesthetics of Japanese Fascism* (Berkeley: University of California Press, 2009).

74. Lippit, *Topographies of Japanese Modernism*, 200–201.

75. Workman, *Imperial Genus*, 176.

76. Workman, *Imperial Genus*, 228.

77. Gordon has written that "Ernst Cassirer was beyond doubt one of the greatest philosophers and intellectual historians to emerge from the cultural ferment of modern Germany. . . . To his admirers as well as his critics, Cassirer stood as the very embodiment of central European liberal culture: his many contributions to the history of science, culture, and epistemology bespoke a robust attachment to the rationalist spirit of the *Aufklärung* and the cultural legacy of German classicism." Gordon, *Continental Divide*, 11. Reading in the Japanese context, Christopher Goto-Jones has pointed out that Nishida immersed himself not only in Buddhist texts, but also in the writings of Kant and neo-Kantian thinkers, including Hermann Cohen, who mentored Cassirer. Christopher S. Goto-Jones, *Political Philosophy in Japan: Nishida, The Kyoto School and Co-prosperity* (New York: Routledge, 2005), 69. Nishida also seems to have had an interest in Cassirer's thought per se: as early as 1917, Nishida mentioned Cassirer in his correspondence, and Goto-Jones has observed that "Cassirer" is a "neo-Kantian name that appears repeatedly in Nishida's diaries." Goto-Jones, *Political Philosophy in Japan*, 69.

78. Ernst Cassirer, *The Philosophy of Symbolic Forms*, vol. 1, *Language*, trans. Ralph Manheim (New Haven, CT: Yale University Press, 1953), 78.

79. Cassirer, *Philosophy of Symbolic Forms*, 82.

80. Cassirer, *Philosophy of Symbolic Forms*, 82. Emphasis in original.

81. Apter described her own study as a response to some reckonings with world literature which she argued "fall prey inevitably to the tendency to zoom over the speed bumps of untranslatability in the rush to cover ground. In a counter-move, I invoke untranslatability as a deflationary gesture toward the expansionism and gargantuan scale of world-literary endeavors." Emily Apter, *Against World Literature: On the Politics of Untranslatability* (London: Verso, 2013), 3.

82. Michael André Bernstein, *Foregone Conclusions: Against Apocalyptic History* (Berkeley: University of California Press, 1994), 96.

83. Yokomitsu, *Teihon Yokomitsu Riichi zenshū*, 8:454.

84. Lippit, *Topographies of Japanese Modernism*, 223.

85. Yokomitsu, *Teihon Yokomitsu Riichi zenshū*, 8:500.

86. Yura wrote that Yokomitsu was related by blood on his mother's side to Bashō. See Yura, *Yokomitsu Riichi no geijutsu shisō*, 5. Inden also discusses Yokomitsu's relationship to

Bashō in his reading of *The Melancholy of Travel*. See Inden, *"Kankaku" to "sonzai,"* 261–62.

87. Yokomitsu, *Teihon Yokomitsu Riichi zenshū*, 8:605.

88. Cheah, *What Is a World?*, 268.

89. Cheah, *What Is a World?*, 268.

90. Cheah, *What Is a World?*, 268.

91. Gary Ebersole has noted that "there were a variety of rituals in early Japan in which poetry played an important part, but all these rituals were based upon the more general belief in the magico-religious efficacy of special words. This belief is generally referred to in the Japanese scholarly literature as *kotodama shinkō*, the belief in the spirit power (*tama*) of words (*koto*)." Gary Ebersole, *Ritual Poetry and the Politics of Death in Early Japan* (Princeton, NJ: Princeton University Press, 1989), 19; see also 19–23. More recently, Tansman has read the writings of Nihon Roman-ha (Japan Romantic School) leader Yasuda Yojūrō (1910–81) through the lens of *kotodama*: "*Kotodama* refers to the power language once possessed to transform the world; and of all Yasuda's works, 'Japanese Bridges' [*Nihon no hashi*, 1936] resonated most powerfully with his readers as an act of *kotodama*, hovering at the border between art and life, rhetorically linking self-immolation and spiritual transformation." Tansman, *Aesthetics of Japanese Fascism*, 61.

92. Yokomitsu, *Teihon Yokomitsu Riichi zenshū*, 8:623.

93. Yokomitsu, *Teihon Yokomitsu Riichi zenshū*, 9:294.

94. Yura, "Yokomitsu Riichi to *Ryoshū* no kōsō," 5.

95. Mogi, *Yokomitsu Riichi no hyōgen sekai*, 69–70.

96. Translated and cited in Harrington, "Miki Kiyoshi and the Shōwa Kenkyūkai," 54.

97. John Namjun Kim, "The Temporality of Empire: The Imperial Cosmopolitanism of Miki Kiyoshi and Tanabe Hajime," in *Pan-Asianism in Modern Japanese History: Colonialism, Regionalism and Borders*, ed. Sven Saaler and J. Victor Koschmann (New York: Routledge, 2007), 151–67. Kim observed that "the political theses of Miki and Tanabe unwittingly demonstrate the ethical ambivalence of cosmopolitanism as a real-world possibility. The promise of cosmopolitan freedom does not necessarily preclude political projects such as imperialism or colonialism. On the contrary, this promise mobilizes such political projects of domination by endowing them with a semblance of ethical legitimacy, of winning the approbation of those who will be subjugated" (152).

98. See Sakai, "Subject and Substratum," 462–530.

99. While noting that the "prewar Japanese government was not fascist," Fletcher has observed that "the leaders of the Shōwa Research Association in 1940 thus attempted to guide the premier of Japan in the building of a political system patterned after European fascism, that is, the Italian corporate state and Nazi economic policies. Three intellectuals were especially enthusiastic about this vision: Rōyama Masamichi (1895–1980), Ryū Shintarō (1900–67), and Miki Kiyoshi (1895–1945)." William Miles Fletcher III, *The Search for a New Order: Intellectuals and Fascism in Prewar Japan* (Chapel Hill: University of North Carolina Press, 1982), 158, 4. Fletcher added: "Fascism appealed to Rōyama, Ryū, and Miki because it presented solutions to serious economic and political problems of industrial society, addressing such concerns as Japan's national role in Asia, social peace, and economic justice. Moreover, fascism promised to break the deadlock of parliamentary democracy, raise productivity, and end economic strife. Rōyama, Ryū,

and Miki believed that even the emotional aspect of fascism, the ethic of national service, could facilitate rational reforms of society" (156–57).

100. Harry Harootunian, *Overcome by Modernity: History, Culture, and Community in Interwar Japan* (Princeton, NJ: Princeton University Press, 2000), 398–99.

101. Miki Kiyoshi, *Miki Kiyoshi zenshū* (Tokyo: Iwanami Shoten, 1967), 8:4.

102. Harootunian, *Overcome by Modernity*, 359.

103. Harootunian, *Overcome by Modernity*, 358.

104. Huxley, *Point Counter Point*, 193–94.

105. Huxley, *Point Counter Point*, 194.

106. Robert Musil, *The Man without Qualities*, trans. Sophie Wilkins (New York: Vintage International, 1996), 1:272.

107. Harrington has pointed out that although "interpretations of the intentions of the Shōwa Kenkyūkai vary from reactionary to communist, and while evaluations of its ultimate goals vary from control of the military to creation of a fascistic mass party organization fully in support of totalitarian military rule, nearly all accounts agree that the group failed to accomplish its goals, whatever the particular interpreter feels these goals to have been." Harrington, "Miki Kiyoshi and the Shōwa Kenkyūkai," 53.

108. Yokomitsu was listed in Odagiri Hideo's well-known essay on literature and war responsibility. See Odagiri Hideo, "Bungaku ni okeru sensō sekinin no tsuikyū," *Shin Nihon Bungaku* 1, no. 3 (May / June 1946): 65. Elsewhere, Nakano Shigeharu wrote: "Yokomitsu Riichi had to invent a 'petty and inferior' straw-man, European wannabe to knock down in his *Ryoshū* [Melancholy journey] for the purpose of proselytizing his pro-Japan ideology." Nakano Shigeharu, "The Humanity of Criticism I: Concerning Hirano Ken and Ara Masahito," trans. Joshua Solomon and Kaori Shiono, in *The Politics and Literature Debate in Postwar Japanese Criticism, 1945–52*, ed. Atsuko Ueda, Michael K. Bourdaghs, Richi Sakakibara, and Hirokazu Toeda (Lantham, MD: Lexington Books, 2017), 112. Toeda Hirokazu has also discussed Yokomitsu's reputation before and after 1945. See Toeda, "From the God of Literature to War Criminal: The Media and the Shifting Image of Yokomitsu Riichi from Prewar and Wartime to the Postwar Era," trans. Atsuko Ueda, in *Literature among the Ruins, 1945–1955: Postwar Japanese Literary Criticism*, ed. Atsuko Ueda, Michael K. Bourdaghs, Richi Sakakibara, and Hirokazu Toeda (Lanham, MD: Lexington Books, 2018), 177–89.

3. Overcome by the Literary

1. Satō Haruo, "Sanbun seishin no hassei," in *Gendai bungakuron taikei dai 3-kan* (Tokyo: Kawade Shobō, 1956), 267.

2. Mikhail Bakhtin, *Problems of Dostoevsky's Poetics*, ed. and trans. Caryl Emerson (Minneapolis: University of Minnesota Press, 1984), 201. This passage is also discussed by Caryl Emerson and Gary Saul Morson. See Morson and Emerson, eds., *Mikhail Bakhtin: Creation of a Prosaics* (Stanford, CA: Stanford University Press, 1990), 34. For a consideration of Bakhtin's *Problems of Dostoevsky's Poetics* in the context of Marxist literary writing in interwar Japan, see Miriam Silverberg, *Changing Song: The Marxist Manifestos of Nakano Shigeharu* (Princeton, NJ: Princeton University Press, 1990), 146–47.

3. As Richard Torrance has observed, "*Sanbun seishin* was the spirit of resistance to all authoritarian discourses, but especially to those propagated by the state." Torrance, "*The People's Library:* The Spirit of Prose Literature versus Fascism," in *The Culture of Japanese Fascism*, ed. Alan Tansman (Durham, NC: Duke University Press, 2009), 67–68. The fascist implications of Yasuda's literary romanticism have been discussed in detail. See Alan Tansman, *The Aesthetics of Japanese Fascism* (Berkeley: University of California Press, 2009), 49–104.

4. Torrance, "*The People's Library*," 57. Torrance also pointed out that although "the journal served as Japan's most articulate, organized, and popular literary opposition to fascism," it was also true that "the pages of the journal contain no sustained definitions or theoretical formulations of fascism" (57). Led by Takeda Rintarō, *The People's Library* group developed its slogan "the spirit of prose" from their readings of the earlier writings by critic and novelist Hirotsu Kazuo, who had argued in a 1924 debate (*ronsō*) with novelist Arishima Takeo that "prosaic art" (*sanbun geijutsu*) forged the most intimate relationship to lived experience. Hirotsu described "the spirit of prose" in the following essays, which appear in *Gendai Nihon bungaku zenshū*, vol. 32 (Tokyo: Chikuma Shobō, 1955): "Sanbun geijutsu no ichi" (1924), 171–74; "Futatabi sanbun geijutsu no ichi ni tsuite" (1925), 174–78; "Sanbun seishin ni tsuite" (1938), 181–82. Torrance has observed in this connection that Hirotsu's main argument was that "'spirit of prose literature' was the highest form of art precisely because it was the most common, immediate, and relevant to human existence." Richard Torrance, *The Fiction of Tokuda Shūsei and the Emergence of Japan's New Middle Class* (Seattle: University of Washington Press, 1994), 186.

5. This approach is indebted to Miriam Silverberg's earlier analysis of leftist language politics in interwar Japan, which elucidated the implicit resonances connecting literary and theoretical texts composed by writers who were not personally in dialogue with one another per se. She described her study of Nakano Shigeharu's poetry in part as an attempt to link his literary writing to the Marxist imagination, writing:

> In the following pages, Nakano's Marxist critique of Taishō culture will be placed alongside the formulations of the leading Marxist theorists of culture in the West, because his changed Marxism bears strong resemblances to the new directions charted by such theorists as Georg Lukács, Walter Benjamin, and Antonio Gramsci. Nakano's Marxism derived from the Marxism of Marx and was also informed by the theory of consciousness set forth by Lukács in the early 1920s. To the extent that the present work can convince the reader that Nakano Shigeharu's criticism of modern culture was Marxist, it is a comparative history. But it must be underscored that Nakano is being placed in relation to, and not in actual dialogue with, the other Marxist thinkers who were his contemporaries. With the exception of the work of Lukács, the writings of the Western Marxist were not available to him until after the war.

Silverberg, *Changing Song*, 5–6.

6. Morson and Emerson, *Mikhail Bakhtin*, 15.

7. This approach is informed by Lucey and McEnaney, who observed that "linguistic anthropology is interested in language-in-use. Language is a social object. Social history is sedimented in language and actualized upon use. Language precedes its use

in some ways, and any given use of language presupposes its prior existence while also entailing the appearance of something new." Michael Lucey and Tom McEnaney, "Introduction: Language-in-Use and Literary Fieldwork," *Representations* 137 (Winter 2017): 8.

8. They wrote:

> Bakhtin's early writings were emphatically *not* sociological, except in the trivial sense in which every meditation on selves and others is sociological. But his writings of the 1930's and 1940's (for example, "Discourse in the Novel" and the book on Rabelais) were deeply sociological. Is it not possible that the encounter with strong Marxist renditions of his own ideas provoked the change? Faced with the challenge of a sophisticated sociological poetics, based to a considerable extent on Bakhtin's own ideas, Bakhtin appears to have responded with theories of language and literature that were sociological without being Marxist; he answered the challenge of his friends with his sociology without theoretism. He seems to have believed that Marxism, for all its help in prodding thinkers to consider sociological questions, falls short in answering them.

Morson and Emerson, *Mikhail Bakhtin*, 118–19.

9. Lucey and McEnaney, "Language-in-Use and Literary Fieldwork," 1.

10. Lucey and McEnaney, "Language-in-Use and Literary Fieldwork," 8.

11. Lucey and McEnaney, "Language-in-Use and Literary Fieldwork," 1.

12. Lucey and McEnaney, "Language-in-Use and Literary Fieldwork," 1.

13. For a detailed examination of the conceptual affinities linking Tosaka's philosophy to that of his Frankfurt School contemporaries, see Fabian Schäfer, *Public Opinion, Propaganda, Ideology: Theories of the Press and Its Social Function in Interwar Japan, 1918–1937* (Leiden: Brill, 2012), 95–123.

14. Interview with Yoshimi Shunya cited in Ikeda Shigekazu, "Tosaka Jun ni okeru 'bungaku' no imi o megutte: Gendai no 'karuchuraru sutadiizu' to no kankei de," in *Yuibutsuron kenkyū nenshi: dai 5 go: Aratana kōkyōsei o motomete* (Tokyo: Aoki Shoten, 2000), 215. Yoshimi also mentions Miki Kiyoshi as a foundational thinker in the field of "cultural studies."

15. Yuriko Furuhata, *Cinema of Actuality: Japanese Avant-Garde Filmmaking in the Season of Image Politics* (Durham, NC: Duke University Press, 2013), 59.

16. Schäfer, *Public Opinion, Propaganda, Ideology*, 99. This led Schäfer to conclude that "Tosaka, in a way that was very similar to the proponents of the early Frankfurt School, saw the most fundamental meaning of both, journalism *and* philosophy, in the critique of the everyday" (108). In a related vein, Furuhata has written: "According to Tosaka, academicism and journalism form two principal ideological apparatuses, which must be dialectically synthesized to produce a viable platform from which to critique existing political and economic conditions." Furuhata, *Cinema of Actuality*, 59.

17. For an analysis of Tosaka's postwar obscurity (despite his wartime lucidity), see H. D. Harootunian, "The Postwar Genealogy of Fascism and Tosaka Jun's Prewar Critique of Liberalism," *Journal of Pacific Asia* 2 (1995): 95–112.

18. Reto Hofmann, *The Fascist Effect: Japan and Italy: 1915–1952* (Ithaca, NY: Cornell University Press, 2015), 72–73.

19. Harry Harootunian, *Overcome by Modernity: History, Culture, and Community in Interwar Japan* (Princeton, NJ: Princeton University Press, 2000), xxviii.

20. Gilles Deleuze and Félix Guattari, "1933: Micropolitics and Segmentarity," in *A Thousand Plateaus: Capitalism and Schizophrenia*, trans. Brian Massumi (Minneapolis: University of Minnesota Press, 1987), 215.

21. My reading of the accretions of a fascist "micropolitics" in language also follows the lead of Alan Tansman, who argued in *The Aesthetics of Japanese Fascism* that "the accumulation of fascist moments over time and in a variety of contexts had an ideological force with real-world implications. They were fleeting, and once past, they were hard to see as belonging to their historical moment. And yet, clearly, they did. Their fascist qualities, though not always overt, are detectable in their very movement toward aesthetic articulation. Each articulation represents a place where aesthetic expression becomes culturally and politically consequential. The ripple effect of those articulations is discernable as the culture of fascism." Tansman, *Aesthetics of Japanese Fascism*, 2.

22. This approach draws on the perspective of Michael Silverstein, who in a different context has analyzed "different kinds of knowledge that are, on the one hand, the begetters of communicative form and, on the other, the begotten results of communication having taken the particular form it did in precipitating textuality-in-context." Michael Silverstein, "How Knowledge Begets Communication Begets Knowledge: Textuality and Contextuality in Knowing and Learning," *Intercultural Communication Review* 5 (2007): 250. Silverstein has shown how certain forms of sociocultural knowledge lead to certain semiotic and lexical expressions, which themselves, in turn, convey specific kinds of sociocultural knowledge. He has called this process "indexically creative": "It requires analysis as part of the fractionation of any so-called language into a union of registers. . . . It is in these terms that the language users experience language from the indexical variability that is both the essential condition of all socio-empirical knowledge and, dialectically, its emergent product" (59).

23. V. N. Volosinov, *Marxism and the Philosophy of Language*, trans. Ladislav Matejka and I. R. Titunik (Cambridge, MA: Harvard University Press, 1973), 9. Emphasis in original.

24. Mikhail Bakhtin, "Discourse in the Novel," in *The Dialogic Imagination: Four Essays*, ed. Michael Holquist, trans. Caryl Emerson and Michael Holquist (Austin: University of Texas Press, 1981), 299. Emphasis in original.

25. Bakhtin, "Discourse in the Novel," 298.

26. As Morson and Emerson put it in their reading of Bakhtin's perspective on poetics: "Whereas the novelist tries to represent, even exaggerate, heteroglossia, the poet escapes it in order to write in a language that is timeless—timeless in the sense that it does not call attention to its specific historical shaping as the point of view of one, merely partial, kind of experience." Morson and Emerson, *Mikhail Bakhtin*, 320.

27. Bakhtin, "Discourse in the Novel," 285. Emphasis in original.

28. As Bakhtin put it, the "poet is a poet insofar as he accepts the idea of a unitary and singular language and a unitary monologically sealed-off utterance." Bakhtin, "Discourse in the Novel," 296.

29. Bakhtin, "Discourse in the Novel," 285.

30. Satō, "Sanbun seishin no hassei," 268.
31. Satō, "Sanbun seishin no hassei," 268.
32. Satō, "Sanbun seishin no hassei," 268.
33. Bakhtin, "Discourse in the Novel," 346.
34. See Tansman, *Aesthetics of Japanese Fascism*, 18–31.
35. Tansman, "Introduction: The Culture of Japanese Fascism," in *Culture of Japanese Fascism*, 13.
36. Other scholars have also discussed what I call "literaturism" (*bungakushugi*) in Tosaka's writing. James Dorsey has translated *bungakushugi* as "literary aestheticism," noting that "in Tosaka's eyes this critical perspective [*bungakushugi*] inverts the proper hierarchy of objective realty over literary representation, and subjugates material realities to the fictional whims of literature. Real-world issues are being evaluated purely in terms of literary aesthetics." James Dorsey, *Critical Aesthetics: Kobayashi Hideo, Modernity, and Wartime Japan* (Cambridge, MA: Harvard University Asia Center, 2009), 151. Alan Tansman translates *bungakushugi* in Tosaka's thought as "ideologies of literature": "Dominating Japanese letters in 1936, critics such as Kobayashi lent their work to smoothing over the economic, political, social, cultural and class conflicts that wracked Japanese society. To Tosaka, it was no coincidence that such ideological work was being done by literature, and it was particularly dangerous that it was being done so, because literary ideas, he argued, easily became 'ideologies of literature (*bungakushugi*)' that rejected positivism and logic and then served up aesthetic models for the social world." Tansman, "Culture of Japanese Fascism," 3.
37. Tosaka Jun, *Tosaka Jun zenshū* (Tokyo: Keisō Shobō, 1966–79), 2:230.
38. Louis Althusser, "Ideology and Ideological State Apparatuses (Notes Towards an Investigation)," in *Lenin and Philosophy, and Other Essays*, trans. Ben Brewster (London: New Left Books, 1971), 158.
39. As Harootunian has put it, "Hermeneutics was a method that appealed to the 'corresponding order of meaning' rather than steeping its claims in a 'realistic order of things.' It was a 'trick,' Tosaka charged, that sought, by sleight of hand, to efface the 'actual world,' that is, the material world, for a fiction of the mind." Harootunian, "Postwar Genealogy of Fascism," 106.
40. Harootunian, "Postwar Genealogy of Fascism," 107.
41. As Harootunian put it, "What troubled Tosaka was the application of a method to classical texts which lacked genuine 'historico-scientific knowledge,' and an operation that led to the subsequent substitution of text for context, philological 'interpretation' for historical inquiry. Tosaka was persuaded that hermeneutics sought to stand-in for history yet claim the truth of history by emplotting the meaning of a vastly different present by appealing to a moment in the remote past." Harootunian, "Postwar Genealogy of Fascism," 107.
42. Volosinov, *Marxism and the Philosophy of Language*, 72, 73.
43. Tosaka made this point explicitly in *The Japanese Ideology*: "If literaturism [*bungakushugi*] operates by an interpretive method that replaces philosophical categories based on reality with literary categories based on literary images, then the ideology of philology [*bunkengakushugi*] is based exclusively on etymological and exegetical interpretations of

texts and language instead of on real things. In the most extreme cases, this native word and that are capriciously selected and passed off as philosophical concepts." Tosaka, *Tosaka Jun zenshū*, 2:231.

44. Tosaka's critique appears in chapter 7 of *Nihon ideorogii ron* (The Japanese Ideology), in *Tosaka Jun zenshū*, 2:299–308.

45. Tosaka, *Tosaka Jun zenshū*, 2:302.

46. Tosaka, *Tosaka Jun zenshū*, 2:301.

47. Tosaka quoted in translation by Furuhata, *Cinema of Actuality*, 59. Emphasis in original.

48. Furuhata, *Cinema of Actuality*, p. 59.

49. Theodor Adorno, *The Jargon of Authenticity*, trans. Knut Tarnowski and Frederic Will (Evanston, IL: Northwestern University Press, 1973), 9–10.

50. Adorno, *Jargon of Authenticity*, 12–13. In a footnote to the last sentence of this citation, Adorno suggests Heidegger's *Being and Time* as an example.

51. Bakhtin, "Discourse in the Novel," 271.

52. Bakhtin, "Discourse in the Novel," 287.

53. Adorno, *Jargon of Authenticity*, 5.

54. Torrance, "*The People's Library*," 56.

55. In this regard, Torrance has remarked on two "clear aspects of fascism in the arts that came to the fore in the mid-1930s: the denigration of Japan's tradition of realism and the neo-romantic exaltation of the poetics of the past, especially in regard to a glorification of the aesthetics of hero worship and death." Torrance, "*The People's Library*," 64–65.

56. Furuhata, *Cinema of Actuality*, 59. Emphasis in original.

57. Kamiya Tadataka, "Shōwa jūnendai no 'sanbun seishin' ron," in *Shōwa no bungaku* (Tokyo: Yūseidō Shuppan, 1981), 100.

58. Quoted by Kamiya Tadataka in "Shōwa jūnendai no 'sanbun seishin' ron," 103.

59. Akutagawa Ryūnosuke, *Akutagawa Ryūnosuke zenshū*, 15:160.

60. My thinking about the "affordance" is broadly informed by James Gibson's "The Theory of Affordances," in *The Ecological Approach to Visual Perception* (Hillsdale, NJ: Lawrence Erlbaum Associates, 1986), 127–43.

61. Odagiri Hideo, *Nakano Shigeharu: Bungaku no kongen kara* (Tokyo: Kōdansha, 1999), 77.

62. Takeuchi Emiko, *Nakano Shigeharu: Hito to bungaku* (Tokyo: Bensei Shuppan, 2004), 65.

63. Nakano's meeting with Akutagawa is described in Takeuchi, *Nakano Shigeharu*, 64–65. Miriam Silverberg also discusses Nakano's relationship with Akutagawa. See Silverberg, *Changing Song*, 90–94.

64. Aono Suekichi, "Sanbun seishin no mondai," in Hirabayashi Hatsunosuke, Aono Suekichi, Kurahara Korehito, and Nakano Shigeharu, *Hirabayashi Hatsunosuke, Aono Suekichi, Kurahara Korehito, Nakano Shigeharu shū: Gendai Nihon bungaku zenshū: 78* (Tokyo: Chikuma Shobō, 1957), 110–11.

65. Etō Jun, *Shōwa no bunjin* (Tokyo: Shinchōsha, 1989), 41. Etō describes commuting through Shinagawa Station on pages 38–39.

66. Odagiri's critique of Etō's reading of Nakano appears in Odagiri, *Nakano Shigeharu*, 242–65. For discussion of the poem "Ame no furu Shinagawa eki" in particular, see 245–53; for discussion of conservatism in particular, see 262–64.

67. Silverberg has written that Bakhtin's essay "Discourse in Life and Discourse in Art (Concerning Sociological Poetics)" "can be used to associate Nakano's Marxist manifestos in verse form with a Marxian theory of poetry," noting in particular that "the Russian theorist argues that art is 'immanently social,' and that the poet works from within society." Silverberg, *Changing Song*, 216–17.

68. Part of Lucey and McEnaney's point about "literary fieldwork" originated in their reading of Pierre Bourdieu's "concept of a field of cultural production," which they observed "involves both makers and critics in conceiving a constantly evolving set of works and the complex indexical relations between those works and also between their makers, relations that themselves become discoverable through critical forms of fieldwork and archival inquiry." Lucey and McEnaney, "Language-in-Use and Literary Fieldwork," 3. Lucey and McEnaney made the point that the novelist can perform this sort of fieldwork, too, as in Proust's prose narratives, when "the narrator also does another kind of fieldwork, performing a kind of archaeological dig on and around the moment of exchange, excavating relevant moments from the pasts of the various interlocutors, bringing in various bits of the surrounding cultural universe that might be indexed in some way by the exchange to hand, and so on" (14). This led them to observe that "there are numerous moments in the novel where the commentary Proust's narrator is able to offer on the speech around him is based on fieldwork of some kind" (15).

69. Lucey and McEnaney, "Language-in-Use and Literary Fieldwork," 18.

70. In this connection, Lucey has written:

> When, in literary studies, we think of context, contextualization, or intertextualiztion, we often dwell in the realm of text-artifacts themselves, weighing what claims we can make for the relations between one text and another or between a text and accounts that have been made of its historical and cultural surroundings. To think of literature as language-in-use is perhaps a slightly different activity. We might characterize the difference as related to a number of slight shifts in emphasis: from the artifactual to the interactive, from the semantic or representational to the pragmatic and social indexical, from context imagined as some kind of fixed surrounding to a sense that context is in a state of continual production—that to make an utterance is to make a claim on context, to make a claim on context is to assert a certain point of view on some aspect of social reality.

Michael Lucey, "Proust and Language-In-Use," *Novel: A Forum on Fiction* 48, no. 2 (2015): 271.

71. Nakano Shigeharu, *Nakano Shigeharu zenshū* (Tokyo: Chikuma Shobō, 1998), 1:51. Silverberg has translated and analyzed this poem, too. See Silverberg, *Changing Song*, 131–33. Silverberg noted that this poem "may well have referred to [Paul] Claudel's arrival in Japan, which was heralded in the Japanese press as the arrival of a 'poet-ambassador'" (131).

72. Tosaka, *Tosaka Jun zenshū*, 2:264. Schäfer has elaborated on this point in his reading of Tosaka's thought: "Journalism, Tosaka explained, from the outset had a

different social function than academic philosophy since it was based on the 'everyday life of the people,' 'inhabiting' a world that is 'quotidan, social, external and sometimes as well profane.' The interest of the common public into journalism is thus directed by its interest into the current, not the persistent matters. To Tosaka, already the etymological origin of the term 'journalism' in the French word 'jour' was indicative of this relationship." Schäfer, *Public Opinion, Propaganda, Ideology*, 99.

73. Furuhata, *Cinema of Actuality*, 66.

74. Furuhata, *Cinema of Actuality*, 66–67.

75. Silverberg, *Changing Song*, 133.

76. Furuhata, *Cinema of Actuality*, 72.

77. Tosaka, *Tosaka Jun zenshū*, 5:126–35.

78. Silverberg, *Changing Song*, 131–32.

79. Michael Silverstein, "The Poetics of Politics: 'Theirs' and 'Ours,'" *Journal of Anthropological Research* 61, no. 1 (Spring 2005): 3.

80. Michael Silverstein, "What Goes Around . . . : Some Shtick from 'Tricky Dick' and the Circulation of U.S. Presidential Image," *Journal of Linguistic Anthropology* 21, no. 1 (2011): 55.

81. Horkheimer and Adorno argued that modern media (including radio broadcasts, pop music, and film) coerce consent through unidirectional communication; in one example, they argued that the radio "turns all participants into listeners and authoritatively subjects them to broadcast programs which are all exactly the same. No machinery of rejoinder has been devised, and private broadcasters are denied any freedom." Max Horkheimer and Theodor Adorno, "The Culture Industry: Enlightenment as Mass Deception," in *Dialectic of Enlightenment*, trans. John Cumming (New York: Continuum, 2002), 122. For Horkheimer and Adorno, the homogenous forms of modern mass culture produced a set of self-identical communicative forms (a veritable "jargon") that instructed its receivers how to think and feel. In formulating this critique, they implied that a poetic kind of cultural enclosure resulted from modern mass media, arguing, "The man with leisure has to accept what the culture manufactures offer him. Kant's formalism still expected a contribution from the individual, who was thought to relate the varied experiences of the senses to fundamental concepts; but industry robs the individual of this function. Its prime service to the customer is to do his schematizing for him" (124).

82. Nakano, *Nakano Shigeharu zenshū*, 1:89. Silverberg has also translated and analyzed this poem. See Silverberg, *Changing Song*, 141–43.

83. Nakano, *Nakano Shigeharu zenshū*, 1:90.

84. Nakano, *Nakano Shigeharu zenshū*, 19:215.

85. Nakano, *Nakano Shigeharu zenshū*, 19:215.

86. See Jonathan Abel, "Personification and a Trope of Writing: Nakano Shigeharu's 'Language of Slaves,'" *Comparative Literature* 65, no. 4 (2013): 470.

87. Abel, "Personification," 470.

88. Nakano, *Nakano Shigeharu zenshū*, 1:78. Silverberg has also translated and analyzed this poem. See Silverberg, *Changing Song*, 101–6.

89. Silverberg has read the repetition of *sayonara* and *sayōnara* as indicative of a Marxist understanding of "the production and reproduction of the working class."

Silverberg argued that the repetition of "Bye" (*sayonara*) and "Good-bye" (*sayōnara*) "introduce[s] the idea of the repetitive nature of capitalist reproduction through the dulling rhythm of the words of the factory girls arriving home from their labors in the textile mills, on New Year's break," and that the poem makes clear how "capitalist society is in constant, repetitive movement, just like the train that stops only to start again along the northern coast of Japan." Silverberg, *Changing Song*, 102.

90. Volosinov, *Marxism and the Philosophy of Language*, 104. Volosinov made this point in the following context: "There are certain expressions like 'so-so,' 'yes-yes,' 'now-now,' 'well-well' and so on that commonly serve as 'safety valves' of that sort. The doubling usual in such expressions is symptomatic; i.e., it represents an artificial prolongation of the sound image for the purpose of allowing the pent up intonation to fully expire. Any one such favorite little expression may, of course, be pronounced in an enormous variety of intonations in keeping with the wide diversity of situations and moods that occur in life" (104).

91. As Volosinov put it: "There is no reason for saying that meaning belongs to a word as such. In essence, meaning belongs to a word in its position between speakers; that is, meaning is realized only in the process of active, responsive understanding. Meaning does not reside in the word or in the soul of the speaker or in the soul of the listener. Meaning is the *effect of interaction between speaker and listener produced via the material of a particular sound complex*. It is like an electric spark that occurs only when two different terminals are hooked together. . . . Only the current of verbal intercourse endows a word with the light of meaning." Volosinov, *Marxism and the Philosophy of Language*, 102–3. Emphasis in original.

92. Nakano, *Nakano Shigeharu zenshū*, 1:80–81.

93. Volosinov, *Marxism and the Philosophy of Language*, 9. Emphasis in original.

94. Volosinov, *Marxism and the Philosophy of Language*, 13.

95. Torrance, "*The People's Library*," 63.

96. Torrance has observed that "although Takeda maintained ultimate editorial control [of *The People's Library*], the managing editor was Honjō Mutsuo, a secret member of the by then clandestine Communist Party. Almost all of the fifty or so contributors were leftists who had been arrested for their political activities. 'We are the leftist survivors,' Naka Kōhei, a regular contributor, declared." Torrance, "*The People's Library*," 56.

97. Torrance, "*The People's Library*," 56.

98. Nakano Shigeharu, "Zensho ni kaete," in *Mori Ōgai kenkyū*, ed. Nakano Shigeharu (Tokyo: Shinchōsha, 1957), 24.

99. For a book-length study of Shibue Chūsai, see Edwin McClellan, *Woman in the Crested Kimono: The Life of Shibue Io and Her Family* (New Haven, CT: Yale University Press, 1985).

100. Marvin Marcus, *Paragons of the Ordinary: The Biographical Literature of Mori Ōgai* (Honolulu: University of Hawai'i Press, 1993), 136.

101. Quoted in translation in Marcus, *Paragons of the Ordinary*, 139.

102. Marvin Marcus has observed that in "Hatori Chihiro," Ōgai "lent his own imprimatur to the memorialization of an obscure but exemplary life. Of course, these are the very terms of his relationship with [Shibue] Chūsai and company, and I would suggest that the Hatori piece, while easily overlooked among the historical novellas and

works of fiction that came out around the same time, is the earliest precursor to the *shiden*." Marcus, *Paragons of the Ordinary*, 133.

103. Marcus, *Paragons of the Ordinary*, 132–33.

104. Nakano, *Nakano Shigeharu zenshū*, 22:423.

105. Nakano, *Nakano Shigeharu zenshū*, 22:429.

106. Nakano, *Nakano Shigeharu zenshū*, 22:430.

107. Nakano, *Nakano Shigeharu zenshū*, 22:433.

108. Nakano, *Nakano Shigeharu zenshū*, 22:433.

109. In a related vein, Marcus observed in his study of Ōgai's historical biographies that "Mori Ōgai all but proclaims himself as the last of his kind, an artist of classical stature." Marcus, *Paragons of the Ordinary*, 281.

110. See Morson and Emerson, *Mikhail Bakhtin*, 36–40.

111. Nakano, *Nakano Shigeharu zenshū*, 22:300. Paragraph break added for clarity.

112. Nakano Shigeharu, "Sōseki to Ōgai to no ichi to yakuwari," in *Ōgai: Sono sokumen* (Tokyo: Chikuma Shobō, 1972), 213.

113. Nakano Shigeharu, "Ōgai ichidzuke no tame ni," in *Ōgai: Sono sokumen*, 126.

114. Amy Vladeck Heinrich, *Fragments of Rainbows: The Life and Poetry of Saitō Mokichi, 1882–1953* (New York: Columbia University Press, 1983), 67.

115. Takeuchi Yoshimi, "Overcoming Modernity," in *What Is Modernity? Writings of Takeuchi Yoshimi*, ed. and trans. Richard Calichman (New York: Columbia University Press, 2005), 130–31. Corresponding Japanese text appears in Takeuchi Yoshimi, *Kindai chōkoku* (Tokyo: Chikuma Shobō, 1983), 90.

116. Takeuchi, "Overcoming Modernity," 131; Takeuchi, *Kindai chōkoku*, 90–91. Emphasis in original.

117. Quotation of Nakano translated by Richard Calichman in Takeuchi, "Overcoming Modernity," 130. Nakano passage quoted by Takeuchi Yoshimi in *Kindai chōkoku*, 90.

118. Key essays from the literature and politics debate are available in English translation. See Atsuko Ueda, Michael K. Bourdaghs, Richi Sakakibara, and Hirokazu Toeda, eds., *The Politics and Literature Debate in Postwar Japanese Criticism, 1945–52* (Lanham, MD: Lexington Books, 2017).

119. Nakano wrote of "the widespread ban on wartime publications" that it had the effect of "writers who once beat the drums for aggressive war [being] viewed by readers now only on the basis of their unbanned works. Their crimes are ironically hidden by the fact that they were criminals." Nakano, "The Humanity of Criticism II: On the Literary Reaction, et Cetera," trans. Joshua Solomon and Kaori Shiono, in Ueda et al., *Postwar Japanese Criticism, 1945–52*, 143.

120. Nakano, "Humanity of Criticism II," 139.

121. Nakano, "Humanity of Criticism II," 140.

122. Nakano, "Humanity of Criticism II," 140–41.

123. Nakano Shigeharu, *Bungaku no koto bungaku izen no koto* (Tokyo: Kaihōsha, 1947), 1.

124. Hirotsu Kazuo, "Shinpan o dasu ni atatte," in *Sanbun seishin ni tsuite* (Tokyo: Sōgeisha, 1950), 259.

125. Ken C. Kawashima, Fabian Schäfer, and Robert Stolz, eds., *Tosaka Jun: A Critical Reader* (Ithaca, NY: East Asia Program, Cornell University, 2013), ix. The editors con-

textualize the translations and critical essays of their volume as part of a broader claim for Tosaka's contemporary relevance, arguing that "Tosaka's critique of cultural liberalism is more useful than ever for a contemporary critique of capitalism and fascism. Indeed, we have likely entered a new period that shares more than just a few ominous family resemblances with the 1930s" (xii).

126. Harootunian, "Postwar Genealogy of Fascism," 112.

127. Lin Shukumi has examined Nakano's postwar critique in *Hihyō no ningensei* with reference to Tosaka's earlier critique of "literary liberalism" (*bungakuteki jiyūshugi*). See Lin, *Hihyō no ningensei: Nakano Shigeharu* (Tokyo: Heibonsha, 2010), 56–115.

128. Lin, *Hihyō no ningensei*, 351.

4. *The Fiction of the Free Market*

1. Friedrich Hayek, *The Fatal Conceit: The Errors of Socialism*, ed. W. W. Bartley III (London: Routledge, 1988), 106. Hayek explained that he had adjusted Arthur Waley's original translation:

> The somewhat simplified quotation by Confucius that stands at the head of this chapter is probably the earliest expression of this concern that has been preserved. An abbreviated form in which I first encountered it apparently stems from there being in Chinese no single word (or set of characters) for liberty. It would also appear, however, that the passage legitimately renders Confucius's account of the desirable condition of any ordered group of men, as expressed in his *Analects* (tr. A. Waley, 1938: XIII, 3, 171–2): "If the language is incorrect . . . the people will have nowhere to put hand and foot." I am obliged to David Hawkes, of Oxford, for having traced a truer rendering of a passage I had often quoted in an incorrect form.

Hayek, *Fatal Conceit*, 109.

2. The historian Quinn Slobodian pointed to two essays that questioned "neoliberalism": Rajesh Venugopal, "Neoliberalism as Concept," *Economy and Society* 44, no. 2 (2015): 165–87, and Bill Dunn, "Against Neoliberalism as a Concept," *Capital and Class* 41, no. 3 (2017): 435–54. But Slobodian also pointed to recent statements declaring not only the existence of neoliberalism, but even positive notions of self-identity that have collected around the term. He noted that in 2016, "the International Monetary Fund (IMF), making international headlines, not only identified neoliberalism as a coherent doctrine but asked if the policy package of privatization, deregulation, and liberalization had been 'oversold.'" Slobodian, *Globalists: The End of Empire and the Birth of Neoliberalism* (Cambridge, MA: Harvard University Press, 2018), 2. Slobodian also noted that "even though the policies described as neoliberal had long been criticized, the IMF report was still significant for recognizing the label 'neoliberalism.' The term appeared poised for the mainstream, appearing in the *Financial Times*, the *Guardian*, and other newspapers. Also in 2016, the Adam Smith Institute, founded in 1977 and a source of guidance for Margaret Thatcher, 'came out as neoliberals,' in their words, shedding their former moniker, 'libertarian'" (3). Responding to those who deny the conceptual purchase of the term "neoliberalism," Slobodian wrote that "labeling neoliberalism helps

us to see it as one body of thought and one mode of governance among others—as a form or variety of regulation rather than its radical Other" (3).

3. Dieter Plehwe, introduction to *The Road from Mont Pèlerin: The Making of the Neoliberal Thought Collective*, ed. Philip Mirowski and Dieter Plehwe (Cambridge, MA: Harvard University Press, 2009), 13.

4. For example, Dieter Plehwe has written:

> Neoliberalism must be approached primarily as a historical "thought collective" of increasingly global proportions. The following chapters focus on what we believe has been the central thought collective that has conscientiously developed the neoliberal identity for more than sixty years now. We will consider any person or group that bears any links to the Mont Pèlerin Society (MPS) since 1947 as falling within the purview of the neoliberal thought collective. Consequently, we will make use of the MPS network of organized neoliberal intellectuals (just over 1,000 members so far) and a closely related network of neoliberal partisan think tanks under the umbrella of the Atlas Economic Research Foundation as a litmus test for identifying the relevant actors and their linkages to other organizations and institutions.

Plehwe, introduction to *The Road from Mont Pèlerin*, 4. Slobodian has written in his survey of scholarship on neoliberalism that "historians have focused, in particular, on the Mont Pèlerin Society, formed by F. A. Hayek and others in 1947, as a group of like-minded intellectuals and policy makers who would meet periodically to discuss world affairs and the contemporary condition of the political cause to which they were devoted." Slobodian, *Globalists*, 4.

In addition, Angus Burgin has described the Mont Pèlerin Society as "an international gathering place for leading philosophers, economists, journalists, politicians, and philanthropists who supported the market mechanism," noting that it "has long been cited as a progenitor of the social philosophy that has become known as 'neoliberalism.'" Burgin, *The Great Persuasion: Reinventing Free Markets since the Depression* (Cambridge, MA: Harvard University Press, 2012), 8. Daniel Stedman Jones has written that after 1945, Hayek and Milton Friedman "first helped to create, and then to synthesize, a neoliberal policy program and political strategy. In 1947, Hayek brought a disparate group of intellectuals together in Switzerland to discuss how liberalism could be defended in the face of the challenge of 'collectivism'—an all-encompassing term that included Nazi and Soviet totalitarianism, New Deal liberalism, and British social democracy. The group adopted the name the Mont Pelerin Society." Jones, *Masters of the Universe: Hayek, Friedman, and the Birth of Neoliberal Politics* (Princeton, NJ: Princeton University Press, 2012), 4. Jones added that their strategy would become clear: "Neoliberal thinkers needed to target the wider intelligentsia, journalists, experts, politicians, and policy makers. This was done through transatlantic networks of sympathetic business founders and ideological entrepreneurs who ran think tanks, and through the popularization of neoliberal ideas by journalists and politicians" (4).

5. My reading of McClellan's translation is indebted to earlier analyses by Keith Vincent and Aida Hirotsugu. See Vincent, *Two-Timing Modernity: Homosocial Narrative in Modern Japanese Fiction* (Cambridge, MA: Harvard University Asia Center, 2012),

86–151, and Aida, "Sōseki, Haieku, Etō Jun: Kokoro no kizuna," *Bungei Shunjū* 86 (2008): 334–41.

6. See Scott O'Bryan, *The Growth Idea: Purpose and Prosperity in Postwar Japan* (Honolulu: University of Hawai'i Press, 2009).

7. O'Bryan, *Growth Idea*, 99.

8. Burgin, *Great Persuasion*, 4.

9. Burgin, *Great Persuasion*, 5.

10. Hayek to Edwin McClellan, March 24, 1971, Friedrich A. von Hayek Papers, Box 37, Folder 26, Hoover Institution Archives, Stanford, California (hereafter cited as Hayek Papers).

11. For example, see the proposal to establish an Institute of Economics and Political Science at Rikkyo University that Matsushita Masatoshi sent to Hayek in 1963, referenced in a letter from Matsushita to Hayek dated August 2, 1963. Hayek Papers, Box 46, Folder 14.

12. For example, see Tanaka Seigen to Friedrich Hayek, July 8, 1964, Hayek Papers, Box 52, Folder 28.

13. Tanaka Seigen to Friedrich Hayek, December 28, 1963, Hayek Papers, Box 52, Folder 28.

14. Friedrich Hayek to James A. Kennedy, President, Earhart Foundation, February 14, 1956, Hayek Papers, Box 17, Folder 37.

15. Burgin has noted that William Volker, a Kansas City furniture manufacturer, had originally endowed the fund to support public works in the Kansas City area. But as the fund came under the control of his nephew, Harold Luhnow, "its priorities began to shift," Burgin wrote, turning "away from regional public works and toward philosophical advocates of economic freedom." Burgin, *Great Persuasion*, 100. Burgin noted that Luhnow took a particular interest in Hayek: "Influenced by Hayek's contention that classical liberal ideals could not be realized without a strong intellectual base, he set out to foster the construction of that base through the strategic allocation of disbursements from his uncle's fund" (100).

16. Friedrich Hayek to R. C. Cornuelle of the William Volker Fund, April 2, 1954, Hayek Papers, Box 58, Folder 18.

17. Edwin McClellan, "Edwin McClellan on Natsume Sōseki and Shiga Naoya," in *Words, Ideas, and Ambiguities: Four Perspectives on Translating from the Japanese*, ed. Donald Richie (Chicago: Imprint Publications, 2000), 15.

18. Adam Bronson, *One Hundred Million Philosophers: Science of Thought and the Culture of Democracy in Postwar Japan* (Honolulu: University of Hawai'i Press, 2016).

19. Jennifer Miller, *Cold War Democracy: The United States and Japan* (Cambridge, MA: Harvard University Press, 2019), 2.

20. For an analysis of early postwar Japanese literary criticism with reference to Cold War anticommunism, see Michael K. Bourdaghs, "Early Freeze Warning: The Politics and Literature Debate as Cold War Culture," in *Literature among the Ruins, 1945–1955: Postwar Japanese Literary Criticism*, ed. Atsuko Ueda, Michael K. Bourdaghs, Richi Sakakibara, and Hirokazu Toeda (Lanham, MD: Lexington Books, 2018), 17–42. For a study of anticommunism, neoliberalism, and the history of the academic field of Japan studies in the United States, see Bourdaghs, "The Ghosts of Anticommunism and Neoliberalism: East

Asian Studies in the Twenty-First Century," in *Reconsidering American Power: Pax Americana and the Social Sciences*, ed. John D. Kelly, Kurt Jacobsen, and Marston H. Morgan (Oxford: Oxford University Press, 2020), 445–64. For a study of "democratic culture" and postwar Japanese art between 1945–1960, see Justin Jesty, *Art and Engagement in Early Postwar Japan* (Ithaca, NY: Cornell University Press, 2018).

21. Harvey began his study of neoliberalism by observing: "Future historians may well look upon the years 1978–80 as a revolutionary turning-point in the world's social and economic history." David Harvey, *A Brief History of Neoliberalism* (Oxford: Oxford University Press, 2005), 1. He later elaborated: "There has everywhere been an emphatic turn towards neoliberalism in political-economic practices and thinking since the 1970s. Deregulation, privatization, and withdrawal of the state from many areas of social provision have been all too common" (2–3).

22. Slobodian has suggested that the Cold War meant little to Hayek: "In his voluminous writings," Slobodian wrote, "the conflict scarcely appears." Slobodian, *Globalists*, 264. Slobodian elsewhere wrote in his study that one of the reasons why "a neoliberal perspective on the history of the twentieth century amounts to an alternative account of the modern era" is that in the eyes of neoliberals, "the Cold War was secondary to the war against the Global New Deal" (16), adding later that "in the neoliberal century, the Cold War was a sideshow to the main event of the rise of mass enfranchisement and the end of empire" (264).

23. See Wendy Brown, *In the Ruins of Neoliberalism: The Rise of Antidemocratic Politics in the West* (New York: Columbia University Press, 2019), and *Undoing the Demos: Neoliberalism's Stealth Revolution* (New York: Zone Books, 2015).

24. Michel Feher, *Rated Agency: Investee Politics in a Speculative Age* (New York: Zone Books, 2018), 11.

25. Philip Mirowski, *Never Let a Serious Crisis Go to Waste: How Neoliberalism Survived the Financial Meltdown* (London: Verso Books, 2013), 38. Emphasis in original.

26. Plehwe, introduction to *The Road from Mont Pèlerin*, 13.

27. In a lecture titled "The Prospects of Freedom," Hayek discussed the difficulty of finding what he called "a statement of those true liberal principles which once seemed destined to conquer the world but during the past two generations have steadily lost their influence," later adding: "There is, of course, John Stuart Mill's noble book *On Liberty*, but there are many reasons which make me hesitate about suggesting Mill as the symbol for a new liberal movement." Hayek, "The Prospects of Freedom," Hayek Papers, Box 107, Folder 7, 16. In an article titled "The Intellectuals and Socialism" (1949), Hayek warned against socialists overtaking liberals: "If we are to avoid such a development we must be able to offer a new liberal program which appeals to the imagination." Hayek, "The Intellectuals and Socialism," *University of Chicago Law Review* 16, no. 3 (Spring 1949): 432.

28. See Slobodian, *Globalists*, 126–27.

29. Friedrich Hayek, "A Rebirth of Liberalism," *The Freeman*, July 28, 1952, 731.

30. Mirowski, *Serious Crisis*, 38. Emphasis in original.

31. Jones, *Masters of the Universe*, 96. Jones added: "The paper [Friedman's 'Neo-Liberalism and Its Prospects,' 1951] is therefore a useful marker of the moment when neoliberalism became a self-conscious political and economic concept in the United States" (96).

32. Burgin, *Great Persuasion*, 10.
33. Burgin, *Great Persuasion*, 9.
34. Slobodian, *Globalists*, 19.
35. Hayek, "Rebirth of Liberalism," 729.
36. Feher wrote:

> The left has not always held a monopoly on melancholy. Without going all the way back to the exiles of the French and Russian Revolutions, the immediate aftermath of the Second World War was arguably a time when the grim mood currently pervading the left side of the political spectrum weighed more heavily on the advocates of free markets. In both cases, we encounter what psychoanalysis diagnoses as melancholia, namely, the inability to mourn a loss. For the Left of today, it is the loss of socialism—made harder to grieve because its once "actually existing" versions were perverted before they were defeated; for yesteryear's stalwarts of economic liberalism, it was the loss of laissez-faire—a motto that originally formed the core of their creed, but was proven unviable by the Great Depression and the war.

Feher, *Rated Agency*, 7.

37. Feher, *Rated Agency*, 15.
38. Leigh Claire La Berge and Quinn Slobodian, "Reading for Neoliberalism, Reading Like Neoliberals," *American Literary History* 29, no. 3 (2017): 607.
39. La Berge and Slobodian, "Reading for Neoliberalism," 611.
40. Slobodian, *Globalists*, 58.
41. Slobodian, *Globalists*, 58.
42. As Slobodian put it: "Perhaps most radical was Hayek's conclusion in that decade, building on an earlier skepticism about statistics cultivated in Viennese debates, that comprehensive knowledge itself would always—and must always—elude the economist because of its necessary dispersal among all members of society. For him, to climb the Lighthouse of the World in search of a synoptic view from which to direct and plan was only the setup for a long fall." Slobodian, *Globalists*, 58.
43. Slobodian made this point in writing that "by placing the economy beyond the space of representation—and, for Hayek, beyond even reason—neoliberalism was born in the late 1930s as a project of synthetic social science in which, as surprising as it might sound, the least important disciplinary approach was that of economics itself." Slobodian, *Globalists*, 86.
44. Friedrich Hayek, "The Principles of a Liberal Social Order," Hayek Papers, Box 85, Folder 9, 15. Hayek noted that this quotation is of Witter Bynner's translation.
45. Nishiyama Chiaki, "Arguments for the Principles of Liberty and the Philosophy of Science," 3, Hayek Papers, Box 85, Folder 9.
46. Nishiyama, "Arguments for the Principles of Liberty," 4.
47. Nishiyama, "Arguments for the Principles of Liberty," 6.
48. Slobodian, *Globalists*, 18.
49. Hayek, "Prospects of Freedom," 4. Paragraph break added for readability.
50. Hayek, "Prospects of Freedom," 6.
51. Hayek, "Prospects of Freedom," 7.

52. Hayek, "Prospects of Freedom," 7–8.
53. Hayek, "Intellectuals and Socialism," 431–32.
54. Hayek, "Intellectuals and Socialism," 432–33.
55. Hayek, "Intellectuals and Socialism," 432.
56. Rob Van Horn and Philip Mirowski, "The Rise of the Chicago School of Economics and the Birth of Neoliberalism," in Mirowski and Plehwe, *Road from Mont Pèlerin*, 161, 159.
57. Cited in Van Horn and Mirowski, "Rise of the Chicago School," 164–65.
58. Van Horn and Mirowski, "Rise of the Chicago School," 165.
59. Mark Greif, *The Age of the Crisis of Man: Thought and Fiction in America, 1933–1973* (Princeton, NJ: Princeton University Press, 2015), 194.
60. Tim Lacy, *The Dream of Democratic Culture: Mortimer J. Adler and the Great Books Idea* (New York: Palgrave Macmillan, 2013), 6.
61. Lacy, *Dream of Democratic Culture*, 6.
62. Lacy, *Dream of Democratic Culture*, 3.
63. See Dwight Macdonald, "The Book-of-the-Millennium Club," in *Masscult and Midcult: Essays against the American Grain*, 135–51, and "Cashing in on Culture," *Time*, April 20, 1962, 94.
64. Greif, *Age of the Crisis of Man*, 39.
65. Greif, *Age of the Crisis of Man*, 40–41.
66. Aida, "Sōseki, Haieku, Etō Jun," 334–41.
67. Russell Kirk, *The Sword of Imagination: Memoirs of a Half-Century of Literary Conflict* (Grand Rapids, MI: William B. Eerdmans, 1995), 90.
68. Russell Kirk, *The Conservative Mind: From Burke to Santayana* (Chicago: Henry Regnery Company, 1953), n.p.
69. Kirk, *Sword of Imagination*, 138.
70. Kirk, *Sword of Imagination*, 173.
71. For an overview of the conservative critique of capitalism with reference to Kirk, see Peter Kolozi, *Conservatives against Capitalism: From the Industrial Revolution to Globalization* (New York: Columbia University Press, 2017), 1–21, 126–30.
72. Melinda Cooper, *Family Values: Between Neoliberalism and the New Social Conservatism* (New York: Zone Books, 2017), 313.
73. Brown, *In the Ruins of Neoliberalism*, 11. Emphasis in original.
74. Brown, *In the Ruins of Neoliberalism*, 13. Brown argued that "only through a return to founding neoliberal ideas and to Hayek in particular is it possible to bring into relief the architecture of reason binding traditional morality to neoliberalism and animating right-wing campaigns today. These campaigns cast as assaults on both freedom and morality all social policy that challenges the social reproduction of gender, racial, and sexual hierarchies or modestly redresses class extremes." (12).
75. Burgin, *Great Persuasion*, 142.
76. Friedrich Hayek to Herbert C. Cornuelle, William Volker Charities Fund, March 28, 1953, Hayek Papers, Box 58, Folder 18. This correspondence is also discussed in Burgin, *Great Persuasion*, 142.
77. Hayek to Herbert C. Cornuelle, March 28, 1953, Hayek Papers, Box 58, Folder 18.

78. Hayek to Herbert C. Cornuelle, March 28, 1953, Hayek Papers, Box 58, Folder 18.

79. Hayek to Herbert C. Cornuelle, March 28, 1953, Hayek Papers, Box 58, Folder 18.

80. In correspondence to Henry Regnery dated April 14, 1953, Hayek stated: "You are welcome to quote any part of the following passage from my report to the Volker people on Russell Kirk's *The Conservative Mind*: 'I can only wish that the book should be read as widely as possible. I fear it is much too scholarly and presumes much too much general education on the part of its readers to receive a wide circulation. But if it were at least read by all the people who can appreciate it, it should do much to shift the general discussion on the right track, and generally on a higher plane." Hayek Papers, Box 24, Folder 19. In his discussion of Hayek's relationship with conservatives in the 1950s, Burgin pointed out that "Hayek declined to write a blurb" for *God and Man at Yale*. Burgin, *Great Persuasion*, 140. Hayek wrote to Regnery: "I am afraid anything friendly I could say about Buckley's book would have to be hedged about by so many qualifications that it would be useless for your purposes. I wish I could, as I almost wanted when I read it, make it the occasion for some discussion of academic freedom, but again, their [*sic*] are more urgent priorities." Hayek to Henry Regnery, November 25, 1951, Hayek Papers, Box 24, Folder 19.

81. Henry Regnery, *Memoirs of a Dissident Publisher* (New York: Harcourt Brace Jovanovich, 1979), 14.

82. Regnery, *Memoirs of a Dissident Publisher*, 193.

83. See Regnery, *Memoirs of a Dissident Publisher*, 170–73.

84. Regnery, *Memoirs of a Dissident Publisher*, 55–56.

85. Hayek to Herbert C. Cornuelle, May 9, 1953, Hayek Papers, Box 58, Folder 18.

86. Hayek to Herbert C. Cornuelle, May 21, 1953, Hayek Papers, Box 58, Folder 18.

87. Hayek to Herbert C. Cornuelle, May 21, 1953, Hayek Papers, Box 58, Folder 18.

88. Hayek to John Nef, May 21, 1953, Hayek Papers, Box 39, Folder 39.

89. Hayek to John Nef, May 21, 1953, Hayek Papers, Box 39, Folder 39.

90. Hayek to John Nef, May 21, 1953, Hayek Papers, Box 39, Folder 39.

91. Hayek to John Nef, May 21, 1953, Hayek Papers, Box 39, Folder 39.

92. Burgin, *Great Persuasion*, 142.

93. Burgin, *Great Persuasion*, 142.

94. Burgin discusses these turns of events in greater detail. See Burgin, *Great Persuasion*, 140–45. Hayek's essay "Why I Am Not a Conservative" appears as a postscript in *The Constitution of Liberty: The Definitive Edition*, ed. Ronald Hamowy (Chicago: University of Chicago Press, 2011), 519–33.

95. Regnery, *Memoirs of a Dissident Publisher*, 159.

96. Burgin, *Great Persuasion*, 144.

97. Burgin has written that Kirk "became notorious for cultivating an anachronistic personal aesthetic at his residence in rural Michigan. He forsook modern appliances and refused to drive automobiles." Burgin, *Great Persuasion*, 141.

98. Burgin, *Great Persuasion*, 140, 141.

99. Burgin, *Great Persuasion*, 142–43.

100. Burgin, *Great Persuasion*, 127.

101. Nathan Shockey, *The Typographic Imagination: Reading and Writing in Japan's Age of Modern Print Media* (New York: Columbia University Press, 2020), 63–64; John

Nathan, *Sōseki: Modern Japan's Greatest Novelist* (New York: Columbia University Press, 2018), 230.

102. Russell Kirk, *The Conservative Mind: From Burke to Eliot*, 7th rev. ed. (Washington, DC: Gateway Editions, 1985), 490.

103. Natsume Sōseki, *Kokoro*, trans. Edwin McClellan (Washington, DC: Regnery Gateway, 1957), 13–14.

104. Komori Yōichi, "*Kokoro* ni okeru hanten suru 'shuki': Kūhaku to imi no seisei," in *Kōzō toshite no katari* (Tokyo: Shinyōsha, 1988), 421.

105. Kirk, *Conservative Mind*, 7th rev. ed., 478.

106. Kirk, *Conservative Mind*, 7th rev. ed., 476–77.

107. Sōseki, *Kokoro*, 50.

108. T. S. Eliot's correspondence with Russell Kirk is quoted by Bradley Birzer in *Russell Kirk: American Conservative* (Lexington: University Press of Kentucky, 2015), 218.

109. Kirk, *Conservative Mind*, 7th rev. ed., 493.

110. Kirk quotation cited in Birzer, *Russell Kirk*, 209.

111. Edwin McClellan, "The Implications of Sōseki's *Kokoro*," *Monumenta Nipponica* 14, no. 3 / 4 (October 1958 / January 1959): 364.

112. McClellan, "Implications of Sōseki's *Kokoro*," 368.

113. Lionel Trilling, *The Liberal Imagination* (New York: New York Review of Books, 2008), xxi.

114. Louis Menand, introduction to Trilling, *Liberal Imagination*, viii.

115. Trilling, *Liberal Imagination*, 301.

116. As Greenwald Smith has summed up, "It is a central argument of this study that assessments of contemporary literary aesthetics that appear politically neutral should be read in the context of the way neoliberal discourse bleeds over into the formal, as well as thematic, mechanisms of literature." Rachel Greenwald Smith, *Affect and American Literature in the Age of Neoliberalism* (New York: Cambridge University Press, 2015), 11.

117. Greenwald Smith described her study as "an argument against the ubiquity of what I call the *affective hypothesis*, or the belief that literature is at its most meaningful when it represents and transmits the emotional specificity of personal experience." Greenwald Smith, *Affect and American Literature*, 1. Her study elaborated on the connection between neoliberal subject formation and "the affective hypothesis" in literary culture:

> Neoliberalism's emphasis on the necessity of personal initiative, along with its pathologizing of structures of dependence, calls upon subjects to see themselves as entrepreneurial actors in a competitive system. These subjective aspects of neoliberalism coincide startlingly with the assumptions underlying the affective hypothesis. While neoliberalism casts the individual as responsible for herself, the affective hypothesis casts feeling as necessarily owned and managed by individual authors, characters, and readers. Neoliberalism imagines the individual as an entrepreneur; the affective hypothesis imagines the act of reading as an opportunity for emotional investment and return. The neoliberal subject is envisioned as needing to be at all times strategically networking; feelings, according to the affective hypothesis, are indexes of emotional alliances.

Greenwald Smith, *Affect and American Literature*, 2.

118. In this connection, Greenwald Smith has observed that "as social institutions, from welfare systems to educational systems, and from media sources to public spaces, increasingly become personalized and privatized, neoliberalism amplifies this tendency for capitalism to individualize, casting individuals as exclusively responsible for themselves." Greenwald Smith, *Affect and American Literature*, 3.

119. In this connection, the political philosopher Wendy Brown has observed that "the normative reign of *homo oeconomicus* in every sphere means that there are no motivations, drives, or aspirations apart from economic ones, that there is nothing to being human apart from 'mere life.' Neoliberalism is the rationality through which capitalism finally swallows humanity—not only with its machinery of compulsory commodification and profit-driven expansion, but by its form of valuation." Brown, *Undoing the Demos*, 44. And as Greenwald Smith sums up her study: "This book has argued that capitalism functions affectively, instigating patterns of behavior that perpetuate the circulation of goods, services, and capital. With the advent of neoliberalism comes an intensification of this tendency as a result of its gathering of aspects of life not explicitly tied to the market under the logic of capitalism." Greenwald Smith, *Affect and American Literature*, 122.

120. Michael K. Bourdaghs, "Property and Sociological Knowledge: Natsume Sōseki and the Gift of Narrative," *Japan Forum* 20, no. 1 (2008): 82. In this essay, Bourdaghs noted that "*Kokoro* (1914) is another work that treats personal experience as a sort of private property" (90).

121. Sōseki, *Kokoro*, 1.

122. Sōseki, *Kokoro*, 248.

123. Atsuko Sakaki, *Recontextualizing Texts: Narrative Performance in Modern Japanese Fiction* (Cambridge, MA: Harvard University Asia Center, 1999), 34. The essay in question is Komori, "*Kokoro* ni okeru hanten suru 'shuki.'"

124. Sakaki, *Recontextualizing Texts*, 34.

125. Nathan, *Sōseki*, 225. As Nathan put it, summing up: "*Kokoro*, then, according to Komori, far from affirming a paternalistic moral code that Sensei successfully imparts to the student, dramatizes a battle between values aligned with nationalism that valorize self-sacrifice and minimize or even disparage (hetero) sexuality, and a new mode of life in which 'two people enter freely into an alliance in which there is no separation between mind and body.'" Nathan, *Sōseki*, 228. For an overview of the "*Kokoro* debates" (*Kokoro ronsō*), see Sakaki, *Recontextualizing Texts*, 29–53.

126. Vincent, *Two-Timing Modernity*, 106.

127. Michael K. Bourdaghs, "Introduction: Overthrowing the Emperor in Japanese Literary Studies," in *The Linguistic Turn in Contemporary Japanese Literary Studies: Politics, Language, Textuality*, ed. Michael K. Bourdaghs (Ann Arbor: Center for Japanese Studies, University of Michigan, 2010), 10–11.

128. Greenwald Smith, *Affect and American Literature*, 6.

129. Ian Watt, *The Rise of the Novel: Studies in Defoe, Richardson, and Fielding* (Berkeley: University of California Press, 1957), 60, 61.

130. Watt, *Rise of the Novel*, 63–64.

131. Watt, *Rise of the Novel*, 64.

132. Sōseki, *Kokoro*, 174.

133. Sōseki, *Kokoro*, 213–14.
134. Sōseki, *Kokoro*, 216.
135. Sōseki, *Kokoro*, 214.
136. Sōseki, *Kokoro*, 215.
137. Sōseki, *Kokoro*, 192.
138. Sōseki, *Kokoro*, 216.
139. Sōseki, *Kokoro*, 238.
140. Duncan K. Foley, *Adam's Fallacy: A Guide to Economic Theology* (Cambridge, MA: Harvard University Press, 2006), xiv–xv.
141. Foley, *Adam's Fallacy*, 2.
142. Foley, *Adam's Fallacy*, xv.
143. Pedro Erber, "Beautiful Money; or, What Can Contemporary Art Teach Us about the Neoliberal Economy?," *Revista Hispánica Moderna* 72, no. 2 (2019): 155.
144. Alan Tansman, "The Pedagogy of the Japanese Novel," *Novel: A Forum on Fiction* 47, no. 1 (2014): 59.
145. Tansman, "Pedagogy of the Japanese Novel," 59–60.
146. Brown has asked:

> What are the implications of the neoliberal vanquishing of *homo politicus* by *homo oeconomicus*? . . . As neoliberalism submits all spheres of life to economization, the effect is not simply to narrow the functions of state and citizen or to enlarge the sphere of economically defined freedom at the expense of common investment in public life and public goods. Rather, it is to attenuate radically the exercise of freedom in the social and political spheres. This is the central paradox, perhaps even the central ruse, of neoliberal governance: the neoliberal revolution takes place in the name of freedom—free markets, free countries, free men—but tears up freedom's grounding in sovereignty for states and subjects alike. States are subordinated to the market, govern for the market, and gain or lose legitimacy according to the market's vicissitudes.

Brown, *Undoing the Demos*, 108.
147. Hayek, "Individualism: True and False," in *Individualism and Economic Order* (Chicago: University of Chicago Press, 1948), 3.
148. Hayek, "Individualism," 11. Hayek qualified this statement: "But even this would be unjust to the very complex and realistic view which these men [earlier identified as "Adam Smith and his group"] took of human nature" (11).
149. Hayek, "Individualism," 18–19.
150. Hayek, "Individualism," 14. Emphasis in original.
151. Hayek, "Individualism," 22.
152. Brown wrote that "for Hayek, markets and morals together are the foundation of freedom, order, and the development of civilization. Both are organized spontaneously and transmitted through tradition, rather than political power." Brown, *In the Ruins of Neoliberalism*, 12. She remarked that "traditional moral systems parallel markets in many ways, Hayek adds, especially in their provision of order without design and their location of justice in rules, rather than in outcomes" (34)."Indeed," as Brown put it else-

where in her paraphrase of Hayek on the role of tradition, "the order generated by markets embodies the evolved, free, incomprehensible, unintentional, voluntary, yet socially integrated order of tradition at its finest. We are disciplined and oriented by market rules; they evolve, change, and develop; yet no one designed them, no one is in charge, and no one coerces us within them" (100).

153. Hayek, *Fatal Conceit*, 76. In the first lines of *The Fatal Conceit* (1988), Hayek brought the threads of morals and markets together:

> This book argues that our civilisation depends, not only for its origin but also for its preservation, on what can be precisely described only as the extended order of human cooperation, an order more commonly, if somewhat misleadingly, known as capitalism. To understand our civilisation, one must appreciate that the extended order resulted not from human design or intention but spontaneously: it arose from unintentionally conforming to certain traditional and largely *moral* practices, many of which men tend to dislike, whose significance they usually fail to understand, whose validity they cannot prove, and which have nonetheless fairly rapidly spread by means of an evolutionary selection—the comparative increase of population and wealth—of those groups that happened to follow them.

Hayek, *Fatal Conceit*, 6. Emphasis in original.

154. Hayek, "Individualism," 32.

155. This point is informed by Szalay's reading of Wallace Stevens, in which context he observed that Stevens "imagines that, like economies and governments, his own poems are testaments to the insufficiency of even the most individuated instances of intentional agency. It is just as impossible to plan a poem, the poet maintains, as to plan the stock market itself." Szalay, *New Deal Modernism: American Literature and the Invention of the Welfare State* (Durham, NC: Duke University Press, 2000), 126–27. Szalay linked this perspective on authorial control and intention to the "New Criticism" of Robert Penn Warren and Cleanth Brooks, writing, "Imagining both poems and stock markets as self-sustaining systems whose motions can be traced and experienced, but never adequately planned or reduced to any one propositional statement—to a 'secret'—Stevens directly anticipates Brooks and Warren's notion of the heresy of paraphrase" (145). Szalay later discussed the intentional fallacy on page 160.

156. Hayek, "Individualism," 11.

157. W. K. Wimsatt Jr. and M. C. Beardsley, "The Intentional Fallacy," *Sewanee Review* 54, no. 3 (July–September 1946): 477.

158. Roland Barthes, "The Death of the Author," in *Image, Music, Text*, trans. Stephen Heath (New York: Hill and Wang, 1977), 147.

159. As Foucault put it, "Basically, Hayek says, it is very simple. The Rule of law, or formal economic legislation, is quite simply the opposite of a plan." Michel Foucault, *The Birth of Biopolitics: Lectures at the Collège de France, 1978–1979*, ed. Michel Senellart, trans. Graham Burchell (New York: Picador, 2008), 172.

160. My thinking about the frames of art is broadly informed by Pedro Erber's *Breaching the Frame: The Rise of Contemporary Art in Brazil and Japan* (Berkeley: University of California Press, 2015).

161. Sōseki, *Kokoro*, 6.

162. Hayek, "Individualism," 5, 11.

163. Adam Smith, *The Theory of Moral Sentiments*, ed. D. D. Raphael and A. L. Macfie (Indianapolis: Liberty Fund, 1982), 113.

164. Smith, *Theory of Moral Sentiments*, 153–54.

165. Smith, *Theory of Moral Sentiments*, 154.

166. Erber, "Beautiful Money," 158.

167. Nussbaum wrote that Smith himself attached "considerable importance to literature as a source of this kind of moral development; and literature is also, for him, an artificial construction of ideal spectatorship, which leads us into the morally good viewpoint naturally, and offers us in that way a model we can refer to in real life." Martha C. Nussbaum, *Love's Knowledge: Essays on Philosophy and Literature* (New York: Oxford University Press, 1990), 339. Nussbaum elaborated: "For frequently, in order to show his reader what he means by a certain claim about the ideal spectator's responses, or in order to support his assertion that the spectator in a certain case will respond this way and not this, [Smith] refers to our experience as readers of stories and watchers of plays, asking us to notice what sentiments we experience in that role" (339).

168. Sōseki, *Kokoro*, 126.

169. Sōseki, *Kokoro*, 128–29.

170. Smith, *Theory of Moral Sentiments*, 146–47.

171. Sōseki, *Kokoro*, 129.

172. Smith, *Theory of Moral Sentiments*, 158.

173. Smith, *Theory of Moral Sentiments*, 158–59.

174. Sōseki, *Kokoro*, 50.

175. Vincent, *Two-Timing Modernity*, 94.

176. Vincent, *Two-Timing Modernity*, 95.

177. Greif, *Age of the Crisis of Man*, 98–99.

178. Greif, *Age of the Crisis of Man*, xii.

179. Friedrich Hayek to Matsushita Kōnosuke, February 26, 1965, Hayek Papers, Box 37, Folder 17.

180. Friedrich Hayek to Tanaka Seigen, November 11, 1967, Hayek Papers, Box 52, Folder 28.

181. Edwin McClellan, "Natsume Sōseki and Shiga Naoya," 5. I have corrected the spelling of David Grene's surname in the quotation, which appears as "Greene" in the published transcription of McClellan's lecture.

182. Burgin, *Great Persuasion*, 50.

183. Henry Regnery to Friedrich Hayek, February 14, 1952, Hayek Papers, Box 24, Folder 19.

184. Friedrich Hayek to Richard A. Ware, Earhart Foundation, October 7, 1958, Hayek Papers, Box 17, Folder 37.

185. Friedrich Hayek to Richard Ware, Relm Foundation, March 2, 1966, Hayek Papers, Box 17, Folder 37.

186. Friedrich Hayek to Richard Ware, Relm Foundation, October 23, 1966, Hayek Papers, Box 17, Folder 37.

Epilogue

1. For a more extensive analysis of Murakami's literature in this context, see Matthew Carl Strecher, *Dances with Sheep: The Quest for Identity in the Fiction of Murakami Haruki* (Ann Arbor: Center for Japanese Studies, University of Michigan, 2002).

2. Vogel wrote that "using measures America has traditionally used to determine success, it is readily demonstrable that in many areas Japanese institutions are coping with the same problems we confront, more successfully than we are. Could we not profit by showing the same eagerness to learn from the East that Japan has shown in learning from the West?" Ezra F. Vogel, *Japan as Number One: Lessons for America* (Cambridge, MA: Harvard University Press, 1979), 8.

3. These statistics were reported by the *New York Times*. See Edwin McDowell, "Two Millionth 'Iacocca' to Roll Off the Assembly Line Today," *New York Times*, July 17, 1985, http://www.nytimes.com/1985/07/17/books/two-millionth-iacocca-to-roll-off-the-assembly-line-today.html?pagewanted=all/.

4. Andrew C. McKevitt, *Consuming Japan: Popular Culture and the Globalization of 1980s America* (Chapel Hill: University of North Carolina Press, 2017), 8.

5. Lee Iacocca, with William Novak, *Iacocca: An Autobiography* (Toronto: Bantam Books, 1984), 343.

6. In this connection, the literary scholar and translator of contemporary Japanese fiction Stephen Snyder has examined Murakami's rise in the international literary marketplace, noting that Murakami's fiction has long been "marketed as the foremost literary representative of what Douglas McGray has called Japan's emergent 'Gross National Cool.'" Snyder, "Insistence and Resistance: Murakami and Mizumura in Translation," *New England Review* 37, no. 4 (October 2016): 134. The McGray essay referenced here is "Japan's Gross National Cool," *Foreign Policy* 130 (May / June 2002): 44–54. Snyder explained the idea of "Gross National Cool" by noting that "at some point after the bursting of its economic bubble at the end of the 1980s, Japan began a transition from being a producer and exporter of industrial and technological products (Honda Civics and Sony Walkmen) to being a producer and exporter of cultural capital." Snyder, "Insistence and Resistance," 134.

7. John Whittier Treat, "Japan Is Interesting: Modern Japanese Literary Studies Today," *Japan Forum* 30, no. 3 (2018): 436.

8. Treat, "Japan Is Interesting," 436.

9. Treat, "Japan Is Interesting," 436.

10. Strecher, *Dances with Sheep*, 206. Dennis Washburn also examined *A Wild Sheep Chase* in the epilogue to his study of modern Japanese literature, arguing that "both the critics and the fans have sold Murakami a little short, for his achievement has been in capturing the temper of his times. I know that phrase sounds hopelessly ponderous and out of date, but I believe it is an accurate statement. Murakami has managed to emanate the aura of art around himself and his fiction. That aura may be a virtual effect, the product of a refusal to get caught in the trap of modern identity, but it makes some form of an ethics of identity possible in a period where belief without conviction is the 'condition' (*guai*) artists live in now." Washburn, *Translating Mount Fuji: Modern Japanese Fiction and the Ethics of Identity* (New York: Columbia University Press, 2007), 247.

11. Strecher, *Dances with Sheep*, 214–15.

12. Lisa Duggan, *Mean Girl: Ayn Rand and the Culture of Greed* (Berkeley: University of California Press, 2019), 5.

13. For example, the anthropologist Anne Allison has explored the social, economic, and environmental precarity of everyday life in neoliberal Japan through the lenses of contingent labor and recessionary restructuring in the millennial years, concluding that "everywhere people are suffering, caught by the instabilities and inequalities of neoliberal globalism run amok. In the acceleration, and spread, of a market logic that has privatized more and more of life and deregulated more and more of capitalism's engine for extracting profits, the struggle—and often failure—of everyday life has become an all too common story for all too many people around the world." Allison, *Precarious Japan* (Durham, NC: Duke University Press, 2013), 5. In addition, Mark Driscoll has studied anticapitalist protests that have organized in opposition to "hyperneoliberalism" in contemporary Japan. See Driscoll, "Hyperneoliberalism: Youth, Labor, and Militant Mice in Japan," *positions: east asia cultures critique* 23, no. 3 (August 2015): 545–64.

14. See Paul Roquet, *Ambient Media: Japanese Atmospheres of Self* (Minneapolis: University of Minnesota Press, 2016), 9–14.

15. Roquet, *Ambient Media*, 9.

16. Roquet, *Ambient Media*, 14.

17. Roquet, *Ambient Media*, 136. Roquet added: "As evidence Ariai notes the popularity of Erik Satie's music; the focus on the minor and inconsequential in novelists like Murakami Haruki, Ikezawa Natsuki, and Yoshimoto Banana; and the 'subtractive merchandise' made popular by brands like Mujirushi ryōhin (literally 'no-label quality goods,' commonly abbreviated as Muji)." Roquet, *Ambient Media*, 136.

18. Roquet, *Ambient Media*, 149.

19. As Brown put it: "The 'shared sacrifice' discourse of neoliberalism's austerity epoch differs sharply from that accompanying the 'trickle-down' economics of the 1980s. The Reagan-Thatcher era promised that wealth generated by the giants would benefit the small; today's sacrificial citizen receives no such promise. Economic ends are delinked from the general welfare of the population but, in addition, as citizens are integrated into these ends via governance, they may be sacrificed to its needs, vicissitudes, and contingencies in a nation, just as they are in a firm. Thus, a political rationality born in reaction to National Socialism (recall that the theories of F. A. Hayek and the Ordo School of neoliberalism were retorts to that formation) paradoxically comes to mirror select aspects of it." Wendy Brown, *Undoing the Demos: Neoliberalism's Stealth Revolution* (New York: Zone Books, 2015), 213.

20. See Allison, *Precarious Japan*, and Hirokazu Miyazaki, "The Temporality of No Hope," in *Ethnographies of Neoliberalism*, ed. Carol J. Greenhouse (Philadelphia: University of Pennsylvania Press, 2010), 238–50.

21. Murakami Haruki, "The Folklore of Our Times," trans. Alfred Birnbaum, *The New Yorker*, June 9, 2003, 91.

22. Strecher, *Dances with Sheep*, 137.

23. *Boku* is a first-person pronoun (I) used in Japanese.

24. Murakami Haruki, *A Wild Sheep Chase*, trans. Alfred Birnbaum (New York: Vintage International, 2002), 9–10. Corresponding Japanese passage in Murakami Haruki,

Murakami Haruki zensakuhin: 1979–1989: 2: Hitsuji o meguru bōken (Tokyo: Kodansha, 1990), 21–22. Hereafter, citations for Birnbaum's English-language translation are indicated after the English-language title of the novel (*A Wild Sheep Chase*), and the corresponding passages in Japanese are indicated after the romanized Japanese title of the novel (*Hitsuji o meguru bōken*).

25. The meaning of Mishima's suicide in *A Wild Sheep Chase* has been analyzed by others. Strecher has noted in his reading that "in retrospect, we may argue that Mishima's death was part of the closure of an era that many were unprepared to see end," adding that the end of Mishima's life and of the 1960s entwine in *A Wild Sheep Chase* such that "to judge from Murakami's text, the reader is uncertain whether Mishima killed the 1960s, or the 1960s killed him." Strecher, *Dances with Sheep*, 172–73. Dennis Washburn has written of Boku and *A Wild Sheep Chase*:

> The narrator is strangely disconnected from the world around him, mainly because he recognizes that in contemporary life everything is equivalent to advertising copy and that the media can create an aura whose presence allows the consumer to experience a virtual world as real. The power of this aura and its disjunctive effects is at work in the reference to Mishima's [suicide], which is given prominent mention at the very beginning of the novel but then treated as an insignificant event, as mere background to the setting. Mishima, whose death was at once a reaction against and an embrace of this aura, is reduced to a media image reproduced in an infinite loop of television replays that diminish the aura of significance surrounding his act.

Washburn, *Translating Mount Fuji*, 244.

26. Murakami, *Wild Sheep Chase*, 24–25; *Hitsuji o meguru bōken*, 37.

27. Murakami, *Wild Sheep Chase*, 25; *Hitsuji o meguru bōken*, 38.

28. Murakami, *Wild Sheep Chase*, 41; *Hitsuji o meguru bōken*, 57.

29. Murakami, *Wild Sheep Chase*, 43; *Hitsuji o meguru bōken*, 58–59.

30. Murakami, *Wild Sheep Chase*, 71; *Hitsuji o meguru bōken*, 86.

31. Murakami, *Wild Sheep Chase*, 99–100; *Hitsuji o meguru bōken*, 112–13.

32. Murakami, *Wild Sheep Chase*, 100; *Hitsuji o meguru bōken*, 113.

33. Murakami, *Wild Sheep Chase*, 114; *Hitsuji o meguru bōken*, 128.

34. Murakami, *Wild Sheep Chase*, 163; *Hitsuji o meguru bōken*, 178.

35. Murakami, *Wild Sheep Chase*, 175; *Hitsuji o meguru bōken*, 190–91.

36. Murakami, *Wild Sheep Chase*, 165; *Hitsuji o meguru bōken*, 180.

37. Treat, "Japan Is Interesting," 436.

38. Murakami, *Wild Sheep Chase*, 113; *Hitsuji o meguru bōken*, 127.

39. Murakami, *Wild Sheep Chase*, 197; *Hitsuji o meguru bōken*, 215.

40. Murakami, *Wild Sheep Chase*, 197–98; *Hitsuji o meguru bōken*, 215–16.

41. Murakami, *Wild Sheep Chase*, 325; *Hitsuji o meguru bōken*, 344.

42. Murakami, *Wild Sheep Chase*, 275; *Hitsuji o meguru bōken*, 292–93.

43. Murakami, *Wild Sheep Chase*, 348; *Hitsuji o meguru bōken*, 367.

44. Paul Roquet raised the question of whether or not there is a return to the social at the conclusions of the literary and cinematic versions of *Tony Takitani*, too. See Roquet, *Ambient Media*, 146.

45. Murakami Haruki, *Dance, Dance, Dance*, trans. Alfred Birnbaum (New York: Vintage International, 1996), 55.

46. In another context, the scholar of Japanese literature and film Baryon Tensor Posadas has drawn on psychoanalytic paradigms that he showed can help us to avoid "relegating the past to something completed and now since overcome," as he put it. Baryon Tensor Posadas, *Double Visions, Double Fictions: The Doppelgänger in Japanese Film and Literature* (Minneapolis: University of Minnesota Press, 2018), 159.

47. In *Undoing the Demos* (2015), Brown wrote that the precarity of neoliberal life today means that "as economic metrics have saturated the state and the national purpose, the neoliberal citizen need not stoically risk death on the battlefield, only bear up uncomplainingly in the face of unemployment, underemployment, or employment unto death" (218). According to Brown, "this citizen releases state, law, and economy from responsibility for and responsiveness to its own condition and predicaments and is ready when called to sacrifice to the cause of economic growth, competitive positioning and fiscal constraints" (219). Brown concluded:

> Thus, again, does a political rationality originally born in opposition to fascism turn out to mirror certain aspects of it, albeit through powers that are faceless and invisible-handed and absent an authoritarian state. This is not to say that neoliberalism is fascism or that we live in fascist times. It is only to note convergences between elements of twentieth-century fascism and inadvertent effects of neoliberal rationality today. These convergences appear in the valorization of a national economic project and sacrifice for a greater good into which all are integrated, but from which most must not expect personal benefit. They appear as well in the growing devaluation of politics, publics, intellectuals, educated citizenship, and all collective purposes apart from economy and security.

Brown, *Undoing the Demos*, 219.

48. Wendy Brown, *In the Ruins of Neoliberalism: The Rise of Antidemocratic Politics in the West* (New York: Columbia University Press, 2019), 8–9.

49. Brown, *Ruins of Neoliberalism*, 9–10.

50. Brown, *Ruins of Neoliberalism*, 10. Emphasis in original.

51. Joseph North, *Literary Criticism: A Concise Political History* (Cambridge, MA: Harvard University Press, 2017), 3.

52. In this connection, the humanities scholar Louis Menand's introduction of Lionel Trilling's classic *The Liberal Imagination* (1950) comes to mind; it began by observing that Trilling's book "made literary criticism matter to people who were not literary critics." Menand, introduction to *The Liberal Imagination*, by Lionel Trilling (New York: New York Review of Books, 2008), vii.

53. As North put it, "Perhaps we can now see something of the dual political character of our period's governing injunction to 'historicize.' Insofar as it led to a critique of the essentialisms and universalism of an old elite, it has been palpably of the left. Yet insofar as it has also asked literary thinkers to give up the wider social function to which 'criticism,' for all its many faults, at least aspired, and has taught them instead merely to observe the culture, however 'critically,' by writing cultural theory and cultural history, it has been a depoliticization: in that sense, of the right." North, *Literary Criticism*, 11.

54. Rita Felski, *The Limits of Critique* (Chicago: University of Chicago Press, 2015), 1.
55. Felski, *Limits of Critique*, 7.
56. Felski, *Limits of Critique*, 5.
57. Felski, *Limits of Critique*, 113, 114.
58. Felski, *Limits of Critique*, 3.
59. *OED Online*, s.v. "academic, n. and adj.," accessed February 1, 2021, www.oed.com/view/Entry/880.
60. Dave Hickey, "Air Guitar," in *Air Guitar: Essays on Art and Democracy* (Los Angeles: Art Issues Press, 1997), 163.

Bibliography

Abel, Jonathan. "Personification and a Trope of Writing: Nakano Shigeharu's 'Language of Slaves.'" *Comparative Literature* 65, no. 4 (2013): 466–86.

———. *Redacted: The Archives of Censorship in Transwar Japan*. Berkeley: University of California Press, 2012.

Adorno, Theodor. *The Jargon of Authenticity*. Translated by Knut Tarnowski and Frederic Will. Evanston, IL: Northwestern University Press, 1973.

Aida Hirotsugu. "Sōseki, Haieku, Etō Jun: Kokoro no kizuna." *Bungei Shunjū* 86 (2008): 334–41.

Akutagawa Ryūnosuke. *Akutagawa Ryūnosuke zenshū*. 24 vols. Tokyo: Iwanami Shoten, 1995–97.

Allardyce, Gilbert. "What Fascism Is Not: Thoughts on the Deflation of a Concept." *American Historical Review* 84, no. 2 (April 1979): 367–88.

Allison, Anne. *Precarious Japan*. Durham, NC: Duke University Press, 2013.

Althusser, Louis. "Ideology and Ideological State Apparatuses (Notes towards an Investigation)." In *Lenin and Philosophy, and Other Essays*, translated by Ben Brewster, 121–73. London: New Left Books, 1971.

———. "Part One: From *Capital* to Marx's Philosophy." In *Reading Capital: The Complete Edition*, translated by Ben Brewster and David Fernbach, 9–72. London: Verso, 2015.

Apter, Emily. *Against World Literature: On the Politics of Untranslatability*. London: Verso, 2013.

Arendt, Hannah. *The Human Condition*. 2nd ed. Chicago: University of Chicago Press, 1998.

Ashiya-shi Tanizaki Jun'ichirō kinenkan shiryōshū (4): Kizō kitaku shokan: Heisei jūhachi-nen-nijūni-nen. Edited and published by Ashiya-shi Tanizaki Jun'ichirō kinenkan, 2011.

Bakhtin, Mikhail. *The Dialogic Imagination: Four Essays*. Edited by Michael Holquist. Translated by Caryl Emerson and Michael Holquist. Austin: University of Texas Press, 1981.

———. *Problems of Dostoevsky's Poetics*. Edited and translated by Caryl Emerson. Minneapolis: University of Minnesota Press, 1984.

Barshay, Andrew. *The Social Sciences in Modern Japan: The Marxian and Modernist Traditions*. Berkeley: University of California Press, 2004.

Barthes, Roland. "The Death of the Author." In *Image, Music, Text*, translated by Stephen Heath, 142–48. New York: Hill and Wang, 1977.

Benjamin, Walter. *Illuminations: Essays and Reflections*. Translated by Harry Zohn. Boston: Mariner Books, 2019.

Berlant, Lauren. *Cruel Optimism*. Durham, NC: Duke University Press, 2011.

Berman, Marshall. *All That Is Solid Melts into Air: The Experience of Modernity*. New York: Penguin Books, 1988.

Bernstein, Michael André. *Foregone Conclusions: Against Apocalyptic History*. Berkeley: University of California Press, 1994.

Birzer, Bradley. *Russell Kirk: American Conservative*. Lexington: University Press of Kentucky, 2015.

Botterill, Steven, ed. and trans. *Dante: De vulgari eloquentia*. Cambridge: Cambridge University Press, 1996.

Bourdaghs, Michael K. "Early Freeze Warning: The Politics and Literature Debate as Cold War Culture." In *Literature among the Ruins, 1945–1955: Postwar Japanese Literary Criticism*, edited by Atsuko Ueda, Michael K. Bourdaghs, Richi Sakakibara, and Hirokazu Toeda, 17–42. Lanham, MD: Lexington Books, 2018.

———. "The Ghosts of Anticommunism and Neoliberalism: East Asian Studies in the Twenty-First Century." In *Reconsidering American Power: Pax Americana and the Social Sciences*, edited by John D. Kelly, Kurt Jacobsen, and Marston H. Morgan, 445–64. Oxford: Oxford University Press, 2020.

———. "Introduction: Overthrowing the Emperor in Japanese Literary Studies." In *The Linguistic Turn in Contemporary Japanese Literary Studies: Politics, Language, Textuality*, edited by Michael K. Bourdaghs, 1–17. Ann Arbor: Center for Japanese Studies, University of Michigan, 2010.

———. "Property and Sociological Knowledge: Natsume Sōseki and the Gift of Narrative." *Japan Forum* 20, no. 1 (2008): 79–101.

Bronson, Adam. *One Hundred Million Philosophers: Science of Thought and the Culture of Democracy in Postwar Japan*. Honolulu: University of Hawai'i Press, 2016.

Brown, Wendy. *In the Ruins of Neoliberalism: The Rise of Antidemocratic Politics in the West*. New York: Columbia University Press, 2019.

———. *Undoing the Demos: Neoliberalism's Stealth Revolution*. New York: Zone Books, 2015.

Brownlee, John S. *Japanese Historians and the National Myths, 1600–1945: The Age of the Gods and Emperor Jinmu*. Vancouver: UBC Press, 1997.

Burgin, Angus. *The Great Persuasion: Reinventing Free Markets since the Depression*. Cambridge, MA: Harvard University Press, 2012.

Carson, Anne. *Economy of the Unlost (Reading Simonides of Keos with Paul Celan)*. Princeton, NJ: Princeton University Press, 1999.

Cassirer, Ernst. *The Philosophy of Symbolic Forms*. Vol. 1, *Language*. Translated by Ralph Manheim. New Haven, CT: Yale University Press, 1953.

Cazdyn, Eric. *The Flash of Capital: Film and Geopolitics in Japan*. Durham, NC: Duke University Press, 2002.

Cheah, Pheng. *What Is a World? On Postcolonial Literature as World Literature*. Durham, NC: Duke University Press, 2016.

Chiba Shunji. "Kindai bungaku no naka no *Genji monogatari*." In *Kindai bungaku ni okeru* "Genji monogatari," edited by Chiba Shunji, 9–28. Kōza *Genji monogatari* kenkyū, dai 6-kan. Tokyo: Ōfū, 2007.

Chowrimootoo, Christopher. *Middlebrow Modernism: Britten's Operas and the Great Divide*. Oakland: University of California Press, 2018.

Cooper, Melinda. *Family Values: Between Neoliberalism and the New Social Conservatism*. New York: Zone Books, 2017.

Dale, Peter N. *The Myth of Japanese Uniqueness*. London: Croom Helm, 1986.

Deleuze, Gilles, and Félix Guattari. *A Thousand Plateaus: Capitalism and Schizophrenia*. Translated by Brian Massumi. Minneapolis: University of Minnesota Press, 1987.

Dorsey, James. *Critical Aesthetics: Kobayashi Hideo, Modernity, and Wartime Japan*. Cambridge, MA: Harvard University Asia Center, 2009.

Driscoll, Mark. "Hyperneoliberalism: Youth, Labor, and Militant Mice in Japan." *positions: east asia cultures critique* 23, no. 3 (August 2015): 545–64.

Duggan, Lisa. *Mean Girl: Ayn Rand and the Culture of Greed*. Berkeley: University of California Press, 2019.

Dunn, Bill. "Against Neoliberalism as a Concept." *Capital and Class* 41, no. 3 (2017): 435–54.

Duus, Peter, and Daniel I. Okimoto. "Fascism and the History of Pre-War Japan: The Failure of a Concept." *Journal of Asian Studies* 39, no. 1 (November 1979): 65–76.

Ebersole, Gary. *Ritual Poetry and the Politics of Death in Early Japan*. Princeton, NJ: Princeton University Press, 1989.

Emmerich, Michael. "The Tale of Genji"*: Translation, Canonization, and World Literature*. New York: Columbia University Press, 2013.

Erber, Pedro. "Beautiful Money; or, What Can Contemporary Art Teach Us about the Neoliberal Economy?" *Revista Hispánica Moderna* 72, no. 2 (2019): 149–59.

———. *Breaching the Frame: The Rise of Contemporary Art in Brazil and Japan*. Berkeley: University of California Press, 2015.

Etō Jun. *Shōwa no bunjin*. Tokyo: Shinchōsha, 1989.

Favret, Mary A. *War at a Distance: Romanticism and the Making of Modern Wartime*. Princeton, NJ: Princeton University Press, 2010.

Feher, Michel. *Rated Agency: Investee Politics in a Speculative Age*. New York: Zone Books, 2018.

Felski, Rita. *The Limits of Critique*. Chicago: University of Chicago Press, 2015.

Finchelstein, Federico. *From Fascism to Populism in History*. Oakland: University of California Press, 2017.

Fletcher, William Miles, III. *The Search for a New Order: Intellectuals and Fascism in Prewar Japan*. Chapel Hill: University of North Carolina Press, 1982.

Foley, Duncan K. *Adam's Fallacy: A Guide to Economic Theology*. Cambridge, MA: Harvard University Press, 2006.

Foucault, Michel. *The Birth of Biopolitics: Lectures at the College de France, 1978–1979*. Edited by Graham Burchell. Translated by Michel Senellart. New York: Picador, 2008.

Fukuyama, Francis. "The End of History?" *The National Interest* 16 (Summer 1989): 3–18.

Furuhata, Yuriko. *Cinema of Actuality: Japanese Avant-Garde Filmmaking in the Season of Image Politics*. Durham, NC: Duke University Press, 2013.

Garon, Sheldon. "Transnational History and Japan's 'Comparative Advantage.'" *Journal of Japanese Studies* 43, no. 1 (Winter 2017): 65–92.

Gibson, James. *The Ecological Approach to Visual Perception*. Hillsdale, NJ: Lawrence Erlbaum Associates, 1986.

Golley, Gregory L. "Tanizaki Junichiro: The Art of Subversion and the Subversion of Art." *Journal of Japanese Studies* 21, no. 2 (Summer 1995): 365–404.

Gordon, Andrew. *Labor and Imperial Democracy in Prewar Japan*. Berkeley: University of California Press, 1991.

Gordon, Peter E. *Continental Divide: Heidegger, Cassirer, Davos*. Cambridge, MA: Harvard University Press, 2010.

Goto-Jones, Christopher S. "The Kyoto School, the Cambridge School, and the History of Political Philosophy in Wartime Japan." *positions: east asia cultures critique* 17, no. 1 (Spring 2009): 13–42.

———. *Political Philosophy in Japan: Nishida, The Kyoto School and Co-prosperity*. New York: Routledge, 2005.

Greenberg, Clement. "Avant-Garde and Kitsch." In *Art and Culture: Critical Essays*, 3–21. Boston: Beacon Press, 1961.

Greenwald Smith, Rachel. *Affect and American Literature in the Age of Neoliberalism*. New York: Cambridge University Press, 2015.

Greif, Mark. *The Age of the Crisis of Man: Thought and Fiction in America, 1933–1973*. Princeton, NJ: Princeton University Press, 2015.

Groethuysen, Bernard. *The Bourgeois: Catholicism vs. Capitalism in Eighteenth-Century France*. Translated by Mary Ilford. New York: Holt, Rinehart and Winston, 1968.

Hamakawa Katsuhiko. *Ronkō Yokomitsu Riichi*. Osaka: Izumi Shoin, 2001.

Harootunian, Harry. *Marx after Marx: History and Time in the Expansion of Capitalism*. New York: Columbia University Press, 2015.

———. *Overcome by Modernity: History, Culture, and Community in Interwar Japan*. Princeton, NJ: Princeton University Press, 2000.

———. "Philosophy and Answerability: The Kyoto School and the Epiphanic Moment of World History." In *Confronting Capital and Empire: Rethinking Kyoto School Philosophy*, edited by Viren Murthy, Fabian Schäfer, and Max Ward, 21–57. Leiden: Brill, 2017.

———. "The Postwar Genealogy of Fascism and Tosaka Jun's Prewar Critique of Liberalism." *Journal of Pacific Asia* 2 (1995): 95–112.

———. *Things Seen and Unseen: Discourse and Ideology in Tokugawa Nativism*. Chicago: University of Chicago Press, 1988.

Harrington, Lewis E. "Miki Kiyoshi and the Shōwa Kenkyūkai: The Failure of World History." *positions: east asia cultures critique* 17, no. 1 (2009): 43–72.

Harvey, David. *A Brief History of Neoliberalism*. Oxford: Oxford University Press, 2005.
Hayek, Friedrich. *The Constitution of Liberty: The Definitive Edition*. Edited by Ronald Hamowy. Collected Works of F. A. Hayek 17. Chicago: University of Chicago Press, 2011.
———. *The Fatal Conceit: The Errors of Socialism*. Edited by W. W. Bartley III. Collected Works of F. A. Hayek 1. London: Routledge, 1988.
———. *Individualism and Economic Order*. Chicago: University of Chicago Press, 1948.
———. "The Intellectuals and Socialism." *University of Chicago Law Review* 16, no. 3 (Spring 1949): 417–33.
———. *Law, Legislation and Liberty*. Vol. 2, *The Mirage of Social Justice*. Chicago: University of Chicago Press, 1976.
———. "A Rebirth of Liberalism." *The Freeman*, July 28, 1952, 729–31.
Hayek, Friedrich A. von. Papers. Hoover Institution Archives. Stanford, California.
Hayter, Irena. "Figures of the Visual: Japanese Modernism, Technology, Vitalism." *positions: asia critique* 25, no. 2 (2017): 293–322.
Heinrich, Amy Vladeck. *Fragments of Rainbows: The Life and Poetry of Saitō Mokichi, 1882–1953*. New York: Columbia University Press, 1983.
Hendrickson, Robert. *The Facts on File Encyclopedia of Word and Phrase Origins*. 4th ed. New York: Facts on File, 2008.
Herf, Jeffrey. *Reactionary Modernism: Technology, Culture, and Politics in Weimar and the Third Reich*. Cambridge: Cambridge University Press, 1984.
Hickey, Dave. *Air Guitar: Essays on Art and Democracy*. Los Angeles: Art Issues Press, 1997.
Hidetoshi Katō. "Middle-Brow Culture." *Journal of Social and Political Ideas in Japan* 2, no. 1 (April 1964): 70–74.
Hirabayashi Hatsunosuke, Aono Suekichi, Kurahara Korehito, and Nakano Shigeharu. *Hirabayashi Hatsunosuke, Aono Suekichi, Kurahara Korehito, Nakano Shigeharu shū: Gendai Nihon bungaku zenshū:* 78. Tokyo: Chikuma Shobō, 1957.
Hirotsu Kazuo. "Futatabi sanbun geijutsu no ichi ni tsuite." In *Gendai Nihon bungaku zenshū* 32, 174–78. Tokyo: Chikuma Shobō, 1955.
———. "Sanbun geijutsu no ichi." In *Gendai Nihon bungaku zenshū* 32, 171–74. Tokyo: Chikuma Shobō, 1955.
———. *Sanbun seishin ni tsuite*. Tokyo: Sōgeisha, 1950.
———. "Sanbun seishin ni tsuite." In *Gendai Nihon bungaku zenshū* 32, 181–82. Tokyo: Chikuma Shobō, 1955.
Hofmann, Reto. *The Fascist Effect: Japan and Italy: 1915–1952*. Ithaca, NY: Cornell University Press, 2015.
Horkheimer, Max, and Theodor W. Adorno. *Dialectic of Enlightenment*. Translated by John Cumming. New York: Continuum, 2002.
Hosoe Hikaru. *Tanizaki Jun'ichirō shinsō retorikku*. Osaka: Izumi Shoin, 2004.
Huxley, Aldous. *Point Counter Point*. New York: Doubleday, Doran, 2009.

Iacocca, Lee, with William Novak. *Iacocca: An Autobiography*. Toronto: Bantam Books, 1984.
Ibuki Kazuko and G. G. Rowley. "The 'Tanizaki Genji': Inception, Process, and Afterthoughts; With Translations by Thomas Harper of Tanizaki Jun'ichirō's 'On Translating

The Tale of Genji into Modern Japanese' (1938) and 'Some Malicious Remarks' (1965)." In *The Grand Old Man and the Great Tradition: Essays on Tanizaki Jun'ichirō in Honor of Adriana Boscaro*, edited by Luisa Bienati and Bonaventura Ruperti, 25–52. Ann Arbor: Center for Japanese Studies, The University of Michigan, 2009.

Ikeda Shigekazu. "Tosaka Jun ni okeru 'bungaku' no imi o megutte: Gendai no 'karuchuraru sutadiizu' to no kankei de." In *Yuibutsuron kenkyū nenshi: dai 5 go: Aratana kōkyōsei o motomete*, 215–35. Tokyo: Aoki Shoten, 2000.

Inaga Shigemi. "Japanese Philosophers Go West: The Effect of Maritime Trips on Philosophy in Japan with Special Reference to the Case of Watsuji Tetsurō (1889–1960)." *Japan Review* 25 (2013): 113–44.

Inden Masashi. *Kankaku to sonzai: Yokomitsu Riichi o meguru konkyo eno toi*. Tokyo: Meiji Shoin, 2014.

Inoue Ken. *Hyōden Yokomitsu Riichi*. Tokyo: Ōfūsha, 1975.

Inoue Ken, Kamiya Tadataka, and Hatori Tetsuya, eds. *Yokomitsu Riichi jiten*. Tokyo: Ōfū, 2002.

Jesty, Justin. *Art and Engagement in Early Postwar Japan*. Ithaca, NY: Cornell University Press, 2018.

Jones, Daniel Stedman. *Masters of the Universe: Hayek, Friedman, and the Birth of Neoliberal Politics*. Princeton, NJ: Princeton University Press, 2012.

Judt, Tony. *The Burden of Responsibility: Blum, Camus, Aron, and the French Twentieth Century*. Chicago: University of Chicago Press, 1998.

Kaffen, Philip. "Nakai Masakazu and the Cinematic Imperative." *positions: asia critique* 26, no. 3 (August 2018): 483–515.

Kamiya Tadataka. "Shōwa jūnendai no 'sanbun seishin' ron." In *Shōwa no bungaku*, 100–105. Tokyo: Yūseidō shuppan, 1981.

Kaneko Motoomi, ed. *Teihon* "Genji monogatari" *shinkai: Jō*. Tokyo: Meiji Shoin, 1925.

Karatani Kōjin. *History and Repetition*. Edited by Seiji M. Lippit. New York: Columbia University Press, 2012.

Kawashima, Ken C., Fabian Schäfer, and Robert Stoltz, eds. *Tosaka Jun: A Critical Reader*. Ithaca, NY: East Asia Program, Cornell University, 2013.

Keene, Donald. *Five Modern Japanese Novelists*. New York: Columbia University Press, 2003.

Kim, John Namjun. "The Temporality of Empire: The Imperial Cosmopolitanism of Miki Kiyoshi and Tanabe Hajime." In *Pan-Asianism in Modern Japanese History: Colonialism, Regionalism and Borders*, edited by Sven Saaler and J. Victor Koschmann, 151–67. New York: Routledge, 2007.

Kim Te-Gyun. *Yokomitsu Riichi to "kindai no chōkoku"*: "Ryoshū" *ni okeru kenchiku, kagaku, shokuminchi*. Tokyo: Kanrin Shobō, 2014.

Kimoto, Takeshi. "Antinomies of Total War." *positions: east asia cultures critique* 17, no. 1 (Spring 2009): 97–125.

Kirk, Russell. *The Conservative Mind: From Burke to Eliot*. 7th rev. ed. Washington, DC: Gateway Editions, 1985.

———. *The Conservative Mind: From Burke to Santayana*. Chicago: Henry Regnery, 1953.

———. *The Sword of Imagination: Memoirs of a Half-Century of Literary Conflict.* Grand Rapids, MI: William B. Eerdmans, 1995.

Klein, Christina. *Cold War Orientalism: Asia in the Middlebrow Imagination, 1945–1961.* Berkeley: University of California Press, 2003.

Kobayashi Masaaki. "Wartime Japan, the Imperial Line, and *The Tale of Genji.*" Translated by Michael Emmerich. In *Envisioning* "The Tale of Genji": *Media, Gender, and Cultural Production*, edited by Haruo Shirane, 288–300. New York: Columbia University Press, 2008.

Kolozi, Peter. *Conservatives against Capitalism: From the Industrial Revolution to Globalization.* New York: Columbia University Press, 2017.

Komori Yōichi. *Kōzō toshite no katari.* Tokyo: Shinyōsha, 1988.

Kōsaka Masaaki, Nishitani Keiji, Kōyama Iwao, and Suzuki Shigetaka. *Sekaishiteki tachiba to Nihon*, edited by Fujita Chikamasa, 1–131. Tokyo: Chūō Kōronsha, 1943.

La Berge, Leigh Claire, and Quinn Slobodian. "Reading for Neoliberalism, Reading Like Neoliberals." *American Literary History* 29, no. 3 (2017): 602–14.

Lacy, Tim. *The Dream of Democratic Culture: Mortimer J. Adler and the Great Books Idea.* New York: Palgrave Macmillan, 2013.

Lady Murasaki. *The Tale of Genji: A Novel in Six Parts.* Translated by Arthur Waley. New York: Modern Library, 1960.

LaMarre, Thomas. *Shadows on the Screen: Tanizaki Jun'ichirō on Cinema and "Oriental" Aesthetics.* Ann Arbor: Center for Japanese Studies, University of Michigan, 2005.

Lemahieu, Michael. "The Novel of Ideas." In *The Cambridge Companion to British Fiction since 1945*, edited by David James, 177–91. Cambridge: Cambridge University Press, 2015.

Lin Shukumi. *Hihyō no ningensei: Nakano Shigeharu.* Tokyo: Heibonsha, 2010.

Lippit, Seiji. *Topographies of Japanese Modernism.* New York: Columbia University Press, 2002.

Long, Margherita. *This Perversion Called Love: Reading Tanizaki, Feminist Theory, and Freud.* Stanford, CA: Stanford University Press, 2009.

Lucey, Michael. "Proust and Language-In-Use." *Novel: A Forum on Fiction* 48, no. 2 (2015): 261–79.

Lucey, Michael, and Tom McEnaney. "Introduction: Language-in-Use and Literary Fieldwork." *Representations* 137 (Winter 2017): 1–22.

Macdonald, Dwight. *Masscult and Midcult: Essays against the American Grain.* Edited by John Summers. New York: New York Review of Books, 2011.

Mack, Edward. *Manufacturing Modern Japanese Literature: Publishing, Prizes, and the Ascription of Literary Value.* Durham, NC: Duke University Press, 2010.

Mann, Thomas. *The Magic Mountain.* Translated by John E. Woods. New York: Vintage Books, 1995.

Marcon, Federico. "Historical Knowledge, Historians' Categories, and the Question of 'Fascism.'" *positions*, February 19, 2020, http://positionswebsite.org/federico-marcon-historical-knowledge-historians-categories-and-the-question-of-fascism/.

Marcus, Marvin. *Paragons of the Ordinary: The Biographical Literature of Mori Ōgai.* Honolulu: University of Hawai'i Press, 1993.

Maruyama Masao. *Nihon no shisō*. Tokyo: Iwanami Shoten, 1961.
McCarthy, Mary. *Ideas and the Novel.* New York: Harcourt Brace Jovanovich, 1980.
McClellan, Edwin. "Edwin McClellan on Natsume Sōseki and Shiga Naoya." In *Words, Ideas, and Ambiguities: Four Perspectives on Translating from the Japanese*, edited by Donald Richie, 3–17. Chicago: Imprint Publications, 2000.
———. "The Implications of Sōseki's *Kokoro*." *Monumenta Nipponica* 14, nos. 3/4 (October 1958–January 1959): 356–70.
McDowell, Edwin. "Two Millionth 'Iacocca' to Roll Off the Assembly Line Today." *New York Times*, July 17, 1985. http://www.nytimes.com/1985/07/17/books/two-millionth-iacocca-to-roll-off-the-assembly-line-today.html?pagewanted=all/.
McKevitt, Andrew C. *Consuming Japan: Popular Culture and the Globalization of 1980s America.* Chapel Hill: University of North Carolina Press, 2017.
Miki Kiyoshi. *Miki Kiyoshi: Tōa Kyōdōtai ronshū*. Edited by Uchida Hiroshi. Tokyo: Kobushi Shobō, 2007.
———. *Miki Kiyoshi zenshū*. 20 vols. Tokyo: Iwanami Shoten, 1966–68.
Miller, Jennifer. *Cold War Democracy: The United States and Japan*. Cambridge, MA: Harvard University Press, 2019.
Minamoto no Tamenori. "Illustration of the Three Jewels." Translated by Edward Kamens. In *Traditional Japanese Literature: An Anthology, Beginnings to 1600*, edited by Haruo Shirane, 214–17. New York: Columbia University Press, 2007.
Mirowski, Philip. *Never Let a Serious Crisis Go to Waste: How Neoliberalism Survived the Financial Meltdown*. London: Verso, 2013.
Miyazaki, Hirokazu. "The Temporality of No Hope." In *Ethnographies of Neoliberalism*, edited by Carol J. Greenhouse, 238–50. Philadelphia: University of Pennsylvania Press, 2010.
Miyoshi, Masao. *Off Center: Power and Culture Relations between Japan and the United States*. Cambridge, MA: Harvard University Press, 1991.
———. "Translation as Interpretation." *Journal of Asian Studies* 38, no. 2 (February 1979): 299–302.
Mizukami Tsutomu and Chiba Shunji, eds. *Tanizaki Sensei no shokan: Aru shuppansha shachō e no tegami o yomu*. Tokyo: Chūō Kōron Shinsha, 2008.
Mogi Masao. *Yokomitsu Riichi no hyōgen sekai: Nihon no shōsetsu*. Tokyo: Benseisha, 1995.
Moretti, Franco. *The Bourgeois: Between History and Literature*. London: Verso, 2013.
Morson, Gary Saul. *Narrative and Freedom: The Shadows of Time*. New Haven, CT: Yale University Press, 1994.
Morson, Gary Saul, and Caryl Emerson. *Mikhail Bakhtin: Creation of a Prosaics*. Stanford, CA: Stanford University Press, 1990.
Motoori Norinaga. *Motoori Norinaga zenshū*. Edited by Ōno Susumu. 23 vols. Tokyo: Chikuma Shobō, 1968–93.
———. "*The Tale of Genji*: A Little Jeweled Comb." Translated by Thomas Harper. In *Reading* "The Tale of Genji": *Sources from the First Millennium*, edited by Thomas J. Harper and Haruo Shirane, 411–506. New York: Columbia University Press, 2015.
Murakami Haruki. *Dance, Dance, Dance*. Translated by Alfred Birnbaum. New York: Vintage International, 1996.

———. "The Folklore of Our Times." Translated by Alfred Birnbaum. *The New Yorker*, June 9, 2003, 91–97.

———. *Murakami Haruki zensakuhin: 1979–1989: 2: Hitsuji o meguru bōken.* Tokyo: Kodansha, 1990.

———. *A Wild Sheep Chase.* Translated by Alfred Birnbaum. New York: Vintage International, 2002.

Musil, Robert. *The Man without Qualities.* Translated by Sophie Wilkins. New York: Vintage International, 1996.

Najita, Tetsuo and H. D. Harootunian. "Japanese Revolt against the West: Political and Cultural Criticism in the Twentieth Century." In *The Cambridge History of Japan.* Vol. 6, *The Twentieth Century*, edited by Peter Duus, 711–74. Cambridge: Cambridge University Press, 1988.

Nakano Shigeharu. *Bungaku no koto bungaku izen no koto.* Tokyo: Kaihōsha, 1947.

———, ed. *Mori Ōgai kenkyū.* Tokyo: Shinchōsha, 1957.

———. *Nakano Shigeharu zenshū.* Tokyo: Chikuma Shobō, 1998.

———. *Ōgai: Sono sokumen.* Tokyo: Chikuma Shobō, 1972.

Nathan, John. *Sōseki: Modern Japan's Greatest Novelist.* New York: Columbia University Press, 2018.

Natsume Sōseki. *Kokoro.* Translated by Edwin McClellan. Washington, DC: Regnery Gateway, 1957.

———. *Natsume Sōseki zenshū.* 29 vols. Tokyo: Iwanami Shoten, 1995.

Ngai, Sianne. *Theory of the Gimmick: Aesthetic Judgment and Capitalist Form.* Cambridge, MA: Belknap Press of Harvard University Press, 2020.

Nishino Atsushi. "Hai o yoseatsumeru: Yamada Yoshio to Tanizaki Jun'ichirō yaku *Genji monogatari.*" In *Kindai bungaku ni okeru* "Genji monogatari," edited by Chiba Shunji, 113–61. Tokyo: Ōfū, 2007.

Nishitani Keiji. "My Views on 'Overcoming Modernity.'" In *Overcoming Modernity: Cultural Identity in Wartime Japan.* Edited and translated by Richard Calichman, 51–63. New York: Columbia University Press, 2008.

Nishiyama Chiaki. "Arguments for the Principles of Liberty and the Philosophy of Science." Friedrich A. von Hayek Papers, Box 85, Folder 9. Hoover Institution Archives. Stanford, California.

North, Joseph. *Literary Criticism: A Concise Political History.* Cambridge, MA: Harvard University Press, 2017.

Nussbaum, Martha C. *Love's Knowledge: Essays on Philosophy and Literature.* New York: Oxford University Press, 1990.

O'Bryan, Scott. *The Growth Idea: Purpose and Prosperity in Postwar Japan.* Honolulu: University of Hawai'i Press, 2009.

Odagiri Hideo. "Bungaku ni okeru sensō sekinin no tsuikyū." *Shin Nihon Bungaku* 1, no. 3 (May / June 1946): 64–65.

———. *Nakano Shigeharu: Bungaku no kongen kara.* Tokyo: Kōdansha, 1999.

Ōiwa Masanaka. "Yamada Yoshio den: Sono go: kan." *Bunpō*, March 1969, 126–29.

———. "Yamada Yoshio den: Sono ichi." *Bunpō*, November 1968, 136–39.
———. "Yamada Yoshio den: Sono ni." *Bunpō*, December 1968, 140–43.
———. "Yamada Yoshio den: Sono san." *Bunpō*, January 1969, 132–35.
———. "Yamada Yoshio den: Sono yon." *Bunpō*, February 1969, 128–31.

O'Neill, D. Cuong. "Tragedy, Masochism, and Other Worldly Pleasures: Reading Natsume Sōseki's *Bungakuron*." *Discourse* 28, no. 2 / 3 (Spring / Fall 2006): 78–97.

Pincus, Leslie. *Authenticating Culture in Imperial Japan: Kuki Shūzō and the Rise of National Aesthetics.* Berkeley: University of California Press, 1996.

Plehwe, Dieter. Introduction to *The Road from Mont Pèlerin: The Making of the Neoliberal Thought Collective*, edited by Philip Mirowski and Dieter Plehwe, 1–42. Cambridge, MA: Harvard University Press, 2009.

Posadas, Baryon Tensor. *Double Visions, Double Fictions: The Doppelgänger in Japanese Film and Literature.* Minneapolis: University of Minnesota Press, 2018.

Rancière, Jacques. *The Emancipated Spectator.* Translated by Gregory Elliott. London: Verso, 2009.

Regnery, Henry. *Memoirs of a Dissident Publisher.* New York: Harcourt Brace Jovanovich, 1979.

Roquet, Paul. *Ambient Media: Japanese Atmospheres of Self.* Minneapolis: University of Minnesota Press, 2016.

Rubin, Joan Shelley. *The Making of Middlebrow Culture.* Chapel Hill: University of North Carolina Press, 1992.

Sakai, Naoki. "Subject and Substratum: On Japanese Imperial Nationalism." *Cultural Studies* 14, no. 3–4 (2000): 462–530.

Sakaki, Atsuko. *Recontextualizing Texts: Narrative Performance in Modern Japanese Fiction.* Cambridge, MA: Harvard University Asia Center, 1999.

Sartre, Jean-Paul. *"What Is Literature?" and Other Essays.* Cambridge, MA: Harvard University Press, 1988.

Sand, Jordan. *House and Home in Modern Japan: Architecture, Domestic Space and Bourgeois Culture, 1880–1930.* Cambridge, MA: Harvard University Asia Center, 2003.

Satō Haruo. "Sanbun seishin no hassei." In *Gendai bungakuron taikei dai 3-kan*, 266–70. Tokyo: Kawade Shobō, 1956.

Satō Kiyoji. "Yamada Yoshio." In *Nihongo gakusha retsuden*, 94–119. Tokyo: Meiji Shoin, 1997.

Satō Takumi. "Kingu" *no jidai: Kokumin taishū zasshi no kōkyōsei.* Tokyo: Iwanami Shoten, 2002.

Schäfer, Fabian. *Public Opinion, Propaganda, Ideology: Theories of the Press and Its Social Function in Interwar Japan, 1918–1937.* Leiden: Brill, 2012.

Shih, Shu-Mei. "World Studies and Relational Comparison." *PMLA* 130, no. 2 (2015): 430–38.

Shimanaka Yūsaku. "*Genji monogatari* no kankō ni atatte." *Chūo Kōron*, January 1939, 328–30.

Shin Nihon no shisō genri. In Miki Kiyoshi, *Miki Kiyoshi: Tōa Kyōdōtai ronshū*, edited by Uchida Hiroshi, 175–193. Tokyo: Kobushi Shobō, 2007.

Shirane, Haruo. *The Bridge of Dreams: A Poetics of* "The Tale of Genji." Stanford, CA: Stanford University Press, 1987.

Shockey, Nathan. *The Typographic Imagination: Reading and Writing in Japan's Age of Modern Print Media*. New York: Columbia University Press, 2020.

Silverberg, Miriam. *Changing Song: The Marxist Manifestos of Nakano Shigeharu*. Princeton, NJ: Princeton University Press, 1990.

Silverstein, Michael. "How Knowledge Begets Communication Begets Knowledge: Textuality and Contextuality in Knowing and Learning." *Intercultural Communication Review* 5 (2007): 31–60.

———. "The Poetics of Politics: 'Theirs' and 'Ours.'" *Journal of Anthropological Research* 61, no. 1 (Spring 2005): 1–24.

———. "What Goes Around . . . : Some Shtick from 'Tricky Dick' and the Circulation of U.S. Presidential Image." *Journal of Linguistic Anthropology* 21, no. 1 (2011): 54–77.

Skya, Walter A. *Japan's Holy War: The Ideology of Radical Shintō Ultranationalism*. Durham, NC: Duke University Press, 2009.

Slobodian, Quinn. *Globalists: The End of Empire and the Birth of Neoliberalism*. Cambridge, MA: Harvard University Press, 2018.

Smith, Adam. *The Theory of Moral Sentiments*. Edited by D. D. Raphael and A. L Macfie. Indianapolis: Liberty Fund, 1982.

Snyder, Stephen. "Insistence and Resistance: Murakami and Mizumura in Translation." *New England Review* 37, no. 4 (October 2016): 133–42.

Sternhell, Zeev, with Mario Sznajder and Maia Asheri. *The Birth of Fascist Ideology: From Cultural Rebellion to Political Revolution*. Translated by David Maisel. Princeton, NJ: Princeton University Press, 1994.

Strecher, Matthew Carl. *Dances with Sheep: The Quest for Identity in the Fiction of Murakami Haruki*. Ann Arbor: Center for Japanese Studies, University of Michigan, 2002.

Suzuki, Tomi. "*The Tale of Genji*, National Literature, Language, and Modernism." In *Envisioning* "The Tale of Genji": *Media, Gender, and Cultural Production*, edited by Haruo Shirane, 243–87. New York: Columbia University Press, 2008.

Szalay, Michael. *New Deal Modernism: American Literature and the Invention of the Welfare State*. Durham, NC: Duke University Press, 2000.

Takeuchi Emiko. *Nakano Shigeharu: Hito to bungaku*. Tokyo: Bensei Shuppan, 2004.

Takeuchi Yoshimi. *Kindai chōkoku*. Tokyo: Chikuma Shobō, 1983.

———. *What Is Modernity? Writings of Takeuchi Yoshimi*. Edited and translated by Richard Calichman. New York: Columbia University Press, 2005.

Takiura Masato. *Yamada Yoshio: Kyōdōtai no kokugaku no yume*. Tokyo: Kōdansha, 2009.

Tanizaki Jun'ichirō. *Tanizaki Jun'ichirō zenshū*. 28 vols. Tokyo: Chūō Kōronsha, 1966–70.

Tanizaki Jun'ichirō, trans., and Yamada Yoshio, ed. *Genji monogatari*. 26 vols. Tokyo: Chūō Kōronsha, 1939–41.

Tansman, Alan. *The Aesthetics of Japanese Fascism*. Berkeley: University of California Press, 2009.

———. "Introduction: The Culture of Japanese Fascism." In *The Culture of Japanese Fascism*, edited by Alan Tansman, 1–28. Durham, NC: Duke University Press, 2009.

———. "The Pedagogy of the Japanese Novel." *Novel: A Forum on Fiction* 47, no. 1 (2014): 57–66.

Toeda Hirokazu. "From the God of Literature to War Criminal: The Media and the Shifting Image of Yokomitsu Riichi from Prewar and Wartime to the Postwar Era." Translated by Atsuko Ueda. In *Literature among the Ruins, 1945–1955: Postwar Japanese Literary Criticism*, edited by Atsuko Ueda, Michael K. Bourdaghs, Richi Sakakibara, and Hirokazu Toeda, 177–89. Lanham, MD: Lexington Books, 2018.

———. "*Ryoshū*—samayoeru honbun." In *Yokomitsu Riichi no bungaku sekai*, edited by Ishida Hitoshi, Shibuya Kaori, and Nakamura Miharu, 130–41. Tokyo: Kanrin Shobō, 2006.

Torrance, Richard. *The Fiction of Tokuda Shūsei and the Emergence of Japan's New Middle Class*. Seattle: University of Washington Press, 1994.

———. "*The People's Library:* The Spirit of Prose Literature versus Fascism." In *The Culture of Japanese Fascism*, edited by Alan Tansman, 56–79. Durham, NC: Duke University Press, 2009.

Tosaka Jun. *Tosaka Jun zenshū*, 5 vols. Tokyo: Keisō Shobō, 1966–79.

Treat, John. "Japan Is Interesting: Modern Japanese Literary Studies Today." *Japan Forum* 30, no. 3 (2018): 421–40.

Trilling, Lionel. *The Liberal Imagination*. New York: New York Review of Books, 2008.

Ueda, Atsuko, Michael K. Bourdaghs, Richi Sakakibara, and Hirokazu Toeda, eds. *The Politics and Literature Debate in Postwar Japanese Criticism, 1945–52*. Lanham, MD: Lexington Books, 2017.

Van Horn, Rob, and Philip Mirowski. "The Rise of the Chicago School of Economics and the Birth of Neoliberalism." In *The Road from Mont Pèlerin: The Making of the Neoliberal Thought Collective*, edited by Philip Mirowski and Dieter Plehwe, 138–78. Cambridge, MA: Harvard University Press, 2009.

Venugopal, Rajesh. "Neoliberalism as Concept." *Economy and Society* 44, no. 2 (2015): 165–87.

Vincent, Keith. *Two-Timing Modernity: Homosocial Narrative in Modern Japanese Fiction*. Cambridge, MA: Harvard University Asia Center, 2012.

Vogel, Ezra F. *Japan as Number One: Lessons for America*. Cambridge, MA: Harvard University Press, 1979.

Volosinov, V. N. *Marxism and the Philosophy of Language*. Translated by Ladislav Matejka and I. R. Titunik. Cambridge, MA: Harvard University Press, 1973.

Ward, Max. "Crisis Ideology and the Articulation of Fascism in Interwar Japan: The 1938 Thought-War Symposium." *Japan Forum* 26, no. 4 (2014): 462–85.

———. *Thought Crime: Ideology and State Power in Interwar Japan*. Durham, NC: Duke University Press, 2019.

Washburn, Dennis. *Translating Mount Fuji: Modern Japanese Fiction and the Ethics of Identity*. New York: Columbia University Press, 2007.
Watt, Ian. *The Rise of the Novel: Studies in Defoe, Richardson, and Fielding*. Berkeley: University of California Press, 1957.
Wimsatt, W. K., Jr., and M. C. Beardsley. "The Intentional Fallacy." *Sewanee Review* 54, no. 3 (July–September 1946): 468–88.
Woolf, Virginia. "Middlebrow." In *The Death of the Moth and Other Essays*, 176–86. New York: Harcourt Brace Jovanovich, 1942.
———. "*The Tale of Genji*: The First Volume of Mr. Arthur Waley's Translation of a Great Japanese Novel by The Lady Murasaki." In *Reading* "The Tale of Genji"*: Sources from the First Millennium*, edited by Thomas Harper and Haruo Shirane, 564–69. New York: Columbia University Press, 2015.
Workman, Travis. *Imperial Genus: The Formation and Limits of the Human in Modern Korea and Japan*. Oakland: University of California Press, 2016.

Yamada Yoshio. "Genji monogatari" *no ongaku*. Tokyo: Hōbunkan, 1934.
———. *Kokugaku no hongi*. Tokyo: Unebi Shobō, 1942.
———. *Renga gaisetsu*. Tokyo: Iwanami Shoten, 1937.
———. "Tanizaki shi to *Genji monogatari*: Kōetsusha no kotoba." *Chūō Kōron*, January 1939, 335–38.
Yoda, Tomiko. *Gender and National Literature: Heian Texts in the Constructions of Japanese Modernity*. Durham, NC: Duke University Press, 2004.
Yokomitsu Riichi. *Teihon Yokomitsu Riichi zenshū*. Edited by Hoshō Masao, Inoue Ken, and Kuritsubo Yoshiki. 16 vols. Tokyo: Kawade Shobō Shinsha, 1981–87.
Yomota Inuhiko. *Sensei to watashi*. Tokyo: Shinchōsha, 2007.
Yura Tetsuji. *Minzoku kokka to sekaikan*. Tokyo: Minzoku Kagakusha, 1943.
———. *Yokomitsu Riichi no geijutsu shisō*. Tokyo: Nihon Tosho Sentā, 1984.
———. "Yokomitsu Riichi to Kawabata Yasunari." In *Yokomitsu Riichi no bungaku to shōgai: Botsugo sanjūnen kinenshū*, edited by Yura Tetsuji, 244–65. Tokyo: Ōfūsha, 1977.

Index

Harvard East Asian Monographs
(most recent titles)

430. Yi Gu, *Chinese Ways of Seeing and Open-Air Painting*
431. Robert Cliver, *Red Silk: Class, Gender, and Revolution in China's Yangzi Delta Silk Industry*
432. Kenneth J. Ruoff, *Japan's Imperial House in the Postwar Era, 1945–2019*
433. Erin L. Brightwell, *Reflecting the Past: Place, Language, and Principle in Japan's Medieval Mirror Genre*
434. Janet Borland, *Earthquake Children: Building Resilience from the Ruins of Tokyo*
435. Susan Blakely Klein, *Dancing the Dharma: Religious and Political Allegory in Japanese Noh Theater*
436. Yukyung Yeo, *Varieties of State Regulation: How China Regulates Its Socialist Market Economy*
437. Robert Goree, *Printing Landmarks: Popular Geography and* Meisho zue *in Late Tokugawa Japan*
438. Lawrence C. Reardon, *A Third Way: The Origins of China's Current Economic Development Strategy*
439. Eyck Freymann, *One Belt One Road: Chinese Power Meets the World*
440. Yung Chul Park, Joon Kyung Kim, and Hail Park, *Financial Liberalization and Economic Development in Korea, 1980-2020*
441. Steven B. Miles, *Opportunity in Crisis: Cantonese Migrants and the State in Late Qing China*
442. Grace Huang, *Chiang Kai-shek's Politics of Shame: Leadership, Legacy, and National Identity*
443. Adam Lyons, *Karma and Punishment: Prison Chaplaincy in Japan*
444. Craig A. Smith, *Chinese Asianism, 1894–1945*
445. Sachiko Kawai, *Uncertain Powers: Sen'yōmon and Landownership by Royal Women in Early Medieval Japan*
446. Juliane Noth, *Transmedial Landscapes and Modern Chinese Painting*
447. Susan Westhafer Furukawa, *The Afterlife of Toyotomi Hideyoshi: Historical Fiction and Popular Culture in Japan*
448. Nongji Zhang, *Legal Scholars and Scholarship in the People's Republic of China: The First Generation (1949–1992)*
449. Han Sang Kim, *Cine-Mobility: Twentieth-Century Transformations in Korea's Film and Transportation*
450. Brian Hurley, *Confluence and Conflict: Reading Transwar Japanese Literature and Thought*